UNLOCK THE POWER

Reverend John Lucas, DMin

UNLOCK THE POWER

HOW TO PRAY SPECIFIC EFFECTIVE SUPERNATURAL PRAYERS

REVEREND JOHN LUCAS, DMIN

UNLOCK THE POWER by Reverend John Lucas, DMin
Copyright © 2024 by John Lucas
All Rights Reserved.
ISBN: 978-1-59755-787-0

Published by: ADVANTAGE BOOKS™
                  Orlando, FL
                  www.advbookstore.com

All Rights Reserved. This book and parts thereof may not be reproduced in any form, stored in a retrieval system or transmitted in any form by any means (electronic, mechanical, photocopy, recording or otherwise) without prior written permission of the author, except as provided by United States of America copyright law.

Publisher and Author's Note: This book is not intended to provide medical or psychological advice or to take the place of medical advice and treatment from your personal physician. Those who are having suicidal thoughts or have been emotionally, physically or sexually abused should seek help from a mental health professional or qualified counselor. Neither the publisher nor the author nor the author's ministry takes any responsibility for any possible consequences from any action taken by any person reading or following the information in this book. If readers are taking prescription medications, they should consult with their physician and not take themselves off prescribed medications without proper supervision of the physician. Always consult your physician or other qualified health-care professional before undertaking any change in your physical regime, whether fasting, diet, medications or exercise.

In teaching this material over many years, a man uses many sources and integrates them with his own material. I have done my best to acknowledge all the sources. If I have failed to acknowledge any borrowings, I hope that the people from whom I have borrowed will understand and forgive.

Unless indicated, Bible quotations are taken from the New International Version of the Bible. Copyright © 1973, 1978, 1984 by New York International Bible Society

Scriptures marked NKJV are taken from the NEW KING JAMES VERSION® Copyright© 1982 by Thomas Nelson, Inc. Used by permission. All rights reserved.

Scripture quotations marked NASB are taken from the NEW AMERICAN STANDARD BIBLE®, Copyright© 1960, 1962, 1963, 1968, 1971, 1972, 1973, 1975, 1977, 1995 by The Lockman Foundation. Used by permission.

Scriptures marked GW are taken from the GOD'S WORD® Copyright© 1995 by God's Word to the Nations. All rights reserved.

Scripture quotations marked GNB are taken from the GOOD NEWS BIBLE© 1994 published by the Bible Societies/HarperCollins Publishers Ltd UK, Good News Bible© American Bible Society 1966, 1971, 1976, 1992. Used with permission.

Scripture quotations marked MSG are taken from THE MESSAGE, Copyright© 1993, 2002, 2018 by Eugene H. Peterson. Used by permission of NavPress, represented by Tyndale House Publishers. All rights reserved.

Scripture quotations marked KJV are taken from THE HOLY BIBLE KING JAMES VERSION which is public domain

Library of Congress Catalog Number: 2024940511

Name:	Lucas, John
Title:	UNLOCK the Power
	John Lucas, Author
	Advantage Books, 2024
Identifiers:	ISBN Paperback: 978159757870
	ISBN eBook: 978159758044
Subjects:	RELIGION: Christian Life – Inspirational
	RELIGION: Christian Life – Prayer
	RELIGION: Christian Life – Spiritual Warfare

First Printing: August 2024
24 25 26 27 28 29   10 9 8 7 6 5 4 3 2

Reverend John Lucas, DMin

What people are saying about Rev Dr. John Lucas and **UNLOCK the Power!**

"UNLOCK the Power" by Rev Dr John Lucas is a strong encouragement to us all to pray diligently and fervently! Rev Lucas is relentless is his exhortation to call God's people not only to spend time with the Lord in prayer and to know the Spirit's leading, but to know how to pray effectively and supernaturally! Ps John provides us 12 detailed chapters on how to pray accurately with power to heal the sick and to cast out demons! There are many detailed patterns of prayer included so that the reader can go back and use this book as a manual for various types of prayer that are needed in different scenarios!

Dr Brendan Kirby
Senior Pastor Hope International Ministries, Adelaide, South Australia
Regional Pastor for HIM in Perth, Australia, Africa, India and Fiji

Rev Dr John & Liz Lucas are a powerful team, who have deep knowledge of the keys to unlocking freedom and healing through the power of authoritative prayer. More importantly their authenticity and experience of this freedom and healing accompanies this knowledge in a way that offers others a way forward that so many have not had before. They complement each other with unique gifting and posture, and I have personally witnessed the freedom and healing that come as a result of the contents of this book in real life. I not only want this book as a regular resource for myself, but I want to share this wisdom with as many as possible to empower others.

Robynne Jeisman, CEO & Founder, Turntable
San Francisco USA

In 2014, John and Liz Lucas were returning to Adelaide, South Australia from Coolangatta, Queensland, Australia. I knew of them but didn't know them but their reputation preceded them and I discovered that they did fragmentation ministry. It's a bit like, as John says, Jesus puts Humpty Dumpty back again.

So, I had ministry, attended his seminars and training for ministry at Walkingfree. Finally, I took my place as a seer under his and Liz's guidance. What an awesome experience that has proved to be, to fulfil both my calling and passion "to heal the broken hearted and set the captives free."

I saw many people healed and delivered from many issues, simple and complex, as John led them through the prayers that are found in the book. I came to respect his knowledge, experience, patience, tenacity, determination, willingness and love to be the instrument of healing for so many broken and wounded lives.

Diane Sampson
Dip Soc Science (Financial Counselling), Spiritual Director, Mindset Life Coach

I came to the ministry of John Lucas in 2014 for help. My life had been out of control for many years. My mother died when I was five and my father was a harsh disciplinarian. I was not successful at school. Though I had a few jobs, my mental health issues began to take over my life. I had depression and anger issues. I struggled with feeling confident in myself and talking to others. I inherited my father's house when he died. Many things were broken inside the house by me and that represented my broken life.

John and his team used the prayer process outlined in chapter 12. It was a long journey with many ups and downs. There were many ministries needed to heal all the broken parts of me that had controlled my behavior. It was deep rooted, but Jesus was patient with me and talked to me as I went along with Him on this journey of healing.

Now my life is getting better. I do not have the anger issues any more. I am attending a Mental Health Support Group and have been appointed to their board of management. Through the sale of my father's house, I have a small house to live in and extra money to support me. I go to church each week and I belong to a life group that meets every week.

I thank God for the healing He has given me through Rev John and his team.

Petar Donjerkovic

God used Walkingfree (Adelaide, South Australia) to bring all my parts together. It specially was the last big healing on my journey from a very fragmented person to a whole person. Learning to live as a whole person also has it challenges but I feel more able to hear God's voice and respond without being bombarded with powerful negative feelings. Your ministry has helped me to want to face life and move into the future.

Gay Buxton

I have worked with John and the prayer team for about 4 yrs. I met John and Liz when they visited my local church to conduct a workshop on healing ministry at Westbourne Park Uniting Church, Adelaide, South Australia. My back-ground in nursing prompted my interest in the theory underpinning healing ministry.

John had completed a Doctorate of Ministry degree which focused on Spiritual Healing. I read it and was hooked! I asked if I could join his prayer team and he cautiously said yes. My role was to speak prayers for particular outcomes. (You will find many of these prayers in this book).

Eventually, I began to assist with interviewing clients, seeking clarification of their statements and offering advice / guidance with 'medical and psychological' issues. John was always present and always 'in charge'.

Being part of the 'Prayer Team' was an honor. I met several women who were 'Seers'. They have a gift of the Holy Spirit to interpret events described by clients. These were 'Mysteries and gifts of the Holy Spirit'. It was fascinating to hear their interpretations of events that just 'made sense' of the client situation. I could go on forever!

I have read, and commented on each chapter of this book as it has been written. Healing Ministry demands faith in our Lord. It also requires commitment to the word of God and a willingness to give yourself to Him. Just 'speaking' a prayer will not do it. Imagine yourself sitting on a sofa with our Lord. Let His presence engulf you; bathed in His love. Then pray.

The book is biblically correct, logical in so many ways and, most importantly, guides you in seeking God's help to resolve those 'sometimes hidden' spiritual problems that many people suffer from. I pray you will read and benefit from this book.

Eric Mapp
Retired Nurse in Mental Health, Nurse Educator in Hospitals and University

It is a great honor for me to indorse the Book called UNLOCK the Power that is written by Rev. Dr. John Lucas. If you want know how to hear God's voice and meaning of the Lord's Prayer and inspiring illustrations and how God healed Sister Liz from cancer and importance of praise and about Jesus Blood and container prayer you should read this wonderful book. If you are looking to be an effective prayer warrior this is the best book for you. It is useful for both pastors and believers. I have been reading Rev John's teaching for many years.

Rev John is gifted Bible teacher. God blessed him with the gift of healing and discerning power. Many people got healing when he had prayed for them. When Rev John came to India first time, we used to have Sunday service at a small thatched house which belongs to one of the believers but God blessed us with a big church building by using Rev John and Sis Liz and Brother Hal and Sis Debbie. Hundreds of Indian Pastors have been so much blessed by his teaching and his ministry. I love this book and I know you will be richly blessed reading this book, Unlock the Power

Devadas Yarraguntla
President of Calvary Mission FOR Christ
Pastor of Calvary Christian Fellowship, Gollaprolu, A.P, India.

My first introduction to the Freedom Life Centre (FLC), Toowoomba, Queensland, Australia where Rev Dr John Lucas worked was a Holy Fire conference that they held which was a great experience for me. It was mostly about intercessory prayer and there was freedom in worship. God had led me to this place after coming out of a cultish type of Christian church in 2005.

I followed up after that at Rangeville church trying to find out more about FLC. Eventually, I started attending the home group which was an intercessory prayer group for the Freedom Life Centre, led by John and his wife Liz Lucas. It was here that I finally got to use my gifts of discernment and the ability to see in the spirit.

My gifts grew and developed and with time I was able to understand the meaning of pictures that I saw and how these gifts could be used to pray for people to set them free. This prayer ministry is effective because it encompasses both deliverance and inner healing and is very thorough. Even the hardest cases where a client had been heavily involved in the occult were set free in a very gentle and calm way, because there were hardly any manifestations.

I learned a lot through training and prayer groups and sitting in on sessions. I also had to have a personal session because I wanted to work at FLC which was life changing for me. I floated around lighter than air for about a week after that session. My old church had taught us to look at our childhood issues and try to process them, but we could not heal ourselves.

While God did some healing it wasn't until I had a prayer ministry that I felt totally free from my issues that I had been tormented by for 25yrs. My husband also had a prayer session too because of the abuse he had experienced at the old church. The fruit of the ministry was amazing because we both had anger issues and after the prayer ministry, we just stopped fighting and our house which had been a war zone was now at peace.

We are still working in the prayer ministry in a new town and a new church, but we are more non-denominational now. It is my experience that God opens the door for his ministry, and he provides the team, and he heals his people, so nothing happens without prayer. I commend this book to you in the hope that it will provide you with the tools to better pray for people and set them free and to give you understanding of how God can heal the broken hearted and set the captives free. Isaiah 61:1

Robyn Webb
President
Breakfree Prayer Ministry Inc

I am so glad and honored to endorse this wonderful book which is called "UNLOCK the Power. If you want to know the experience of God's Goodness and the power of prayer...you must read this book!

First time I met Rev Dr John in 2011 at a village in India, I had many confusions in my life. He prayed for me ...amazing I was delivered from all my Confusions.

Second time Rev Dr John came to our church which is in very remote place in India. He prayed for all people personally! In that time, one sister, her name Kotamma. She has no children for 18 years. He prayed for children for her.

God blessed her a first child!

In that time another brother called Gallaiah had major surgery in his body. He has been suffering with sickness for many years. After prayer he was healed completely. Now he is very active in our church at Vaddipadu.

We are being so encouraged by reading Rev Dr John literature's and he helps us to build a church and house in Narasaraopet at Andhra Pradesh in India,

We are so grateful and thankful to God for Rev Dr John Lucas and Sister Liz and their ministry. We praise God for this wonderful book about prayer.

Pastor CH. Devadas, Walking Free Church, Narasaraopet, A.P. India

It's my great pleasure to endorse above prayer book on behalf of Walking Free Ministry Church (Kenya). By God's grace we give ourselves as much as possible to your success and fruitfulness in His great purpose as we still recall your 2018 visit. You preached a very powerful message about spiritual warfare to pastors / leader's conference meetings. You taught us the basket prayer (Container Prayer) which has still left a mark in our lives remembering you as a spiritual gifted servant of the Most High.

Lastly the good man brings good things out of the good stored up in him (Matthew 12:35). Well done! May His grace continue to take you higher and deeper in Him as He leads you to lead others in prayer book. Onto the next level.

Pastor Isaac Newton
Walkingfree Church
Kegan and Homa Bay, Kenya

"Informative and Inspirational"
Debra Grady
Associate Publisher, Advantage Books

Table of Contents

ACKNOWLEDGEMENTS 15

INTRODUCTION 17

1: UNLOCKING THE POWER OF GOD'S VOICE 21

The power to pray is to learn to pray as Jesus did: praying as the Father has shown Him. This chapter explores the ways that God speaks to us and how you can distinguish between God's voice, Satan's voice and your own feelings and desires that can influence us.

2: UNLOCKING THE POWER OF THE LORD'S PRAYER 43

We look at the foundation principles for every believer who wants to pray more effectively. These are Relationship with God, Reverence for God, Right Kingdom Focus for our prayers, Right Requests, Repentant Heart, Resistance to Satan.

3: UNLOCKING THE POWER OF YOUR AUTHORITY AND FAITH 63

Jesus gave the disciples and us the authority that came from him. What is that authority and how we are to use it is the theme of the first part of the chapter. Then we explore the faith that is required to move mountains.

4: UNLOCKING THE PRAYER POWER TOOLS 83

The Bible records many ways to effectively pray for specific situations. There are numerous prayer tools that are to be used to pray more powerfully and effectively, viz working with Jesus and the Holy Spirit to bring about transformation.

5: UNLOCKING THE POWER OF FASTING

The Bible records a number of fasts that help to release God's answer that may have been delayed or bring change to a situation that may be dire. This chapter explores what is the Biblical purpose for fasting, the type of fasts and practical advice about fasting

6: UNLOCKING THE POWER TO DEFEAT DEMONS 143

If we are going to overcome the enemy, we need to know Satan and His army, how he works and how to overcome him. We need to know the legal rights and remove them so that Satan has no might.

7: UNLOCKING THE POWER TO HEAL THE SICK 171

This chapter explores the nature of sickness from physical sickness to mental sickness and how it might be linked to sin, the heart, lack of forgiveness and Satan and why some are not healed. Finally, we look as to how we can pray for the sick.

8: UNLOCKING THE POWER TO CANCEL CURSES 187

The old saying "Sticks and stones may break my bones, but words will never hurt me" is not true. Words hurt! This chapter examines the nature of words and curses, how you can determine whether a curse is acting on you and how to cancel them. This chapter also examines self-cursing or inner vows and how to undo them.

9: UNLOCKING THE POWER TO SET YOUR PROPERTY FREE 201

Many farms struggle to be productive. Many businesses struggle to become successful. Some classrooms struggle to be an environment of learning. Many homes struggle to have peace in them. We have found that in some cases there are spiritual reasons that are causing this struggle. This chapter examines how properties may become defiled and enable the enemy to impact and affect them. Prayers are given to enable the owners to set the property or business or classroom or home free

10: UNLOCKING THE POWER TO PROTECT ONESELF AND OTHERS 221

We live in a world where we are becoming more under attack from various sources. We ask for God's protection. But what does it mean? We explore the meaning of God's protection and give a prayer of protection to cover you and your family from spiritual attack.

11: UNLOCKING THE POWER TO BRING BACK REBELS 231

One of the most heartbreaking issues to deal with is when people walk away from their family and friends because of family conflict or getting involved with the "wrong crowd" or some form of addiction or mental health issues. The only answer is prayer. But it must be targeted prayer that works with the Holy Spirit to achieve a good outcome. The Rebel Prayer that is given and explained has had a lot of success in bringing back peple from darkness into the light by the power of Jesus.

12: UNLOCKING THE POWER TO SET THE CAPTIVE FREE 241

This last chapter is the prayer process that I have developed and used over many years to set the captive free. It covers the many ways that people are held captive to sickness and Satan: Family or Generational patterns; word curses and vows; sin; unforgiveness; bitter roots; demonic strongholds; trauma and the associated impact through fragmentation or dissociation of the soul. Explanation is given for each area and prayers given that set the captive free in each area.

GLOSSARY OF PRAYERS 277

REFERENCES 311

Reverend John Lucas, DMin

ACKNOWLEDGEMENTS

I wish to thank God for calling me into His ministry of prayer, healing and deliverance. It has not been an easy journey but it has changed me for the better. I have been privileged to hear His love words and guidance and experience His presence when I pray for people as He has set them free.

I wish to thank my wife, Liz, for all her love, sacrifice, courage, forbearance and prayers that have covered me and my ministry. I thank her for being the woman of God and partner in God's ministry.

I wish to thank my children, Naomi, Jess and Dave who have loved and supported me, kept their faith in Jesus though I was caught up with praying for other people then being sent to Queensland so that they had to look after each other while Liz and I were away.

I wish to thank Chris Hams, Joan Weeding, Helen Burchall and Jenny Lock who supported and prayed with me at the beginning of ministry at Peterborough, South Australia.

I wish to thank Ann Piper, Stephanie Lunn and Tim Andrew who supported and prayed with me at Tusmore Park Uniting Church, Adelaide, South Australia.

I wish to thank the many people who supported me and prayed with me when Pools of Healing was started at Tusmore Park Uniting Church, Adelaide, South Australia, especially Kath Croser, Tony Green and Maureen Harris

I wish to thank the people who supported me at the beginning of Walkingfree in Toowoomba, Queensland, Australia, especially Jamie and Robyn Webb, Hal and Debbie Hopper, Craig Brunkhorst, Jenny Dunn, Rod and Narelle Faddy.

I wish to thank all the people especially Liz Lucas, Lindy Collie, Rosalie Cameron, Robyn Webb, Barbara Hall, Diane Sampson and Eric Mapp who have joined me in the prayer room to pray for the damaged people that have come into our lives. Their spiritual anointing and insight have been God's gift to the ministry of freedom for people and a blessing to me.

I wish to thank all the people who have sponsored Walkingfree over the years. Words are inadequate to thank them for their generosity and obedience to God to support the work financially and prayerfully.

I wish to thank the prayer warriors that have prayed for us over the journey to sustain the ministry. Their prayers have impacted the lives of our clients in ways that they may never know but God will show them on that day.

Reverend John Lucas, DMin

In particular I wish to thank Hal and Debbie Hopper, Jamie and Robyn Webb, the team at Coolangatta Healing Rooms (Queensland, Australia), Liz Lucas, Diane Sampson, Margaret Wallace, Lesley Vizzard, Valda Burleigh, Eric Mapp and Julie Butterick.

I wish to thank all the people who came to Pools of Healing and Walkingfree for prayer, trusting us with their pain and struggle, and being open to the new ways of praying that they encountered so that they could be set free.

I wish to thank Tim Piper, Eric Mapp and Mary Hawkes for reading the manuscript and giving me valuable advice and changes to the final product.

INTRODUCTION

I am not a good pray-er! I am not an intercessor. I don't have a worldwide ministry. I am not a pastor of a large church. I have spent most of my ministry, pastoring small churches in rural regions.

So why am I writing a book on prayer.

In 1986, my ministry and life were turned around by God when Dr Peter Wagner came to Adelaide, South Australia, to lecture on Church Growth for people wanting to begin a Doctorate of Ministry from Fuller Theological Seminary located Pasadena, Los Angeles USA.

My intention and hope were to get a degree so that I may become a lecturer in a Bible/Theological College. Little did I know that this idea was a million miles away from what God had intended for me.

Dr Wagner offered to pray for people in the breaks, especially with those with bad backs. While I did not have a bad back, I came and watched and something happened to me. I felt giddy. I ignored this but this giddiness again came upon me when I was walking down the main street to buy some lunch. I approached Dr Wagner about this and he suggested that this experience was the Holy Spirit coming upon me.

In 1987, I moved to a country railway town, Peterborough, South Australia, with my wife and children. I went to Fuller Theological Seminary to further my studies, went to various churches in Los Angeles involved with the healing ministry and came back to explore this area of ministry. I changed my topic of my thesis from *Growing Small Churches to Foundations for the Healing Ministry of Christ in the Uniting Church in Australia.*

In the early years at Peterborough (South Australia), I was a minister of two denominational churches, Anglican (Church of England or Episcopal) and Uniting Church in Australia (Methodist, Presbyterian and Congregational churches combined in 1977).

Two events happened while I was involved with the Anglican Church. Jeremiah 29:11 *(I know the plans that I have for you.....)* was the scripture to start the Anglican service on one Sunday. As I read out this scripture, it was as if God was speaking to me. I was shaken by this and it took all my effort to gather myself and go ahead with the service.

The other thing that happened when I was with some ladies from the Anglican church. We were praying and a demon manifested in one of the ladies and spoke with a male voice, saying: *she is mine and you are not having her!* I prayed for her and nothing happened! They did not teach me anything about this in theological college! I decided that I would not get caught short again.

Soon I attended a John Wimber conference in Melbourne, Australia, and the Lord gave me a dream that rocked my boat on the night before the final day. During the final day, the message of that dream became clear and there were issues that I had to sort out. I went forward for prayer but there was more to do.

I ended up in the gardens of Ballarat, Victoria, Australia, being prayed for by the people that I took with me. It was a huge cleanout of my sin and life that was needed if I was going to fulfil Jeremiah 29:11. I ended up doing many deliverance sessions for people who lived within a 100-mile radius from Peterborough, South Australia, where I lived. I also conducted teaching sessions, training people in prayer and prophecy and learning to pray to bring down the strongholds of sin and suicide around Peterborough (South Australia)

In 1997, I was called to Tusmore Park Uniting Church in Adelaide, South Australia. In 1998, my wife contracted cancer and nearly died. But we prayed and learnt more about praying and having faith and belief to pray. The church grew in numbers and again people came wanting healing.

I started a ministry called Pools of Healing at Tusmore Park Uniting Church where I trained teams to pray for healing and people came for healing. Some of these people had complex issues that forced us to increase our knowledge and ability to pray because they came with mental health and abuse issues. I devised a ministry model of praying that could be used by others to bring healing to shattered lives.

In 2004, I was called to Freedom Life Centre at Toowoomba, Queensland (Australia). This was a ministry started by Rev. Dr Colin Warren and he wanted to hand the baton over to someone. The appointment lasted three years. Yet in that time, we learnt how the power of worship and prayer released the presence of the Holy Spirit in the three conferences that I organized.

While it was sad that the appointment was terminated in difficult circumstances, the Lord used this to expose me to many ways of ministry including phone ministry. My wife, Liz, was "dumped into the deep end" to pray for people with me as we went to churches, teaching and praying for people. She has become a warrior woman of prayer for healing, deliverance and intercession.

In 2007, the Lord said that Liz and I were not to return to South Australia but stay in Toowoomba, Queensland, where, with the help of a few people, we started the ministry called Walkingfree. We set it up as a charity to gain sponsorship and waited to see what the Lord will do. Again, people came to our doorstep wanting help. People were raised up by the Holy Spirit to sponsor this ministry and very quickly we had a halftime paid ministry with benefits (approximately $60,000) for a minister in the Uniting Church in Australia. The other half was to be supplied by being a pastor of a church on a half time basis.

In 2011 we were led to go to India to teach and pray for the sick and in 2017 we went to Kenya. We have raised money to build a church and home for two pastors in India and a church and school for a pastor in Kenya. I ran seminars for the local pastors, teaching them about prayer, healing, deliverance and how to contend against the negative prayers (curses) from unbelievers.

In 2014, we returned to South Australia, pastoring a church half time and continuing with Walkingfree, learning to pray for people from interstate and overseas using the phone, skype and zoom technology. We have travelled to Elcho Island (a first people's community) off the coast of the Northern Territory, Australia, to teach on deliverance from demons and pray for healing for our Aboriginal brothers and sisters.

Since 1986, we have prayed for many people, for many places, many cultures and the Lord has shown us how to pray to set people, property and churches free!

This book is about what I have learnt about prayer and how to pray to release God's presence and power in a situation.

It is in part my testimony of how God has used me but it also a request from God to write this book/prayer manual so what I have learnt will not be lost.

So, I invite you to come on this journey about how to pray so that God's presence and power is released as you pray for people, their property and businesses.

Like me, God wants to use an ordinary person to do extraordinary things when they pray specifically, effectively and supernaturally

Rev Dr John Lucas

Reverend John Lucas, DMin

1

UNLOCKING THE POWER OF GOD'S VOICE

Jesus gave them this answer: "Very truly I tell you, the Son can do nothing by himself; he can do only what he sees his Father doing, because whatever the Father does the Son also does. For the Father loves the Son and shows him all he does. Yes, and he will show him even greater works than these, so that you will be amazed. For just as the Father raises the dead and gives them life, even so the Son gives life to whom he is pleased to give it. Moreover, the Father judges no one, but has entrusted all judgment to the Son, that all may honor the Son just as they honor the Father. Whoever does not honor the Son does not honor the Father, who sent him. (John 5:19-23)

He who belongs to God hears what God says. The reason you do not hear is that you do not belong to God. (John 8:47)

When the shepherd has brought out all of his own, he goes ahead of them, and his sheep follow him because they know his voice. (John 10:4)

In my reading of the Bible and the ministry of Jesus, what struck me was that God spoke and those He spoke to, heard Him in some way.

This became apparent to me when I started my Doctorate of Ministry course from Fuller Theological Seminary, Pasadena, USA. The first session was at the Bible College in Adelaide, South Australia, with Dr Peter Wagner.

One hundred men and women from Australia attended this two-week course on Church Growth. Each session was started in prayer and Dr Wagner would ask an attendee to pray. He said that each time he would seek God the night before about who was to open in prayer.

A few days in, I heard a pastor behind me say to his companion that he knew who the person was to be asked to pray. He said his name to his companion. To my surprise, Dr Wagner asked that person to pray!

The companion asked the pastor how did he know the name and he replied that the Holy Spirit had revealed the person to him.

This was a revelation to me and started a journey of discovering how God speaks to an individual. I had experienced God "speaking" to me when I became a Christian at 18 and sense that He loved me. I experienced God calling me to become a minister through a sermon and an altar call for ministry. I knew that God speaks through the Bible.

But these were occasional occurrences, not every day and not in a personal way.

In 1989 I came across the book Dialogue with God (1) by Mark Virkler. He also wrote a course called Communion with God. This material taught me that hearing from God was possible and how to do it.

This ability to hear from God was the key to Jesus'ministry. If it was a key to Jesus'ministry, then it must be a key for my ministry and indeed every Christian's ministry.

The following is what I discovered about how to hear from God, consistently, every day.

Stilling our Spirit

Psalm 46:10 says *Be still and know that I am God.*

Be still means cease striving and relax. Other translations have *Let go of your concerns* (God's Word); *Stop fighting* (Good News) and *Step out of the traffic* (Message Bible). We need to practice the art of being still inside.

I have found that worship music to start my session of being still is very helpful. It begins with a song or two of praise to God for what He has done, followed by a song or two about Jesus, and what He has done, then a song of love to God and/or Jesus.

The praise music has a strong tempo but the tempo changes to a slower one with the songs about Jesus and then a slow love song.

This flow is based upon the Old Testament pattern of the temple. The temple had courts where people would gather and approach God with praise and thanksgiving. They would come to the Holy Place which housed the table of showbread, the menorah and the incense censor. This is where the priest enters. Then he comes to the veil where the Ark resides, called the Holy of Holies. He can only enter on the Day of Atonement.

But Jesus has split the veil and we now have access to the Holy of Holies (Hebrews 10:19-23) We can now enter in through praising God, thanking Jesus for what He has done for us on the Cross, and then expressing our love to Him through song.

While each generation sing new songs to the Lord, you can select the songs that speak to you and enable you to share your praise and love to God. These songs take the focus off you and put your focus on God through Jesus.

Some use the gift of tongues to still their spirit and connect with the Holy Spirit. These are spoken softly so that you are able be still and then tune in to what Jesus may be sharing with you.

A Clean Heart

The second thing that God was dealing with was my heart. In Mark 7:1-23, Jesus in talking about clean and unclean things to the Pharisees

After he had left the crowd and entered the house, his disciples asked him about this parable. "Are you so dull?" he asked. "Don't you see that nothing that enters a person from the outside can defile them? For it doesn't go into their heart but into their stomach, and then out of the body." (In saying this, Jesus declared all foods clean.) He went on: "What comes out of a person is what defiles them. For it is from within, out of a person's heart, that evil thoughts come—sexual immorality, theft, murder, adultery, greed, malice, deceit, lewdness, envy, slander, arrogance and folly. All these evils come from inside and defile a person." (Mark 7:17-23)

Mark Virkler (1) talks about the heart being like a satellite dish upon which the Spirit of God alights with God's message and then directs the message to the intuitive side of your brain for you to comprehend and understand.

If your heart is clogged up or messed up, the message cannot get through nor can it be beamed up to your brain in a cognizant way.

Jesus talks about what comes out of the heart that makes it unclean in the passage above.

To be an effective prayer-er, one must have a clean heart. Why?

Firstly, the heart is that satellite dish receiving the message from God through the Holy Spirit. If the heart is dirty with sin, then its ability to pick up what God is saying is very limited. The sin, whatever it is, blocks or filters or jumbles the message from God. If you don't have a clean heart, it will be a problem to hear from God clearly.

Secondly, sin, in whatever form, hinders or even breaks our relationship with God. Unresolved sin can build up a wall between God and the person praying. Unless the sin is recognized and repented, the communication from God may be misunderstood or filtered by our own desires or even not received.

What are the main problems of the heart?

a. Pride: where your heart and will is not submitted or surrendered to God and hence is self-oriented.

b. Control: where the person wants to be in control of everything, sometimes because everything is going out of control in their life and they struggle to let Jesus be in control i.e. be Lord.

c. Rebellion: where there is a default position to respond with No and go against all forms of authority including God's authority. It signifies a willingness to go after false gods.

d. Fear: where there have been many situations that have caused fear in a person's life and hence a lack of trust has found its way in.

e. Doubt: where broken promises have been experienced, questions have been raised and disappointments experienced that have affected one's relationship with God.

f. Unbelief: where there has been a refusal to believe what God has said in His Word and a refusal to believe that God can turn life around.

g. Unforgiveness: where the action of another has been so soul and life destroying that a person continues to hold that person accountable but in so doing destroys the relationship and themselves.

h. Bitter roots: where hurt that was experienced has turned into a deep root that can evolve into bitterness, resentment, anger, hatred, criticism and judgement to name a few

Will God hear the prayers of sinners? I am sure He does. Will He answer the prayers of sinners? In some way He will.

But I am speaking to people who want to be effective for others in their praying. The point that I am making is the necessity of a clean heart to have a close, intimate relationship with God and hence the ability to hear from Him clearly and be used by Him.

We need to come to Jesus, repent of any sin and have our hearts washed clean by His precious blood and then seek with the help of the Holy Spirit not to repeat that sin again.

So how clean is your heart? Do you do a weekly heart inventory to make sure that it is clean?

If we are to hear God's voice clearly, our hearts need a good clean out through confession and repentance of sin allowing that sin to be washed away by the blood of Jesus.

Jesus also came to heal the broken hearted. He stood up in the synagogue and read out Isaiah 61:1-2 that speaks about binding up the broken hearted. A broken heart through the trauma of life leading to rejection, abuse, hurt, bitterness and resentment, control, rebellion and so forth also becomes a blockage from hearing God's voice.

The four hours of cleansing my heart and life in the Ballarat gardens (see Introduction) was painful and confronting but necessary if I was going to hear from God. We will all need our hearts cleansed and then continue to be cleansed, if we want to know what God is saying to us.

Healing prayer may be needed to heal and clean your heart so that you are able to hear God clearly.

The "sound" of God's voice – the Rhema Word

And the word of the Lord came to him: "What are you doing here, Elijah?" He replied, "I have been very zealous for the Lord God Almighty. The Israelites have rejected your covenant, torn down your altars, and put your prophets to death with the sword. I am the only one left, and now they are trying to kill me too. The Lord said, "Go out and stand on the mountain in the presence of the Lord, for the Lord is about to pass by."

Then a great and powerful wind tore the mountains apart and shattered the rocks before the Lord, but the Lord was not in the wind. After the wind there was an earthquake, but the Lord was not in the earthquake. After the earthquake came a fire, but the Lord was not in the fire. And after the fire came a gentle whisper. When Elijah heard it, he pulled his cloak over his face and went out and stood at the mouth of the cave. Then a voice said to him, "What are you doing here, Elijah?" (1 Kings 19:9-13)

After six days Jesus took Peter, James and John with him and led them up a high mountain, where they were all alone. There he was transfigured before them. His clothes became dazzling white, whiter than anyone in the world could bleach them. And there appeared before them Elijah and Moses, who were talking with Jesus. Peter said to Jesus, "Rabbi, it is good for us to be here. Let us put up three shelters— one for you, one for Moses and one for Elijah." (He did not know what to say, they were so frightened.) Then a cloud appeared and covered them, and a voice came from the cloud: "This is my Son, whom I love. Listen to him!" (Mark 9:2-7)

The third thing that I had to learn was to recognize the "sound" of God's voice to my heart.

The experience of the people in the Bible was that when God spoke, they heard a sound that contained words that they could hear and understood in their own language. In most cases, the person that God wanted to communicate to, was the only person who heard it. The experience of Peter, James and John on the Mount of Transfiguration where a number of people heard the voice of God was not common.

To understand the "sound" of God's voice, I started to dialogue with God in an exercise book. I would write *Jesus, I praise you. I love you. What would you like to say to me today?* Initially the thought would come into my mind. *John, I love you. You are My son.* As I received these thoughts, I would write them down straight away. Then I would read them again to see whether this would be Jesus speaking to me.

Every day, I would repeat this process. Initially, Jesus would reaffirm His love for me, speaking in the first person. Slowly, Jesus would start to add more to the conversation than just *I love you.*

I came to realize that Jesus wanted me to really know that He loved me. He used my name to personalize the relationship.

Then He started to speak to me about my life, my ministry, my family. These became cherished times of intimacy with Jesus. Over time, I recognized the unique sound of Jesus' voice in my heart and trusted that it was Jesus speaking to me through the Holy Spirit.

God speaks to us through a **rhema word**, the still small voice that gently lights upon us. It can come to us when we are doing something routine like ironing, walking, mowing, driving. It comes to us when we are still, i.e. when our spirit has slowed down enough to be connected to God's Spirit. We can train ourselves to be still (cease striving, relax) and know God and know His voice.

From my experience, the voice is the voice of Jesus that I hear. It is a voice that is gentle and soft to my heart and mind and I have learnt over the years that it sounds different than my voice, my thoughts and the enemy's voice and accusations.

But it always sounds the same, like my wife's voice always sounds the same to me. Jesus speaks to me in a language that I understand and reflects my vocabulary on the whole. Occasionally, He will use a word that I am not familiar with. He does not speak in the King James language but often I get a *thus says the Lord* at the end of the message to indicate both that it is Jesus that is speaking and it is the end of the message.

On one occasion, I was praying for a client and I received the word *discombobulate*. It is a word that I do not normally use but I have heard one of my clients use it to describe her situation some time before (in fact it was many months before). It shocked me and my team. We had to look it up to know the meaning.

When we uncovered the meaning, it helped us to pray more specifically for the client.

But there is a condition to hearing God/Jesus speak to us. It is a willingness to be totally obedient to what we have heard.

Initially it is to believe totally that Jesus loves you, not just intellectually but in every cell of your being. Then Jesus will ask to you to serve Him in some way. We may be asked to do something for God. It may be to cross the road and speak and pray with a neighbor that you do not know very well. It may be to pray for a person in church or take a position on the church.

Jesus spoke to my daughter in the midst of her struggle with chronic fatigue. He told her to apply for a graduate diploma of nursing. The application was to close in a few days. She obeyed God and did the course that not only opened up more opportunities for work and an increase in pay but helped her cope with her recovery.

When God does speak and asks you to do something for Him, you do wonder if it is God speaking. You do have a decision to make. You wonder whether God has got it right as you come to grips with what He has said to you, as you struggle to believe it.

But before God drops the big bombshell (at least what it seems to you), He wants intimacy and He wants conversation with you so that you know, deep within your heart, that God loves you and He wants to say that to you, again and again.

So, we practice listening to God's unique "voice" for us to have a chat with our Maker and He has a chat with us. He wants you to know His voice for words of encouragement, for words of insight and help. He wants you to know His voice for words of warning to prevent you from getting into a situation that could be diabolical for you.

As God walked and talked with Adam and Eve in the garden, so He wants to walk and talk with you in the everyday of your life, business and social life.

God speaks to us through vision.

Peter fell into a trance. He saw heaven opened and something like a large sheet being let down. (Acts 10:9)

A close look at the Old Testament and New Testament reveals that God often spoke through vision. Acts 2:17 quoting Joel refers to young men seeing visions. God speaks to us through the eyes of our heart through vision; a spiritual picture given to us while we are awake, giving us a message from God.

Steven was given a vision of heaven when he was about to be stoned (Acts 7:55-56). Ananias was given a vision by God to go to Paul (Acts 9:10-18). Peter was put in a trance as he prayed and was given a vision of a great sheet coming down from heaven with all kinds of animals (Acts 10:9-23). Paul was given numerous visions to direct his ministry.

It seems that the vision comes when a person is praying and they are given a picture with a message. They were able to talk with God about what they were given to understand the message of the vision.

Vision comes to people who are more intuitive in their nature and more visual in their thinking. It is important to note all that you see in the vision, especially the detail, as it may give clarity to the message from God.

Vision is not the primary way that God speaks to me but it is for other people. What is most important is to discover the message of the vision. We can be caught up with the experience of receiving a vison from God and not understand that it is a message to be received and even given to someone.

I encourage people to check with Jesus that it is a vision from Him. I encourage people to explore the vision with Jesus by asking further questions about the vision and each aspect of it.

We were praying about our next move to a church. It was a large regional church. I had an interview and suggested that 10% of my time there could be devoted to the healing ministry. A lady we knew from South Australia rang me about a vision that she had received while praying for me. She was given a vision of Jesus trying to drill into hard ground and getting nowhere. We understood that this church would be hard going for the ministry that I offered and we decided not to move there.

God speaks to us through dream.

Joseph had a dream, and when he told it to his brothers, they hated him all the more. (Genesis 37:5)

The angel of the Lord appeared to Joseph in a dream (Matthew 1:20; 2:13)

God speaks to his people through dreams. From Jacob's ladder to Pilate's wife's dream about Jesus, God has spoken to many people through their dreams. Dreams are the language of the emotions and often contain much symbolism. There are symbolic actions, colors, creatures, directions, names, numbers, objects. Dreams can come from God or Satan or the soulish realm of our heart and mind.

Remember do not be dazzled by dreams and visions but be dazzled by God who wants to communicate with you. Write down the dream straight away, and then seek God about its meaning. Not everything in a dream is part of God's message unlike a vision where everything in the vision is important.

As the dreams are more symbolic than vision, it is important to explore the dream with Jesus. What parts of the dream are relevant? What parts can be left out? What is the message of the dream?

In 1987, after beginning the Doctorate of Ministry the previous year where I experienced the presence of the Holy Spirit when I attended the John Wimber conference in Melbourne. The night before the final day, I received a dream from God where I was in the spirit next to John Wimber.

A lady came and kissed my cheek and John Wimber said *"Beware the Ides of March"*. I woke up trembling about the strong warning that I received.

The message of the dream was played out during the next day when I had to deal with the sin in my heart if I was to enter the ministry that God has for me.

I continue to receive God's message through dreams. They usually come in the last hours of my sleep.

God speaks to us through prophecy.

When Agabus came to us, he took Paul's belt, bound his own hands and feet and said "Thus says the Holy Spirit: So, shall the Jews of Jerusalem bind the man who owns this belt, and deliver him into the hands of the Gentiles. (Acts 21:11)

But the one who prophesies speaks to people for their strengthening, encouraging and comfort. Anyone who speaks in a tongue edifies themselves, but the one who prophesies, edifies the church. I would like every one of you to speak in tongues, but I would rather have you prophesy. (1 Corinthians 14:3-5)

God speaks to us through the prophetic word both spoken and acted out by people. This word always is to be tested but it can be a powerful word to the church or individual.

In June, 1998, my family attended Hillsong in Sydney, Australia. My wife went to the Sunday School Conference session. At the end everyone was prayed for. While most received a positive word about the growth of their Sunday School, the person giving the prophecy saw a large mountain that my wife would have to climb. In fact, my children and I would have to climb that mountain too but in a different way.

We returned home and in the September of that year, Liz started her battle with uterine cancer that became lung cancer and then a brain tumor. It took strong chemotherapy, surgery, a lot of prayer and faith to finally climb the mountain and see that her life was not to end.

While praying early one morning after two years of treatment and prayer, the sun came through the window and there was a rainbow on her leg. As there was no more flood to cover the earth, so there will be no cancer to flood her life. Twenty-five years later she is still alive serving God in a powerful prayer ministry.

The challenge for all of us is to attend church or a conference that values the prophetic word of God. It comes through a person who is given a picture or words to share or a combination of both.

The prophetic word is a message from God to help you understand your life, the challenges that you may face, any correction that needs to be given. The outcome is dependent upon God fulfilling His prophetic word and our obedience to that Word.

The danger, I have seen, is people continually looking for a prophetic word for their life from a prophetic person. Thus, the prophetic person becomes an "oracle" for the individual rather than the individual resting in the first word that was given and seeing it fulfilled. Thus, the person relies more upon the word of prophet rather than the Word of God through personal revelation and the Bible.

God speaks through the Bible (Logos word).

All Scripture is given by inspiration of God and is profitable for doctrine, for reproof, for correction, for instruction in righteousness, that the man of God may be complete, thoroughly equipped for every good work. (2 Timothy 3:16-17).

The Bible is God's Word and is the primary way in which God speaks to us. Reading the Bible, ruminating on it and reflecting upon its application for your life enables God to meet with you and speak to you. It does not mean that God will give you a now word or there will be a supernatural encounter every time that you read it, but more often than not, God will speak to you in little ways through your bible reading. He will also use the Bible to communicate His word to you by giving you chapter and verse to look up.

We worked with an older lady in our prayer/healing team in Queensland, Australia. She would give chapter and verse that would always correspond to the fundamental issue to be addressed in the person. We regularly marveled at what God showed her, even from some obscure Old Testament reading.

I was pondering about where God was leading me in ministry. My move to Queensland, a northern state of Australia, did not prove to be the lifelong ministry that I had hoped. I had to start again. Walkingfree was birthed and started to grow but it would only pay a half time position. I needed to pastor a church to supplement my income.

I was approached by a large church to consider being their minister. We went through all the interviews. One morning I woke up early to pray and talk to the Lord about this position. The following scripture came into my heart:

No one can serve two masters. Either you will hate the one and love the other, or you will be devoted to the one and despise the other. You cannot serve God and money (Matthew 6:24)

God's message was not about money. It was about serving two masters: a large church or a growing demanding healing ministry. I had to make a choice. God would bless either but I could not do both.

The church or Walkingfree had to be my "master". I chose Walkingfree and the healing ministry of Christ.

God continues to speak through the Scriptures and this must be the plumbline for all words, vision and prophecies received. If what you get is contrary to Scripture or the tenet of Scripture, then it must be dismissed as being not from God.

God speaks to us through the Church.

His intent was that now, through the church, the manifold wisdom of God should be made known to the rulers and authorities in the heavenly realms, according to His eternal purpose which he accomplished in Christ Jesus our Lord (Ephesians 3:10,11)

Certain people came down from Judea to Antioch and were teaching the believers: "Unless you are circumcised, according to the custom taught by Moses, you cannot be saved." This brought Paul and Barnabas into sharp dispute and debate with them. So, Paul and Barnabas were appointed, along with some other believers, to go up to Jerusalem to see the apostles and elders about this question. (Acts 15:1,2)

While many of us may be discouraged or disillusioned about Church as an institution and as an entity, God has always and continues to speak through the Church even when its pastors or people are sinful. God has never stopped speaking through His church whether it be through church leaders, church worship or church people.

Paul had come across a major problem: to be saved you must be circumcised. This was not just a local problem. It was a teaching that had come from Judea. The issue needed to be addressed not just locally but by the whole Christian church as the teaching would affect the whole ministry amongst the Gentiles.

Paul and Barnabas decided to go to Jerusalem and sort this out with the apostles and elders there. For some of the believers in Jerusalem, who came from the Pharisees, wanted the new believers to be circumcised and follow the Law of Moses.

The whole church gathered and listened to the report from Paul and Barnabas about their Gentile mission. Peter stood up, drawing upon his experience with Cornelius where the Holy Spirit fell upon Cornelius and his household, and spoke to affirm that people are to be saved by the grace of Jesus and not by Jewish law.

James, the brother of Jesus, and the elder of the church at Jerusalem, stood up and spoke. He outlined a way forward to have the Gentiles be welcomed into the church of Jesus. The only conditions were that Gentiles were to abstain from food polluted by idols, from sexual immorality, from the meat of strangled animals.

The people gathered came into agreement and sent Paul and Barnabas back with a letter outlining the policy of ministry with gentiles: *It seemed good to the Holy Spirit and to us.*

Throughout history, God used gathered leaders of the church, to reveal His answers to the many heresies that had been spreading about Jesus and the Holy Spirit. From these gatherings, we have the Apostles Creed and the Nicene Creed that provided the parameters to what we believe about God, Jesus, His birth, His death and resurrection, the Holy Spirit and to counter any further heresies.

God constantly uses His church to communicate His will. The struggle is the ability for the church and its leaders to seek the will of God, clear of personal bias or popular belief. God continues to speak to His people as we gather for worship through what is sung, prayed or preached.

The problem is that we miss it each Sunday because we come to church with the wrong mindsets, with the wrong attitudes and with the wrong expectations. God speaks to us through the worship songs, the prayers, the preached word, and our fellow believers.

Chapter 1: Unlocking the Power of God's Voice

Finally, whenever God's people gather for church, they make a powerful heavenly statement to the powers of darkness that their time is coming to an end. We come together to declare the victory of Jesus through His death and resurrection, over sin, sickness and Satan.

It is God's message to all the powers of darkness that would want to rob people of the life that God wants to give to His creation.

God speaks through the Preached Word

Then Peter stood up with the Eleven, raised his voice and addressed the crowd: "Fellow Jews and all of you who live in Jerusalem, let me explain this to you; listen carefully to what I say. These people are not drunk, as you suppose. It's only nine in the morning! No, this is what was spoken by the prophet Joel. When the people heard this, they were cut to the heart and said to Peter and the other apostles, "Brothers, what shall we do? (Acts 2:14-16, 37)

Throughout history, from Peter's first sermon to now, God has chosen to speak to people and bring conviction of sin and salvation through the preached word of God.

Whether it be a sermon preached to thousands or a few, God speaks through that sermon. Whether it be the best crafted sermon that was ever written or one that has hastily been prepared, God speaks through that sermon.

I have attended conferences where the speaker has not given a great presentation. Indeed, it seemed that he was all over the place. Yet when the call was given, over half of the attendees came forward to respond to the call of God to their lives.

Through the best prepared or the worst prepared, the best orator or one who struggles to put a few words together, the grace of God is that He speaks through the preached Word.

Every preacher is humbled and grateful that God would speak to the people through what he or she has prepared and delivered.

God speaks through books, devotional material, art and songs

We will tell the next generation the praiseworthy deeds of the Lord, his power, and the wonders he has done. (Psalm 78:4)

One of the amazing things is that God speaks to us and is happy to use many things that have been written.

He speaks to us through the devotional writings of Christians from the past and present. God uses their experience to speak into our experience. He speaks to us through the many Christian books written on many topics by different authors, female and male, past and present.

He speaks to us through the songs and hymns that have been written over hundreds of years.

He speaks to us through Christian art depicting the life and times of Jesus and Christianity. From the pictures in the Sistine Chapel to the paintings in every art gallery, God speaks to us about His glory, His suffering and His love for all people.

During World War 2, a team of people sought to save the art that had been stolen by the Nazis. One piece was the Altarpiece of Ghent in Belgium. In 2016 I visited Ghent to see that altarpiece. On that trip in Europe, I took the opportunity of seeing many altarpieces in various churches and God's message to all who saw them.

The amazing thing is that God is not limited to Christian writings. There have been times when God has spoken to me through a secular pop song, a line from Shakespeare or a novel.

We must not limit God speaking to us through Christian sources only. God wants to speak to us and will use anything to get His message across.

God speaks through Truth.

I am the Way, the Truth and the Life. (John 14:6)

But when the Spirit of Truth comes, he will guide you into all truth. (John 16:13)

God speaks to us through truth because He is truth. He speaks truth to our hearts about every aspect of our life: our mind, our actions, our ethics, our relationships, our work practices.

Sometimes God will speak his truth through Christians and sometimes He will speak it through potential Christians, even his enemies. For Truth stands whoever speaks it because God is truth.

There have been times when I have been pulled up about my language or actions by another person. What they said was true. It was not pleasant but needed to be said to me to make the adjustment I needed to make. Our spouses are very good at speaking truth into our lives.

God speaks through His Creation

The heavens declare the glory of God; the skies proclaim the work of his hands. Day after day they pour forth speech; night after night they reveal knowledge. They have no speech; they use no words; no sound is heard from them. Yet their voice goes out into all the earth, their words to the ends of the world. (Psalm 19:1-3)

The creation of heaven and earth began with God speaking. The psalmist acknowledges that the very creation of God speaks about His majesty and glory. Though they use no words or sound, they communicate to all who would listen.

Brent D Earles (2), a Christian author, says:

The stars are God's fingerprints. The sun is a mere smidgen of His radiance. The moon is to remind us that He doesn't sleep at night. The vastness of space proclaims the infinity of His wisdom, while the sand pebble indicates His thoroughness with the puniest details. The lion hints at His fearlessness, the bear at His power, the hawk at His keen insight. And yet, those possess only a titbit of God's omnipotence and omnipresence. Every tree points towards heaven; every bird has a song to sing; even every moment of wind goes in some direction. There is nothing chaotic about our beautiful designed world. All creation has a message to tell. It says, "Listen, there is a God. There is a God!"

God speaks to us through His peace

The peace of God, which passes all understanding, keep your heart and mind in Christ Jesus. (Philippians 4:7)

In seeking direction for your life, God's peace will affirm whether you have made the right decision or are going in the right direction. Sometimes if you are unsure, make a decision in your mind then wait and see whether God's peace continues in your heart. If there is no peace, then revisit your decision or possible direction with God. This method can be used in the process of testing or confirming a word from God.

There is always a question of whether you are hearing right from God. There have been times when I sought God's peace before I acted on what I received.

God speaks through circumstances

Paul and his companions travelled throughout the region of Phrygia and Galatia, having been kept from preaching the word in the province of Asia. When they came to the border of Mysia, they tried to enter Bithynia but the Spirit of Jesus would not allow them to go (Acts 16:6,7)

The key to understand circumstances is to see what the Father is doing as Jesus did. (John 5:19) For circumstances can be misread and misunderstood and should always be balanced by the word of truth from God.

In Exodus 5-6, after a few miracles, Moses went to Pharaoh to challenge him to let God's people go. To his astonishment and the Israelites, Pharaoh did not let them go but added to their punishment. It would be easy to interpret the circumstances that you had got it wrong. But the truth was that God wanted to harden Pharaoh's heart.

In Paul's missionary journey in Acts 16, he was prevented from entering the province of Asia and Bithynia to preach the word by the Holy Spirit. We are not told how that happened. But what seemed a godly thing to do was denied to Paul. Paul was guided by hindrance. The Holy Spirit often guides as much by the *closing* of doors as He does by the *opening* of doors.

David Livingstone wanted to go to China, but God sent him to Africa. William Carey wanted to go to Polynesia, but God sent him to India. Adoniram Judson went to India, but God guided him to Burma.

Reverend John Lucas, DMin

Recognize the Promptings of the Holy Spirit

But the Counsellor, the Holy Spirit, whom the Father will send in my name, will teach you all things and will remind you of everything that I have said to you. (John 14:26)

We need to be aware of the promptings of the Holy Spirit.

The word, *Prompt,* means "to incite, move person to action (to do); to supply with the words that come next; to assist with suggestion; to inspire, give rise to feeling, thought, action, thing said to help the memory."

The feeling associated with Prompting is a gentle tug, light touch, soft sound, use of all senses.

In a stage play, a person is employed with the script to prompt the actors when they have forgotten their lines. They are usually on the side lines and are in earshot of the actors but not the audience.

It is a gentle communication. In the same way, it is the Spirit that brings the message of God or Jesus to our hearts so that this message can be registered in our minds. But the sound level of this message is soft and not loud and if you are focusing too hard, you can miss it.

This is a major problem for those who wish to hear from God. They try so hard and in their trying they miss the gentle voice of God. They actually shut themselves down rather than opening up to God's voice. Sometimes they have been distracted by other things and God's voice can't penetrate them.

I was leaving to go to Oakey near Toowoomba in Queensland, Australia. I said goodbye to Liz who was outside. As usual I pressed the garage door remote to close the garage door but I did not realize that Liz had no way to get into the house.

She prayed to Jesus to prompt me to return to open up the house. Jesus' answer was that I was not listening! I had the radio on and my mind was on driving the 20 miles to Oakey from our house.

Fortunately, we had left a key with a friend nearby and Liz walked there, found the friend home and got the key. I would have been in a pretty pickle if the friend was not home!

I have found that the Holy Spirit uses a number of ways to get Jesus' message across.

Know your Spiritual Gifts

Now to each one the manifestation of the Spirit is given for the common good. To one there is given through the Spirit a message of wisdom, to another a message of knowledge by means of the same Spirit, to another faith by the same Spirit, to another gifts of healing by that one Spirit, to another miraculous powers, to another prophecy, to another distinguishing between spirits, to another speaking in different kinds of tongues, and to still another the interpretation of tongues. All these are the work of one and the same Spirit, and he distributes them to each one, just as he determines. (1 Corinthians 12:7-11)

Finally, the Holy Spirit gives people specific supernatural abilities to hear God's message, to discern the supernatural realm and equip people to praise Him. These gifts are to be used to minister to the church and people though one (speaking in tongues) can be used for personal worship of God.

The word of wisdom, the word of knowledge, the word of prophecy, speaking in tongues and their message by a word of interpretation are still valid today and God uses these Holy Spirit giftings in people to communicate His message to people. Though it would be true that not every church would practice these gifts. I have found that seeking to hear from God opens us up to these Holy Spirit speaking giftings to not only hear better but minister to people with the other giftings like healing.

When I became a Christian at 18, the gift of tongues was being released in the people in the mainline churches like Methodists and Baptist in South Australia. I had the opportunity to receive this gift but I was young and arrogant, believing that tongues were given to people who needed it. I decided that I did not need it because I was OK! Little did I realize that I was not ok. Going to a Baptist church who believed that spiritual gifts died with the apostles did not help.

Later I did receive this gift and found it very necessary in the ministry of deliverance that I was called to, as well as to connect with the Holy Spirit to praise Jesus.

However, I have seen Tongues used in an unhelpful way as a group of people burst into tongues while praying for healing for a person. The person had no idea what was being prayed for and they had no idea what was being said so that they could participate.

Paul in 1 Corinthians 14 outlines some of the common problems and how to use Tongues.

As I listen to Jesus when I pray for a person, words come to my mind and as I speak them out, God touches the heart of the person being prayed for.

Recently, I was praying for a person who had come forward for prayer at the front of the church. She was struggling about God's direction for her life. She was a musician and a relief teacher. As I prayed, the words came like a prophecy that encouraged her and gave her some direction and answers for her struggles. The most important thing was the touch of Jesus and the knowledge that He was on her case!

Remember that even though you may have a prophetic word for someone, it does not make you a prophet. Prophets are an office of the church (Ephesians 4:11-13) and not everyone who has a prophecy gifting is a prophet. Prophecy is about encouragement, comfort and strengthening (1 Corinthians 14:3) and the apostle Paul would prefer people have the gift of prophecy. (1 Corinthians 14:3-5)

Testing what you hear

Do not quench the Spirit. Do not treat prophecies with contempt but test them all; hold on to what is good, reject every kind of evil. (1 Thessalonians 5:19-22)

Beloved, do not believe every spirit, but test the spirits to see whether they are from God, for many false prophets have gone out into the world. By this you know the Spirit of God: every spirit that confesses that Jesus Christ has come in the flesh is from God, and every spirit that does not confess Jesus is not from God. This is the spirit of the antichrist, which you heard was coming and now is in the world already. (1 John 4:1-3)

So how do you know if it is God who is speaking to you? For we know that demons have the capacity to speak into our minds. We also know that we can hear other voices from our own selfish desires and our fractured self. Then our world and culture speak to us as well.

Mark Virkler (3) in his training book *Communion with God* offers the following about the voices we can hear and how we can test them. (I have used his key points but with my descriptions. I have used his description of testing. The test of belief is my addition.)

It is a helpful guide to discern and distinguish the "voices" that may come to you with their content, intent and purpose.

1) Voice of the World.

Do not love the world or the things of the world. If anyone loves the world, the love of the Father is not in him. For all that is in the world – the lust of the flesh, the lust of the eyes and the pride of life – is not in the Father but is of the world. (1 John 2: 15,16)

The world that we live in has different values that seek to force themselves upon us. It is like a voice seeking to convince us that the world's values are better than the biblical values. In some of them the values are contradictory to what the Bible teaches. These values are presented to us through all forms of media.

The apostle John categorized these values as fundamentally lust and self-centeredness where all our senses are tempted to succumb to these values. But it is done in such a way that is *Enticing, Alluring, Desiring and Convincing.*

As you live in the world, are you listening to the voice of the World and succumbing to its values and adopting them.

Are you being enticed to believe what these voices are saying?

It is not just the prevalent materialism of the world or its blatant sexual overtones. At the time of writing, we encounter a voice that wants to cancel out what you want to say, a voice that accuses you that you are racist or wrong if you do not adopt what they are saying. Their voice is the only voice and will not tolerate any other voice that is different.

Are you discerning the Voice of the World and what it may be saying to you?

2) Voice of Satan.

Now the serpent was more cunning than any beast of the field which the Lord God had made. Has God indeed said, "You shall not eat of every tree of the garden?" (Genesis 3:1)

We live in a spiritual world. As we seek to live spiritually and be open to the Holy Spirit, there is another player. He is known as Satan. For most of us, we will not encounter Satan but we will encounter some of his demonic army that have been taught well by their master.

Chapter 1: Unlocking the Power of God's Voice

They attack the mind of the person by sowing thoughts that *twist what God has said, create doubt, deceive, lies and accuses or slander the individual.* They seek to undermine the person's belief about themselves and their life. They prey on the person's vulnerabilities.

The voice is subtle and cunning and knows how to play to the individual's weaknesses and their faulty belief about themselves and their situation.

Like the experience of Jesus in the wilderness, Satan knows the Bible, is able to quote it and change the context for his own ends. There is an element of truth in what is suggested but it is not the total truth. There is always an element that is not true that needs to be understood.

The aim of the enemy is to lead you away from God and his plans for you.

Are you discerning the voice of the enemy and his army? Do you know what it sounds like in your ear?

3) Voice of Self.

I will ascend into heaven, I will sit on the mount of God, I will be like the Most High. (Isaiah 14:13,14)

So, Elijah said, "I have been very jealous for the Lord God of Hosts; for the children of Israel have forsaken Your covenant, torn down your altars, and killed Your prophets with the sword. I alone am left; and they seek to take my life." (I Kings 19:10)

The voice of self comes from our fallen nature that seeks to rebel against God and desires to be in control. It comes out of our hearts that may not be totally surrendered to God.

The first scripture, above, from Isaiah, is a window into the heart of Satan. He was an archangel, created by God, mighty and powerful. But he decided that he wanted to be God. He was not happy with what he was given.

His arrogance and pride in himself and his abilities took over. His heart was corrupted by his pride and his desire to be like God caused him to be cast out of heaven.

The voice of self can be strong in its desires to want everything and be everything. Unless the heart is surrendered and the voice of self, dethroned, it can be a real problem in the life of a person.

The second scripture is from the life of Elijah, where Jezebel has threatened to kill him after he had destroyed all the prophets of Baal. It seems that this threat overwhelmed him in such a way that it cancelled out all that God had done through him.

Now the voice of self takes over in the form of a pity party! He prayed that he had had enough and wanted to die. *Take my life. I am no better than my ancestors. (1 Kings 19:4,5)*.

Later he would complain that all that he had done for the Lord was to no avail, The Israelites had rejected the covenant, broken down all the altars, killed all the prophets and that he was the only one left. But the Lord reminded him that seven thousand had not bowed to Baal. (1 Kings 19:14,18)

Our own thinking about our self and situation becomes a hindrance to hearing what God wants to say to us.

4) Voice of God

He who belongs to God hears what God says. (John 8: 47 a)

We "hear" and "see" God with the ears and eyes of our heart! The heart is like a satellite dish receiving the "video" and "sound waves" from heaven. The mind helps us to process and understand these "video and sound waves"

The ability to hear the voice of God involves developing an intimate love relationship and nurturing that love relationship. The "voice of God" is gentle and encouraging and affirming.

When it is a message of warning or judgment of your behavior, it is done in such a way that you do not feel condemned.

It is happy to be tested again and again to assure you that you are hearing right. Is this you Jesus? Is this you Jesus? Any other voices do not stay strong when they are tested and questioned *"Is this you, Jesus?"*

SOURCES OF REVELATION

The Scriptures indicate that there are three sources of spiritual revelation or communication: Holy Spirit, Self or the human Soul or Satan.

Holy Spirit: True source (2 Peter 1:21)

Human Soul: capable of voicing thoughts, ideas and inspirations out of the unsanctified portion of the soul (mind, emotions and will) (Ezekiel 13:1-6; Jer. 23:16)

Satan: appears to be a good voice but when it is scrutinized and tested, the voice lies, slanders, condemns and makes you feel guilty.

TESTING THE REVELATION

We are called to test the "spirit" and the message that comes to us. We have outlined the different voices that could be heard. Now we need to test the voice and the message by asking specific questions.

Firstly, we need to check to see if *our self has the right perspective and position to receive*.

So, we ask the following

- Is there any evidence of influences other than the Spirit of God in my life?
- What is the essence of the "vision" or "word" or revelation?
- Was I under the control of the Holy Spirit when I received the revelation?
- Did I present my life to Jesus?
- Was I obedient to His Word?
- Was I enlightened with His inspiration?
- Was I committed to doing His will no matter what it is?
- Was I yielding my life to the praises of God?
- Was I waiting humbly, quietly and expectantly before Him?

Secondly, we need to check the source. What may be the origin of this message. John warns in his letter

Dear friends, do not believe every spirit, but test the spirits to see whether they are from God, because many false prophets have gone out into the world. (1 John 4:1)

If the origin is SELF, we need to ask the following
- Is the voice/message born in the mind? Does it feed my ego or exalt Jesus?
- Does it appeal to my ego? Is the self on the throne of my heart or Jesus?
- Does it elevate man or Jesus? Does it display the fruit of the flesh (Galatians 5:19-21)

If the origin is Satan, we need to ask the following
- Is the Word or image destructive? Does it lure me away from God?
- Is it negative, destructive, pushy, fearful, and accusative?
- Is it a violation of the nature of God, the Word of God?
- Is it afraid to be tested or confirmed?
- Am I fearful, compulsive, in bondage, anxious, confused?

If the origin is the Spirit of God, we need to ask the following
- Does it help me focus on Jesus?
- Is there a living flow from my heart?
- Is it instructive, uplifting, and comforting?
- Does it accept testing or confirmation?
- Does it encourage me in my walk with God?
- Do I sense a quickened faith, power, peace, good fruit, enlightenment, knowledge, humility?

Thirdly, we can apply the Scriptural Test by asking the following
- Does the revelation edify, exhort or console? (1 Corinthians 14:3)
- Is it in agreement with God's Word? (2 Timothy 3:16)
- Does it exalt Jesus? (John 16:14)
- Does it have good fruit? (Matthew 7:15-16)
- Does it come to pass? (Deuteronomy 18:22-30)
- Does it turn you to God or away from God? (Deuteronomy 13:1-5)
- Does it produce liberty or bondage? (Romans 8:15)
- Does it produce life or death? (2 Corinthians 3:6)
- Does the Holy Spirit bear witness that it is true? (John 16:13)

Test of Belief

Then the word of the Lord came to him: "This man will not be your heir, but a son who is your own flesh and blood will be your heir." He took him outside and said, "Look up at the sky and count the

stars—if indeed you can count them." Then he said to him, "So shall your offspring be." Abram believed the Lord, and he credited it to him as righteousness. (Genesis 15:4-6)

When God spoke to Abraham, he believed what God said and obeyed, leaving his homeland not knowing his destination. Then later after having no children yet, God appeared to Abraham. Abraham commented, even complained, that his servant would inherit his estate.

But God again spoke and told him that he would have a child. Then God showed him the stars and reiterated that he would have many offspring. Abraham believed the Lord.

God spoke to Moses and told him that he was going to Pharoah and cause him to release the people of God. God answered all his concerns and finally Moses believed God and did what He was told.

God spoke to Joshua and gave him each strategy to take each city. Joshua believed what he heard and implemented them.

Gideon was working in the wine press and God revealed that he was to save God's people from the Midianites. Gideon looked at who he was, the least in his family, and suggested to God that He has the wrong man. Gideon wanted proof and received it a number of times until he believed God and believed that he was chosen to free God's people from the Midianites.

As we look at all the conversations that God had with people. The challenge for the people was to believe what they heard and then act on it.

It is one thing to receive a vision or word from God, but it is another to believe what you have heard or seen and do what God had asked you to.

One night I was awakened by God to go to the house of the Salvation Army officer in Peterborough South Australia. I was to walk around it, praying as I went. I was aware that the Officer was struggling with some issues that threatened his ability to be an officer. He was a former trucker and he smoked. As a Salvation Army Officer, he was not allowed to smoke but it still had control over him. He was struggling with His calling and there were family issues.

So, I did what God asked of me. I did have many questions, thoughts and many what ifs. What if the family wakes up? What if someone comes along or the dog barks? What if this does not work? What if I look like a fool?

But I did what I was asked to do by God. The dog next door did bark at my presence but nobody woke up. I finished the task.

It is vital to believe what God has told you or shown you or ask you to do. On many occasions, it will stretch you and seems to be beyond you.

Believing and obeying what God has revealed is essential to have a long-term ability to hear from God even if you do not know all the reasons as to why you should believe and obey.

Are you willing to believe what you hear? Are you willing to obey what Jesus has said and asked you to do and speak?

PRACTICE LISTENING

I have found that the best way to learn to listen to God was to talk to God through writing. I would get an exercise book and a pen. I would spend about ten minutes listening to worship music that focuses on God, His goodness and what He has done through Jesus.

As the music is playing softly in the background, I would write
Lord Jesus, I love you. What would you like to say to me today?

I would wait with pen in my hand, ready to write down the thoughts that came to me in my mind. I would write them all down and then assess whether this is Jesus speaking to me.

Initially it would be, *I love you, John. You are my son.* Then it would be a little more as I asked different questions.

It started off small but doing this every day, the conversation grew and I learned that these thoughts were Jesus, speaking to me in my heart and then being registered in my mind for me to understand. Every time, I tested what I had heard with the tests that I have outlined above.

The more that I practiced, the more I recognized the "sound" of Jesus' voice in my heart. Then I was able to speak to Jesus and hear Him spontaneously without the need of having a book and pen on hand.

Over the years, I have accumulated many exercise books containing my conversations with Jesus which are now a record of my journey with Jesus, the issues that I faced and the answers that I was given, along with all the words of love and encouragement from Jesus.

Hearing from Jesus and praying what He shows you is critical to unlocking the power of your praying. Then you will experience God working through you, powerfully, effectively and supernaturally.

On one occasion, one of the disciples asked Jesus to teach them to pray as John the Baptist had taught his disciples (Luke 11:1). Jesus gave them a prayer that we now know as the Lord's prayer.

In the next chapter, we explore the importance of that prayer for every disciple of Jesus who wants to pray specifically, effectively and supernaturally.

Reverend John Lucas, DMin

2

UNLOCKING THE POWER OF THE LORD'S PRAYER

One day Jesus was praying in a certain place. When he finished, one of his disciples said to him, "Lord, teach us to pray, just as John taught his disciples." He said to them, "When you pray, say: "'Father, hallowed be your name, your kingdom come. Give us each day our daily bread. Forgive us our sins, for we also forgive everyone who sins against us. And lead us not into temptation. (Luke 11:1-4)

This, then, is how you should pray:'"Our Father in heaven, hallowed be your name, your kingdom come, your will be done, on earth as it is in heaven. Give us today our daily bread. And forgive us our debts, as we also have forgiven our debtors. And lead us not into temptation, but deliver us from the evil one.' For if you forgive other people when they sin against you, your heavenly Father will also forgive you. But if you do not forgive others their sins, your Father will not forgive your sins. (Matthew 6:9-15)

The disciples asked Jesus to teach them how to pray. Jesus gave them a simple prayer that we know as the Lord's Prayer. Often it is recited in the liturgy of a number of denominations. But it is more than a prayer to be recited. It is the starting point in unlocking the power to pray specifically, effectively and supernaturally.

This prayer equips us with foundational principles that every Christian must embrace if they are to be a powerful prayer warrior. I would like to share with you these foundational principles that I have found enables me to pray specifically, effectively and supernaturally.

RELATIONSHIP: Our Father who is in Heaven

For what father of you, if the son asks for bread, will he give him a stone? Or if he asks for a fish, will he give him a snake for a fish? Or if he shall ask for an egg, will he give him a scorpion? If you then, being evil, know how to give good gifts to your children, how much more shall your heavenly Father give the Holy Spirit to those who ask Him? (Luke 11:11-13)

Behold the birds of the air; for they sow not, nor do they reap, nor gather into barns. Yet your heavenly Father feeds them; are you not much better than they are? For the nations seek after all these things. For your heavenly Father knows that you have need of all these things. (Matthew 6:26, 32)

Jesus turned prayer upside down by stating that our relationship with God is primarily a relationship with a Heavenly Dad. Jesus used the term *Abba*, which means Daddy, and this brought intimacy into the relationship and the understanding that a dad delights to give good things to his children.

Jesus had to change the mindsets of the disciples about who God is. Their view of God was dominated by distance, discipline and "don't touch!" God to the Jews was unreachable and unknowable. God to the Jews was about rules and regulations as typified by the Mosaic Law but further complicated by the Pharisees with their additions. God to the Jews was not to be experienced or else you would die!

Sadly, our relationship with God has mirrored the Jewish experience where over the years the God of Christianity was also distant and not caring and not hearing. The God of Christianity was a killjoy with all the rules and regulations that were developed to constrain a person's life. Certainly, the God of Christianity was not expected to be experienced each Sunday even though there had been some experiences of the out pouring of God's Spirit from time to time.

Our relationship with God is influenced by two things: our picture of God and our relationship with our parents, primarily, with our human father.

Our picture of God is formed first of all by what has been heard and received as a child growing up. Bible stories and Sunday School are the first places for developing a picture of who God is and what He is like. The stories that you heard and the way that they were selected and told were part of the picture. The experience and relationship with Sunday School teachers also contributed to this picture. The minister/pastor and his/her preaching also contributed to this picture.

The Bible gives us many pictures or aspects of God. In The Old Testament, God is a Creator, caring for His creation and His creatures and yet able to punish quite severely those who broke His laws, especially the commandment of not having another god. We see God as judge, jury and executioner and yet able to forgive those who transgress His laws.

He is a God who speaks to bring creation into being and also speaks to certain individuals about His plans and purposes. He even uses pagan rulers to bring about His purposes. He is a God who gives rules and regulations to live by and woe betide any who break those rules.

In the Old Testament we have two polarities to understand: God's love on the one hand and God's judgment or wrath on the other hand.

In the New Testament, Jesus comes onto the scene and presents a radically different picture of God as Abba Father. He presents God as compassionate and caring, seeking those who are lost in their lives. He presents God as healer of sickness and deliverer from Satan's oppression of people's lives.

Jesus becomes the new Moses teaching people the ways of God's Kingdom and inviting them to follow Him. He has stern words for the Scribes and the Pharisees who have locked people into a religious understanding of the God of rules and regulations.

Later in the Acts of the Apostles and the Letters of Paul, John and Peter, God is the Savior of people's sin who offers forgiveness and a second chance to all who would repent and claim Jesus as their Lord.

Chapter 2: Unlocking the Power of The Lord's Prayer

To be effective about your praying you need a personal relationship with the God of Jesus. He is your Abba Father who loves you and yet He is willing to pull you up when you go off track in your walk with Him. He wants to walk and talk with you, every day. Like Jesus, we learn to hear from Him and do what He tells us to do, especially when we pray for others.

My picture of God had many missing pieces. I did not grow up as a church goer. I went to Sunday School when I was young for two years. I attended religious instruction in the early years of High School. I believed in the existence of God. I believed the Easter story that Jesus lived, died and rose again. But for most of my first 18 years there was no connection with God and Jesus.

Things changed when I went to a Baptist Church with my brother. We were told that there were some nice girls there! I did not meet a girl for a wife but did meet God who said to me that He loved me. This was spoken to my heart and I felt loved. I gave my life to Jesus and I was given a love for the Bible.

I grew up not feeling loved by my parents though they did love me in their own way. There were some rejection issues in my life that needed to be addressed and healed. I needed to know the truth that even if everybody rejected me, for whatever reason, true or false, God has not rejected me and even loved me, personally.

This leads me to the next issue. Our view of God is colored by our view of our human Dad. If our relationship with our human father is in any way dysfunctional, then our relationship with our heavenly Father will be distorted in some way. We will need a change of mindset to embrace God as father and talk to Him as Daddy.

In my case, I did not have a close relationship with my dad. We were different. He was very practical and I was more intellectual. Though I enjoyed playing sport, he was more interested in playing His sport. We did fish together and I helped him with his floor covering business in high school. But he could not say that he loved me or was proud of me.

I went to live with my grandmother in the 4th and 5th year of High School. Looking back that did not help our relationship. Then when I became a believer but he was not, life became different for both of us. I became more and more independent as I studied at University and became involved with the church.

Rejection was my life script reinforced by my perception of my parents and upbringing though it was not all bad because of my grandmother's love. It was only later in life as I came to understand my parent's background and life, that I came to understand them better and why I felt the way I did.

In the thirty odd years of being involved with healing of people's lives, their relationship with God was infected and affected by their relationship with a parent or pastor or church leader.

It seems that people's perspective of God is formed through the prism of a person in authority over them. They interpret God as that person. There may have been some distance in the relationship. There may have been some form of abuse or perceived abuse. There may have been a sense of abandonment due to the early death of a parent or being adopted out. They say *If God is like that, I will have nothing to do with Him!"*

There may be a lot of bitterness and anger about the way that they have been treated and Satan has a hold on them and they struggle to let go of all the deep hurt that they carry.

We have to work hard to demonstrate that God is not like their father or mother or church leader who have abused their position of authority. We have to work hard to help these people see that God is not like them but is like Jesus. We get them to read the gospels to get to know Jesus and help them to see that God is not like what they thought or experienced or believed.

They will need to forgive their parent or pastor or church leader to be set free from this tainted picture of God and in some cases, they will need to forgive God for giving them their parents or allowing His church leaders to affect their lives.

So, God had to break through my rejection façade and communicate that He loves me and accepts me as I am and that was a real turning point when I was 18. It was a life changing experience to know that God loves me. His joy filled my life and I could not get enough of knowing Him through the scriptures. But it did not last. So, there was still another lesson to learn and another situation to deal with.

In Revelation 2, to the church at Ephesus, Jesus said

Yet I hold this against you: You have forsaken the love you had at first. Consider how far you have fallen! Repent and do the things you did at first. If you do not repent, I will come to you and remove your lampstand from its place. (Revelation 2:4-5)

By 1986, fifteen years after I became a Christian, I had lost my first love! The busyness of life, study and a parish meant that my devotional life was minimal and intellectual. I had lost my first love!

So, it was back to the drawing board, recognizing, repenting and recovering my first love. Two things helped me; the desire to hear God and the worship music of the Vineyard that encouraged people to sing and express love to and for God.

The ability to hear from God, talk with Him and learn from Him helped me to pray for people and situations more effectively and specifically. The worship music drew me into the presence of God and nurtured my love relationship with Him.

Suffice it to say that the start to becoming an effective prayer warrior is to have a living, vital relationship with God where you walk and talk with Him and God walks and talks to you. If you focus on that first, your prayers will become very powerful and achieve what God wants.

REVERENCE: Hallowed be Your name

While our relationship with God is to be intimate like a father-child relationship, we should not lose our respect or reverence for our God. Jesus says, repeatedly, "Holy is the name of God"

And each one of the four living creatures had six wings about him, and within being full of eyes. And they had no rest day and night, saying, Holy, holy, holy, Lord God, the Almighty, who was and is and is to come. And whenever the living creatures gave glory and honor and thanks to Him who sat on the throne, who lives forever and ever, the twenty-four elders fell down before the One sitting on the throne. (Revelation 4:6-11)

Holiness is the core part of God's being and we are called to worship a Holy God. Part of our praying is to be reverent and to worship a Holy God.

We need to rediscover two things: Holiness of God and the name of God. For we live in a time where these have been lost.

Firstly, the Bible describes Holy as separate, other or different from something else. So, when the Bible speaks about God's holiness, the primary thrust is to refer to God's transcendence, His magnificence which is higher and above all things. He is superior to anything there is in all of creation.

And in His presence, we experience His touch that is both indescribable and filled with awe and fear. But we experience Him as Creator and we as His creatures; His sinlessness and our sinfulness.

It is like the experience of the prophet Isaiah who experienced the holiness of God in the temple and at the same time felt his sinfulness.

"Woe to me!" I cried. "I am ruined! For I am a man of unclean lips, and I live among a people of unclean lips, and my eyes have seen the King, the Lord Almighty. (Isaiah 6:3)

It is like the experience I had in the gardens of Ballarat (see Introduction) when my sin was paraded before me after I had an experience of the presence of God in the conference the previous night. I was lifted onto and into another plane that I still remember to this day that I had tasted the presence of the Holy God in my life and I never want to forget it.

This experience changed the way that I approach God whenever I pray. I knew His place and I knew my place and never should those places be confused or changed.

While we rejoice in what Jesus has done for us:

Therefore, brothers and sisters, since we have confidence to enter the Most Holy Place by the blood of Jesus, by a new and living way opened for us through the curtain, that is, his body, and since we have a great priest over the house of God, let us draw near to God with a sincere heart and with the full assurance that faith brings, having our hearts sprinkled to cleanse us from a guilty conscience and having our bodies washed with pure water. (Hebrews 10:19-22)

We should not forget our place and barge in to the Holy Place of God, forgetting who we are and who He is. And let us not forget what we need to do before we enter: having a sincere heart that has been cleansed of all its sin; a heart that is in accord with God.

So, we approach God not with any rights of our own but with the permission of God through Jesus.

Secondly, we should understand the importance of God's name.

Names are important to us because they often do more than just identify an individual; they can actually reveal who a person is, and what he or she is like. Knowing a person's name establishes a relationship with that person and can also be a means of exercising power over them.

The term for name in the Old Testament means "individual mark" and it communicated an individual's essence. In the New Testament, the word for name comes from a verb that means "to know." To know the name of God means to have an intimate relationship with God.

In the Old Testament, God revealed his name to individuals. There were many names given that revealed many aspects of who God was and corresponded to the need or experience of the person with God.

Abraham looked up and there in a thicket he saw a ram caught by its horns. He went over and took the ram and sacrificed it as a burnt offering instead of his son. So, Abraham called that place The Lord Will Provide. And to this day it is said, "On the mountain of the Lord it will be provided. (Genesis 22:13,14)

God revealed himself as Jehovah Jireh when He provided a ram to sacrifice rather than Isaac.

Moses said to God, "Suppose I go to the Israelites and say to them, 'The God of your fathers has sent me to you,' and they ask me, 'What is his name?' Then what shall I tell them?" God said to Moses, "I am who I am. This is what you are to say to the Israelites: 'I am has sent me to you.' (Exodus 3:13,14)

God revealed His name to Moses, Yahweh, (I am who I am), so that Moses could tell the people who had sent him.

Later the prophet Ezekiel commented:

But when they came to the nations, wherever they came, they profaned my holy name, in that people said of them, 'These are the people of the Lord, and yet they had to go out of his land.' But I had concern for my holy name, which the house of Israel had profaned among the nations to which they came. (Ezekiel 36:20-23)

As you can see, the problem arose when God's people profaned His holy name. The word "profane" is not necessarily derogatory or negative, it just means common or ordinary, no different from anything else in that category.

All holiness flows from the LORD, the one who is uniquely other, separate and exalted above everyone and everything. He is utterly distinct from all other things and His name cannot be classed among other things or other gods. He can never be profane or common because He could never be one in a class of many. He is in a class all by Himself, which is the very definition of Holiness.

Thus, to take the Lord's name in vain is to make the Lord's name common; to use it in such a way that its meaning and significance is lowered. We bring God and His name down to our level by the way we treat it and the way we live and the way we go after "other gods". In both the church and the community, we have lost our sense of the Holiness of God and we have profaned His name.

Chapter 2: Unlocking the Power of The Lord's Prayer

If we are to powerfully, we must learn to:

Pray with respect and honor – Hallowed be Your name

RIGHT FOCUS: Your kingdom come, Your will be done, on earth as it is in Heaven

I have found that to pray effectively and powerfully is to have the right focus: the will and perspective of God. Often, we start with our agenda and not God's agenda.

But Jesus taught His disciples to pray God's agenda

Your Kingdom come, Your will be done, on earth as it is in Heaven (Matthew 6:10)

The power of Jesus' praying and ministry was found in the right focus of God's Kingdom will.

Very truly I tell you, the Son can do nothing by himself; he can do only what he sees his Father doing, because whatever the Father does the Son also does. (John 5:19)

When you have lifted up the Son of Man, then you will know that I am he and that I do nothing on my own but speak just what the Father has taught me. (John 8:28)

But seek first the kingdom of God and His righteousness; and all these things shall be added to you. (Matt. 6:33)

And this is the confidence that we have toward Him, that if we ask anything according to His will, He hears us. (1 John 5:14)

The power of our prayers lies in praying God's Kingdom will. His Kingdom will be found in the heart of God in heaven. So, when we pray, we need to ask God first: *What is Your Kingdom will for this person or situation?*

Then we wait and listen to His response to our heart through the Holy Spirit. Through the Holy Spirit, we will be given His answer through a scripture or pictures, words or impressions or a combination of some or all. Then it will be our task to pray them out aloud to fulfill God's kingdom will.

I was praying for a lady who had been hurt badly and this hurt was like a poison that was in many areas of her body. After she had forgiven the people who had hurt her, the word "drain" came into my mind and then a memory of giving blood where a drip attached to a bag was put in my arm to collect the blood.

So, I asked Jesus for a drip to be put in and the poison to be emptied into a bag. Then the picture came of this drip and the poison filling the bag. Once it was finished, the drip was removed and the bag was taken to the foot of the cross to be destroyed. The lady felt much better and the hurt had disappeared.

In our ministry of healing at Walkingfree, we had a prayer process and ways of praying to work through the many doors to ill health including generational doors, curses and inner vows, unforgiveness etc. While we had this process and ways of praying, Jesus could intervene in the process so that He could lead us to the crucial areas that we needed to deal with on that day. On some occasions, the process is laid aside altogether because it was important to do what Jesus wanted to do rather than a pre-determined process!

It is God's Kingdom intersecting the lives of people and the world that is to be the focus of our praying. It is God's Kingdom intersecting our lives that gives the right focus for our praying. Then as we see that Kingdom coming into being, we give God all the glory, honor and praise!

Pray with an expectant heart – Your Kingdom come

He told the crowd to sit down on the ground. When he had taken the seven loaves and given thanks, he broke them and gave them to his disciples to distribute to the people, and they did so. They had a few small fish as well; he gave thanks for them also and told the disciples to distribute them. The people ate and were satisfied. Afterward the disciples picked up seven basketfuls of broken pieces that were left over. (Mark 8:6-8)

Jesus saw God doing great things around him and through him. He was excited about what God was going to do next. He saw God's Kingdom rule entering into people's lives and circumstances. Sometimes it upset them as it did with the Pharisees but God was still at work and **in control**. We are called to pray with the same expectations that God was up to something good. Sometimes it starts with a mess but He soon sorts it out.

How expectant are you that God will work through your praying? I have found over the years when there is a high level of expectancy, God will be present and something good will happen, and we are not disappointed. I have organized a few conferences in my time and attended many others. There have often been powerful times of God's presence. But the key was that all the attendees would come with great expectation that God will appear, meeting the needs of those who will be present.

Pray with a servant attitude – Your will be done on earth as it is in heaven

For even the Son of Man did not come to be served, but to serve, and to give His life as a ransom for many (Mark 10:45)

Jesus was always at the disposal of His Father. He came to serve and not to be served. Humility was His major characteristic trait.

We pray to serve the purposes of God and experience the privilege of working with Him to achieve those purposes. It is God's agenda that we serve and not our own. He invites us to join Him in His Kingdom work and we get a front row seat through our praying.

But there is a warning for all of us. God can work through our praying in a powerful way. We can become intoxicated by the power of God working through us. Very quickly, we can claim the glory rather than give all the glory to God.

We have seen a number of pastors, over the years, who have had a successful ministry but have fallen from grace because their success has "justified" or covered their sinful behavior.

They thought that their success made them "untouchable". Soon their sinful behavior was uncovered and many ministries that started well with God, ended very badly and sadly. Many people left the church disillusioned with the pastor and God.

I have seen many people healed through the ministry of Walkingfree and my preaching and speaking. It is easy to take it all for granted. It is easy to claim a little bit of the glory as you pray and see people healed. But it all belongs to God and nothing belongs to us.

The challenge for all of us is to remain humble before our God, recognizing ALWAYS that it is God who does it and we have the privilege of seeing Him work through our praying and ministry.

Pray with a confident heart – Yours is the Kingdom and the power and the glory forever

One day Peter and John were going up to the temple at the time of prayer—at three in the afternoon. Now a man who was lame from birth was being carried to the temple gate called Beautiful, where he was put every day to beg from those going into the temple courts. When he saw Peter and John about to enter, he asked them for money. Peter looked straight at him, as did John. Then Peter said, "Look at us!" So, the man gave them his attention, expecting to get something from them. Then Peter said, "Silver or gold I do not have, but what I do have I give you. In the name of Jesus Christ of Nazareth, walk." Taking him by the right hand, he helped him up, and instantly the man's feet and ankles became strong. He jumped to his feet and began to walk. (Acts 3:1-8)

Jesus prayed with the confidence that His Father would act through his prayers. Peter would also pray in the same manner. The episode at the Gate Beautiful in Acts 3 demonstrates that Peter was confident that he had the ability to pray and command healing in the name of Jesus. Paul was confident that God would act when he prayed and preached the gospel.

This confidence was and is found in their relationship and the calling of God in their lives. This confidence grew as they prayed and saw God answer and act. Their confidence grew as God in Christ continued to use them to minister to people.

We need that same confidence that God will use our prayers to bring about His Kingdom by releasing His power and glory.

Confidence is a big issue in our lives affecting every aspect of them. If we are confident, we can scale mountains but if we lose our confidence, the smallest task seems impossible.

So do not throw away your confidence, it will be richly rewarded. (Hebrews 10:35)

Reverend John Lucas, DMin

REQUESTS: Give us this day our daily bread

So do not worry, saying, 'What shall we eat?' or 'What shall we drink?' or 'What shall we wear?' For the pagans run after all these things, and your heavenly Father knows that you need them. But seek first his kingdom and his righteousness, and all these things will be given to you as well. Therefore, do not worry about tomorrow, for tomorrow will worry about itself. Each day has enough trouble of its own. (Matthew 6:31-34)

"Do not be anxious about anything, but in every situation, by prayer and petition, with thanksgiving, present your requests to God. And the peace of God, which transcends all understanding, will guard your hearts and your minds in Christ Jesus." (Philippians 4:6,7)

God is concerned about our daily needs and his desire is to provide for them.

Dr. Helen Roseveare (1), a missionary to Zaire, told the following story.

"A mother at our mission station died after giving birth to a premature baby. We tried to improvise an incubator to keep the infant alive, but the only hot water bottle we had was beyond repair. So, we asked the children to pray for the baby and for her sister.

One of the girls responded. 'Dear God, please send a hot water bottle today. Tomorrow will be too late because by then the baby will be dead. And dear Lord, send a doll for the sister so she won't feel so lonely.'

That afternoon a large package arrived from England. The children watched eagerly as we opened it. Much to their surprise, under some clothing was a hot water bottle! Immediately the girl who had prayed so earnestly started to dig deeper, exclaiming, 'If God sent that, I'm sure He also sent a doll!'

And she was right! The heavenly Father knew in advance of that child's sincere requests, and 5 months earlier He had led a ladies' group to include both of those specific articles."

We have moved interstate two times. On both occasions we had to buy our own home. On both occasions, I presented my requests to God for not only a home but everything that I would like in it and one that I could afford.

On the first occasion, my requests included four bedrooms, two bathrooms with a spa in one of them and remote-controlled garage doors. The home that I saw on the internet had everything that I wanted including all my requests but it was too expensive. Soon the owners dropped their price significantly to get a quick sale as they had bought another property.

Needless to say, we praised God and bought the house.

The Lord is vitally interested in every request that we have. Some are needs and some are wants. Some are basic and some may seem extravagant.

But if you do not ask, you do not receive! So, I have continued to ask for big things and small things. Many are necessities but some are luxuries. I am surprised that while God does provide for our needs, He also loves to bless and spoil His beloved children.

Our focus is to take one day at a time and pray for each day's needs. These needs include our basic needs like food, clothing, housing, work and finance. They also include the answers to our prayers. They also include not going ahead of God but being prepared to be patient and wait for God's provision.

Pray with dependence – Give us this day our daily bread

And Jesus said to him, Foxes have holes, and birds of the air have nests, but the Son of Man has nowhere to lay His head. (Luke 9:58)

Jesus relied upon the Father to provide for all his needs. He travelled depending upon the provision of God. This came from the generosity of those who were following Him. It came from invitations from certain wealthy people and even pharisees wanting to know more.

It came from miraculous provision when the loaves and fishes were multiplied (Matthew 14:17-20) or the coin in the fish to pay for the temple tax (Matthew 17:23-27).

That same provision was given to Jesus' disciples as they travelled to spread the gospel. It was given to the apostle Paul and his fellow travelers as they spread the gospel.

The ministry of Walkingfree depended upon donations to pay for insurance, salaries and administration. We depended upon the Lord for His provision to pay all the bills. It came in surprising ways but it always came.

Pray with expectation – Give us this day our daily bread

Ask:

Ask and it will be given to you; seek and you will find; knock and the door will be opened to you. For everyone who asks receives; the one who seeks finds; and to the one who knocks, the door will be opened. (Matthew 7:7,8)

One of the main things that Jesus encourages his disciples to do is to ask. This sounds simple but we lose the art of asking as we grow up. We are reluctant to ask because we do not know whether we can, whether we have a right to and whether it is appropriate. But a child simply comes up and asks: "Dad, can I have this? Can I go there?"

Jesus pointed out a number of times to ask with the expectancy that what you ask for, you will most likely get, more often than not!

As I have shared above, I have learnt to ask for my material needs like a house. On the second occasion of moving, I again asked for a house with certain specifications: a front room for ministry, a room for an office, bedrooms and bathrooms but with no spa this time!

My wife asked for a garden to enjoy. Well, that garden was more like the garden of Eden with stone fruit and citrus fruit trees, a vegetable garden and a flower garden. It turned out to be a house that was over 100 years old, with a shopping center within walking distance and its location near our children and grandchildren.

Jesus expands this principle of asking with certain criteria:

Agreement of two.

"Again, truly I tell you that if two of you on earth agree about anything they ask for, it will be done for them by my Father in heaven." (Matthew 18:19)

Agreement releases God's power and purposes, as when two or more gathers and agrees on a matter, Jesus is present. This is said in the context of disputes within the church.

In My name

And I will do whatever you ask in my name, so that the Father may be glorified in the Son. (John 14:13 cf. John 15:16;16;23,24,26)

Prayer is to be offered in the name of Jesus. That prayer is in accordance with His character and must be presented in the same spirit of dependence and submission that marked Him. Prayer offered in the name of Jesus is offered with his authority and imprimatur.

Belief

If you believe, you will receive whatever you ask for in prayer." (Matthew 21:22)

Belief is a key ingredient of prayer. It is a part of faith and we will tackle this important area in the next chapter. Remember that doubt and unbelief can rob your power to pray and ask.

Pray Specifically

And when you pray, do not keep on babbling like pagans, for they think they will be heard because of their many words. Do not be like them, for your Father knows what you need before you ask him. (Matthew 6:7-8)

The way that the Pharisees prayed, was an object lesson in praying the wrong way. There were too many words! Praying the Jesus way meant praying simply and specifically. Prayers are not meant to be shot gun pellets sprayed into the spiritual realm hoping to hit something. Rather they are to be like missiles with a homing device that lock into the target with maximum effect.

Pray with Persistence

Then Jesus said to them, "Suppose you have a friend, and you go to him at midnight and say, 'Friend, lend me three loaves of bread; a friend of mine on a journey has come to me, and I have no food to offer him.' And suppose the one inside answers, 'Don't bother me. The door is already locked, and my children and I are in bed. I can't get up and give you anything.' I tell you, even though he will not get up and give you the bread because of friendship, yet because of your shameless audacity he will surely get up and give you as much as you need. (Luke 11:5-8)

Jesus encourages his disciples and us to be persistent in our praying. The point of the story was the willingness of the person to persist until what was needed, was granted. We live in an instant society that wants everything yesterday, the first time that they ask for it. People struggle with being persistent with their prayers and thus struggle to continue to pray until the answer arrives.

Daniel prayed for three weeks to receive God's answer to His prayer (Daniel 10:12-14) Daniel did not know the kind of spiritual warfare going on behind the scenes until the angel told him. He was able to receive an answer to his prayer because he did not give up praying. Imagine if Daniel had given up and stopped praying after a couple of days?

Hannah wanted a child. She was provoked and made fun of by her husband's second wife. But Hannah did not give up praying for a child and went to the temple regularly to ask for a son. In the end she promised that if God would give her a son, she would dedicate him to the Lord's service. Samuel was born and given to God to become a great prophet. (1 Samuel 1)

When I was at Peterborough, South Australia, I knew a lady in another church who had been praying for her husband's salvation for many years. In my ninth year at Peterborough, he still had not committed his life to Jesus. I invited an Adelaide pastor to come for a weekend conference to speak about the Holy Spirit. The lady and her husband came on the Saturday night to listen to this pastor. The pastor invited people to give their lives to Jesus and this husband came forward to do just that.

It was twenty years in the making but it was worth the wait and the praying! A number of years later, I saw the couple at the beach and he was still following Jesus.

But God encourages us to knock on the door and keep on knocking until the door is opened.

REPENTENCE: Forgive us our debts as we also have forgiven our debtors

Forgiveness of sin is one of the main concerns of God, if not His main concern. It is the reason He sent Jesus to die on a cross. Sin kills relationships with God and with each other. Forgiveness of sin gives life to relationship with God and others.

For the wages of sin is death, but the gift of God is eternal life in Christ Jesus our Lord. (Romans 6:23)

It begins with us receiving the forgiveness of God for what we have done in breaking the relationship. Recognition of what we have done to break the relationship with God, admitting it and seeking God's forgiveness is called confession.

If we confess our sins, He is faithful and just to forgive us our sins, and to cleanse us from all unrighteousness. (1 John 1:9)

But it does not stop there. We are expected to repent: make a complete turn around and act like God and not man by forgiving the sin of others who have wronged us, those close to us and any others.

For if you forgive other people when they sin against you, your heavenly Father will also forgive you. But if you do not forgive others their sins, your Father will not forgive your sins. (Matthew 6:14,15)

Jesus strongly warns us that our relationship with God is jeopardized even broken if we ask for forgiveness for our sin but do not forgive other people's sin. Many people's prayers go unanswered because of unforgiveness in their hearts towards others.

Pray as a sinner – Forgive us our debts

To some who were confident of their own righteousness and looked down on everyone else, Jesus told this parable: "Two men went up to the temple to pray, one a Pharisee and the other a tax collector. The Pharisee stood by himself and prayed: 'God, I thank you that I am not like other people—robbers, evildoers, adulterers—or even like this tax collector. I fast twice a week and give a tenth of all I get.' "But the tax collector stood at a distance. He would not even look up to heaven, but beat his breast and said, 'God, have mercy on me, a sinner'. "I tell you that this man, rather than the other, went home justified before God. For all those who exalt themselves will be humbled, and those who humble themselves will be exalted." (Luke 18:9-14)

The parable of the Pharisee and the tax collector was spoken to people who were confident in their own righteousness and looked down on everybody else. We have to guard against a religiosity such that self-righteousness that can creep into our lives. We must be consciously aware of what we think, say and do as a Christian in all circumstances and relationships.

Our nature is in the process of being refined by the Holy Spirit (the work of consecration) but, and there is a but! We live in a toxic culture that does not reflect many Christian values, especially through social media. We can easily get caught up in the toxic atmosphere of criticism and judgment expressing anger and hatred towards people who attack or affect us, using malicious gossip, hurtful remarks, and unjust actions and thus we get sucked in and taint our soul (i.e. Sin)

Or we can become overconfident, thinking that nothing can touch us, even thinking we are above it all. We become supercilious and super-Christian, and so pride can enter in and when pride comes, so does the fall. It can be a huge fall and loss.

Things can happen in our lives and they can have a profound effect upon us. They threaten our Christian values and behavior and encourage us to walk away from them and God in some way.

My focus is *"there but for the grace of God go I!"*. I am conscious that I am a sinner, saved by the grace of God in Christ, and yet know that I am not perfect and just when I think I have some attitude in control, I am conscious that I may be very vulnerable.

It is a balance of knowing that you are forgiven but conscious that you could trip up and you will only reach perfection in heaven once Jesus has stripped away all the dross of your human life.

Pray with a forgiving heart – as we also have forgiven our debtors

Then Peter came to Jesus and asked, "Lord, how many times shall I forgive my brother or sister who sins against me? Up to seven times?" Jesus answered, "I tell you, not seven times, but seventy-seven times.

"Therefore, the kingdom of heaven is like a king who wanted to settle accounts with his servants. As he began the settlement, a man who owed him ten thousand bags of gold[h] was brought to him. Since he was not able to pay, the master ordered that he and his wife and his children and all that he had be sold to repay the debt. "At this the servant fell on his knees before him. 'Be patient with me,' he begged, 'and I will pay back everything.' The servant's master took pity on him, canceled the debt and let him go.

"But when that servant went out, he found one of his fellow servants who owed him a hundred silver coins. He grabbed him and began to choke him. 'Pay back what you owe me!' he demanded. "His fellow servant fell to his knees and begged him, 'Be patient with me, and I will pay it back.' "But he refused. Instead, he went off and had the man thrown into prison until he could pay the debt. When the other servants saw what had happened, they were outraged and went and told their master everything that had happened.

"Then the master called the servant in. 'You wicked servant,' he said, 'I canceled all that debt of yours because you begged me to. Shouldn't you have had mercy on your fellow servant just as I had on you?' In anger his master handed him over to the jailers to be tortured, until he should pay back all he owed.

"This is how my heavenly Father will treat each of you unless you forgive your brother or sister from your heart." (Matthew 18:21-35)

Jesus hung on the cross, battered and bruised after terrible torture and he looked down to the screaming crowd, baying for blood, and asked God to forgive them. That is the standard for all Christians to pray and say *"Father forgive them for they do not know what they do"*.

Lack of forgiveness is a major problem in our culture and our churches. People carry hurt from others that morphs into either bitterness and resentment, envy and jealousy, anger, hatred or rage and revenge. These can then morph into various physical and debilitating diseases and destructive actions that will not only impact others but the person as well.

We don't have to go too far outside the church to see this play out. Hurting people hurt people but we struggle to deal with the hurt caused by others. It may be what someone has posted on social media, or a leader or pastor's comment or action, or it may be a family member's attitude towards another, holding a grudge or whatever.

Paul had to deal with this in the churches he established. Paul had to deal with many people issues in most of the early churches.

For example, in the Galatian church we read

You were running a good race. Who cut in on you to keep you from obeying the truth? That kind of persuasion does not come from the one who calls you. "A little yeast works through the whole batch of dough." I am confident in the Lord that you will take no other view. The one who is throwing you into confusion, whoever that may be, will have to pay the penalty. You, my brothers and sisters, were called to be free. But do not use your freedom to indulge the flesh; rather, serve one another humbly in love. For the entire law is fulfilled in keeping this one command: "Love your neighbor as yourself." If you bite and devour each other, watch out or you will be destroyed by each other. (Galatians 5:7-15)

The danger is we can get caught up with the people issues and find ourselves either taking sides or even worse being caught in the middle and both sides then attack you.

Unforgiveness is a major blockage and often is why prayers have little power and may be left unanswered. In our prayers for the healing of people in many areas, we have to deal often with the sin and hurt by others that the person has held on to and thus has given Satan and his demons a strong hold.

Until the person has truly given that hurt etc. to Jesus, then it will remain a blockage and prevent God from acting. Unless you live and forgive easily, you will struggle in your life and have few prayers answered for yourself and others.

Jesus' words on the cross are my guide:

Jesus said, "Father, forgive them, for they do not know what they are doing." (Luke 23:24)

Finally, a warning from Jesus about holding on to unforgiveness which also guides me.

For if you forgive other people when they sin against you, your heavenly Father will also forgive you. But if you do not forgive others their sins, your Father will not forgive your sins. (Matthew 6:14,15)

RESISTANCE TO SATAN: And lead us not into temptation, but deliver us from evil (the evil one)

Pray Against Temptation -Lead us not into Temptation

No temptation has taken you but what is common to man; but God is faithful, who will not allow you to be tempted above what you are able, but with the temptation also will make a way to escape, so that you may be able to bear it. (1Corinthians 10:13)

A small boy, forbidden by his mother to swim in the local river on his way home from school, was later discovered in his room with damp hair, working studiously at his homework. Enthusiasm for mathematics assignments never figured largely in his usual late-afternoon activity.

"Did you go swimming after school today?" his mother asked. He nodded, then added, "I couldn't help it. The devil tempted me." "How come you had your swimmers with you?" persisted his mother. "Oh", said the boy, "I took them along in case I got tempted."

Temptation is unfortunately an inevitable part of being human, but we have a choice about how to deal with it. We can try to be stoic, steeling ourselves against its persistent invitations to be deflected from God's purpose, and becoming hard, rigid and intolerant of others' weaknesses. In the process we can act like the boy in the story, preparing to meet temptation halfway while knowing inside ourselves that our excuses are not authentic. Or we can be like Jesus in his response.

While Satan's temptation of our Lord has many similarities to his attack against the Christian, it must be remembered that our Lord's temptation was a unique event in history. It was Satan's attempt to nullify the purpose of Christ's first coming, to prevent the establishment of God's kingdom on earth, where God's will would be done, even as it is done in heaven. It was also the temptation of our Lord to use God's power for his own benefit.

The temptations of our Lord were those which could only be pressed on one who was divine. Mere man could not be "tempted" to make stone into bread for this is something which only God can do. Satan's temptation was direct and obvious. It was obvious that Satan was the source of the temptation. Our temptations are more indirect, coming most often through the world and the flesh. Yet it may be that a demon is behind the temptation using our flesh against us.

Finally, our Lord's temptation was unique in that He, unlike all of us, provided Satan with no "inner ally," no "fallen flesh" to which Satan could appeal. There was no inner inclination to rebel against God and no inner desire to sin. For us it is an entirely different matter, as Romans chapter 7 makes abundantly clear.

We must recognize, then, that the term "temptation" is employed in two very different senses, each of which can be seen from the temptation of our Lord.

Temptation is, on the one hand, a solicitation to sin, to do that which is contrary to the will and the word of God. Temptation is an attempt to cause a person to sin. Satan's efforts at temptation always fall into this category.

But "temptation" when viewed from God's point of view is a "test," like an exam, or an opportunity for one to be proven righteous. Thus, in the case of Job (cf. especially chapters 1 and 2) Satan sought to bring Job to the point of forsaking his faith, to the point of sinning, but God's purpose was to deepen Job's faith. It was also to demonstrate to Satan that Job's love for God was not based upon the material blessings which God bestowed upon him. These two meanings of the same term have long been recognized by biblical scholars.

We might therefore maintain that Jesus was "tempted" in two senses in our text. From the vantage point of Satan's intended purpose, our Lord was tempted. Satan wished to prompt the "Son of God" to act in disobedience to the Father, thus terminating His ability to fulfil His mission.

From the viewpoint of God, and the author (Luke), however, this was a "test" of Jesus Christ, proving Him to be suited and qualified to fulfil His mission as the Son of God.

In our case there are the temptations of living in this world: gluttony, greed, lust, sloth, envy, pride, and wrath and the struggle of our own sinful nature. As Paul confesses to the Roman church and us:

So, I find this law at work: Although I want to do good, evil is right there with me. For in my inner being I delight in God's law; but I see another law at work in me, waging war against the law of my mind and making me a prisoner of the law of sin at work within me. What a wretched man I am! Who will rescue me from this body that is subject to death? Thanks be to God, who delivers me through Jesus Christ our Lord! (Romans 7:21-25)

But there are also temptations that we can fall into when we pray.

Keep back thy servant also from presumptuous sins; Let them not have dominion over me: Then shall I be upright, and I shall be innocent from the great transgression. (Psalm 19:13) (KJV)

The "great transgression" of Psalm 19:13 is disobedience in the name of the Lord. It is the sin of presumption, to act without authority or permission, supposing that God is still somehow obligated to support you in your chosen venture.

Webster's Dictionary tells us that presumption is "marked by headstrong confidence; it is unreasonable adventurousness; it is venturing to undertake something without reasonable prospect of success, or against the usual probabilities of safety." Our Lord does not want us to be presumptuous. He wants us to follow him and to pray and act within the boundaries he sets.

We do not pray *My kingdom come.* Our praying must be in the boundaries of God. I can pray for a car but maybe a Lamborghini or Rolls Royce is a prayer too far.

In taking the promised land, Joshua inquired of the Lord and was given a different strategy to take each city. What he did around the walls of Jericho was not repeated around the walls of the other cities.

The temptation in praying is to find a one prayer that fits all situations rather than doing the hard work of inquiring and seeking God's way. Yes, there are some basic ways of praying and we need to be fluent in all these ways and we will explore these in another chapter. But they are tools to be used for specific tasks of praying rather than thinking that the one prayer will suit every occasion.

The Holy Spirit will teach us how to pray not just the content but the method.

And He was there in the wilderness forty days, tempted by Satan. (Mark 1:13)

And when the Devil had ended every temptation, he departed from Him for a time. (Luke 4:13)

Jesus was in constant battle with Satan. It began in the wilderness and continued throughout His life, even to the cross.

For our struggle is not against flesh and blood, but against the rulers, against the authorities, against the powers of this dark world and against the spiritual forces of evil in the heavenly realms. (Ephesians 6:12)

Jesus asks us to take Satan seriously and to pray to resist the temptation that comes from Satan through others (those who are against us and those who love us) and ourselves (both our weaknesses and strengths).

This is a challenge today as many churches and mission organizations do not take Satan and his demonic army seriously. There is little teaching about spiritual warfare and the strategies of Satan to steal, kill and destroy (John 10:10)

While there is not a demon behind every bush, there are many behind most bushes! We must have a healthy respect of Satan and his army but not be fixated on him nor ignore him.

We must learn to pray in ways that address the spiritual and demonic strongholds over our lives, other people's lives, our church, community and even country. This will be addressed in later chapters.

Peter warns the early church and us:

Be alert and of sober mind. Your enemy the devil prowls around like a roaring lion looking for someone to devour. (1 Peter 5:8)

Pray to have a discerning spirit – And do not lead us into temptation, but deliver us from the evil one

He then began to teach them that the Son of Man must suffer many things and be rejected by the elders, the chief priests and the teachers of the law, and that he must be killed and after three days rise again. He spoke plainly about this, and Peter took him aside and began to rebuke him. But when Jesus turned and looked at his disciples, he rebuked Peter. "Get behind me, Satan!" he said. "You do not have in mind the concerns of God, but merely human concerns." (Mark 8:31-33)

Satan lurks to trap, entice and deceive. His major strategy is through lies. However, they are not bold face lies but truth mixed with worldly wisdom and a lying twist in the tail! We need to pray to discern Satan's lies and deception.

While we say Satan is lurking, for most of us it will be one or more demons trying to attack us. Discernment is never easy. Diagnosis of a problem is not straightforward. Just ask anyone in the health industry! But there are usually tell-tale signs where there is evil activity by a demon(s).

These tell-tale signs include unresolved and unrepentant sin in its many forms. It may also include the sins that are passed on from generation to generation or the sin of unforgiveness. It may include bitterness and resentment, envy or jealousy that can't be let go. It may be uncontrollable anger. It may include addictions like alcohol or pornography that can't be easily shaken.

Then there are patterns of behavior and thinking that can't be humanly broken and changed but constantly hold the person in captivity known as strongholds.

Finally, it is being aware of which demon(s) are operating. Knowing the name of the demon grabs their attention and prevents them from hiding or not responding.

More will be given in the chapter UNLOCKING THE POWER TO DEFEAT DEMONS.

Reverend John Lucas, DMin

Pray with the Armor of God on – Deliver us from the Evil One

I put on the whole armor of God. On my head I place the helmet of salvation to protect my mind, upon my heart the breastplate of Christ's righteousness, around my waist the belt of truth, on each of my feet the gospel shoes of peace, on my arm the shield of faith and in the other hand the sword of the Spirit. Lord Jesus, please repair or replace any part of my armor that has been damaged or now non-existent due to the warfare that I have been knowingly or unknowingly been involved in. (Ephesians 6:10-20)

Praying is going into battle for someone or something. It is coming against the enemy in some way. He does not like you praying and will do anything he can to stop you praying.

Praying is connecting you to God and he does not want you to be connected and he will attack you in some way.

We pray on the armor every day, to protect our minds, our hearts, our knowledge of the truth and to enable us to stand and not run away. For the armor covers our front but not our back.

We go into battle everyday as a Christian and there are days when we get beat up and our armor is damaged. Thus, it is important to ask God to repair or replace our armor. It is foolish to go into battle without our armor being perfect and ready for the next onslaught by the enemy.

We now turn to two more foundational principles that unlock the power of our praying: our authority and faith.

3

UNLOCKING THE POWER OF YOUR AUTHORITY AND FAITH

The people were all so amazed that they asked each other, "What is this? A new teaching—and with authority! He even gives orders to impure spirits and they obey him." (Mark 1:27)

Then Jesus came to them and said, "All authority in heaven and on earth has been given to me. Therefore go and make disciples of all nations, baptizing them in the name of the Father and of the Son and of the Holy Spirit, and teaching them to obey everything I have commanded you. And surely I am with you always, to the very end of the age (Matthew 28:18-20)

Truly I tell you, if you have faith as small as a mustard seed, you can say to this mountain, 'Move from here to there,' and it will move. Nothing will be impossible for you. (Matthew 17:20)

If you believe, you will receive whatever you ask for in prayer." (Matthew 21:22)

UNLOCKING THE POWER OF YOUR AUTHORITY

In 2004 I moved to Toowoomba, Queensland (north-eastern state in Australia) to take up a new role with Freedom Life Centre as its CEO. In one of my first ministry sessions, I was commanding some demons to go to the feet of Jesus for judgment. One of my team, Lindy, burst out laughing as she saw the reaction of the demons and heard their comments:

"Who is this person? We have not met him before? But he does have authority to order us to go!

One of the important areas for people who pray is to understand their authority in Jesus together with its areas of limitation. For as we participate in prayer, we enter the spiritual realm with its principalities and powers. As Paul said to the Ephesian church:

For our struggle is not against flesh and blood, but against the rulers, against the authorities, against the powers of this dark world and against the spiritual forces of evil in the heavenly realms. (Ephesians 6:12)

In my work as a pastor visiting people, the expectation is for the minister to pray for them. But do I pray a general prayer or pray in such a way that has authority and connects people to Jesus.

Many Christians feel that they lack power in their praying and even power to pray. They do not recognize that power to pray is connected to their authority that they have in Jesus.

Let's unpack these two concepts authority and prayer.

"*Power*" and "*Authority*" (*Dunamis* and *Exousia* in the original Greek) are two key words that help us to understand what Jesus is doing today.

"*Power*" or *Dunamis* (Greek) comes from a root word which means to be able or have the capacity and means, the ability to carry out something or to bring something to conclusion.

In the Old Testament it meant military power or force. The central proof of God's power was the miraculous deliverance of Israel at the Red Sea (Exodus 15:6,13). For Jeremiah (Jeremiah 27:5; 32:17), the great power of God was at creation. In Micah 3:8, Micah talks of God's power being at work in him and that power is the Holy Spirit.

In the New Testament "*Dunamis*" is found 118 times. In the Synoptics (Matthew, Mark, Luke) and Acts "*Dunamis*" denotes the power of God (Mark 14:62). "*Dunamis*" is also used in reference to "powers" which are evil and powerful but their power has been broken or will be abolished. (Matthew 12:29, 1 Corinthians 15:24)

A third way that "*Dunamis*" is used is in reference to Jesus' "*mighty deeds*". Jesus' miracles are worked by power within Himself (Mark 5:30), and Luke links the power that Jesus had with the Holy Spirit. (Luke 4:14)

The servants of Jesus have this same power of the Spirit given to them to perform mighty acts. This can be seen in the Acts of the Apostles.

Paul lays great emphasis on the experience of God's power. For Paul the central proof of God's power was raising Jesus from the dead. He also talked about the power of the gospel (Romans 1:16). He sees this power coming from Christ Himself. (1 Corinthians 1:24). The ability to preach for Paul came from God's power (1 Corinthians 2:2-4). He also connects power with the Holy Spirit who is the power of the resurrection and who works *Signs and Wonders* (Romans15;9; Galatians 3:5)

The power comes through the Holy Spirit's anointing. Jesus was anointed with that power at His baptism and He gives us that power through the Holy Spirit. Through this power we are transformed into the likeness of Jesus and we are also anointed for ministry through the gifts given to us through the Holy Spirit.

The power is not located in what we do but in God, through the Holy Spirit and what He does in and through us, especially in the power to pray specifically to bring about God's purposes, to heal people of their sickness and deliver them from the strongholds of Satan and his demons.

"*Authority*" or *Exousia* (Greek) denotes the unrestrained right or freedom of action. It signifies the right of a king to rule or the authorization of an officer or messenger to carry out a task.

In the Old Testament, the book of Daniel helps us to understand the New Testament use of the word authority. The authority of world rulers originates from a supernatural realm. Their authority is delegated by God and it is God who installs and removes kings (Daniel 2:21) and can take their dominion away from them all (Daniel 7:12).

In the New Testament, "*Exousia*" appears 108 times. It is characteristic for the New Testament that "*Exousia*" and "*Dunamis*" are both related to the work of Christ, the consequent new ordering of cosmic power structures and the empowering of believers.

Jesus' "*Dunamis*" has its foundation in His anointing by the Holy Spirit but His "*Exousia*" has its foundation in Him being sent by God.

Thus "*Exousia*" or authority is that power, authority and freedom of action which belongs (1) to God alone (2) to Christ (3) to believers.

1. To God alone.

God's authority is linked with his role as the Architect of world history and as Judge of the world. He has fixed the dates and times of the end (Acts 1:7). He has the power to consign people eternal ruin (Luke 12:5). He is the potter who can do what He likes with the clay (Romans 9:21 cf. Isaiah. 29:16; 45:9; Jeremiah 18:6). God delegates His authority to heavenly creatures like the angel who punishes at the judgment (Revelation 6:8) and the other creatures listed in Revelation (Revelation 9:3, 10, 19).

2. To Christ.

Jesus is the One, sent by God, who has the authority to destroy the works of the devil and snatch men and women from his rule. Exorcism is therefore attributed to the authority of Jesus (Luke 4:36) which He can also pass on to the disciples He sends out (Matthew 10:1; Mark 3:15; Luke 9:1; Mark 6:7; Luke 10:19)

Jesus is the One sent by God who has the authority to forgive sins which is confirmed by the power of His word through a healing miracle. (Matthew 9:2-8; Mark 2:3-12; Luke 5:18-26 cf. Psalms 103:3)

Jesus is the One sent by God who has the authority to teach (Mark 1:22,27; Matthew 7:29; Luke 4:32) not like the scribes who are guided by the teaching tradition (Matthew 7:29). Jesus received His words from the mouth of God like Moses and the prophets and He spoke with unique authority as God's Son. (John 5:19-23).

Jesus is the One sent by God who has the authority to judge at the end time (John 5:27).

3. To Believers

The authority of the believer is founded on both the rule of Christ and the commission of Christ to the believer. Christ commissions his disciples, you and me, to carry on His work.

We are sent by Jesus and in this act of sending we have Jesus' power and authority
- a) to go and make disciples (Matthew 28: 16-20)
- b) to heal every disease and infirmity and cast out demons (Matthew 10:1-8, Luke 9:1-6)
- c) to do greater works than Jesus (John 14:12)
- d) to use the keys of the Kingdom – both to bind and to loose. To bind something means to put fetters or a bond on it. It is like closing and locking the door to a room. To loose something is to release or set it free. It is similar to opening the door to a room. (Matthew 16:17-19)
- e) to forgive sins (John 20:23)

The power and authority to pray, heal and deliver comes from Jesus through the power of the Holy Spirit. This power and authority are centered in Jesus who bestows that same power and authority on the first disciples and every disciple that followed down through the ages.

In the Gospel of John, Jesus said to His disciples in the upper room, *Very truly I tell you, whoever believes in me will do the works I have been doing, and they will do even greater things than these, because I am going to the Father. (John 14:12)*.

In Luke 9:1, Jesus sends the twelve out and gives them power and authority over all demons and to cure all diseases.

In Luke 10:1-24, Jesus sends out seventy, two by two, ahead of Him and they return and report that even the demons were subject to them in His name.

In Acts 1:8, Jesus promised the disciples power from the Holy Spirit and the end result was inspired preaching and *signs and wonders* where many responded to the gospel.

In Matthew 28:18-20, Jesus, after His resurrection, affirms that all authority has been given to Him and commands the disciples to go and make more disciples of all nations, teaching them all that Jesus has taught them. The going, the making, the teaching was all armed with the authority of Christ and they were to act with no other authority.

The problem for many Christians today is that they are unaware of their power and authority to pray, to heal, to cast out demons and to witness and so they do not exercise it. They do not understand what Jesus has given to them to serve Him and His purposes.

The challenge for every Christian is to discover that power and authority of Christ, especially in every area of prayer and to begin to exercise it for Christ's sake and the Gospel's sakes.

The power and the authority of the name of Jesus

Then Peter, filled with the Holy Spirit, said to them: "Rulers and elders of the people! If we are being called to account today for an act of kindness shown to a man who was lame and are being asked how he was healed, then know this, you and all the people of Israel: It is by the name of Jesus Christ of Nazareth, whom you crucified but whom God raised from the dead, that this man stands before you healed. Jesus is "'the stone you builders rejected, which has become the cornerstone. Salvation is found in no one else, for there is no other name under heaven given to mankind by which we must be saved." (Acts 4:8-12)

In Genesis 42, Pharaoh had a dream about seven fat cows and seven thin cows by the Nile followed by seven full heads of grain and seven thin and scorched heads of grain. The local magicians had no idea what the dream meant.

The cup bearer remembered Joseph who had correctly interpreted his dream whilst in prison and saved the cup bearer's life. Joseph was summoned and correctly interpreted the meaning of the dream (seven years of plenty followed by seven years of drought) and he suggested that the Pharaoh put someone in place to save grain for the years of famine.

And Pharaoh did. He chose Joseph and gave Joseph his signet ring to signify that he had the authority of the Pharaoh to act and do what must be done.

In the book of Nehemiah, chapter 2, Nehemiah went to the King to ask to be released from his job as cup bearer to go to Jerusalem to rebuild the walls. In addition, he asked for letters from the King to provide safe conduct and to procure the timber to make the beams for the gates, the city wall and his home.

The ring and the letters were tangible evidence that this person had the authority of the ruler and was acting on behalf of the ruler and his wishes.

Christians do not have a letter in their wallet or a ring on their finger but they do have the name of Jesus.

The name had great significance to the Hebrews.

The name could record some aspect of a person's birth or situation (for instance, the naming of the place, Bethel (house of God) when Jacob dreamt and saw the ladder to heaven with the angels coming and going.

The name could express the parent's reaction to the birth of the child (Sarah laughing when she heard that she was going to have a child at her age: hence Isaac that means laughter)

The name could communicate God's message or purpose (for instance the angel instructing Joseph to call his son Jesus (Yeshua): to save people from their sins)

The name can also indicate a new beginning, identity and purpose. For example, Simon being renamed by Jesus as Peter (the rock) on which God will build His church.

The name was also to establish authority and reveal intimacy. When God created man, Adam, his first job was to name all the animals and in so doing to establish his authority over them.

In Genesis 16:14, when Hagar was wandering in the wilderness and near death, she was rescued by God and gave God the name "The One who sees me".

In John 10, Jesus said that He was the good shepherd who knows his sheep and the sheep know Him. He calls them by name and they can hear His voice.

And being found in appearance as a man, he humbled himself by becoming obedient to death—even death on a cross! Therefore, God exalted him to the highest place and gave him the name that is above every name, that at the name of Jesus every knee should bow, in heaven and on earth and under the earth, and every tongue acknowledge that Jesus Christ is Lord, to the glory of God the Father. (Philippians 2:8-11)

Jesus gives us His name, which is like the signet ring of the Pharaoh given to Joseph or the letter of introduction by the king to Nehemiah, to gain safe passage or procure what we need to do the task.

But it is much more! So, in what ways does the name of Jesus give us power and authority?

1. Presence of Jesus

For where two or three gather in my name, there am I with them. (Matthew 18:20)

One cannot underestimate the presence of Jesus when you pray with another or in a team. With that presence comes enormous power to achieve what needs to be achieved.

In our healing prayer room, whether we are praying for a person face to face or online or on the phone, we can be overwhelmed by Jesus' presence. We sense his presence, feel the increase in temperature, gain revelation and understanding of the person's issues, see Jesus working to heal and then finally escorting the demons out to His feet for judgment.

Recognizing Jesus being present, showing the way to pray, doing the work and allowing people to participate and share in a small way in the victory can never be underestimated or taken for granted.

When you gather for prayer in a small group, for your church or community, you gather in the name of Jesus i.e. recognizing His presence. You are then ready to be led by His Spirit and be empowered by that same Spirit. You are ready to pray out loud (i.e. raise your voice as the disciples did in Acts 4) for His Kingdom purposes with faith and with boldness.

So, at the beginning of the meeting, we pray for the presence of Jesus as we deliberately gather in His name and pray in His name for protection, power and faith to confront the big issues that are brought for prayer, revelation as to how to pray and strength to persist in praying for as long as needed until Jesus says that it is finished.

2. Power to Ask

Very truly I tell you, whoever believes in me will do the works I have been doing, and they will do even greater things than these, because I am going to the Father. And I will do whatever you ask in my name, so that the Father may be glorified in the Son. You may ask me for anything in my name, and I will do it. (John 14:12-14)

Again, truly I tell you that if two of you on earth agree about anything they ask for, it will be done for them by my Father in heaven. (Matthew 18:19)

What have you ever asked God for?

As I said previously, we moved to Toowoomba, Queensland in 2004. We needed a house to live in and so I searched the internet for an appropriate house. As I have shared previously, I asked for many things to be in the house and to be in my budget.

As I prayed, I put my requests to God: 4 bedrooms, one for an office, main bedroom with ensuite and it would be really good if there was a spa bath there, modern kitchen for my wife, garage for the two cars with remote controls, reasonably close to my work and within our budget.

I found the house that fitted all my requests but it was $25,000 over my budget. A couple of months later, the house was still there but now the owners who had bought another property, lowered their price by $25,000. So, I put an offer in and it was accepted.

We moved and life was good enjoying the house and spa. In the second year of our stay, a drought came and the dam that provided water to Toowoomba was at 14% capacity. Water restrictions were placed on the town for the next three years. We showered in a large basin to collect the water for use on our garden. The spa became useless as we were not permitted to use it during the drought!

I share this story not to illustrate that you can ask for anything but to raise the vexed question of what do you ask for from God, what is He going to provide and what does the above message of Jesus to his disciples in the upper room really mean?

Was asking for a spa wrong? It was a bit "cheeky" but it was not necessarily wrong. For God loves to bless His children and grant their requests. We did use it after the drought!

I found that the key to asking is to ask in line with God's Kingdom purposes and being attuned to that. So, part of your asking must include God's Kingdom purposes and be willing to ask and pray with that in mind.

Thus, God's Kingdom purpose was to provide a house for us, with all our needs met and with a price that we could afford. The spa was a bonus and a reminder that God loved us even if we did not use it for a number of years.

The key to asking includes the wisdom of the request, to be certain that it would be granted and will be granted if it should be. This includes when two agree as in Matthew 18:19 and not just agreeing to pray the request together.

In 2006, my position at Freedom Life in Toowoomba was not renewed in controversial circumstances. I felt that there was no reason to terminate my position because of what God had done in the three years through me. Yet the leadership of the church had a different opinion. We spent two weeks at Coolum Beach, on the Sunshine Coast of Queensland, grieving and seeking God, thinking that we would return to South Australia. However, God had other ideas and wanted me to set up the healing ministry that eventually became Walkingfree.

We were starting from scratch and it was to be a faith ministry. I had the capacity to work as a Uniting Church Minister but what were God's Kingdom purposes? What did I need to ask for?

I asked God how much would He provide? He replied that he would supply half a Uniting Church minister's salary with its benefits and in a very short time, we had sponsors that provided for half a stipend and benefits. The other half came from being a parish minister where I could preach, teach and pray to help Christians become better and closer to Jesus.

After we started, we had enough finances to employ a ministry coordinator for 20 hours/week, booking in clients and sending information that was needed for their ministry.

Thus, to ask in the name of Jesus is to ask for the Kingdom purposes of God in your praying not just for others but yourself, not just for big things but also in the little things for God is interested in every aspect of your life.

To ask in the name of Jesus is to believe that what you asked for will be realized and far more than just wishing and hoping.

3. Power to save

Everyone who calls on the name of the Lord will be saved (Romans 10:13)

But what does it mean to call on the name of the Lord? Is it just a poetic way of referring to prayer or trusting in the Lord? In Hebrew, the original language of the Old Testament, the word translated as *call* in English means *to call out to* or *to cry unto*. And in Greek, the original language of the New Testament, the word means *to invoke a person, to call a person by name*. So, by definition, calling on the Lord is audible. It's to say His name aloud.

For example, when a little child falls off a swing, they immediately call out, "Mum!" When the mother hears the cry, she runs to the child, wipes away the tears, and soothes them.

Children call out to their mothers when they're hungry, tired, or scared; they call because they're helpless and need to be cared for.

In the same way, we can cry out to the Lord when we're spiritually hungry or thirsty, or when we need His care. We can call on Him in every kind of situation we find ourselves in. We can call upon Him to save us!

Firstly, this saving is from sin and estrangement from God. It is the act of salvation when we become a follower of Jesus, a Christian. It is believing in your heart that Jesus died on the cross for your sin that controls you. It is also believing in the resurrection three days later that Jesus was no ordinary man or mere mortal but that He is the Son of God and that He did come alive to die no more.

To call upon the name of Jesus is to beseech and receive His salvation from sin. It is inviting Jesus into your heart to be your Savior and Lord.

Calling upon the name of Jesus has the power to save you.

The second thing is to call upon the name of the Lord when we are in trouble.

"Lord, if it's you," Peter replied, "tell me to come to you on the water." "Come," he said. Then Peter got down out of the boat, walked on the water and came toward Jesus. But when he saw the wind, he was afraid and, beginning to sink, cried out, "Lord, save me!"

Immediately Jesus reached out his hand and caught him. "You of little faith," he said, "why did you doubt?" (Matthew 14:28-31)

In its early days, Dallas Theological Seminary was in critical need of $10,000 to keep the work going. During a prayer meeting, renowned Bible teacher Harry Ironside, a lecturer at the school, prayed, "Lord, you own the cattle on a thousand hills. Please sell some of those cattle to help us meet this need."

Shortly after the prayer meeting, a cheque for $10,000 arrived at the school, sent days earlier by a friend who had no idea of the urgent need or of Ironside's prayer. The man simply said the money came from the sale of some of his cattle! (1)

Jesus knows our needs but we have to call out to Him, especially in our time of trouble. Yet we have to be careful that we don't use or treat Jesus as a vending machine satisfying every whim that we have.

Rather it is in desperation that we call and it is in our desperation that Jesus answers.

4. Power to heal

Then Peter said, "Silver or gold I do not have, but what I do have I give you. In the name of Jesus Christ of Nazareth, walk!" (Acts 3:6)

Peter and John were going up to the temple to pray as good Jews did. Remember that they were Jews who had now believed that Jesus was the promised Messiah. They came across a beggar who was there every day seeking money to live and the beggar asked them for money.

In that moment, that interaction, something clicked, connected inside Peter. We are not told but I suspect it was the Holy Spirit impressing upon Peter to offer something more than just the money for the man to exist for that day or maybe a couple of days later.

Peter began *"In the name of Jesus Christ of Nazareth"* and then gave the command *"Walk!"* and lifted the man onto his feet. The man felt his ankles and feet getting stronger and acted on what he sensed by jumping and walking, the very thing he was not previously able to do.

We will go further in another chapter about praying for the sick, but suffice here to say that healing prayer done in the name of Jesus releases His presence and His power to heal.

The early church saw that the use of the name of Jesus was the key to praying for healing and that nothing happened without that name.

All healing prayer must be done in the name of Jesus and it is best quoted at the beginning of the prayer along with the command to heal/act (*In the name of Jesus, I command ....*)

5. Power to set free

Just then a man in their synagogue who was possessed by an impure spirit cried out, "What do you want with us, Jesus of Nazareth? Have you come to destroy us? I know who you are— the Holy One of God!" "Be quiet!" said Jesus sternly. "Come out of him!" The impure spirit shook the man violently and came out of him with a shriek. (Mark 1:23-26)

Once when we were going to the place of prayer, we were met by a female slave who had a spirit by which she predicted the future. She earned a great deal of money for her owners by fortune-telling. She followed Paul and the rest of us, shouting, "These men are servants of the Most High God, who are telling you the way to be saved." She kept this up for many days. Finally, Paul became so annoyed that he turned around and said to the spirit, "In the name of Jesus Christ I command you to come out of her!" At that moment the spirit left her. (Acts 16:16-18)

Since the time of Jesus, people have been and continue to be demonized. In other words, there is a demon(s) that have a hold on them in a certain area. This has become a stronghold that needs prayer to release the person from the hold of the demon(s).

Some Bible translations use the word possessed but that is incorrect. The correct terminology is demonized i.e. have a demon(s). The extent of the demonization will be seen by the influence or control that the demon(s) exert over the person.

In most cases, people who are demonized, can appear normal and can go about their normal business. However, the demon can be exposed through prayer or worship or recognition that there is an area of sin that controls them and their behavior.

Then it is not simply a matter of trying harder to break free but rather asking for help and prayer to be set free.

Thus, a deliverance prayer offered in the name of Jesus releases the power of Jesus to confront and release the demon(s). However, one must remember that the demon is there for a reason. If the reason has not been addressed, confession of sin and/or forgiveness sought, a long battle may ensue before the person is released.

In the early days of deliverance ministry, there were many long battles and sometimes there was no victory and a demonized person was left exhausted.

In fact, this does not need to be so. If the right or reason for the demon being there is addressed first, then the prayer for deliverance in the name of Jesus will not need to take a long time. More on this later in the chapter on demons.

Understanding the limits of your authority

Some Jews who went around driving out evil spirits tried to invoke the name of the Lord Jesus over those who were demon-possessed. They would say, "In the name of the Jesus whom Paul preaches, I command you to come out." Seven sons of Sceva, a Jewish chief priest, were doing this. One day the evil spirit answered them, "Jesus I know, and Paul I know about, but who are you?" Then the man who had the evil spirit jumped on them and overpowered them all. He gave them such a beating that they ran out of the house naked and bleeding. (Acts 19:13-16)

A number of years ago, a colleague with many years of experience in the deliverance ministry was in Canberra and visited parliament house. For some reason, he decided to pray and seek to shift the spiritual atmosphere over the government at the time. He entered into spiritual warfare against the strong demonic powers over parliament. However, the end result was a major heart attack and the weakening of his heart.

He was lucky to be alive for God had saved him. But he learnt a valuable lesson that was passed on to other people. He had overstepped the bounds of his authority in the spiritual realm and nearly lost his life, prematurely.

The account in Acts 19 of the Seven sons of Sceva was to remind the early church of the power of the demons and how they could attack people trying to remove them. It was also a reminder that while the power of Jesus name was very great, it was not to be used inappropriately or by people who had no permission from Jesus to use His name.

Ephesus, in Paul's time, was a strategic commercial port that had the Temple of Artemis (Diana) (one of the Seven wonders of the ancient world) and the Library of Celsus. It was a place of wealth and a place of sexual and occult practice. The worship of the goddess Artemis was centered in Ephesus but had spread throughout the province of Asia.

Silver statues were sold by many of the locals who made a good living. But with Paul's preaching that trade dropped off dramatically. The trade in sorcery also dropped off when books and scrolls worth 50,000 drachmas (one drachma was a day's wage) were burned.

As Paul walked around the city, he saw all the wealth, the idolatry of Artemis with its sexual practices and prostitution, the practice of sorcery by many people. He concluded that the spiritual atmosphere was not linear but layered and extremely powerful.

Writing to the Ephesians (Ephesians 6:10-20) of his experience, he described this as *principalities and authorities, against the powers of this dark world and against the spiritual forces of evil in the heavenly realms,* all part of a spiritual army that is organized and established into ranks and is under the headship of Satan who comes against Christians, Churches, Communities and Countries.

He was more than aware of the spiritual battle that he was entering into and respected their power and authority. While he was happy to pray for people so that they were healed and set free from evil spirits it is important to understand that he did not take on specific prayer against the principality Artemis.

In fact, towards the end of his time in Ephesus (Acts 19), Demetrius, a silver shrine maker, stirred up opposition to Paul and caused a major problem for Paul. Fortunately, the city clerk, restored order and sense but it was the sign to Paul that he needed to move on.

While we need to understand what evil we are up against, we also need to understand our authority in Jesus and what we can do and can't do. In other words, understand the limits of our authority in Jesus.

All Christians, I believe, have the authority needed to pray for people for healing and deliverance of demons. They just need to learn how to! All Christians can pray to see God move through their praying. It is about linking into the power of Jesus with your prayers.

Some Christians have been given special or super-natural gifts by the Holy Spirit, according to 1 Corinthians 12: 7-11 that increase their authority and ability to pray for healing or deliverance of demons or pray with Holy Spirit insight for people to give them a word of prophecy or encouragement.

A very few Christians, because of their faithfulness and obedience to what God has given to them, have another level or an increase of authority that goes across cultures and countries not only in the area of healing and deliverance but also evangelism, teaching, prophecy and planting churches (Ephesians 4:11-12)

The challenge for many Christians is to understand the level of authority that God has actually given to them rather than what they want to have. It is easy to make a business card with Apostle or Prophet with your name attached but that does not make it so.

I am fully aware of what authority God has given me and it is very humbling to see the fruit of that in my ministry. I am also fully aware that before I pray into the spiritual realm to tackle the powers of darkness over people and situations, that I must always ask Jesus how far can I go; what are my limits?

I have travelled to different communities and cultures in Australia and overseas where I have had to teach, and pray for healing and freedom from demons. I have learnt to pray before each occasion or session to create a barrier to prevent the local forces of darkness from infiltrating and upsetting what God wants to do.

So, ask Jesus what you can pray for or can't pray for before you go gung-ho into your praying for whatever situation you face. For there are always spiritual powers of darkness lurking to counter your prayers and make the most of any overstepping of your authority.

Don't underestimate your power and authority in what God has given you in Jesus. You do need to take it up in your being and KNOW that you have the authority and power of Jesus when you pray.

How you pray, with confidence and certainty in your voice, will demonstrate that you know your authority in Christ rather than just saying words and wishing and hoping that something will happen!

UNLOCKING THE POWER OF YOUR FAITH

Truly I tell you, if you have faith as small as a mustard seed, you can say to this mountain, 'Move from here to there,' and it will move. Nothing will be impossible for you. (Matthew 17:20)

If you believe, you will receive whatever you ask for in prayer. (Matthew 21:22)

A few days later, when Jesus again entered Capernaum, the people heard that he had come home. They gathered in such large numbers that there was no room left, not even outside the door, and he preached the word to them. Some men came, bringing to him a paralyzed man, carried by four of them. Since they could not get him to Jesus because of the crowd, they made an opening in the roof above Jesus by digging through it and then lowered the mat the man was lying on. When Jesus saw their faith, he said to the paralyzed man, "Son, your sins are forgiven." (Mark 2:1-5)

When Hudson Taylor (2) went to China, he made the voyage on a sailing vessel.

As it neared the channel between the southern Malay Peninsula and the island of Sumatra, the missionary heard an urgent knock on his stateroom door. He opened it, and there stood the captain of the ship.

"Mr. Taylor," he said, "we have no wind. We are drifting toward an island where the people are heathen, and I fear they are cannibals."

"What can I do?" asked Taylor. "I understand that you believe in God. I want you to pray for wind."

"All right, Captain, I will, but you must set the sail."

"Why that's ridiculous! There's not even the slightest breeze. Besides, the sailors will think I'm crazy."

But finally, because of Taylor's insistence, he agreed. Forty-five minutes later he returned and found the missionary still on his knees.

"You can stop praying now," said the captain. "We've got more wind than we know what to do with!"

Faith is defined in the dictionary as "complete trust or confidence in something or someone". It can also mean a strong belief in the doctrines of religion, based on spiritual conviction rather than proof.

Hebrews 11:1 states *"Now faith is confidence in what we hope for and assurance about what we do not see"*.

It then goes on to list the people of God that had great faith and the way they exercised it.

If you are going to be effective and powerful as a pray-er, then you will need to have faith, even great faith.

So, what is this faith that unlocks God's power and presence? If we look at Hebrews 11, the writer commends the heroes of faith, found in the Old Testament, and in so doing highlights certain characteristics of the people who had faith.

1. God focused

These heroes like Noah, Abraham and the like had a faith based in who God was and is and what he had done.

There was, and is, One God and He created the universe that they lived in. They believed that God was behind all of creation and the source of all creation. Though there were many theories going around, and many gods attached to these theories, their conclusion was that there was one God and He was and is behind it all.

Today there are many theories still, like evolution or the big bang theory, about who and how the universe was created and how long it has been in existence. We can easily be led down the rabbit holes of creation theories and miss the point that God existed in the beginning and He created the universe, full stop. This is a statement of faith and, as such, it is central to a person's faith

2. God connected

In all these examples of people of faith, there was a connection with God, where God spoke and they heard what He had said. It was a clear, two-way connection where communication was developed. This was extremely important and an essential foundation of having faith. It starts with a relationship with God and a willingness to listen and obey.

As outlined in chapter One, God speaks in a number of ways and it is very important to hear/sense/understand what He is saying. A strong connection with God through Christ and the Holy Spirit was, and is, an important component of having a strong faith.

3. God believed

In all the examples of faith, the people believed what God was saying. This is amazing!

Noah was asked to build a large boat in the middle of the desert, nowhere near water. This reminds me of a minister colleague who worked at Karoonda (a country town, 91 miles east of Adelaide, SA) and built a sailing boat in his back yard, 40 miles from the river Murray (a major river that travels through South Australia). His parishioners regularly came and asked whether he knew something that they did not know about any rain!

Abraham was asked to pack up his family and chattels and go to where God will show him. On top of that, he was promised that he would be a father even though his wife was barren. Then when his son was born and became a young lad, he was asked to sacrifice him to God! In all these things he believed what God said was correct and true, no matter how improbable or even impossible they must have seemed!

And so, the list goes on. God asked people not only to hear him but also to believe what He said. This was a key ingredient of faith.

4. God obeyed

It is one thing to believe what God has told you, but quite another to obey it. For what God asks you to do creates a crisis of belief inside every individual; a crisis of whether they are hearing right and a crisis of whether they are the right person for the job.

When God revealed himself to Moses in the burning bush, he told Moses to go to Pharoah and tell Pharoah to let God's people go. Moses thought up many reasons why he should not go, but God had the final say and Moses went.

The walls of Jericho would not have fallen down if Joshua did not obey what God told him to do: march around the city once for six days then seven times on the seventh day, with the priests blowing the trumpets and the people giving a loud shout when they hear a long blast!

The Gentile mission would not have been understood or started if Peter had not gone to Cornelius' house and preached the good news about Jesus.

Many times, what God asks us to do seems "out there", "crazy", or "does not make sense" and thus we question whether we have got it right. Many times, we are like Moses when he said "send someone else because I am not good enough to carry out the task".

People who exercise great faith have a history of believing what God has said and obeying God and his instructions, no matter how "crazy" it seems or how unqualified they think they are. For they have realized that they never do anything alone but always with God, through God and for God.

5. God trusted

People of faith have learnt to trust God and His word. It is a relationship of trust and knowing that God is able. It is a belief that defies the present circumstances. It is a belief that trusts in God no matter what, whatever the outcome.

Shadrach, Meshach, and Abednego were brought before King Nebuchadnezzar. They had been "dobbed in" for not bowing down to the gold statue of Nebuchadnezzar. They fronted up to the King and were given a final chance to bow down to the statue. They refused and the King ordered the fire of the furnace to be increased so much that the soldiers who threw Shadrach, Meshach and Abednego into the fire, were themselves burnt.

Before they were thrown into the fire, they said to the King:

"King Nebuchadnezzar, we do not need to defend ourselves before you in this matter. If we are thrown into the blazing furnace, the God we serve is able to deliver us from it, and he will deliver us from Your Majesty's hand. But even if he does not, we want you to know, Your Majesty, that we will not serve your gods or worship the image of gold you have set up." (Daniel 3:16-18)

Their trust in God was not based on whether he delivered them or not but their trust was in God alone. Their faith was in God alone.

Hebrews 11: 32-35 outlines the many nameless people who trusted God and gained glorious deliverances and victories, and also many nameless people who trusted God and yet suffered, were ill-treated, imprisoned and died for their belief in God.

For all of them, their trust in God was not based on what God did for them but who He was to them.

6. God persisted

The gospels link faith with persistence in doing all that it takes to get God's attention and help.

The story of the paralyzed man being healed by Jesus in Mark 2 highlights that faith includes doing all that is necessary to bring their friend to Jesus. Jesus is in Capernaum preaching. He is in the main room of the house that is filled with people including some teachers of the Law. There are people outside standing six deep just to hear what Jesus is saying. Along come four men with their friend who is a paralytic.

Imagine being in their shoes, with the room and door jammed with people and the street also filled with people. It would be easy to walk away because there is no way that they can get to Jesus. But there was a way. Up the steps alongside of the house onto the roof. Then removing the tiles and thatching that the roof consisted of. This was no easy task. They tied the man to the stretcher and then lowered him down to Jesus. The four friends knew that only Jesus could heal their friend.

But their friend also had to have faith to respond to what Jesus said to him, that his sins were forgiven, and doing what Jesus commanded him to do: to get up off the mat, stand up and walk!

Luke relates in his gospel (Chapter 18:1-8), the Jesus parable of the widow who wanted justice from the judge who did not care for people or fear God. But she did not take no for an answer and continued to pester the judge until she got what she wanted.

Jesus told this parable to his disciples to show them that they always should pray and not give up. The widow was an example of a person of faith.

In 1998 my wife contracted uterine cancer that nearly took her life as it metastasized into her lungs then brain. During the next year many people from many churches prayed and prayed for her healing. At my church we prayed each week after the church service plus many other times.

Many people exercised persistent faith, knocking on God's door, day and night for her healing.

We pestered God for her healing. One lady prayer warrior even suggested that God has to heal her because of the many prayers and faxes sent to Him!

One day after church, a lady came to visit. She prayed with all of us, laying her hands upon Liz. Liz felt the power of God go through her and the cancer being destroyed. One can only wonder if Liz was going to be healed if we had not set up these prayer sessions for her after the church service.

We continue to persist in faith and prayer for we do not know when God will answer our prayers.

Then Jesus said to them, "Suppose you have a friend, and you go to him at midnight and say, 'Friend, lend me three loaves of bread; a friend of mine on a journey has come to me, and I have no food to offer him.' And suppose the one inside answers, 'Don't bother me. The door is already locked, and my children and I are in bed. I can't get up and give you anything.' I tell you, even though he will not get up and give you the bread because of friendship, yet because of your shameless audacity he will surely get up and give you as much as you need. (Luke 11:5-8)

How do we increase our faith?

So how do you increase your faith? Like the disciples, you can ask God to increase your faith (Luke 17:5). Faith is like a muscle and so our faith needs to be exercised every day.

How do you do that?

Pray, pray, pray and still pray. Pray for people, for their healing, for their circumstances. Pray specifically, asking specifically for God to work in specific situations. Then continue to pray until the prayer is answered in a specific way!

John Wimber recounts that for the first year of his praying for healing, no one was healed. That can be discouraging. However, he persisted and prayed and learnt to work with God, listening to His directions through the Holy Spirit, and it all started to change. People were being healed.

The 1904–1905 Welsh Revival was the largest Christian revival in Wales during the 20th century. While by no means the best known of revivals, it was one of the most dramatic in terms of its effect on the population, and it triggered revivals in several other countries. "The movement kept the churches of Wales filled for many years to come, seats being placed in the aisles in Mount Pleasant Baptist Church in Swansea for twenty years or so, for example. Meanwhile, the Awakening where people discovered their need of God swept the rest of Britain, Scandinavia, parts of Europe, North America, the mission fields of India and the Orient, Africa and Latin America". (3)

It began with good faithful men praying in the early hours of every morning crying out to the Lord in prayer. The great awakenings began with earnest prayer, as they waited for the Lord to come.

Listening to the Holy Spirit, praying out loud what He has shown you, seeing the fruit before your eyes increases your faith. It is not about what you can get or have, but rather what God can do through you as you are open to the Spirit and be willing to pray what the Holy Spirit has shown you.

Over the years, my faith has increased because of the many people and situations that I have prayed for and then seen those prayers answered by God.

But my faith is linked to my relationship with God through Jesus and the Holy Spirit. It is about asking how I should pray for a particular person or situation, and then praying out what I have been shown. Seeing the prayer answered, that is God doing what He has shown me He will do as I pray, gives me confidence that my faith connection is strong. Confidence in God and faith are linked together.

This is the confidence we have in approaching God: that if we ask anything according to his will, he hears us. And if we know that he hears us—whatever we ask—we know that we have what we asked of him (1 John 5:14,15)

Confidence, asking according to His will, believing that God hears us, whatever we ask, and increasing our faith are all linked together. It becomes an increasing cycle as we grow in confidence, we increase in knowing God's will for each situation by asking for it and then praying as God has shown us.

The faith component is actually believing and trusting what God has shown you and praying it out. For God often gives some "out of the box" pictures or thoughts to you to pray. They seem "quite out there" to us but they are not "out there" for God.

I have been given some unusual pictures or thoughts to pray. Yet as I trust what I have been shown and pray what I see and discern, God moves, helps and heals every time.

In my early days of praying for an individual, God gave me a medical picture. It was a colostomy bag with a tube. I knew that the bag was used to help people to remove waste from their body. As I prayed for this bag to be connected to the client's body, I prayed for the Lord to fill the bag with the poison/waste of the hurt and pain from a broken relationship.

I saw the bag being filled and then another one connected until all the hurt and pain had been emptied out of the person's life. The client felt different, better, lighter, released of all that was inside.

The next time this happened, I did not question the "crazy" picture that God used to help me pray for the person. My faith increased through my trust and belief in what God showed me, and what God did through my praying.

Thus, the first chapter about Hearing from God is crucial to becoming a person of faith. It is all about belief and trust in God and what He shares with you.

In Genesis 15, we read

But Abram said, "Sovereign Lord, what can you give me since I remain childless and the one who will inherit my estate is Eliezer of Damascus?" And Abram said, "You have given me no children; so, a servant in my household will be my heir." Then the word of the Lord came to him: "This man will not be your heir, but a son who is your own flesh and blood will be your heir." He took him outside and said, "Look up at the sky and count the stars—if indeed you can count them." Then he said to him, "So shall your offspring be." Abram believed the Lord, and he credited it to him as righteousness. (Genesis 15:2-6)

Abram, later called Abraham, was childless at the time. He was getting older, with little chance of having children. Yet when God told him that his flesh and blood son and not his servant would inherit everything, and that he would have as many offspring as the stars that he saw in heaven, Abraham believed God.

Now time passed and Abraham took matters in his own hand with the help of Sarah, his wife, and Ishmael was born. He tried to fulfill the promise in his own way and not God's way. But none of this diminished what he believed. He just went about it the wrong way.

Later Isaac was born, in God's way that was even more miraculous!

Belief and trusting God are the keys to faith and increasing faith. Then, giving God permission to act His way and not take matters into our own hands is also important. The model is Jesus who only did what the Father had shown and told Him to pray. (John 5:19,20)

Faith's enemy- Disbelief

A week later his disciples were in the house again, and Thomas was with them. Though the doors were locked, Jesus came and stood among them and said, "Peace be with you!" Then he said to Thomas, "Put your finger here; see my hands. Reach out your hand and put it into my side. Stop doubting and believe." (John 20:26,27)

But when you ask, you must believe and not doubt, because the one who doubts is like a wave of the sea, blown and tossed by the wind. That person should not expect to receive anything from the Lord. Such a person is double-minded and unstable in all they do. (James 1:6-8)

Doubt is every Christian's nightmare. The Oxford dictionary defines doubt as "a lack of conviction, a feeling of uncertainty". But when it is linked with faith, we have another perspective.

The account of "doubting" Thomas in John 20 is not about doubting but rather about disbelieving. Thomas did not believe the disciples when they said that they had seen the Lord. He wanted proof, and until he had that proof, he would not believe. So, the lack of believing undermines the faith and belief of a person.

In James' letter, he links asking with believing in a way that you do not doubt i.e. waver from what you are asking and believing for. He describes this wavering as like a wave being tossed and blown by the wind.

So, to ask and pray in faith is to believe in what you are asking for and not wavering from that even though it seems to be a "big ask"! We have a big God who is happy with big asks!

Remember what God said in Psalm 2:9; *Ask me, and I will make the nations your inheritance, the ends of the earth your possession.*

I think that for many Christians, the challenge is *"Can I ask God for that?"* But the problem does not lie with God's ability as much as our ability to believe that we can ask for this or that, so that God can answer. The main problem is that we lack the faith to believe for big things!

While we may be happy to pray and believe for a headache to go, it becomes another matter to believe that we can pray for eyes to be opened and for the dead to come alive!

For me and I suppose for everyone, I had to get over the false modesty (pride) and believe that God wanted to use me to change the world. And the only thing that was stopping God was me!

So, I started to pray, believing and not wavering, that God could use my prayers to help and heal another or change the world. For if I did not pray and believe then I was not much help to God.

So, over time, I improved not just in my faith and belief that God can do it in and through me, but I learnt to pray better and for bigger things. My praying became more specific and targeted to the person's need.

In my devotions, I use a very old book, God Calling, that I found in a box of books from a retired minister. I still use this today. I came across this word from Jesus to the writer (4)

Pray daily for faith. It is My Gift. It is your only requisite for the accomplishment of mighty deeds. Certainly, you have to work, you have to pray, but upon Faith alone depends the answer to your prayers- your works.

I give it to you in response to your prayer, because it is the necessary weapon for you to possess for the dispersion of evil – the overcoming of all the adverse conditions, and the accomplishment of all good in your lives, and then you having Faith, give it back to me. It is the envelope in which every request to Me should be placed.

And yet, "Faith without works is dead." So, you need works, too, to feed your Faith in Me. As you seek to do, you feel your helplessness. You then turn to Me. In knowing Me, your faith grows – and that faith is all you need for My Power to work.

The next chapter is what I learnt about the "prayer power tools" that enable people to pray specifically, effectively and supernaturally.

4

UNLOCKING THE PRAYER POWER TOOLS

If you go to a mechanics garage, you will find either on the wall or in a mobile case many tools that enable him to fix up your car. There is a tool for everything from removing a spark plug to removing a wheel. The job is easily done if you have the right tool for the right problem. It is frustrating to use a tool that is not just right. The job takes longer or else is not completed.

In the same way, God has given us prayer tools to achieve the task of praying. It is not the case that one prayer fits all situations. Rather the right prayer will achieve the required outcome.

The following are a basic set of tools that will help the Christian be more effective in their praying for themselves and/or with or for others.

PRAYER OF PRAISE

Praise is a powerful tool for prayer. The ability to praise God and/or Jesus through word and song or the gift of tongues is an important tool to have in your prayer kit.

Praise facilitates the presence of God coming upon a group or into a prayer situation.

Yet you are holy, enthroned on the praises of Israel (Psalm 22:3)

Praise releases the presence of Jesus into a meeting or a situation. Too often we want to go straight into the asking or need rather than welcoming Jesus into the situation first. In our prayer meetings, we begin with 15 minutes of songs that lead people into the presence of Jesus. They are a combination of praising God then finish with songs of adoration towards God.

Our praying has power when we begin with praise of God/Jesus and also continues with praise and thanksgiving as we pray for a person or situation. Paul encouraged us to always praise and give thanks to God (Ephesians 5:19,20)

Praise is a warfare weapon to bring victory

After consulting the people, Jehoshaphat appointed men to sing to the Lord and to praise him for the splendor of his holiness as they went out at the head of the army, saying: "Give thanks to the Lord, for his love endures forever."

As they began to sing and praise, the Lord set ambushes against the men of Ammon and Moab and Mount Seir who were invading Judah, and they were defeated. (2 Chronicles 20:21,22)

About midnight Paul and Silas were praying and singing hymns to God, and the prisoners were listening to them, and suddenly there was a great earthquake, so that the foundations of the prison were shaken. And immediately all the doors were opened, and everyone's bonds were unfastened. (Acts 16:25, 26))

The account from 2 Chronicles 20 describes Jehoshaphat's battle with Moab and Ammon. Jehoshaphat begins by standing before God with the people and declaring the greatness of God, His deliverance from past enemies and calling out for help.

The Word of God then came through the Holy Spirit on Jahaziel that God will deliver them and they will not need to fight. But they will need to take up their positions and stand firm.

The following morning, Jehoshaphat rallied the troops to have faith in God.

They took up their position but it was not with swords but with song. They marched forward praising God for His goodness and mercy and it was God who set ambushes and the two enemy armies turned on each other and killed each other's men!

We do not have enemy armies attacking us like Jehoshaphat but we do have an enemy Satan with his army of demons. Praising Jesus and the name of Jesus keeps the enemy at bay.

The account of the release of Paul and Silas from prison suggests that it happened through the praising and singing of hymns to God.

In your situation, do you turn to praise and songs to God to change your situation, the strongholds in your life like Paul and Silas?

In our early days of deliverance ministry, we would praise the name of Jesus to facilitate the liberation of the person from demons. As we got better at deliverance ministry and understood how to pray to remove the demons grasp, we still used "praise the name of Jesus" through word of song to release the person from the demons' stronghold.

Praise enables people to endure hardship and suffering

His speech persuaded them. They called the apostles in and had them flogged. Then they ordered them not to speak in the name of Jesus, and let them go. The apostles left the Sanhedrin, rejoicing because they had been counted worthy of suffering disgrace for the Name. (Acts 5:40,41)

Consider it pure joy, my brothers and sisters, whenever you face trials of many kinds because you know that the testing of your faith produces perseverance. Let perseverance finish its work so that you may be mature and complete, not lacking anything. (James 1:2-4)

Suffering and hardship are one of the great challenges of the Christian walk. This comes in a variety of forms and for each person it is different. It may be physical, emotional or mental suffering. It may come from the loss of spouse, family or work. It may come from the persecution of being a Christian in overt or covert ways, through social media or being overlooked for promotion.

I have not been free of suffering and hardship. My wife's fight with cancer where she nearly died and the ongoing consequences of the chemotherapy, radiotherapy and brain tumor operation has been a challenge not only for her but for me, even though it was and is in different ways.

My loss of my employment at Freedom Life Centre in Toowoomba, Queensland, and the challenge of starting a new ministry, Walkingfree, from scratch was not easy. It meant spending days away from home each week to earn a living and support my wife.

While many churches emphasize the blessings of God in the Christian life and there are many, Christians need to know how to live through the other side of blessings viz hardship and suffering.

Praising and thanking God not for the hardship and suffering but for being there carrying you through the hardship and suffering. Praising and thanking God changes the focus from hardship to the hand of God in your life; from suffering to the sense of His presence.

The disciples in the Acts 5 passage, above, rejoiced not in their suffering as masochists but with the idea that for a brief moment, they were counted worthy, privileged, to experience something of what the Master, Jesus, went through and did for them.

James in his letter confronted the issue of hardship and suffering in the first few words of his letter. His perspective was that there was and is a purpose in all the trials; faith, perseverance and spiritual maturity. And the way to go through this was joy; that good feeling in us based on who Jesus is and the work of the Holy Spirit in us rather than any dire circumstance.

So, when you are going through a tough time praise and thank God not for the tough time but for His strength and grace, His presence to carry you through and get you to the other side.

Praise should be continually on our lips

Rejoice in the Lord always. I will say it again: Rejoice! Let your gentleness be evident to all. The Lord is near. Do not be anxious about anything, but in every situation, by prayer and petition, with thanksgiving, present your requests to God. (Philippians 4:4-6)

Rejoice always, pray continually, give thanks in all circumstances; for this is God's will for you in Christ Jesus. (1 Thessalonians 5:16-18)

Finally praise and thanksgiving should be the constant disposition of every Christian. For we have so much to be thankful for: the forgiveness of sins; our salvation and eternal life; the gift of the Holy Spirit in us; the ability to hear from God through the Holy Spirit; God's help in every time of trouble; His provision for every aspect of our life and the ones that we love and so the list goes on.

Praise and thanksgiving on our lips makes us a pleasure to be with. Without it, we can easily become a pain to live with!

Reverend John Lucas, DMin

PRAYER OF THE BLOOD OF JESUS

But when Christ came as high priest of the good things that are now already here, he went through the greater and more perfect tabernacle that is not made with human hands, that is to say, is not a part of this creation. He did not enter by means of the blood of goats and calves; but he entered the Most Holy Place once for all by his own blood, thus obtaining eternal redemption. The blood of goats and bulls and the ashes of a heifer sprinkled on those who are ceremonially unclean sanctify them so that they are outwardly clean. How much more, then, will the blood of Christ, who through the eternal Spirit offered himself unblemished to God, cleanse our consciences from acts that lead to death so that we may serve the living God! In fact, the law requires that nearly everything be cleansed with blood, and without the shedding of blood there is no forgiveness. It was necessary, then, for the copies of the heavenly things to be purified with these sacrifices, but the heavenly things themselves with better sacrifices than these. (Hebrews 9:11, 12; 22-24)

The blood of Jesus is pivotal to God's plan of salvation. What does the blood of Christ achieve for us?

1. It remits sins (Matthew 26:28).
2. It gives life to those who consume it (John 6:53).
3. It causes us to dwell in Christ and He in us (John 6:56).
4. It is the means by which Jesus purchased the church (Acts 20:28).
5. It is the means by which Jesus becomes our atonement through faith (Romans 3:25
6. It justifies us and saves us from wrath (Romans 5:9).
7. It redeems us (Ephesians 1:7; 1 Peter 1:18-19; Revelation 5:9).
8. It brings those who were far away from God near to Him (Ephesians 2:13).
9. It brings peace and reconciliation to God (Colossians 1:20).
10. It has obtained eternal redemption for us (Hebrews 9:12).
11. It cleanses our conscience from dead works to serve the living God (Hebrews 9:14).
12. It is the means by which we enter the most holy place with boldness (Hebrews 10:19).
13. It speaks a better word than the blood of Abel (Hebrews 12:24).
14. It sanctifies us (Hebrews 13:12).
15. It makes us complete for every good work (Hebrews 13:20-21).
16. It cleanses us from all sin (1 John 1:7).
17. It bears witness in the earth along with the Spirit and the water (1 John 5:8).
18. It is the means by which Jesus frees us (Revelation 1:5; 7:14).
19. It is the means by which Jesus makes us to be His kingdom and priests to serve God (Revelation 1:5; 7:14).
20. It is the means by which we overcome the accuser of the brethren (Revelation 12:11).

The blood of Jesus does so much for us. It gives us so much in every area of salvation and eternal life.

But we must learn to apply this power to not only our life but to the lives of people. We are to pray the blood of Jesus over us and others. Some talk about "pleading the blood".

Jack Hayford (1) writes (his words are in italics under the headings The Blood ....)

When we talk about "pleading" the blood of Jesus, we are not talking about "begging." "Pleading the blood" should not be considered a desperation exercise; God has not called us to come begging before Him. Pleading the blood of Jesus is not the superstitious application of a magic formula of words. Rather, a spiritual dynamic is being applied. The power of the blood of Jesus Christ is greater than both the energy of our own humanity and that of our Adversary. The power that saves is also the power that releases, delivers, and neutralizes the enterprises of hell and the weaknesses of the flesh. The appropriation of the power of the Blood in tough situations is intended for every believer in Christ to know, to understand, and to employ.

He goes on to say, citing the experience of Israel and the first Passover (Exodus 12:13,14) that the blood provides four things:

The Blood Provides Protection

First, the blood provided protection. The Lord was providing a way, not only for Israel's protection on that occasion, but also for the ultimate protection of all humankind from the judgment of death that is upon everyone unless we come under the protective cover of the Blood.

The Blood Provides A Means Of Deliverance

By the blood of the lamb, there came the breaking of the yoke of Pharaoh's strength to retain them, and God's covenant people were released from bondage, literally overnight. It was a miracle by every measure and has become the central point of worship to this day in Jewish tradition. Every time you and I come to the Lord's Table, we're celebrating in Jesus Christ, the Lamb of God, the same thing that the Passover lamb provided—protection and deliverance.

Today we have bondages to sickness (e.g. cancer); bondages to mental illness; bondages to people (e.g. co-dependency). These bondages can be and, in most cases, have demonic attachments or elements that hold back the healing.

The Blood Provides The Promise Of A New Day

The Lord makes the Passover an important beginning point: "This month shall be your beginning of months; it shall be the first month of the year to you" (Exodus 12:2). Our children will ask about it; it relates to future generations. He's saying that what happens through this blood is going to open the door to a new day for you. Like Israel, you may be right now at what seems to be the end of your own hope and strength. But through the power of the Blood, there comes the promise to you, just as it came to Israel so long ago: this will be the beginning of days to you. In addition to protection and deliverance, there's fresh hope in the Blood.

The Blood Provides A Witness

As the blood was put over the door, it was a testimony that there was a place of safety for anybody who wanted to come in from out of the circle of death. The record of Scripture is that there were some Egyptians who did. Seeing the power of the God who had already visited fierce judgments upon their land, they believed that He was the God of all, and they fled into the Jewish households.

We're not people who simply make recitations of creeds. We're people who have tasted of a power. And that power, having come into our lives, is to penetrate our homes. It is the power of the Blood that protects, that delivers, that opens a new day, and that becomes a witness and an invitation to others.

So how can we plead the blood of Jesus?

We can pray for its protection.

I cover us here by the blood of Jesus. I cover all our family and friends, pets, possessions and property, wherever they are and whatever they are doing by the blood of Jesus for our and their protection

We can pray for its saving power.

I confess all sin committed by me, including fear, anxiety, doubt, unbelief, frustration, anger, lack of trust in Jesus, knowingly or unknowingly. I ask You, Lord Jesus, to forgive me and wash me clean by Your precious blood and take back the ground that I have given to Satan.

We can pray for its healing power.

Lord Jesus, I ask that You to place Your blood on every cancer cell to destroy the power of the cancer that is controlling this person.

Lord Jesus, pour Your blood through the diseased parts of the body of ………. (name of person) so that the body may be healed.

We can pray for its delivering power.

I bind in the name of Jesus, all head spirits, powers and principalities. I bind their power and their control in the name of Jesus. I place them in chains unbreakable and cover them with the blood of Christ and the anointing oil of the Spirit. In the name of Jesus, I bind, gag all demonic spirits and confound all their prayers; we stop up their ears, blindfold their eyes, shine the light of the Lord on them and shrink them to their proper size.

We can pray for the cancelling of curses.

In the name of Jesus, I cover with the blood of Jesus, all curses, hexes, spells, ungodly prayers against us. In the name of Jesus, I negate them all, ask Jesus to retrieve any blood that was shed in the making of them and return it to Himself. I pull out all instruments used in the making of these curses, put them in a pile and call down the fire of God to destroy all instruments and curses and send their ashes to the flames of the pit.

Pleading the blood of Jesus is not an optional extra but central and critical for every Christian to practice and pray to release the supernatural power and presence of Jesus in every situation.

PRAYER IN THE NAME OF JESUS

And I will do whatever you ask in my name, so that the Father may be glorified in the Son. You may ask me for anything in my name, and I will do it. (John 14:13,14)

Therefore, God exalted him to the highest place and gave him the name that is above every name, that at the name of Jesus every knee should bow, in heaven and on earth and under the earth, and every tongue acknowledge that Jesus Christ is Lord, To the glory of God the Father. (Philippians 2:9-11)

Salvation is found in no one else, for there is no other name under heaven given to mankind by which we must be saved. (Acts 4:12)

In ancient Hebrew culture, names carried great significance. They might refer to an individual's personality, relate to an event surrounding a person's birth, or indicate a way that God would use the child's life. A name conveyed the very character and nature of a person.

The birth stories of Jesus highlight the importance of naming the son of Mary and Joseph. The angel spoke to Joseph in a dream about the pregnancy of Mary. Joseph knew that this boy was not his son but the angel explained to Joseph the origin of the birth and that he was to name this boy, Jesus (Yeshua, the Lord saves). (Matthew 1:20,21)

The angel Gabriel spoke to Mary that she was to have a child and she is to call him Jesus (Luke 1:31-33)

Jesus taught the disciples that they could ask for anything and if they use His name, it will be done for them. They did not understand the significance of this until Jesus's death and resurrection where He commissioned them to carry out His ministry to bring salvation, healing and deliverance of demons.

It was not too long before Peter standing in the temple on the day of Pentecost spoke and encouraged the crowd to believe in the name of Jesus to be saved. Then on another day, Peter went to the temple to pray and he was accosted by a beggar for money. But Peter offered him something better.

Peter said *Silver or gold I do not have, but what I do have I give you. In the name of Jesus Christ of Nazareth, walk. (Acts 3:6)* Peter lifted the man up and his feet and ankles became strong and not only did he walk but he leapt and praised God.

The early church realized that using the name of Jesus brought salvation, healing and deliverance to people. The early church realized that praying in the name of Jesus released God's answers to their prayers.

That knowledge of using the name of Jesus has continued throughout the centuries, releasing the power of God to save, heal, deliver, have prayers answered. (See chapter 3 Unlocking the power of your authority)

So, we pray in the name of Jesus. We command bodies to be healed in the name of Jesus. We command in the name of Jesus all demons to go to the feet of Jesus. As we pray, we ask, seek and find in the name of Jesus.

Using the name of Jesus gives us the authority to act and minister on His behalf. Using the name of Jesus gives us access to the throne of God so that our requests and prayers can be heard.

However, there is a warning about using the name of Jesus. The sons of Sceva in Acts 19:13-16 found out that invoking the name of Jesus to command demons to go without a personal relationship with Jesus landed them in all sorts of trouble. They were beaten up by the man who had demons! They escaped from the house naked and bleeding.

The name of Jesus is not a magic talisman for anyone to use. Rather it is the personal authority and power of Jesus that is given to every believer to use for His Kingdom's sake.

Lord Jesus, in Your name I ....
In the name of Jesus, I ....

PRAYER OF CONFESSION

Four preachers met for a friendly gathering. During the conversation one preacher said, "Our people come to us and pour out their hearts, confess certain sins and needs. Let's do the same. Confession is good for the soul." In due time all agreed.

One confessed he liked to go to movies and would sneak off when away from his church. The second confessed to liking to smoke cigars and the third one confessed to liking to play cards.

When it came to the fourth one, he wouldn't confess. The others pressed him saying, "Come now, we confessed ours. What is your secret or vice?"

Finally, he answered, "It is gossiping and I can hardly wait to get out of here." (2)

The practice of confession has either been formalized or ignored. In the liturgical denominations it is an essential part of the liturgy but in the non-conformist denominations or charismatic or Pentecostal churches it rarely appears.

Whatever your denomination or church, every Christian needs to understand what confession is and what it can do. Every Christian needs to know how to confess and how to lead a person to confess. Every Christian needs to know how confession can unlock the door to healing and deliverance of every situation.

Let us look at the definition of confess explained in Vine's Complete Expository Dictionary of Old and New Testament Words (3)

Firstly, to confess means to speak the same thing, to assent, accord, agree with, denotes

a) To confess with the meaning of declare or admit is found in the words of John the Baptist: *He did not fail to confess, but confessed freely, "I am not the Messiah." (John 1:20)*

b) To confess by way of admitting oneself guilty of what one is accused of, the result of inward conviction is found in the well-known passage from John's first letter. *If we confess our sins, he is faithful and just and will forgive us our sins and purify us from all unrighteousness. (1 John 1:9)*

c) To declare openly by speaking out freely, such confessing being the effect of deep conviction of facts is found when Jesus said *Then everyone who shall confess Me before men, him, I will confess him before My Father who is in heaven. (Matthew 10:32) (NASB 1977)*

In the intensive form, the word confession means to confess forth and is used

a) Of a public acknowledgement or confession of sins; *Confessing their sins, they were baptized by him in the Jordan River. (Matthew 3:6)*

b) To profess or acknowledge openly *"and that every tongue should confess that Jesus Christ is Lord, to the glory of God the Father." (Philippians 2:11) (KJV)*

c) To confess by way of celebrating, giving praise *and that the Gentiles might glorify God for His mercy, as it is written: "For this reason I will confess to You among the Gentiles, and sing to Your name." (Romans 15:9) (NKJV)*

The power of confessional prayer releases God's power to do many things.

Confession to Cleanse People from their Sins

If we confess our sins, He is faithful and just to forgive us our sins, and to cleanse us from all unrighteousness. (1 John 1:9)

Confession of sin is crucial to find forgiveness of sin and restore relationships with God and people. Confession is about admitting to God and yourself, what you have done wrong or said that has broken the relationship.

It may include how you have been wronged that has impacted and affected you and caused you to sin in the areas of bitterness, resentment, anger, hatred, envy, jealousy, rejection, criticism and judgment to name a few.

At the heart of sin is pride (excessive love of self or self-centeredness); rebellion (desire to be disobedient to God and His authority); and control (the desire to be in control and manipulate others)

It also includes sinful behaviors that arise out of the flesh which include sexual sin like lust, pre-marriage sexual relationships; adultery; same sex sexual relationships; pornography, masturbation to name a few. It includes behaviors that come from the misuse of the tongue like lying, boasting, criticizing, gossiping, manipulating and deceiving to name a few.

It includes participating in alternative religions, philosophies and practices that lead you to worship something other than the One True God. It includes following the way of the world that is obsessed with money, image, and social media in its various forms that takes a person away from following God.

To summarize it includes everything that has broken the Great commandment of loving God and neighbor. Neil T Anderson (4) has a comprehensive resource with prayers, *Steps to Freedom in Christ*, that enables a person to check out every area of their life and confess to God their sin so that they may be cleansed by the blood of Christ and be set free from sin.

It is important that you know how to lead a person to confess their sin with a simple prayer that they can identify with and follow your lead. It is an essential part of your prayer tool kit where you lead a person to confess their sin.

It is essential that you memorize a prayer of confession so that you are able to help a person to confess their sin and invite Jesus in their life to be Lord and Savior. This can be done by slowly reciting the confession prayer in phrases so that they can repeat after you.

It is important that they name the sin(s) before God so that nothing is hidden and they own what they have said and done wrong.

Lord Jesus, I confess to you my sin(s) of .... I ask for your forgiveness through your precious blood and I ask you to wash away my sin(s) and its affect upon every part of my being and relationships. I thank you that you died on the cross for my sin(s) and invite you to come into my life and be my Savior and Lord. Help me not to repeat these sin(s) any more. In Jesus name.

If they are a Christian but need help to confess, the following prayer that you memorize is helpful:

Lord Jesus, I confess to you my sin(s) of .... I ask for your forgiveness through your precious blood and I ask you to wash away my sin(s) and its affect upon every part of my being and relationships. I thank you that you died on the cross for my sin(s), that I am forgiven and have been given a clean slate. I surrender again my life to you, Lord Jesus, and recommit to serve you. Help me not to repeat these sin(s) any more. In Jesus name Amen.

Chapter 4: Unlocking the Prayer Power Tools

Confession to Bring Forgiveness

Then Peter came to Jesus and asked, "Lord, how many times shall I forgive my brother or sister who sins against me? Up to seven times. Jesus answered, "I tell you, not seven times, but seventy-seven times!" (Matthew 18:21-22)

For if you forgive other people when they sin against you, your heavenly Father will also forgive you. But if you do not forgive others their sins, your Father will not forgive your sins. (Matthew 6:14-15)

Linked to the concept of confession of sin is forgiveness. Forgiveness itself is defined as the letting go of sin. In the Bible, this includes forgiving everyone, every time, of everything, as an act of obedience and gratefulness to God. It acknowledges the sacrifice God made through His Son Jesus who died on the cross to restore the relationship between God and man.

It covers all that people have said and done to you and what they haven't said and haven't done for you that has caused you hurt and grief.

Neil Anderson (5) points out in his Steps to Freedom in Christ;

- *It is a choice that we make even if we do not feel like it. It is letting them off your hook even if they are never off God's hook. If we wait to feel like forgiving, we will never get there. It is a willingness to give people a clean sheet in the same way that God gives us a clean sheet when he remembers our sin no more.*
- *Forgetting will be a process for many but if we wait to forget before we forgive, we will struggle to forgive wholeheartedly or maybe never.*
- *Forgiving will also include bearing the consequences of the sin that has impacted your life. This will not be easy because the very nature of sin is to ruin life. The consequences are for both the sinner and for those affected by that person's sin. The good news is that God can restore what sin has ruined but we will need the grace of God to work through all the fallout!*

Forgiveness will not only include people or persons in authority but institutions like a company, church, hospital or government agency that has wronged you. Remember that the perception and/or reality of the wrong need to be considered and forgiven.

Again, a simple prayer that needs to be a part of your prayer tool kit. You need to memorize this and be ready to lead a person to forgive not only another person but themselves. It is important to forgive yourself and receive the grace of Jesus for your wrongdoing.

*I choose to forgive .... (name of the person, themselves, church, institution) for all that they said and did (*Invite person to name any specific sins that have ruined their life*) and for all that has not been said and done* (Invite person to name any specific sins that have ruined their life).

I release my judgment of them to you, Jesus, and I place them and the situation into your hands. Lord Jesus, wash me clean by your blood of all hurt and pain, bitterness and resentment, envy and jealousy, criticism and judgment, frustration, anger and rage. In Jesus name. Amen.

Confession to Cleanse the Family Line-Prayer of Identification Confession/Repentance

You shall not bow down to them or worship them; for I, the Lord your God, am a jealous God, punishing the children for the sin of the parents to the third and fourth generation of those who hate me. (Exodus 20:5)

When I heard these things, I sat down and wept. For some days I mourned and fasted and prayed before the God of heaven. Then I said: Lord, the God of heaven, the great and awesome God, who keeps his covenant of love with those who love him and keep his commandments, let your ear be attentive and your eyes open to hear the prayer your servant is praying before you day and night for your servants, the people of Israel. I confess the sins we Israelites, including myself and my father's family, have committed against you. We have acted very wickedly toward you. We have not obeyed the commands, decrees and laws you gave your servant Moses. "Remember the instruction you gave your servant Moses, saying, 'If you are unfaithful, I will scatter you among the nations, but if you return to me and obey my commands, then even if your exiled people are at the farthest horizon, I will gather them from there and bring them to the place I have chosen as a dwelling for my Name.'" They are your servants and your people, whom you redeemed by your great strength and your mighty hand. Lord, let your ear be attentive to the prayer of this your servant and to the prayer of your servants who delight in revering your name. Give your servant success today by granting him favor in the presence of this man. (Nehemiah 1:4-11)

In my first years at Tusmore Park Uniting Church, a lady came to my office. She was quite distraught. She had done some family research and she showed me her family tree. On every branch was an example of child sexual abuse. This pattern of sexual abuse had now infected her family.

When you visit a medical practitioner for the first time, they ask for your family history of medical issues. When you visit a counsellor or psychologist or psychiatrist, they also ask for your family history related to emotional and mental issues, trauma and life in general. They are looking to see if there are any repetitive patterns in your family history.

Your family history gives you a window into what you are and may become, good and bad. Families are good at business or sport or the arts like music etc. Families also contain secrets, patterns of bad behavior towards members of the family and participation in various addictive behaviors and non-Christian organizations.

In particular, family members who have or are members of various groups like Freemasonry, alternative religions, new age or occult groups can impact other family members, through their vows and prayers that they have made, affecting the health, marriage, finances and even the lives of family members

Chapter 4: Unlocking the Prayer Power Tools

The good news is that Jesus died on the cross to forgive and cancel the negative family patterns that are in your family line.

Like Nehemiah, you pray to stand in the gap (to identify and own your family patterns especially the sin patterns) and confess/repent of the sin of your family members past and present. In some families there are not only birth parents, but step, adoptive and foster parents that are involved. In some cases, a parent has remarried and so one includes both birth and step parents even if there is not a close relationship with the person whom your parent has married.

The prayer to pray looks like this:

I stand in the gap, on behalf of my family, and repent of all sin committed by previous generations on my (birth/adoptive/step or foster) mother's side and my (birth/adoptive/step or foster) father's side.

I ask, Lord God, for Your forgiveness through the blood of the Lord Jesus Christ.

In particular I name the patterns of _____
(physical illness like cancer or heart disease),
(mental illness like depression and anxiety, dementia etc.),
(relationship issues like abuse (all forms), abandonment, control etc.)
(financial issues)
(suicide)
(addiction to alcohol, gambling, pornography etc.)
(participation in Freemasonry, alternative religions, New Age and witchcraft/occult groups)

I ask you, Lord Jesus, to cleanse my family line through Your blood, through my (birth/adoptive/step or foster) mother's side and my (birth/adoptive/step or foster) father's side to my children _____ (names of any children) (or any children that I may have) and every succeeding generation.

I ask you, Lord Jesus, to take back the ground that Satan has gained through my family line on my (birth/adoptive/step or foster) mother's side and my (birth/adoptive/step or foster) father's side and fill every place with the presence, power, love, joy and peace of the Holy Spirit. In Jesus' name, Amen

As the above prayer indicates, you need to cover all your bases regarding future generations. You may have no children now but you may in the future either through normal birth or step children through marriage.

Once you have prayed this prayer of confession, the following prayer needs to be prayed by another person or a team of people to cancel and stop the family patterns of sin, sickness and Satan's impact upon you.

I cover by the blood of Jesus the family line through the (birth/adoptive/step or foster) mother's side and the (birth/adoptive/step or foster) father's side back to the beginning of the generations.

Lord Jesus, has there been any blood shed in any of the generational lines? If yes, pray:

In the name of Jesus, I cover all blood shed, with the blood of Jesus and I ask Jesus to recover all the blood and return it to Himself?

Lord Jesus, have there been any instruments used in the generational lines? If yes, pray:

In the name of Jesus, I cover all instruments used, with the blood of Christ and I ask Jesus to remove them and throw them into His holy fire to be destroyed.
Then pray:

In the name of Jesus, I break the power of all generational sin in every area that Satan has had a hold in the family line on the (birth/adoptive/step or foster) mother's side and the (birth/adoptive/step or foster) father's side and through the (birth /adoptive/step or foster) children .... (names of any children) or any children that they may have to every succeeding generation

In the name of Jesus, I take the sword of the Spirit and I sever all negative generational connections from the (birth/adoptive/step or foster) mother's side and the (birth/adoptive/step or foster) father's side through the (birth/adoptive/step or foster) children............. (names of any children) or any children that they may have and to every succeeding generation

In the name of Jesus, I command every demon attached to the family line to go to the feet of Jesus for judgment.

I ask you, Lord Jesus, to take back the ground that Satan has gained in the family line and fill those places with Your presence, power, love and peace.

As the above prayer indicates, there are issues related to blood and instruments. The enemy, Satan, is about power and control. He generates this power by copying the power of God.

God's power is found in the shed blood of Jesus on the cross. Satan will use any blood that was shed in the generations to gain power over the family line. This blood may be spilt innocently through accidents etc. or purposely by an occult group or part of a ceremony.

God's power is found also in the words that He speaks. There is enormous power in the words what we share both for good and sadly for evil. Often, we say hurtful words out of the hurt that we experience.

Thus, words that are spoken negatively against others are instruments of pain and suffering. Prayers that are prayed against another, especially against Christians by non-Christian groups are also instruments that need to be dealt with. Finally, any vows that are made or words that are spoken in rituals entrap people and need to be removed by God to set the family line free.

In the specific instance of Freemasonry, there are additional prayers that need to be made to free the family line from the power of Freemasonry over the family line.

There are a number of resources available to renounce the impact of Freemasonry upon the family. One such resource is from www.jubilee.org.nz.

While it is helpful to go through all the renouncements to cancel Freemasonry that are given by these groups (and I would encourage you to do that), in some cases they do not address the deeper spiritual impact upon the family.

There needs to be further prayers to be made to totally set free the family line from the influence and impact of Freemasonry upon the family.

To gain total power of the family, Freemasonry copies what God has done.

As your name is written in the Lamb's book of Life, so the family name is written in the Freemasonry book to claim ownership.

As you are married to Christ, so there are Masonic ceremonies which include rings and marriage certificates to marry family members to the demon behind Freemasonry.

As you have committed to the way of Christ through baptism and make various promises to Christ and being given a Bible, Freemasonry has various rituals of entry that include a noose around the neck and a dagger to the heart that is a part of the ritual that holds curses of sickness, financial ruin and even death if the person chooses to walk away from Freemasonry and they are given a Masonic bible with all the rituals that can be used to be promoted in the order up to the Grand Master.

Unless these issues are specifically addressed, Freemasonry can still impact the person even if all the renouncements are made. It has been our experience that if we address these issues then the renouncements may not be needed.

To address these issues, we pray the following:

Lord Jesus, is there Freemasonry in the family line? If you have the sense of Yes, then proceed. (Sometimes you may not have a sense of Yes or No, so assume that there is present)

Lord Jesus, is the family name written in the Freemasonry Book?
If yes, (Sometimes you may not have a sense of Yes or No, so assume that there is present)

Then pray:

Lord Jesus, please remove the family name and all names of the family from the Book and destroy the page(s) on which they have been written

Then wait. Then pray: *Lord Jesus, has it been done?* Wait for His Yes.

Lord Jesus, are there any marriage rings and certificates?

If yes, (Sometimes you may not have a sense of Yes or No, so assume that there is present)

Lord Jesus, please remove all rings and certificates, destroy them by fire and put the ashes into the pit.

Then wait. Then pray: *Lord Jesus, has it been done?* Wait for His Yes.

Lord Jesus, are there any books and Masonic instruments and paraphernalia like ropes, daggers etc.?

If yes, (Sometimes you may not have a sense of Yes or No, so assume that there is present)

Lord Jesus, please remove all books and Masonic instruments and paraphernalia, destroy them by fire and put the ashes into the pit.

Then wait. Then pray: *Lord Jesus, has it been done?* Wait for His Yes.

There is also the need to address the possible presence of the Occult/Witchcraft in the family.

While it may not be a "witch" problem, there may have been family members who have participated or dabbled in the practice of Tarot, Séance, Psychic readings, horoscopes etc. It is a way of gaining power over the family.

The consequences of a family history of Witchcraft/Occult are similar to Freemasonry: sickness, family problems, finances, anti-Christian impact.

Similarly, to gain power over the family the occult has certain practices they use: ceremonies/rituals that are performed to gain power; the use of various objects like crystals, shells, hair, photographs to pray over and gain power and sadly the sacrifice of animals and even humans to gain power.

Lord Jesus, is there Occult/Witchcraft in the family line? If you have the sense of Yes, then proceed. (Sometimes you may not have a sense of Yes or No, so assume that there is present)

Lord Jesus, are there ceremonies still present in the family line?

If yes, (Sometimes you may not have a sense of Yes or No, so assume that there is present)

Then pray:

Lord Jesus, please destroy all ceremonies by fire and put the ashes into the pit!

Then wait. Then pray: *Lord Jesus, has it been done?* Wait for His Yes.

Lord Jesus, are there any instruments still active in the family line?

If yes, (Sometimes you may not have a sense of Yes or No, so assume that there is present)

Lord Jesus, please remove all instruments, destroy them by fire and put the ashes into the pit.

Then wait. Then pray: *Lord Jesus, has it been done?* Wait for His Yes.

Lord Jesus, are there any sacrifices still active in the family line?

If yes, (Sometimes you may not have a sense of Yes or No, so assume that there is present)

Lord Jesus, please destroy all sacrifices by fire and put the ashes into the pit.

Then wait. Then pray: *Lord Jesus, has it been done?* Wait for His Yes.

Knowing how to cancel the patterns of sin, sickness and Satan's hold on the family line will enable these patterns to stop influencing and infecting future generations.

Confession to Heal People

Therefore, confess your sins to each other and pray for each other so that you may be healed. (James 5:16)

Part of the benefit of confession of sin is the effect of healing in a person's life. We have seen many examples where people have come to us for physical healing but the root cause is not a physical breakdown of the body but an emotional or relational breakdown where sin has been the cause that needs to be removed for the healing to take place.

A lady came for healing. As we talked, it became apparent that there were some issues with family members. One of her siblings had sexually abused her and now she was suffering with anxiety and insomnia. Her parents had taken the brother's side and she was angry with them.

There was hurt, bitterness and resentment that had now affected her back and walking.

We led her in a prayer of forgiveness for her brother and parents and a confession of what she had held onto for many years using the Container prayer. After that, her back pain was less.

In the area of healing, especially physical, there may be a sin that needs to be revealed either by asking a person some questions about their life and/or revelation from God.

Then a prayer of confession and/or forgiveness may need to be employed to unlock the healing of God.

Then the container prayer (see later in this chapter) to download the sin and hurt feelings into the container. Once it is filled, the container with all its contents is taken to the cross to be destroyed.

Then a healing and deliverance prayer may be needed. (we will see later for how to do this)

Confession to Change Your Perspective of Yourself

Do two walk together unless they have agreed to do so? (Amos 3:3)

Reverend John Lucas, DMin

Let us hold unswervingly to the hope we profess, for he who promised is faithful. (Hebrews 10:23)

Confession' means: 'to say the same thing as.' To confess God's Word is to say the same thing as God, to speak His Word as the ultimate truth concerning our lives, to be in agreement with Him.

It is to declare God's promises over our lives as true and established. God gives us His promises and tells us who we are in Christ, and we are to agree with Him in our heart and say out loud, both in our believing and in our speaking.

It's all about walking in fellowship-agreement with God.

The aim of confession (whether confession of our sin or confession of His promises) is to get ourselves into greater agreement with God, to line up our lives with His Word, so that we can have a closer faith-walk with Him and see His promises come powerfully to pass in our lives.

When you go to the doctor for a sickness, he will give you some pills to take at a regular interval to overcome the sickness and restore the body.

In the same way, God's Word needs to be taken each day to change the perspective in your soul. These are "*gospills*"!

People come to us struggling with a number of feelings due to what has happened to them. It might be fear or rejection, shame or guilt, loneliness or abandonment to name a few.

We encourage the person to find four verses of scripture to confess or declare out loud over their life which counters what they are feeling and to change their thinking about themselves and their circumstances.

These scriptures are to be confessed out loud 4X4X4! Four scriptures, four times a day (breakfast; lunch; dinner and bedtime) for four weeks. They are *gospills* to transform the feelings and thinking in a person about some aspect in their life. It takes this repetition and this length of time to sink in!

For example: fear.

The Bible has a lot to say about fear and how to counter it. The following are such verses.

When I am afraid, I put my trust in you. In God, whose word I praise—in God I trust and am not afraid. What can mere mortals do to me? (Psalm 56:3,4)

When you pass through the waters, I will be with you; and when you pass through the rivers, they will not sweep over you. When you walk through the fire, you will not be burned; the flames will not set you ablaze. (Isaiah 43:2)

He will not let your foot slip—he who watches over you will not slumber; indeed, he who watches over Israel will neither slumber nor sleep. The Lord will keep you from all harm— he will watch over your life; the Lord will watch over your coming and going both now and forevermore. (Psalm 121:3,4,78)

Surely, he will save you from the fowler's snare and from the deadly pestilence. He will cover you with his feathers, and under his wings you will find refuge; his faithfulness will be your shield and rampart.

You will not fear the terror of night, nor the arrow that flies by day, nor the pestilence that stalks in the darkness, nor the plague that destroys at midday. (Psalm 91:3-6)

Confessing these scriptures as your *gospills*, *4X4X4*, will transform your feelings and thinking about fear as you align your life with God's Word and His Truth for you to conquer fear.

Confession to Heal the Land

If My people, who are called by My name, shall humble themselves and pray, and seek My face, and turn from their wicked ways, then I will hear from Heaven and will forgive their sin and will heal their land. (2 Chronicles 7:14)

I looked for someone among them who would build up the wall and stand before me in the gap on behalf of the land so I would not have to destroy it, but I found no one (Ezekiel 22:20)

The promised land was a gift to Israel. It was integral to their identity as a nation. Before they were to enter it, they were given specific instructions.

If you fully obey the Lord your God and carefully follow all his commands I give you today, the Lord your God will set you high above all the nations on earth. All these blessings will come on you and accompany you if you obey the Lord your God: You will be blessed in the city and blessed in the country. The fruit of your womb will be blessed, and the crops of your land and the young of your livestock—the calves of your herds and the lambs of your flocks. Your basket and your kneading trough will be blessed. You will be blessed when you come in and blessed when you go out. The Lord will grant that the enemies who rise up against you will be defeated before you. They will come at you from one direction but flee from you in seven. (Deuteronomy 28:1-7)

However, there were the consequences of not obeying God's commands.

However, if you do not obey the Lord your God and do not carefully follow all his commands and decrees, I am giving you today, all these curses will come on you and overtake you: You will be cursed in the city and cursed in the country. Your basket and your kneading trough will be cursed. The fruit of your womb will be cursed, and the crops of your land, and the calves of your herds and the lambs of your flocks. You will be cursed when you come in and cursed when you go out. The Lord will send on you curses, confusion and rebuke in everything you put your hand to, until you are destroyed and come to sudden ruin because of the evil you have done in forsaking him. (Deuteronomy 28:15-20)

Sadly, the people of Israel did not heed the commandments of the Lord and followed after other gods and the outcome was subjugation by foreign kings and armies until freedom in 1949 to rule themselves.

For many people from a western mindset, there is a lack of awareness of how sin and breaking of God's commandments can affect and ruin the land and people's lives. However, for many indigenous tribes, in many countries, the land was and is integral to their identity and they know how the land can be affected by acts done upon the land or the inhabitants, even if they did not follow the One True God of the Israelites (and Christianity).

This sin can be in the form of sinful acts including robbery, removal of boundary markers, rape and murder. It can also include curses placed upon the land by people who have been wronged by authorities or subsequent owners. Sadly, some of these sinful actions have been done in the name of Christ, by invaders who were in name, Christian, or carrying out the orders of a "Christian" King.

As I write, Russia has invaded Ukraine and carried out many atrocities on the land. There will be not only the physical destruction of infrastructure, property and lives but also the spiritual impact where these atrocities have created strongholds in the future that will need to be addressed or else the consequences will continue for generations to come.

This will be the case with Hamas attacking Israel, carrying out many atrocities and Israel retaliating. The retaliation by Israel upon Gaza will not only destroy the infrastructure, property and people but also create the spiritual strongholds that will need to be addressed or else the consequences will continue for generations to come.

In our ministry, we have been called to people's properties that either have become unproductive or have recurring problems that need to be addressed; churches that have not been and still are not fruitful for the Lord and businesses that have been having things go wrong!

So, what can be done! A later chapter will go into more detail about what can be done. But the key is the willingness for people who have some ownership of the land, church, business, to stand before God, humbly, confess the sin that has happened, ask God to forgive the sin and then to cleanse everything by the blood of Jesus.

Confession to Heal the Nation

While Ezra was praying and confessing, weeping and throwing himself down before the house of God, a large crowd of Israelites—men, women and children—gathered around him. They too wept bitterly. Then Shekaniah son of Jehiel, one of the descendants of Elam, said to Ezra, "We have been unfaithful to our God by marrying foreign women from the peoples around us. But in spite of this, there is still hope for Israel. Now let us make a covenant before our God to send away all these women and their children, in accordance with the counsel of my lord and of those who fear the commands of our God. Let it be done according to the Law. (Ezra 10:1-3)

In 2018 we were invited to Galiwin'ku (Elcho Island), an Aboriginal community off the northern coast of Australia, to run seminars on deliverance ministry and pray for the local people who came for prayer. On one occasion, we were privileged to be taken to special places of spiritual importance by a local elder.

One place was where the elders had gathered in 1979 to pray and seek the Lord. It was a difficult time; suffering hardship and persecution. Government money was available and many people began to have many material possessions. But with this came also alcohol consumption that led to families fighting and deaths caused by excessive drinking. The community was in chaos.

So, the elders gathered at this sacred place to pray, to confess the sins of the people and ask for God's forgiveness. At the same time, a local aboriginal Uniting Church minister (5) started a bible study for about 8 people. The local Christians had been praying for revival; for God to heal and change their community, their Yolngu nation.

The Holy Spirit swept through the community. The spirit of revival not only affected the Uniting Church communities and the parishes, but Anglican churches in Arnhem Land as well, such as in Angurugu, Umbakumba, Roper River, Numbulwar and Oenpelli. (These are Aboriginal communities in the Northern Territory, a large state in central, north Australia). These all experienced the revival, and were touched by the joy and the happiness and the love of Christ.

What we read in the Old Testament about the Israel nation and individuals repenting of the sin of the nation so that renewal and revival and healing can touch the nation has been true also in the modern era.

We have seen in various communities when local churches gather together for prayer and repent of the sin that is going on in their community that God has answered in a powerful way to turn the community around and deal with the local sin that is present through ordinary people and prayer.

When the leaders of the church and community come together and pray to heal the problems of the local community, we see God pour out His Spirit for revival of community and nation.

Sadly, today, we do not have the degree of unity needed, the priority of prayer by the leaders, the desperate intercession by the leaders and people to want God to heal their community and nation. Until we move into desperate times, will enough people become desperate enough to seek God to heal their community and nation?

Confession to Change the Circumstances

When I heard these things, I sat down and wept. For some days I mourned and fasted and prayed before the God of heaven. Then I said: "Lord, the God of heaven, the great and awesome God, who keeps his covenant of love with those who love him and keep his commandments, let your ear be attentive and your eyes open to hear the prayer your servant is praying before you day and night for your servants, the people of Israel. I confess the sins we Israelites, including myself and my father's family, have committed against you. We have acted very wickedly toward you. We have not obeyed the commands, decrees and laws you gave your servant Moses. (Nehemiah 1:4-7)

Finally, the prayer of confession of sin can open the doors for God's purposes to be fulfilled. Nehemiah was hurting. His nation was in disarray and the walls of Jerusalem were in disrepair. He was a cup bearer to Artaxerxes in the citadel of Susa, Persia. He had heard the report about the walls and fasted and prayed so that God would give him favor in King Artaxerxes presence.

Four months of fasting, praying, confessing the sin of Israel, and planning what he would say if God gives him an opportunity with the King had passed. The King saw his sad countenance and inquired about this. Nehemiah explained, though fearful of speaking, that the walls of Jerusalem were down and he wanted to go there, to Jerusalem, to rebuild them.

He outlines his plan and the materials that were needed and lo and behold, the King grants his request. The King gave him finances to rebuild and sent his soldiers to accompany Nehemiah to get what was needed.

If we want a change in our circumstances, we need to understand the blockages and strongholds that may be there caused by sin and deal with them through private or corporate confession.

In my work as a church minister, I applied this principle of confession to change the circumstances of my church and ministry. Each church I pastored had a history where past sin was blocking the present ministry that I wished to fulfill for the Lord. I would gather the elders and we would pray to understand and deal with the sin blockages and through confession see those blockages removed and ministry developed.

In one church, after this type of prayer, we started a second contemporary service where young adults came back into the life of the church and began using their gifts.

People's spiritual lives were increased and a belief in the power of prayer was developed amongst young and old, alike. A healing ministry was started and developed called Pools of Healing where we were able to help many people. God gathered people from other churches to be a part of this ministry.

It was a significant period of growth, healing and spiritual renewal that not only affected the local church but later, many of the young adults became leaders in other churches as they married and moved on.

What are the blockages or strongholds that are preventing your family, church, business growing and moving forward with God? Maybe a time of fasting and praying, confessing the sin blockages and asking God to change the circumstances, open new doors may be your answer.

CONTAINER PRAYER

One of the most powerful prayer tools that the Lord has revealed to me is what I call the Container Prayer. This prayer facilitates the download of all that the person is carrying that is holding back their lives.

It may be anger, anxiety, fear, worries, troubles, hurt, bitterness, resentment, envy, jealousy or it may a combination of many of the above. It may be challenges in the work place or bullying by other colleagues. It may be financial issues. It may be anything and everything.

In my early days as a Christian, we were told to take it to Jesus or take it to the cross. While the principle was correct, there was seemingly no transaction taking place where the person still carried the problems.

Once I started praying for people, the Lord showed me a way of praying that enabled a spiritual transaction to take place where the person experienced an earthly impact: they felt lighter and the load was not there anymore.

The prayer process to use this method began with explaining to the person what is to happen.

We are first going to pray a prayer of confession where you confess any wrongdoing, forgive the person involved, forgive yourself or confess the emotions that you are struggling with. We are then going to ask you to close your eyes, and then ask Jesus to give you a container that you will recognize to put everything in that you are struggling with.

Sometimes people get a picture or a word to identify the container so that they can work with Jesus. Some people are not as spiritually attuned, so I "prime the pump" suggesting that they imagine a large box.

Once that container is recognized, we then ask Jesus to empty all the problems etc. into the container.

Once filled, keeping our eyes closed but spiritually seeing, we will close it and then take it to the cross for Jesus to destroy it. We will not determine the way Jesus will destroy it so that you know by what you see, that the container with all its contents is destroyed. Most people will experience a difference inside them, when the container and all its contents are destroyed.

When I went overseas to Africa, I renamed it the Basket Prayer as the people were used to having baskets and putting their goods in one to carry. They seem to identify more with this concept. What I found was that the Lord gave them baskets that were different each time. This then became more than they were imagining it!

Lord Jesus, I ask for a container for ......

Ask the person to describe what the container looks like.

Has it got a lid? (Lids need to be open)

Lord Jesus, could you please tell .... what this container is for?

In the name of Jesus, I bring the power of the blood of Jesus and the oil of the Holy Spirit against all ungodly soul ties that .... has had with .... (other people)

I cut them off with the sword of the spirit and put them into the container.

Once this is indicated,

Lord Jesus, please download into the container everything that has happened between .... and .... (e.g. Thoughts, words, hurts, feelings, traumas issues with other people or groups).

Ask the person if they need another container or a bigger one.

Ask the person to tell you when the container is full.

Ask Jesus to close and seal the container.

Lord Jesus, please help............. to take the container to the cross.

(If too heavy you can ask Angels or Jesus to help the person take it to the cross.)

Is the container at the cross yet? Ask the person. Do they sense or see it there?

If it is there, pray:

Lord Jesus, please destroy the container with all its contents.

Once it is destroyed

Ask the person how it has been destroyed (e.g. fire, disappeared crushed or exploded)

Lord Jesus, please put anything that is left over (like ashes) in the place that you have appointed. I wash the area clean with the blood of Jesus and the living water of God.

I close and seal that place with the blood of Jesus. Amen

PRAYER OF COMMAND

He looked around at them in anger and, deeply distressed at their stubborn hearts, said to the man, "Stretch out your hand." He stretched it out, and his hand was completely restored. (Mark 3:5)

Jesus was in the stern, sleeping on a cushion. The disciples woke him and said to him, "Teacher, don't you care if we drown?" He got up, rebuked the wind and said to the waves, "Quiet! Be still!" Then the wind died down and it was completely calm. He said to his disciples, "Why are you so afraid? Do you still have no faith?" They were terrified and asked each other, "Who is this? Even the wind and the waves obey him!" (Mark 4:39-41)

He shouted at the top of his voice, "What do you want with me, Jesus, Son of the Most High God? In God's name don't torture me!" For Jesus had said to him, "Come out of this man, you impure spirit!" (Mark 5:7,8)

Jesus replied, "Truly I tell you, if you have faith and do not doubt, not only can you do what was done to the fig tree, but also you can say to this mountain, 'Go, throw yourself into the sea,' and it will be done. If you believe, you will receive whatever you ask for in prayer." (Matthew 21:21-22)

To command is give an authoritative order, to speak in a forceful and official way.

What people noticed about Jesus was his ability to command, to speak with authority in every situation. It was seen as He taught that Jesus had authority unlike the Scribes and Pharisees.

But in the Scripture examples that begin this section, Jesus commanded the hand to be healed, the storm to abate and the demons to come out of the Gerasene demoniac. There was an authority that was linked to His forceful speaking. He gave an order to the withered hand, the storm and the demons and they obeyed and did what Jesus commanded them to do.

He taught His disciples to speak to the mountain. In other words, give the mountain the order to move!

The command prayer is to pray in the same way with the authority that Jesus has given to all believers. We are to pray in such a way that we mean what we pray, with the authority that we have.

While I have not been able to command a storm to abate, I have commanded legs to be lengthened, demons to be removed, the human body to be healed, the mountain of sickness to be removed.

I liken this prayer of command to giving orders to a dog to sit, roll over, to come and stand at your feet, to give the ball back.

The tone of the voice is important. The authority in the voice is important. The words are short and sharp and are meant to be obeyed. You mean what you say and you expect to be obeyed.

Thus, when praying for sickness, we command the sickness to go in Jesus' name. When praying to remove demons, we command, in the name of Jesus, the demons to go to the feet of Jesus for judgment.

Thus, the prayer of command is giving an order to someone or something e.g. a body or a demon or whatever with the expectation that the command would be listened to and obeyed.

Don't be afraid to repeat the command a few times until that which is spoken to listens and obeys!

In the name of Jesus, I command ....
- *the body to be healed*
- *The headache to leave (name of person)*
- *The demons of ....to go to the feet of Jesus*
- *The mountain of .... (name the mountain e.g. confusion, boss's attitude or hindrances in your life) to be moved into the sea.*

PRAYER OF THE LORD'S NET

Therefore, this is what the Sovereign Lord says: As surely as I live, I will repay him for despising my oath and breaking my covenant. I will spread my net for him, and he will be caught in my snare. I will bring him to Babylon and execute judgment on him there because he was unfaithful to me. All his choice troops will fall by the sword, and the survivors will be scattered to the winds. Then you will know that I the Lord have spoken. (Ezekiel 17:19-21)

Once again, the kingdom of heaven is like a net that was let down into the lake and caught all kinds of fish. When it was full, the fishermen pulled it up on the shore. Then they sat down and collected the good fish in baskets, but threw the bad away. This is how it will be at the end of the age. The angels will come and separate the wicked from the righteous and throw them into the blazing furnace, where there will be weeping and gnashing of teeth. (Matthew 13:47-50)

Jeremiah 52:6-9 tells the story of how Zedekiah and some other high-ranking men of the government tried to escape when the Babylonians came against Jerusalem. They did not succeed, because God had spread His net over him.

In our passage from Ezekiel 17, the prophet is declaring that the Lord will place His net around Zedekiah and take him to Babylon because he has broken covenant with Nebuchadnezzar by looking to Egypt to free him from the yoke of Babylon. And that is what happened.

In Matthew 13, the parable of the net is a parable of judgment where again the Lord will cast his net, collect all people, keeping the righteous but disposing the wicked into hell.

In our ministry of deliverance, the Lord has shown me that I can pray for the net of Christ to be placed over all the demons and take them to the feet of Jesus for judgment. I found this especially helpful when the demons do not easily respond to the command prayer to go to the feet of Jesus for judgment.

In the name of Jesus, I place the net of Christ over all demons attacking and afflicting .... (person's name) and I send them to the feet of Jesus for judgment.

PRAYER OF BINDING AND LOOSING

"Truly I tell you, whatever you bind on earth will be bound in heaven, and whatever you loose on earth will be loosed in heaven." (Matthew 18:18)

To bind means to bind or tie up or to fetter. Prayer of binding and loosing seeks to stop the enemy's attack (binding) and release or permit God's will to enter the situation because God has willed that His purposes be carried out, by asking in prayer.

The binding is done in the name of Jesus and has the same power and force as the prayer to command.

Binding

"Or again, how can anyone enter a strong man's house and carry off his possessions unless he first ties up the strong man? Then he can plunder his house." (Matthew 12:29)

Before one can see effective results in prayer, it is often necessary to bind the power of Satan's demons so they are hindered from working in a person's life or situation. Binding is a temporary means of restraining Satan and his army and often needs to be done each day. Some situations require more than just one person to do the binding and needs to be coupled with the weapon of the prayer of agreement.

In every prayer situation, we are aware that the enemy seeks to hinder, block and stop God's purposes. In every prayer situation, the enemy has a team of demons seeking to harass and attack a person or a particular situation with the intent of negating our prayers and their spiritual outcomes.

In our ministry of healing, we always bind every demon over the person especially pride, rebellion and control as well as blocking and deceiving spirits. The prayer is to negate the influence of the demons upon the person or situation and minimize or negate any demonic manifestation in a person. This type of prayer has made it safe for people who have been severely demonized to be helped without the demonic manifestations like rolling on the ground or sounds coming out of their mouths.

From our experience in the area of healing, we seek to bind all the demons that may be present at the beginning of the session.

The following is an example of binding

In the name of Jesus, I bind all head spirits, powers and principalities. I bind their power and their control in the name of Jesus. I place them in chains unbreakable and bring the power of the blood of Jesus and the oil of the Holy Spirit against them and shrink them to their proper size.

In the name of Jesus, I bind all the strongmen of pride, rebellion and control, sickness and infirmity, doubt and unbelief, deception and Antichrist, lying and blocking Spirits.

In the name of Jesus, I bind and gag all demonic spirits and confound all their prayers;

I stop up their ears, blindfold their eyes and command them not to interfere with anyone on earth.

In the name of Jesus, I bind all watcher and listener spirits sent by Satan to spy and report back what we are doing. I bring the power of the blood of Jesus and the oil of the Holy Spirit against them, I bind them in chains unbreakable, erase their memories and I command them to go to the feet of Jesus for judgment.

I call down the fire of God to destroy all listening, scrambling, recording and looking devices and all infrastructure that they have left behind and send their ashes to the flames of the pit.

When I pray at the altar for a person who has come forward with a need, I pray a simple prayer of binding over the person and their situation.

Loosing

The Lord answered him, "You hypocrites! Doesn't each of you on the Sabbath untie your ox or donkey from the stall and lead it out to give it water? Then should not this woman, a daughter of Abraham, whom Satan has kept bound for eighteen long years, be set free on the Sabbath day from what bound her?" (Luke 13:15-16)

On their release, Peter and John went back to their own people and reported all that the chief priests and the elders had said to them. When they heard this, they raised their voices together in prayer to God.

Reverend John Lucas, DMin

"Sovereign Lord," they said, "you made the heavens and the earth and the sea, and everything in them. You spoke by the Holy Spirit through the mouth of your servant, our father David:

"'Why do the nations rage and the peoples plot in vain? The kings of the earth rise up and the rulers band together against the Lord and against his anointed one." Indeed, Herod and Pontius Pilate met together with the Gentiles and the people of Israel in this city to conspire against your holy servant Jesus, whom you anointed. They did what your power and will had decided beforehand should happen. Now, Lord, consider their threats and enable your servants to speak your word with great boldness. Stretch out your hand to heal and perform signs and wonders through the name of your holy servant Jesus." *(Acts 4:23-30)*

Loosing is releasing the purposes of God into a person's life or a situation. Thus, it is important to know what the purposes of God are! In other words, what is in heaven for that person or the circumstance or situation that needs to be released on earth.

As we look at the ministry of Jesus, He stated that He only did what the Father was doing (John 5:19). We see this when He went to the pool, Bethesda, and only healed one person though there were many there wanting to be healed. We see this with the woman caught in adultery (John 8) and Jesus wrote on the ground waiting for the Father to guide Him to what to say.

It was the purpose of God to release the daughter of Abraham (Luke 13) even though it was the Sabbath. She had been bound by Satan for eighteen years until Jesus came and prayed.

We note that there was no command of demons to go like other situations but Jesus knew that she was bound by Satan. The laying on of hands by Jesus was all that was needed for the healing to be released and the bonds of Satan loosed!

As we look at the ministry of the apostles, Peter's sermon at Pentecost caused about three thousand to become believers in Jesus. Then the healing of the beggar and the further sermon about Jesus and His resurrection caused more people to be saved and Peter and John to be imprisoned by temple guards. They appeared before the Sanhedrin, questioned then flogged.

Peter and John were released and returned to the gathered disciples. They prayed to God, quoting King David's words, and asked for God's power to speak with boldness and for God to stretch out His hand to heal and perform miraculous signs and wonders.

Immediately the Holy Spirit came upon them and they spoke the Word of God boldly. Then in the following days and weeks more healings, miraculous signs like the death of Ananias and Sapphira and more people being raised up like Stephen and Philip to continue the work of Jesus.

It was the purpose of God to continue the ministry of Jesus, first to the Jews and then to the Gentiles so that all people could be saved.

What is the will of heaven for an individual or circumstance? Many of our prayers do not seem to be answered because we have assumed what the will of heaven is rather than know what the will of heaven is.

Chapter 4: Unlocking the Prayer Power Tools

In my ministry with the sick, especially those who may die, I ask the Lord about this sickness and its possible outcome. If the Lord's outcome is that the person will recover, then I pray for that. But if the Lord's outcome is that the person will not recover, then my prayer for them is tailored accordingly so that they may know Jesus and experience Him.

There are times when the person is to die, sometimes because of their wish which God honors. I make sure that they have the opportunity to know Jesus as Lord and Savior if they don't know Him and to know His comfort and strength to face whatever the future holds. I do not drop the bombshell that you will die because God told me. Rather my counsel and prayer are to lead them closer to Jesus at this time.

Scripture and its promises give us some insight into what Heaven thinks about a circumstance or situation. It can be the basis for our praying. I have encouraged people to pray out loud Psalm 23, personalizing it and believing that the truth of this Psalm is true for them, especially as they go through tough times as David did.

Knowing the Scriptures and their promises, praying them out loud is one way of "loosing"heaven. The challenge is to make sure that the scriptures you pray are applicable to your situation and you have a sense that this scripture promise is for you personally.

The Lord may have the cattle on a thousand hills but praying this for yourself does not necessarily give you the finances that you think you need. You can ask/pray for financial provision but unless it is part of God's purposes i.e. in heaven, you may be disappointed.

When I started Walking Free, I knew that it would be a faith ministry where God will provide for our financial needs. However, I had the foresight to ask further of God: "How much will you provide for me and my wife".

It is an important question to ask. Many have started faith ministries, churches or businesses, believing that God will provide everything but are very disappointed when that provision does not materialize in the way that they had thought or believed.

His answer to me was that it will be a half time ministry where I will be paid half of what I would be paid as a Uniting Church minister. I knew exactly where I stood and what I had to do. I worked, three days a week, as a half time church minister with a church that could only afford to pay half time. This enabled Walking Free to grow to where it could pay me the other half. The exciting thing was it took only a few months to generate the income through sponsorship and ministry donations!

In Acts 4 passage above, the believers gathered and prayed:

And now, Lord, behold their threatening, and grant to Your servants that with all boldness they may speak Your Word, by stretching forth of Your hand for healing, and miracles, and wonders may be done by the name of Your holy child Jesus.

Luke records that:

After they prayed, the place where they were meeting was shaken. Now, Lord, consider their threats and enable your servants to speak your word with great boldness. Stretch out your hand to heal and perform signs and wonders through the name of your holy servant Jesus." (Acts 4:31)

In 2004, I was appointed the CEO Freedom Life Centre in Toowoomba, Queensland. I had inherited a conference to plan, to put into place and speak at. Many came to hear the speakers. It was a powerful time for many people when the presence of the Holy Spirit was loosed amongst the people gathered.

This happened in two ways.

Firstly, we loosed heaven on earth through the worship.

I organized the worship and the selection of songs to begin every session. It has been my experience that if we modelled worship in the light of the Tabernacle of Moses, we could lead people into the presence of God, into the Holy of Holies.

I selected 4-5 songs that led the people through praise and thanksgiving to God, then focusing on what God had done through Jesus and finally the last song expressing our love and adoration for God. Then we waited in silence or soft songs for the Holy Spirit to minister to everyone in the conference. The 20–25-minute bracket of worship led people to experience the presence of the Holy Spirit.

I organized two more conferences using a similar pattern of songs to lead people into the presence of God. It was life changing for everyone. This had been my practice in Adelaide, South Australia, to help people to experience God through worship in our second service.

Secondly, we loosed heaven on earth through the waving of worship banners.

In the first conference as a last act of going out, we had two lines of people waving worship banners and invited the whole conference to walk through the avenue of banners. There were 6-8 people on either side waving banners depicting salvation, healing, freedom, the glory of God to name a few.

As the people started to walk through, the manifest presence of God came upon them. Many could only crawl on hands and knees, or walk like "drunken sailors" as God loosed heaven on earth through the Holy Spirit.

In the subsequent conferences, we had similar out pouring of the Holy Spirit as we worshipped, waved banners and walked through an arch made of people raising their hands and joining together.

Through seeking God's purposes and implementing what He asked us to do through worship, banner worship and a "fire tunnel" (the line of people with arms raised to form an arch) His power and presence was loosed and people were touched by heaven at the conferences.

Finally, a word of knowledge or wisdom or prophecy can also loose God's purposes for a person, church or situation.

In a recent visit to India to bless the church building that we had funded, I prayed for the pastor and his family. The pastors were two brothers who had married sisters. I prayed for the younger sister.

As I was praying for her, the Lord said that she was to move out of her older sister's shadow. She was not to compare herself to her older sister but realize that she is very special to God.

At the 2023 Hope Church Conference, the guest speaker gave a word of prophecy that the Holy Spirit will be poured out in the church. The intercessors and people are now praying for that word to be "loosed" upon the church.

PRAYER OF INTERCESSION

Then the Lord said, "The outcry against Sodom and Gomorrah is so great and their sin so grievous that I will go down and see if what they have done is as bad as the outcry that has reached me. If not, I will know." The men turned away and went toward Sodom, but Abraham remained standing before the Lord. Then Abraham approached him and said: "Will you sweep away the righteous with the wicked? What if there are fifty righteous people in the city? Will you really sweep it away and not spare the place for the sake of the fifty righteous people in it? Far be it from you to do such a thing—to kill the righteous with the wicked, treating the righteous and the wicked alike. Far be it from you! Will not the Judge of all the earth do right?" The Lord said, "If I find fifty righteous people in the city of Sodom, I will spare the whole place for their sake." (Genesis 18:20-26)

I looked for someone among them who would build up the wall and stand before me in the gap on behalf of the land so I would not have to destroy it, but I found no one (Ezekiel 22:20)

I urge, then, first of all, that petitions, prayers, intercession and thanksgiving be made for all people—for kings and all those in authority, that we may live peaceful and quiet lives in all godliness and holiness. This is good, and pleases God our Savior, who wants all people to be saved and to come to a knowledge of the truth. (1 Timothy 2:1-4)

As I mentioned previously when I moved to Toowoomba in 2004, I inherited a conference to organize and speak at. I reported that the experience of God in the Conference was due to the worship and the banner waving. There was one added and very important ingredient to releasing the presence and power of God. It was intercession.

A lady came and offered to pray for the Conference while the Conference was on. Each day we talked to each other about what God was revealing and what we need to adjust to fulfil the revelation from God. It was an extraordinary gift of time and sacrifice in prayer. But God blessed her praying and her.

We enacted that same principle for the next two conferences by having a team of people praying at the same time as the conference. Like previously, we had constant communication with the people praying to ascertain what the Lord may be saying and whether we needed to modify anything to fit in with what God wanted to do.

The word intersession comes from the verb intercede. The English word is derived from Latin *intercedo*, "to come between," which strangely has the somewhat opposed meanings of "obstruct" and "to interpose on behalf of" a person, and finally "to intercede."

The Old Testament words that are translated intercede are *paga* and *pawlal* which imply the sense of urging, to assail with petitions for another but can be also for the individual.

In the New Testament, all prayer necessarily takes a new form from its relation to our Lord Jesus. At the outset, Christ teaches prayer on behalf of those "which despitefully use you" (Matthew 5:44).

How completely does this change the entire spirit of prayer! We breathe a new atmosphere of the higher revelation of love. The Lord's Prayer (Matthew 6:9-13) is of this character. Its initial word is social, domestic; prayer is the address of children to the Father.

We find the spirit of intercession in the pleas of those who sought Christ's help for their friends, which He was always so quick to recognize: the centurion for his servant (Matthew 8:13); the friends of the paralytic (Matthew 9:2-6), where the miracle was wrought on the ground of the friends' faith. Of a similar character are the requests of the woman for her child and the Lord's response (Matthew 15:28); of the man for his lunatic son (Matthew 17:14-21).

The place of intercession in the work of Christ is seen clearly in our Lord's intercessory prayer (John 17) and now being seated at the right hand of the Father interceding for us. (Romans 8:34)

In the Epistles we may expect to find intercession more distinctly filled with the relation of prayer through Christ. Paul gives us many examples in his letters to the churches offering prayer for them.

In 1 Timothy 2:1,3 Paul instructs Timothy and us to intercede for all men and for kings and those in authority.

Intercession is prayer on behalf of another. It can arise from the prompting of the Holy Spirit to pray and can arise from the instinct of the human heart—where there is great concern for another person or situation.

We see one type of intercession for another between Abraham and God over Sodom and Gomorrah in Genesis 18:16-33 seeking to save the cities if ten righteous people could be found. Sadly, there were not ten righteous people and the only people saved was Lot and His family before the city was destroyed. The account also includes Lot's wife who looked back when told not to and she was turned into a pillar of salt.

The act of intercession is being prepared to stand in the gap (on behalf of another) for a situation and pray so that God can achieve his purpose. It is a willingness to be available to God so that His purposes can be achieved.

We see another type of intercession for self by Hannah, wanting a child in 1 Samuel 1:10-16. She poured her heart out to God, urging God to give her a baby, and being willing to dedicate the baby to the Lord.

This way of intercession, urging, imploring, and pouring one's heart out for a situation has been adopted by many people who are very concerned about the dire nature of a situation and asking God to intervene. This type of intercession, prayed in the secret places by committed individuals willing to sacrifice time and energy to pray has brought revival, changed the course of history and led many people to the Lord.

I am reminded of the men who got up in the early hours of each night praying for revival in Wales. I am reminded of Rees Howell whose intercession brought revival to Southern Africa from 1915-20. Later he was used by God during World War 2 to help change the course of the war.

But I am also reminded of Susannah Wesley who would put her apron over her head to create a space of prayer and give the message to the children that Mum was praying. I am also reminded of ordinary people with their written lists that focus their prayers and guide their praying. As they set aside a time each day and a space to pray, they would diligently bring their concerns to God.

And I am reminded also of the intercessions that are a part of some denominational worship liturgies that bring before God and the people what Paul had instructed Timothy to pray for all men and for kings and those in authority (1 Timothy 2:1-4)

From these many examples it is clear that intercession, viz praying for people, those in authority, nations and specific situations, can take many forms from being spontaneous to an intense, emotional outpouring of the heart, beseeching God to intervene; from using a list or waiting upon the Holy Spirit.

In the book of Revelation in chapter 5:8 we read

And when he had taken it, the four living creatures and the twenty-four elders fell down before the Lamb. Each one had a harp and they were holding golden bowls full of incense, which are the prayers of God's people.

And then in Revelation 8:5

Another angel, who had a golden censer, came and stood at the altar. He was given much incense to offer, with the prayers of all God's people, on the golden altar in front of the throne. The smoke of the incense, together with the prayers of God's people, went up before God from the angel's hand. Then the angel took the censer, filled it with fire from the altar, and hurled it on the earth; and there came peals of thunder, rumblings, flashes of lightning and an earthquake.

What we conclude is simply is that God hears our prayers, stores them and uses them to achieve His own purposes as well as His purpose for people and situations.

PRAYER OF THE SPIRIT

For anyone who speaks in a tongue does not speak to people but to God. Indeed, no one understands them; they utter mysteries by the Spirit. (1 Corinthians 14:2)

When they heard this sound, a crowd came together in bewilderment, because each one heard their own language being spoken. (Acts 2:6)

Reverend John Lucas, DMin

And pray in the Spirit on all occasions with all kinds of prayers and requests. With this in mind, be alert and always keep on praying for all the Lord's people. (Ephesians 6:18)

When I first became a Christian in 1971, I started University. I joined the Christian Fellowship and many people started to speak in tongues. It was the beginning of the charismatic movement that touched many people. I was a young Christian and made the observation that tongues were for those who needed it. I decided that if God would give it to me, that would be Ok but really, I thought I did not need it.

I was a "wee bit" arrogant and looking back, this was a major part of the reason that I did not need it. It did not help that I went to a Baptist church who believed that all spiritual gifts died with the apostles. It was much later, over 17 years later, that God gave me the gift of tongues for the ministry that He called me to.

Praying in the Spirit is normally described as "praying in tongues". I have spoken about this in Chapter 1 as one of the ways that God speaks to us. But this is only a part of what can be described as praying in the Spirit. Praying in the Spirit is one of the means given to us by God to ascend above rationalism. It is one avenue for opening up the spiritual realm.

But what if you do not have the gift of Tongues?

Praying in the Spirit means that it is the Holy Spirit, who leads, inspires and takes control of the prayer. It is opening up to the Spirit of God so that there is a spiritual synergy between the Holy Spirit and the individual. It enables the Holy Spirit to speak to you and through you; to reveal how you are to pray and what you need to share with a person that you may be praying for.

It may morph into what we know as a word of knowledge or a word of prophecy or a word of discernment even though the individual may not operate in those giftings on a regular basis.

Fundamentally, there is a connection and synergy with the Holy Spirit as you are praying and there is a sense at the end that something special happened that was God inspired and God used.

There have been many occasions while praying for people that the Holy Spirit has revealed insights to me for the client. On one occasion, I was talking over the phone with a client and praying for her. She was battling with a terminal disease and she felt that she was heading for a storm. But the Holy Spirit reminded me of a secular song that I heard back in the 1960's and the lyrics were God's message and encouragement for her.

So, it is important that at the beginning of your prayer or prayer time you invite the Holy Spirit to come and superintend over your praying.

Come Holy Spirit and guide me as I pray.

What follows may be in tongues to open up your spiritual connection or it can happen as you pray in English but the end result is a flow of the Holy Spirit in you, leading and joining in with your praying.

PRAYER OF UNITY

Again, truly I tell you that if two of you on earth agree about anything they ask for, it will be done for them by my Father in heaven. For where two or three gather in my name, there am I with them. (Matthew 18:19,20)

When they heard this, they raised their voices together in prayer to God. "Sovereign Lord," they said, "you made the heavens and the earth and the sea, and everything in them. You spoke by the Holy Spirit through the mouth of your servant, our father David:

'Why do the nations rage and the peoples plot in vain? The kings of the earth rise up and the rulers band together against the Lord and against his anointed one. Indeed, Herod and Pontius Pilate met together with the Gentiles and the people of Israel in this city to conspire against your holy servant Jesus, whom you anointed. They did what your power and will had decided beforehand should happen. Now, Lord, consider their threats and enable your servants to speak your word with great boldness. Stretch out your hand to heal and perform signs and wonders through the name of your holy servant Jesus.

After they prayed, the place where they were meeting was shaken. And they were all filled with the Holy Spirit and spoke the word of God boldly. (Acts 4:24-31)

God's power through prayer is released when people come into unity with the Holy Spirit and with each other. They listen to what the Spirit is saying, how the Spirit is leading the others and how what you might be led to pray is in unity with the theme and flow of the meeting.

Too often people come with their agenda rather than being open to God's agenda. Too often the flow of the Spirit is quenched when people pray in such a way that the subject of prayer is changed. Remember we want to see what is in heaven so that we can pray it on earth.

Thus, if you are praying with another or a small group, it is important that you talk and agree on what you are praying for. Agree on the prayer points and then stay focused on praying about each point until that subject is exhausted, then pray for the next point.

This enables everyone to be on the same page and be in unity as you pray rather than jumping from one topic to another then going back later to the first topic. This also enables the Holy Spirit to guide and inform your praying as you focus on the one subject.

PRAYER OF PROTECTION

The Lord watches over you. The Lord is your shade at your right hand; the sun will not harm you by day, nor the moon by night. The Lord will keep you from all harm. He will watch over your life; the Lord will watch over your coming and going both now and forevermore. (Psalm 121:5-8)

In my first parish in country South Australia, I was travelling home late at night after a meeting. There were two rail crossings, one with lights and one without. I was coming home and the crossing without lights was the closest for me. I arrived at the crossing and something inside prompted me to stop. As I stopped, a freight train roared past.

I remember staying there for a moment, shaking and thinking how close I was to being killed.

The Lord had protected me from being killed.

To protect means to keep safe, defend; guard a person, thing from danger.

The promise from Psalm 121 of God protecting us is a complex issue. Is it protection from everything and anything or is it most things or is it from certain things? Is it complete protection from any harm?

As my wife contracted cancer in three ways, uterine, lung and brain, one wonders about God's protection. Thankfully, God healed her, but what does it mean to be protected by God.

From our experience, it is not a carte blanche protection for everything. In fact, Jesus said

Whoever wants to be my disciple must deny themselves and take up their cross and follow me. (Mark 8:34)

Suffering and sorrow are a part of the Christian walk. Paul talks about his sufferings that have been a part of his ministry (2 Corinthians 11:23-29) and the thorn in the flesh (2 Corinthians 12:7) that God did not remove.

James writes:

Consider it pure joy, my brothers and sisters, whenever you face trials of many kinds, because you know that the testing of your faith produces perseverance. Let perseverance finish its work so that you may be mature and complete, not lacking anything. (James 1:2-4)

So how do we marry the promise found in Psalm 121 with the experience of the apostles, the early church, Christians down through the centuries.

God's protection can be found in different ways in various circumstances. Certainly, that is what I have found.

When I started in the deliverance ministry, I ask God to protect my wife and family for I knew that I was being led into a very dangerous and life-threatening ministry. The words of Jesus in John 10:10 were loud and clear for me; *The thief comes only to steal and kill and destroy.*

God has answered my prayer for the many years that I have served Him. My wife, family and I have been protected. But we have still experienced life-threatening illnesses, sickness, loss of job, car accidents and close shaves!

There is protection but it is conditional on us. In other words, we have a significant part to play. We have to lead a life of holiness and obedience to God for the protection to stay in place.

So, what undermines God's protection?

Firstly, unconfessed sin undermines God's protection. It is important to realize that sin is serious. So serious that God sent Jesus to die for it. We must learn to hate sin and how it infects our life. It is not just the "big" sins like murder and adultery that we should watch out for but our negative reactions to people and the way that they treat us and the hurt that we deeply feel.

Thus, envy and jealousy, resentment and bitterness, anger, hatred and rage, unforgiveness and holding a grudge, lying, gossiping and spreading rumors, i.e. the sins of the flesh that Paul enumerates in his letters.

All this and more gives Satan an opportunity to send his demons to attack and have a hold upon the person. They become an open door and undermine the protection that God wants to give us.

Secondly, generational sin also undermines God's protection. In the book of Exodus, we have seen, previously, the problems of sin passing down through the generations.

You shall not bow down to them or worship them; for I, the Lord your God, am a jealous God, punishing the children for the sin of the parents to the third and fourth generation of those who hate me. (Exodus 20:5)

We see this in King David's life. He had an adulterous relationship with Bathsheba that made her pregnant. He tried to cover it up inviting Uriah, back from the battle front, to have sex with his wife. When Uriah chose not to, David ordered the soldiers to withdraw from Uriah as they were taking the city and he was killed.

The consequences of David's sin were that the child died, Amnon, David's son, had sex with Absalom's sister, Tamar then Absalom murders Amnon in retaliation and then flees the wrath of the other brothers. Later Absalom seeks to usurp David's throne which ended in a battle where Absalom was slain. The sin of the father visited the next generations.

Our family history paints a picture of both good and bad. The doctor asks for this picture to see whether there are any physical illnesses that are passed down through the family. The psychologist and psychiatrist also ask for a family history to ascertain what patterns of abuse, suicide, mental illness and emotional problems that may be present.

Unless the family history is addressed before God and healed by God, it becomes an open door for problems in health, mental health, relationships, finances to name a few.

Thirdly, words in the form of criticism and judgment, prayers and curses (words to bring destruction in some form) that are spoken against a person can undermine God's protection if not dealt with immediately.

James, in speaking about the tongue and its evil power, describes the tongue as

Likewise, the tongue is a small part of the body, but it makes great boasts. Consider what a great forest is set on fire by a small spark. The tongue also is a fire, a world of evil among the parts of the body. It corrupts the whole body, sets the whole course of one's life on fire, and is itself set on fire by hell. We use it to give thanks to our Lord and Father and also curse our fellow man, who is created in the likeness of God. Words of thanksgiving and cursing pour out from the same mouth" (James 3:5,6,9,10)*

Words are seeds of destruction that are planted in our life and if not dealt with, will grow and dominate our thinking about ourselves and our destiny. Sadly, our own words and thoughts about ourselves can add fuel to the fire and continue the destruction of our lives.

Prayers can come from anti-Christian people and groups trying to pull us down. Sadly, even Christians can pray against another Christian. The one who answers these prayers is not God but Satan. All these words, prayers and curses can open the door for sickness, suffering and Satan's attack.

Fourthly, disobedience to God's commandments and guidance also causes a loss of protection.

But since you refuse to listen when I call and no one pays attention when I stretch out my hand, since you disregard all my advice and do not accept my rebuke, I in turn will laugh when disaster strikes you; I will mock when calamity overtakes you— when calamity overtakes you like a storm, when disaster sweeps over you like a whirlwind, when distress and trouble overwhelm you. (Proverbs 1:24-27)

One of my clients has had a very difficult marriage for many years. She admitted to me that the Lord had warned her right at the beginning not to marry this man. Being young and not a strong Christian, she ignored the prompting and advice from God. He was and is an angry and abusive man. Her six children have been a delight but each have had major health problems. She herself has had to manage her own self esteem issues.

Sadly, her story of not heeding the advice from God, His commandments found in the Bible, or the godly advice from ministers, priests or godly people has been repeated often in the lives of people.

If you ignore the direction of God, if you disobey his commandments, you will reap the whirlwind. The good news is that if you recognize what you have done and repent of your disobedience, God can and will turn things around for you. But there will be consequences that you may have to wear because of your disobedience.

Finally, Satan's attack through demons can seek to undermine God's protection for an individual. Paul writing to the Ephesian church points out that

Put on the full armor of God, so that you can take your stand against the devil's schemes. For our struggle is not against flesh and blood, but against the rulers, against the authorities, against the powers of this dark world and against the spiritual forces of evil in the heavenly realms. (Ephesians 6:11,12)

Peter writing to the persecuted church points out

Be alert and of sober mind. Your enemy the devil prowls around like a roaring lion looking for someone to devour. Resist him, standing firm in the faith, because you know that the family of believers throughout the world is undergoing the same kind of sufferings. (1 Peter 5:8,9)

Satan works overtime to attack Christians especially those committed to following Jesus. He does this through temptation. The experience of Jesus' temptation with Satan in the wilderness gives us some clues.

Firstly, Jesus was tempted to doubt the *Welfare of God* and take matters in His own hands and misuse His power to satisfy His need. The second temptation was to misuse the power of the *Word of God*. The third temptation is about the *Worship of God*. The last and final temptation is about who will Jesus serve i.e. worship: Satan or God?

Satan also seeks to defeat believers in their individual and corporate life and service.

He does this by:

- Waging warfare (Ephesians 6:10-18);
- Accusing and slandering (Revelation 12:10);
- Planting doubt (Genesis 3:1-5);
- Tempting to sin through lies (Acts 5:3),
- Sexual sin (1 Corinthians 7:5),
- Occupation with this world (1 John 2:15-17),
- Relying on human wisdom and strength (Matthew 16:21-23),
- Pride in spiritual matters (1 Timothy 3:6),
- Discouragement (1 Peter 5:6-10);
- Inciting persecution (Revelation 2:10),
- Preventing service (1 Thessalonians 2:18),
- Infiltrating the church through false teachers (2 Corinthians 11:13-15),
- False disciples (Matthew 13:38-39)
- Promoting division (2 Corinthians 2:10-11).
- Creating Offence (Matthew 17:24-27)

Unless you aware of the enemy's schemes and attacks and make your stand and withstand the ways of the enemy, you can walk out of the umbrella of the Lord's protection.

So, what can we do and pray to enhance the Lord's protection? (Chapter 10 will go into more detail)

Cover with the blood of Jesus

Then they are to take some of the blood and put it on the sides and tops of the doorframes of the houses where they eat the lambs. (Exodus 12:7)

As the blood of the lamb over the door posts and doors of the houses protected the people of God from the angel of death, so the power of Christ's blood offers the same protection and more.

Now have come the salvation and the power and the kingdom of our God and the authority of his Messiah, for the accuser of our comrades has been thrown down, who accuses them day and night before our God. But they have conquered him by the blood of the Lamb and by the word of their testimony, for they did not cling to life even in the face of death. (Revelation 12:10-11)

There is power in the blood of Jesus for many things: a new covenant with God (Mark 14:24); cleansing and purifying our lives (1 John 1:7; Hebrews 9:14,22); redemption from the slavery of sin (Revelation 1:5,6); makes peace and reconciliation with God (Colossians 1:20; Ephesians 2:13); gives us confidence and assurance (Hebrews 10:19)

In the name of Jesus, I cover with the blood of Jesus my family, pets, property and possessions and I ask you Lord Jesus to keep them and me safe

Cover with the Armor of God

Finally, be strong in the Lord and in his mighty power. Put on the full armor of God, so that you can take your stand against the devil's schemes. For our struggle is not against flesh and blood, but against the rulers, against the authorities, against the powers of this dark world and against the spiritual forces of evil in the heavenly realms. Therefore, put on the full armor of God, so that when the day of evil comes, you may be able to stand your ground, and after you have done everything, to stand. Stand firm then, with the belt of truth buckled around your waist, with the breastplate of righteousness in place, and with your feet fitted with the readiness that comes from the gospel of peace. In addition to all this, take up the shield of faith, with which you can extinguish all the flaming arrows of the evil one. Take the helmet of salvation and the sword of the Spirit, which is the word of God. (Ephesians 6:10-17)

Paul recognizes that the enemy can attack us in many ways. He had seen what a Roman soldier wears and this became a prophetic model of protection against the enemy. Much has been written about the armor of God by many people.

Suffice it to say that each part of the armor protects a certain part of the body.

The helmet protects the mind as the enemy attacks us with thoughts of doubt and unbelief. The breastplate protects our hearts from the hurtful words of others. The belt of truth is to give us discernment of the truth so that we don't get deceived. The shoes enable us to stand firm and face our foes and not allow fear to overwhelm us and make us run away where we become most vulnerable.

The shield is to protect us from the prayers and curses of others that come against us. The sword is God's word that can used to counter the lies.

What may not be known is that this armor can be damaged because of the battle that we are involved in. Rather than going around with damaged armor, we can ask Jesus to repair and/or replace that part of the armor that has become useless.

During the seminars that I conduct about spiritual warfare, we ask Jesus to show the people their armor. Many are surprised about the poor condition their armor is in or some have no armor on!

Thus, it is important to regularly pray your armor on for protection.

I put on the whole armor of God. On my head, I place the helmet of salvation to protect my mind, upon my hears the breastplate of Christ's righteousness to protect me from hurtful words, around my waist the belt of truth so that I will not be deceived, on each of my feet the gospel shoes of peace so that I may stand and face my foes without fear, on my arm the shield of faith to ward off the prayers and curses of others and in the other hand the sword of the Spirit to know the truth to counter the lies.

Lord Jesus, please repair or replace any part of my armor that is damaged.

Ask for God's Angels to protect you

For he will command his angels concerning you to guard you in all your ways; they will lift you up in their hands, so that you will not strike your foot against a stone. (Psalm 91:11,12)

My God sent his angel, and he shut the mouths of the lions. They have not hurt me, because I was found innocent in his sight. Nor have I ever done any wrong before you, Your Majesty." (Daniel 6:22)

God has an innumerable number of angels. We see from scripture that angels are
- Spiritual beings (Hebrews 1:13,14)
- Created (Psalm 148:2,5; Colossians 1:16)
- Immortal (Luke 20:36)
- Holy (Matthew 25:31)
- Innumerable (Hebrews 12:22; Revelation 5:11)
- Wise (2 Samuel 14:17,20)
- Powerful (Psalm 103:20)
- Elect (1 Timothy 5:21)
- Respectful of authority (Jude 9)
- Invisible (Numbers 22:22-31)
- Obedient to God (Psalm 103:20)
- Possessing emotions e.g. joy (Luke 15:10)
- Concerned to know heavenly mystery (1 Peter 1:12)
- Incarnate in human form at times (Genesis 18:2-8; Hebrews 13:2)
- Freewill (Ezekiel 28:12-17)
- Organized in ranks or orders (Isaiah 6:1-3; 1 Thessalonians 4:16)

We see that they have a number of roles that are ordered by Jesus.
- Worship at the throne of God (Cherubim and Seraphim- Revelation 4:6-9; Isaiah 6:1-8)
- Gabriel – stands at the throne of God (Luke 1:19) – God's messenger giving interpretation of vision, dream and prophecy (Daniel 8:16-27;9:21-27) – announces John's and Christ's birth.
- Archangel (chief prince) Michael – protector of Israel (Daniel 12:1) warrior angel (Daniel 10:12-13) Other archangels have responsibility for different nations and regions

- Watch over churches (Revelation 2,3)
- Ministry to believers (Hebrews 1:14)
- Guidance (Genesis 24:7,40)
- Provision (1 Kings 19:5-8)
- Protection (Psalm 34:7)
- Deliverance (Daniel 6:22; Acts 12: 6-11)
- Gathering (Matthew 24:31)
- Directing activities (Acts 8:26)
- Comfort (Acts 27:23,24)

One of the roles of God's angels is to guard and protect God's people. Psalm 34:7 says

The angel of the Lord encamps around those who fear him, and he delivers them.

But there are criteria for their protection: *Those who fear the Lord.* Your walk with God, your obedience to God; your righteous life and your prayer life enables God's protection through His angels.

While we are not meant to talk with angels and should not, we have found that the angels are strengthened through our praises, words and songs including the playing of worship music while we are at home, we are praying to God for family, friends, church and other intercessions (1 Timothy 2:1-4) and asking God to heal and restore our angels because we have been going through difficult times when the enemy has come against us.

Lord Jesus, I ask you to appoint angels on the boundary markers and over my house for protection. I ask you to strengthen them and renew them during times of personal struggle and attacks from the enemy.

The Hedge of Protection

Then the Lord said to Satan, "Have you considered my servant Job? There is no one on earth like him; he is blameless and upright, a man who fears God and shuns evil." "Does Job fear God for nothing?" Satan replied. "Have you not put a hedge around him and his household and everything he has? You have blessed the work of his hands, so that his flocks and herds are spread throughout the land. But now stretch out your hand and strike everything he has, and he will surely curse you to your face." The Lord said to Satan, "Very well, then, everything he has is in your power, but on the man, himself do not lay a finger." Then Satan went out from the presence of the Lord. (Job 1:8-12)

The beginning of Job sets the scene for the whole drama regarding the eternal question of bad things happening to good people. It appears that God had protected and blessed Job and his family through Job's relationship with God described as blameless and upright, fearing God and shunning evil.

Satan negotiates with God to remove the hedge of protection to prove that Job's upright life was dependent upon the hedge of protection and blessing. Remove the hedge and blessing and Job's true colors would appear. He would curse God!

Praying for the hedge of protection is connected with one's life and relationship with God like Job: blameless and upright; fearing God and shunning evil! If one or most of those characteristics of your walk with God is missing, it would be fair to say that God may not offer his hedge of protection for you.

But on the other hand, leading a blameless and upright life, fearing God and shunning evil does not guarantee that bad things do not happen to you. But like Paul and others that followed him, God's protection enabled him and everyone who followed, to fulfil God's purpose for their lives though it was not trouble free.

This should not discourage us from praying for God's hedge of protection for our lives and our loved ones.

Lord, I ask that you place your hedge of protection around my family, property, friends and business.

Now you have a prayer tool kit to use the right prayer for each occasion as the Holy Spirit leads you. The task is to be familiar with all the prayer tools in your prayer tool box.

Go through each prayer that has been listed and be familiar with the words that you may need to use to pray for each situation. Once you are familiar with all the prayer tools, the Holy Spirit will bring to your memory, as He has promised, what prayer to use for each situation.

We now move to another power source to your praying: the power of fasting.

Reverend John Lucas, DMin

5

UNLOCKING THE POWER OF FASTING

Is not this the kind of fasting I have chosen: to loose the chains of injustice and untie the cords of the yoke, to set the oppressed free and break every yoke? (Isaiah 58:6)

In 1995 I was finishing writing my thesis on healing for my Doctorate of Ministry. I retreated to my mother's home to finish the thesis. God spoke to me about fasting to finish the writing. It was to be an Esther fast where I do not eat or drink for three days. It was a challenge and my mother was concerned when I refused food and drink. But I managed this command from God.

Over the years, especially in the healing ministry, we have fasted to prepare to pray for a challenging client that has Occult history. We have gone without food for the day. Some churches call the congregation to fast at the beginning of the year to seek God and understand His purposes for that year. They would outline what type of fast and for how long.

WHAT IS FASTING

Fasting can include different things, but basically, it is going without food. Fasting provides both release from and release into what is humanly impossible. It is the key to what seems to be the impossible.

The purpose of fasting is to draw a person from the natural realm into the spiritual. It is the seeking of the fulfilment of the purposes that God intended for humankind. It is the experience of a new freedom and the release from the oppression of Satan, with a release into peace of mind and soul as its end.

It is vain/sinful for a person to fast for the purpose of self-gain, to be revered by men for merely selfish reasons. The desire must be from a deep compassion for the suffering of humanity. It should seek the decrease of self, the increase of Jesus Christ, and must be dedicated solely to the Lord for the glory of God.

We must with all sincerity search our hearts, be repentant and confess our sins and come before our Lord with humility when we fast. This is the key to fasting and prayer. The only acceptable motive recognized by God, that releases mighty power from and into all things.

WHY SHOULD WE FAST?

      a.   There is biblical warrant for it.
      b.   It allows extra time for prayer.

c. Releases spiritual power.
d. Brings increased emphasis on the spirit and decreases concern for the physical.

WHEN SHOULD WE FAST?
a. When God specifically calls.
b. When in crisis - seeking special guidance.
c. As a regular discipline - especially when preparing to speak, sing, play an instrument, any time when seeking a release of spiritual power.
d. When ministering at the level of healing or deliverance.

VALUE OF FASTING

- Fasting was an expected discipline in both the Old and New Testament eras. For example, Moses fasted at least two recorded forty-day periods. Jesus fasted 40 days and reminded His followers to fast, "when you fast," not if you fast.
- Fasting and prayer can restore the loss of the "first love" for your Lord and result in a more intimate relationship with Christ.
- Fasting is a biblical way to truly humble yourself in the sight of God (Psalm 35:13; Ezra 8:21). King David said, "I humble myself through fasting."
- Fasting enables the Holy Spirit to reveal your true spiritual condition, resulting in brokenness, repentance, and a transformed life. The Holy Spirit will quicken the Word of God in your heart and His truth will become more meaningful to you!
- Fasting can transform your prayer life into a richer and more personal experience.
- Fasting can result in a dynamic personal revival in your own life-and make you a channel of revival to others.
- Fasting and prayer are the only disciplines that fulfill the requirements of 2 Chronicles 7:14: *If my people, who are called by my name, will humble themselves and pray and seek my face and turn from their wicked ways, then will I hear from heaven and will forgive their sin and will heal their land.*
- If you fast, you will find yourself being humbled. You will discover more time to pray and seek God's face. And as He leads you to recognize and repent of unconfessed sin, you will experience special blessings from God.

Fasting has been a major emphasis in the lives of many of the great spiritual leaders throughout history. John Wesley, the founder of the Methodist denomination, fasted every Wednesday and Friday and required all of his clergy to do the same. Effective ministers of God from the apostle Paul to Martin Luther to John Calvin made it a continual part of their walks with God.

None of those men had a "formula for fasting" that was the only "right" way. Fasting is about the condition of the heart, not the number of days. Each time that I have, it was because I felt impressed by God to do so.

So, start slowly. Fast for one meal a day, or one day a week, or one week a month. Build up your spiritual muscles so that you will be prepared in a period of several months to fast for an extended 40-day period.

A partial fast is described in the book of Daniel. Although the water fast seemed to be the custom of the prophet, there was a three-week period in which he only abstained from "delicacies," meat, and wine (Daniel 10:3).

The two primary types mentioned in the Bible are the "absolute" and "supernatural absolute" fasts. These are total fasts-no food (solid or liquid) and no water. Paul went on an absolute fast for three days following his encounter with Jesus on the road to Damascus (Acts 9:9). Moses and Elijah engaged in what must be considered a supernatural absolute fast of forty days (Deuteronomy 9:9; I Kings 19:8).

So, I strongly advise you to drink plenty of liquids. Obviously, if God leads you to undertake an absolute fast, you should obey. If so, be certain, without doubt, that God is leading you.

Water-only fasts that last for more than several days need to be undertaken with complete rest and under medical supervision because of the extreme danger of over-toxification, breakdown of vital body tissues, and loss of electrolytes.

I personally recommend and practice water and juice fasting, especially if you are going to fast for an extended period of time. This type of fast will provide you with more energy than absolute or water-only fasts and still lead you into the humbling experience of denying your desire for solid food that you can chew.

When it comes to making your final decision about what type of fast is right for you, the best advice I can give you is to follow the leading of the Holy Spirit. He will guide your heart and mind as to what is best for you. Remember, the most important consideration in fasting is your motive. Why are you fasting? To seek something personally from God's hand or to seek His face in worship, praise and thanksgiving?

Spiritual Preparation

In preparation for this special time with God, I strongly urge you to examine your heart, and detect any unconfessed sin. Scripture records that God always requires His people to repent of their sins before He will hear their prayers. King David said:

Come and hear, all you who fear God; let me tell you what he has done for me. I cried out to him with my mouth; his praise was on my tongue. If I had cherished sin in my heart, the Lord would not have listened; but God has surely listened and has heard my prayer. Praise be to God, who has not rejected my prayer or withheld his love from me! (Psalm 66:16-20)

In your prayers, confess not only the obvious sins, but the less obvious ones as well. We call them the sins of omission as well as the sins of commission experiences. Sin includes doing things you should not do and not doing things you should do.

These may be experiences like worldly-mindedness, self-centeredness, spiritual indifference, and unwillingness to share your faith in Christ with others. It may include not spending sufficient time in God's Word and in prayer, a poor relationship with your spouse, your children, your pastor, or other members of your church.

Another great way to prepare for your fast is to practice what I call "Spiritual Breathing." The concept is simple. Like physical breathing, Spiritual Breathing is a process of exhaling the impure and inhaling the pure. If you knowingly sin, breathe spiritually to restore the fullness of God's Holy Spirit in your life.

You exhale by confessing your sins immediately you become aware of them, and you inhale by inviting the Holy Spirit to re-take control of your life. As an act of faith, trust Him to empower you. During the fast, spiritual breathing-constant reliance on the Holy Spirit- will enable you to resist the temptation to sin or abandon your fast.

Physical Preparation

Although fasting is primarily a spiritual discipline, it begins in the physical realm. It is important that you know your medical issues and consult with your doctor or specialist to make sure that you are medically able to fast.

You should not fast without specific physical preparation. If you plan on fasting for several days, you will find it helpful to begin by eating smaller meals before you abstain altogether. Resist the urge to have that "last big feast" before the fast. Cutting down on your meals a few days before you begin the fast will signal your mind, stomach, and appetite that less food is acceptable.

Some health professionals suggest eating only raw foods for two days before starting a fast. I also recommend weaning yourself off caffeine and sugar products to ease your initial hunger or discomfort at the early stages of your fast.

All the experts agree that "breaking the fast" is the critical phase of fasting. While your body is in the resting mode, your stomach shrinks and your intestines become idle, so solid food must be re-introduced very slowly to avoid kidney failure or digestive distress. In fact, after a 40-day fast, you should make a careful transition for at least three days before returning to eating meats or fats or normal foods.

Further, if you end your fast gradually, the beneficial physical and spiritual effects will linger for days. But if you rush into solid foods, you may lose much of your deep sense of peace and experience physical problems such as diarrhea, sickness, fainting, and frankly even death in some cases, due to shock!

Chapter 5: Unlocking the Power of Fasting

Dr. Paul Bragg and his daughter Patricia have conducted fasting clinics for many years. Their book *The Miracle of Fasting* (1) gives a specific daily food plan for breaking a 7-day fast that could be adapted and stretched out over several more days for a 40-day fast.

Most experts agree that breaking a fast with vegetables, either steamed or raw, is best. Your stomach is smaller now, so eat lightly. Stop before you feel full. Stay away from starches like pastas, potatoes, rice, or bread (except for "Melba toast") for at least a week. Also avoid meats, dairy products, and any fats or oils for a week or more. Introduce them very slowly and in small amounts.

Extended fasts are not the only fasts which need to be ended with caution. Even a 3-day fast requires reasonable precautions. It is wise to start with a little soup -- something thin and nourishing such as vegetable broth made from onion, celery, potatoes, and carrots -- and fresh fruits such as watermelon and cantaloupe.

In terms of resuming any sort of exercise routine, the advice is the same. Start out slowly, allowing time for your body to re-adjust to its usual regime

BREAKING STRONGHOLDS

"Is not this the kind of fasting I have chosen: to loose the chains of injustice and untie the cords of the yoke, to set the oppressed free and break every yoke? Is it not to share your food with the hungry and to provide the poor wanderer with shelter—when you see the naked, to clothe them, nd not to turn away from your own flesh and blood?" (Isaiah 58:6,7)

The chapter begins with God urging the prophet to expose the sins of his people (Isaiah 58:1) by raising his voice like a shofar (musical horn typically made of a ram's horn, used for Jewish religious purposes). Although the people appear to be acting in sincere desire for the Lord's favor (Isaiah 58:2), they feel that God has not noticed or answered them.

The Lord responds that this is because they are actually seeking after their own desire and exploiting workers (Isaiah 58:3). Such fasting does not merit God's attention. God has not chosen fasting to be a day for merely humbling oneself outwardly, as shown by the bending of the head and lying in sackcloth and ashes.

Such displays seem to not even merit the title of fast, as the concluding question of Isaiah 58:5 suggests:

Is this the kind of fast I have chosen, only a day for people to humble themselves? Is it only for bowing one's head like a reed and for lying in sackcloth and ashes? Is that what you call a fast?

Instead, God has chosen a fast in which one will make restitution for injustice, "to loosen the bonds of wickedness, to undo the bands of the yoke, and to let the oppressed go free, and break every yoke" (Isaiah 58:6). Additionally, it is a day for sharing food with the hungry and clothing the naked (Isaiah 58:7).

The purpose of the fast was to connect with God and his power so that together through the human act of abstaining and the God act of breaking strongholds, yokes were broken.

The purpose was to remove sinful chains; tear away ropes of burden; to set free those who are oppressed and to break the yokes that are burdensome.

To loose the chains of injustice: These bands initially referred to unjust court decisions, contracts and bonds that were entered into. They could also refer to religious matters where forms of worship and conduct were imposed upon the lives of people. We continue to see, today, forms of worship and particular conduct imposed by religious leaders which the Word of God has not made necessary.

To untie the cords of the yoke: The Septuagint render it, "dissolve the obligations of violent contracts." It regards the loosing or freeing people from all obligation to all human prescriptions and precepts. In the same way that Jesus spoke against the traditions of the Scribes and Pharisees that had become "heavy burdens, grievous to be borne" (Matthew 23:4)

We see these impositions not only in churches but in cults and other groups

To set the oppressed free: Initially it referred to the oppression of the person's spirit and their finances through fines, and confiscation of goods. It also referred to those who have been cast into prisons and detained for a long time in filthy dungeon by secular and religious persecution. Later it came to include the oppression of sin, sickness and Satan.

And break every yoke: The yoke is the yoke of church power and tyranny. It is everything that is not enjoined and authorized by the Word of God. It is all human precepts, commands and obedience to them. The only yoke to be put upon the neck of Christ's disciples is the yoke of Christ's commands and obedience to them.

The yoke of church power with its human precepts and commands with obedience to them are the strongholds in humans and over humans that need to be broken. These need more than just confessing, praying, healing and delivering. The fasting has a broader application than the emotional, physical and spiritual side of an individual.

It has a political and institutional impact that can affect change and transformation in a church or society. Isaiah 58:7 states that the power of the fast will include the person who is fasting to provide out of their abundance in some way.

Is it not to share your food with the hungry: The food that you have saved should not be laid up but given away to those in need. It includes spiritual bread, imparting the Gospel to those who are hungering and thirsting after righteousness, which is an acceptable service to God. The fast has a focus for God to supply humanitarian needs.

And to provide the poor wanderer with shelter: The person who fasts is to be open provide refuge, food and shelter to those fleeing persecution, especially Christian exiles.

When you see the naked, to clothe them: The person who fasts is also encouraged to provide better clothing to preserve people from the cold and wet than what they have on them. We are again reminded by the words of Jesus in the parable of the sheep and goats (Matthew 25:31-46) about feeding the hungry, clothing the naked, visiting the prisoner. The fast has a focus to supply material needs.

The fruit of the fast will be:

Then your light will break forth like the dawn, and your healing will quickly appear; then your righteousness will go before you, and the glory of the Lord will be your rear guard. Then you will call, and the Lord will answer; you will cry for help, and he will say: Here am I. (Isaiah 58:8,9)

Then your light will break forth like the dawn: The fast seeks to bring light and clarity and a new perspective to the individual or group.

And your healing will quickly appear: The prayers will be answered and health be given quickly.

Then your righteousness will go before you: The one who fasts will have the righteousness of God in Christ given to them and it will become obvious to all

And the glory of the Lord will be your rear guard: The very presence of God and the brightness of God's glory will surround you and protect you as a reward for the fasting.

Then you will call, and the Lord will answer; you will cry for help, and he will say: Here am I: The promise is that God will hear your cries, answer your prayers and make His presence known to you through His personal Word to you: *I am here with you.*

FURTHER BIBLICAL PERSPECTIVE ON THE PURPOSE OF FASTING

Each example of fasting in the Bible is attached to a purpose to be achieved. Each example of fasting was either conducted by a person or a group of people to seek God's favor. Each example of fasting had a time period.

Forty Day Fasts – For God's Spiritual Preparation

Moses was there with the LORD forty days and forty nights without eating bread or drinking water. And he wrote on the tablets the words of the covenant—the Ten Commandments. (Exodus 34:28)

Moses had been given the Ten Commandments by God on Mount Sinai. However, in their impatience, waiting for Moses' return, they built a golden calf and worshipped it. Moses in his anger, threw down the tablets of stone with the Commandments written on them and broke them.

God was angry with the people and put a plague amongst them as a punishment for their sin. He threatened not to go with them into the promised land. But because of His servant Moses, God promised to go with Moses and the people.

So, Moses went a second time up to Mount Sinai with two stone tablets for God to write upon them the words that were on the original tablets. Moses was there with God for forty days and nights without food and water, sustained by the very presence of God while God wrote down again the Ten Commandments on the stone tablets.

It was a time to establish again the nation of Israel through Moses and the giving of the Ten Commandments. The spiritual purpose was to reset in stone the Ten Commandments to form the covenantal relationship with God and Israel.

Then Jesus was led by the Spirit into the wilderness to be tempted by the devil. After fasting forty days and forty nights, he was hungry. The tempter came to him and said, "If you are the Son of God, tell these stones to become bread." (Matthew 4:1-3)

We now move forward to the beginning of Jesus' ministry. After being baptized in the river Jordan by John and hearing God speak to Him personally, the Holy Spirit sends Him out into the wilderness for a time of spiritual preparation. It was to be a testing time with Satan.

During this time Jesus did not eat for forty days but we do not know whether He drank any water. At the end of the forty days, Satan came to challenge Him about being the Son of God by using His Sonship for selfish reasons.

After three tests, Jesus was ministered to by God's angels and now was ready to inaugurate the Kingdom of God.

Forty Days is seen as a time of testing or trial or some significant call or work of God. The flood of Noah was for forty days and nights. Eilijah, after being threatened by Jezebel, escaped to a place in the wilderness, a day's journey from Beersheba. He was met by an angel and fed then travelled to Mt Horeb for forty days to deal with his depression and be given his charge to anoint Elisha.

When God called me into the ministry of healing and deliverance, He asked me to do a 40 day fast as a time of preparation for the ministry that He was calling me to. It was not at the level of going without food or water but it was to go without certain foods and coffee for the forty days.

It was a challenging, cleansing time but at the same time it gave me a closer walk with God and the ability to hear Him on a daily basis. It was a time of learning to be obedient to what God shared with me.

It was also a preparation time to enable me to understand Satan's ways and power and know how to contend against him with the power of Jesus.

If God is calling you into ministry of some kind, He may ask you to do a forty day fast to prepare you for that ministry, especially if that ministry is to contend against Satan.

Twenty-One Day Fast- For Spiritual Waiting for Revelation

In the third year of Cyrus king of Persia, a revelation was given to Daniel (who was called Belteshazzar). Its message was true and it concerned a great war. The understanding of the message came to him in a vision. At that time, I, Daniel, mourned for three weeks. I ate no choice food; no meat or wine touched my lips; and I used no lotions at all until the three weeks were over. On the twenty-fourth day of the first month, as I was standing on the bank of the great river, the Tigris, I looked up and there before me was a man dressed in linen, with a belt of fine gold from Uphaz around his waist. (Daniel 10:1-3)

Daniel sets the stage for the spectacular prophecy of Daniel 11, which described a time of great persecution and testing for the people of Israel. The reasons for the mourning are unclear. Some think that Daniel was in mourning because so few Jews had returned with Ezra from exile. Others believe it was because Ezra faced severe opposition in rebuilding the temple. Daniel was 84 at the time and may have felt it better to stay in his position of power rather than go back with Ezra.

We are told that the understanding of the vision was delayed because of a heavenly battle between the archangel Michael and the Principality (Head Demon) over Persia.

While some see this fast for a time of distress and mourning, it seems that the focus was to wait upon God for understanding of any revelation of vison or dream that He has given you.

It seems that this type of fast was instigated by Daniel and so we can assume that this fast may be instigated by a follower of Christ to wait upon the Lord for discernment and revelation of the purposes of God.

Fourteen Day Fast- For Spiritual Protection and Wisdom

Just before dawn Paul urged them all to eat. "For the last fourteen days," he said, "you have been in constant suspense and have gone without food—you haven't eaten anything. Now I urge you to take some food. You need it to survive. Not one of you will lose a single hair from his head." After he said this, he took some bread and gave thanks to God in front of them all. Then he broke it and began to eat. They were all encouraged and ate some food themselves. (Acts 27:33-36)

Paul is now a prisoner being taken to Rome. The boat sets out. So, Paul warns them that the voyage will be disastrous and bring great loss to ship and cargo, and to their lives also. But the centurion, instead of listening to what Paul said, followed the advice of the pilot and of the owner of the ship.

The storm came and the boat was caught up in it. The men secured the boat with ropes wound around the hull. The boat went aground but all 276 on board were able to make the shore safely,

For some reason they went without food for fourteen days. It was after this period; an angel came and spoke to Paul and stated that he would get to Rome.

Technically going without food for a period of time is a fast. If you feel your life is being threatened in some way either physically or financially or spiritually, a fourteen day fast may be God's way to give you protection and wisdom for your circumstance as you pray.

Ten Day Fast- Spiritual Commitment to God and His ways.

Daniel then said to the guard whom the chief official had appointed over Daniel, Hananiah, Mishael and Azariah, "Please test your servants for ten days: Give us nothing but vegetables to eat and water to drink. Then compare our appearance with that of the young men who eat the royal food, and treat your servants in accordance with what you see." So, he agreed to this and tested them for ten days. At the end of the ten days, they looked healthier and better nourished than any of the young men who ate the royal food (Daniel 1:11-15).

Daniel was taken into captivity to Babylon along with his friends. Their talents were recognized and they were being trained to be diplomats/bureaucrats to serve the King. The training regime included being fed with the finest delicacies and wine from the King's provisions. But the food was not kosher, so Daniel negotiated with his overseers to only eat vegetables and drink water for 10 days. It seems that Daniel and his friends were important enough to negotiate.

After 10 days, Daniel and his friends were healthier in body and mind than the men who were served from the king's provisions.

Daniel was not vague in his objection and had a clear solution. It seems that the King's food was against Jewish dietary laws. Daniel and his friends may have made vows against partaking of wine. The food most likely had been offered to idols.

It seems that there are two principles here: (1) Daniel felt that it was a religious test of his faith (he would not defile himself) (2) Daniel had a desire to still have a strong body and mind.

This is not a fast to lose weight or become healthy but a spiritual commitment to God. It was a time to draw near to God and make sure that there is nothing in his life that would defile him. This defilement was not just about food but covered the whole of his life.

The Daniel fast is a time to detox our mind, heart and body from our self-centered life, our wrong thinking, our poor attitudes, our lack of thankfulness in our life. It is a time to reset our lives and draw near to God.

One church near me, invited the whole congregation to undertake a Daniel fast in January to cleanse the body, mind and heart and seek God for His revelation for the coming year.

Seven Day Fast – For Spiritual Grief and Mourning

When the people of Jabesh Gilead heard what the Philistines had done to Saul, all their valiant men marched through the night to Beth Shan. They took down the bodies of Saul and his sons from the wall of Beth Shan and went to Jabesh, where they burned them. Then they took their bones and buried them under a tamarisk tree at Jabesh, and they fasted seven days. (1 Samuel 31:11-13)

The Philistines attacked Israel. Saul, his sons and army were overrun. Saul's sons were killed and Saul was critically wounded by arrows. When his armor bearer refused to kill Saul, Saul fell on his sword. Saul and his sons' beheaded bodies were then placed on the wall of Beth Shan. The men of Jabesh Gilead took down the bodies of Saul and his sons from their place of humiliation and gave them a proper burial.

When David heard of Saul's death, he did not rejoice. In fact, he mourned and composed a song in honor of Saul and Jonathan. In spite of all that Saul did against David, David spoke well of Saul after his death.

The fast was to commemorate the death of Saul and his sons. It was a time of mourning.

You may choose to fast for seven days to mourn the death of a family member or friend.

Three Day Fasts- Spiritual Breakthrough

Then Esther sent this reply to Mordecai: "Go, gather together all the Jews who are in Susa, and fast for me. Do not eat or drink for three days, night or day. I and my attendants will fast as you do. When this is done, I will go to the king, even though it is against the law. And if I perish, I perish. (Esther 4:15,16)

Esther was a Hebrew maiden that was living in the land of Persia where Israel had been taken into captivity. She was a beautiful girl raised by her older cousin Mordecai. Queen Vashti displeased King Xerxes and so Esther and a number of young girls were taken to the palace as possible replacements. God saw that Esther was chosen over all the other girls but Esther did not reveal her identity as a Jew.

Haman, the prime minister, hated the Jews because Mordecai would not bow down to him. He plotted to slaughter all the Hebrews living in Persia. Mordecai sought Esther's help to appeal to the King. The problem was that she could not just enter the King's presence but had to be summoned. If she did go in without the King's approval, she would be killed.

Esther sought the help of Mordecai and all the Israelites by asking them to fast for three days without food or water. The Israelites responded. At the end of the three days, Esther approached the King and he extended his staff towards her indicating his acceptance. She proposes a banquet for the King and Haman. They come but she does not give her request but offers another banquet.

Haman goes home extremely proud of his status of being invited twice to the Queen's banquet. On the way he meets Mordecai who does not bow down to him. Haman's wife and friends suggest that gallows be built for Mordecai.

That night the King cannot sleep and he orders the book of Chronicles, the record of his reign, to be read. He discovers that he is indebted to Mordecai and has not honored him for what Mordecai did. He asks Haman how a man should be honored. Haman thinking that it was for him, says a parade needs to be organize for all the people to honor this man.

The King orders Haman to organize this for Mordecai much to Haman's displeasure but he can't afford to say no to the King. The second banquet is held and Esther reveals to the King her Israelite identity and what Haman was plotting. The King was furious and hanged Haman on the gallows that Haman had prepared for Mordecai. The Jews in Susa killed all the people engaged to kill the Jews including the ten sons of Haman. But the Jews did not take any plunder. The Feast of Purim was born and is still celebrated today.

The men traveling with Saul stood there speechless; they heard the sound but did not see anyone. Saul got up from the ground, but when he opened his eyes, he could see nothing. So, they led him by the hand into Damascus. For three days he was blind, and did not eat or drink anything. (Acts 9:7-9)

Paul had been met by Jesus on the road to Damascus. He was blinded by the light. He was taken to Damascus and did not eat or drink for three days. During that time, he received a vision from Jesus stating that a man named Ananias would come, lay hands on him and his eyesight would be restored.

This period of fasting without food or water enabled Saul to work through what had happened to Him on the road to Damascus. For Jesus had told him that he had been appointed not to persecute and kill Christians but speak to the Gentiles to convert them to Christianity. He was given revelation that a man named Ananias would come to Him. All of this happened as it was spoken. It was a life changing and ministry changing moment for Saul who became known as Paul.

In 1995, I went away to finish writing my thesis on healing and deliverance for my Doctorate of Ministry. While praying, the Lord called me for a three day fast without food and water as part of my writing my thesis.

Unbeknown to me but known to God, this was an important thesis to be written for a spiritual breakthrough that was to be printed and shared with people who wanted to learn about how to pray for the sick effectively.

What is the spiritual breakthrough that you need in your life? It may be for healing. It may be a new business venture. It may be a new ministry or church plant. Whatever it may be, the Lord may call you to an "Esther Fast" so that the spiritual breakthrough can happen to you.

The breakthrough may need extra spiritual power to overcome the enemy and his desire to thwart God's purposes for you.

Fasting to solve a problem of your own making

There, by the Ahava Canal, I proclaimed a fast, so that we might humble ourselves before our God and ask him for a safe journey for us and our children, with all our possessions. I was ashamed to ask the king for soldiers and horsemen to protect us from enemies on the road, because we had told the king, "The gracious hand of our God is on everyone who looks to him, but his great anger is against all who forsake him." So, we fasted and petitioned our God about this, and he answered our prayer. (Ezra 8:21-23)

The Jews were going back from captivity in Persia in 538BC. First, Zerubbabel led the people back to begin work on the temple. The surrounding nations caused trouble, so the work went slowly, even stopping for several years. The temple was finally finished in 515BC.

Ezra, the priest, attempted to lead a second group back to Jerusalem.

Though these people were returning from captivity, they were not poor and had their household goods and treasures with them. They also had the wealth given to them by King Cyrus. It amounted to 25 tons of silver; 100 vessels of silver valued at three and three-quarter tons of gold; 20 gold bowls weighing eighteen and a half pounds; 2 vessels of bright red copper, as valuable as gold.

They were to travel through places where marauders and thieves lived and attacked caravans and they would be sitting ducks!

Ezra had religiously declared that God would look after them but then he had second and third thoughts about this. But pride, shame and embarrassment took over and he felt that he could not go back to the King for an army of protection.

He was in a pretty pickle because he did not want to lose people or the wealth that they carried.

So, they reached the river and faced with a significant problem, Ezra called a fast. A private problem needs a private fast. A group problem needs a group fast. As we examine the account, there were a number of steps that Ezra took.

Ezra called a fast to solve the problem of his own making. He proclaimed that God will protect their journey and possessions but now he has had second thoughts as they were travelling though dangerous country.

But it was more than just fasting. They agonized in prayer as they understood the seriousness of their situation. For a meaningful fast, people must not only withhold food, but they must also agonize in prayer. This involves spiritual introspection; spiritual examination; spiritual confession; spiritual intercession.

After discussing the situation with the elders, they waited three days for the priests to arrive as they were part of the solution.

We often approach a problem with the traditional problem-solving strategy. But Ezra did something before even discussing the problem with his elders. They gathered at the river for three days until the Levites had joined them. Note that he did not fast as he travelled; he did not fast before all had gathered; he did not try and solve the problem before fasting. Many times, we seek a solution to our problems and when nothing works, then we fast. The timing of the fast is just as important as its mechanics!

Then I set apart twelve of the leading priests, namely, Sherebiah, Hashabiah and ten of their brothers, and I weighed out to them the offering of silver and gold and the articles that the king, his advisers, his officials and all Israel present there had donated for the house of our God. .... I said to them, "You as well as these articles are consecrated to the Lord. The silver and gold are a freewill offering to the Lord, the God of your ancestors. Guard them carefully until you weigh them out in the chambers of the house of the Lord in Jerusalem before the leading priests and the Levites and the family heads of Israel." (Ezra 8:24-29)

God showed Ezra not only the way he should travel but also a plan to distribute the wealth so that if attacked all would not be lost. By dividing the wealth, Ezra made each priest accountable for an exact amount of treasure.

If we face big problems in our family life or business life or private life, we can fast for God's solution to solve the problem. But we must fast and wait upon the Lord for the solution, then implement it.

Fasting to repent and gain God's forgiveness

When Jonah's warning reached the king of Nineveh, he rose from his throne, took off his royal robes, covered himself with sackcloth and sat down in the dust. This is the proclamation he issued in Nineveh:

By the decree of the king and his nobles: Do not let people or animals, herds or flocks, taste anything; do not let them eat or drink. But let people and animals be covered with sackcloth. Let everyone call urgently on God. Let them give up their evil ways and their violence. Who knows? God may yet relent and with compassion turn from his fierce anger so that we will not perish.

When God saw what they did and how they turned from their evil ways, he relented and did not bring on them the destruction he had threatened (Jonah 3:6-10)

Jonah finally reached Ninevah and began preaching about the destruction of Ninevah by the Lord God. The King heard about this and instructed all his people to fast, pray and change their ways of evil and violence.

The Lord God heard their prayers and their acts of repentance and was moved to not bring on them the destruction He had threatened, much to Jonah's disgust.

Fasting, prayer and acts of repentance show God that you are serious about changing your life to avert His judgment whether you are an individual or a community or a church or a nation.

Fasting to bring Deliverance from Demons

A man in the crowd answered, "Teacher, I brought you my son, who is possessed by a spirit that has robbed him of speech. Whenever it seizes him, it throws him to the ground. He foams at the mouth, gnashes his teeth and becomes rigid. I asked your disciples to drive out the spirit, but they could not." When Jesus saw that a crowd was running to the scene, he rebuked the impure spirit. "You deaf and mute spirit," he said, "I command you, come out of him and never enter him again." The spirit shrieked, convulsed him violently and came out. The boy looked so much like a corpse that many said, "He's dead." But Jesus took him by the hand and lifted him to his feet, and he stood up. After Jesus had gone indoors, his disciples asked him privately, "Why couldn't we drive it out?" He replied, "This kind can come out only by prayer (and fasting (other ancient authorities))" (Mark 9:17-18;25-29)

The incident in the above scripture records the one place where deliverance from demons involved more than just a prayer or a command to go. It required the possibility of the need to fast.

Privately the disciples asked Jesus why they could not remove the demon. In Mark's account the problem was prayer. Some manuscripts add fasting. In Matthew's account, it was the problem of little faith. In Luke's account, Jesus attributed the reason for failure to deliver the child was a faithless and perverse generation.

While the scriptural text may be vague, fasting to pray for people who have a demon(s) gives power to the prayer for deliverance.

On a number of occasions, we have fasted when we have prayed for people who have been involved with the occult in some way. Their involvement with the enemy has given the enemy a very strong hold on their lives. On some occasions, God has called us to fast when we awake as we have prayer ministry that day that needs the spiritual power that fasting releases.

Praying with fasting can break the strong hold that the enemy has on the person's life.

Fasting for Spiritual Growth

When you fast, do not look somber as the hypocrites do, for they disfigure their faces to show others they are fasting. Truly I tell you, they have received their reward in full. But when you fast, put oil on your head and wash your face, so that it will not be obvious to others that you are fasting, but only to your Father, who is unseen; and your Father, who sees what is done in secret, will reward you. (Matthew 6:16-18)

The three great religious practices among the Jews were giving, praying, and fasting. Jesus' own ministry began with an epic forty-day fast. Jesus begins, "Whenever you fast," because He probably expected His followers would fast, though neither He nor of any of the New Testament writers command it.

Jesus offers no technical instructions on when or how to fast, only that fasting should not be for outward show. Apparently, many who fasted made a point of wearing tattered clothing, scrubbing their head with ashes, and stumbling about as though carrying a great burden.

Jesus offers two instructions.

First, when fasting, look normal,- cheerful! *"put oil on your head and wash your face."* The oil and water treatment were the everyday norm in Jesus' day. That's just what people did before going out. In fact, since oil was synonymous with gladness (Isaiah 61:3), a person should look not only normal but cheerful!

Second, Jesus taught, when fasting, fast for God, *so that your fasting may be seen not by others but by your Father who is in secret.*

Scripture does not command Christians to fast. God does not require or demand it of Christians. At the same time, the Bible presents fasting as something that is good, profitable, and beneficial. The book of Acts records believers fasting before they made important decisions (Acts 13:2; 14:23).

Fasting and prayer are often linked together (Luke 2:37; 5:33). Too often, the focus of fasting is on the lack of food. Instead, the purpose of fasting should be to take your eyes off the things of this world to focus completely on God. Fasting is a way to demonstrate to God, and to ourselves, that we are serious about our relationship with Him. Fasting helps us gain a new perspective and a renewed reliance upon God.

Fasting has a number of benefits for the Christian. It can help us hear from God. It can reveal our hidden sin. It can strengthen intimacy with God. It can teach us to pray with right motives. It can build our faith.

Not only does fasting and prayer help us focus on God, but through that time, it brings us closer to Him and changes our hearts.

If we do fast, especially for a particular situation, we need to be prepared for spiritual attacks. Thus, praying the prayer of protection that is discussed in a future chapter would be helpful.

Victory is not instantaneous but is a process that is only won through diligent and consistent praying.

Barbara Gordon (2) talks about her first time fasting.

She fasted one day a week for 9 weeks. She was led to pray for 9 individuals that had requested prayer. At the end she said, "God moved in many ways during that time. While most of the answers didn't appear during the 9 weeks, God increased my faith that they would come.

Within a year of that first fast, my lost friend came to Christ. Another friend was delivered from a long-standing addiction. A couple whose marriage seemed doomed is still married several years later. My unmarried friend is still single, but I see her enjoying new peace.

I learned that fasting is not a guarantee that every request will be answered. It is, however, a way to prepare ourselves to pray more in line with God's will. The most important personal result of my first fast was that I felt more in love with my Savior. Circumstances were indeed changed, but more importantly, I was changed."

We now move to understand Satan and his demon army, the way they operate and how to defeat them.

6

UNLOCKING THE POWER TO DEFEAT DEMONS

At once the Spirit sent him out into the wilderness, and he was in the wilderness forty days, being tempted by Satan. He was with the wild animals, and angels attended him. (Mark 1:12-13)

Just then a man in their synagogue who was possessed by an impure spirit cried out, "What do you want with us, Jesus of Nazareth? Have you come to destroy us? I know who you are— the Holy One of God!" "Be quiet!" said Jesus sternly. "Come out of him!" The impure spirit shook the man violently and came out of him with a shriek. (Mark 1:23-26)

Put on the full armor of God, so that you can take your stand against the devil's schemes. For our struggle is not against flesh and blood, but against the rulers, against the authorities, against the powers of this dark world and against the spiritual forces of evil in the heavenly realms. (Ephesians 6:11,12)

In 1988, I was the minister over two denominational congregations; Anglican (Church of England or Episcopal) and Uniting Church (Methodist, Presbyterian, Congregational). It was a joint ministry. I attended a prayer meeting of some Anglican ladies. As we were praying, a male voice came out of one of the ladies and said *"She is mine, you are not going to have her!"*

I had been a parish minister for 6 years, and a Christian for 17 years and this was my first experience of a demon manifesting through a person. I prayed for her but nothing happened and I resolved that day to learn as much as I could so that I would not be caught again.

Since that time, I have been on a learning curve, dealing with demons in many situations. My first learning was to adjust my theological understanding to incorporate the reality that demons actually exist and inhabit people in some way. This was not taught or emphasized in my theological training. Much of ministerial training has a western world view which minimizes or neglects or fails to believe in the existence of Satan and his demons.

For me, there was and is no doubt that Satan and his army exists. Jesus believed in his existence, confronted him in the wilderness when Satan tried to thwart Jesus and His destiny and then set people free from the demons that had impacted and affected their lives. If we are to defeat Satan and his demons, we need to know his character and modus operandi.

Reverend John Lucas, DMin

KNOW YOUR ENEMY

The downfall of many armies is their lack of knowledge of their enemy and how that enemy attacks and counter attacks. We have seen wars in Vietnam and Afghanistan which have not reached any conclusion except a great loss of life. The assumption by those who invaded those countries was that fighting would be done in a conventional way as in previous wars. But these wars were far from conventional and different tactics were employed to fight and delay the advance of the army.

If we are to defeat Satan, we need to know him, his tactics and how to defeat him. We must be aware of the fact that most of us would not encounter Satan per se as Jesus did in the wilderness. Most of us are not that important or strategic enough for Satan to bother with us. But while the majority would not have an encounter with Satan, we do have encounters with many powerful demons and we should not underestimate their power.

We must also be aware that as we travel overseas, we may encounter powerful demons attached to the religious worship of the people of the land via their many idols and ancestor worship. These demons have been positioned geographically to contend with the local population and any who visit.

In the following description of Satan, we use the name, Satan, even though many of us would not encounter him. However, what we describe not only applies to the archangel called Satan or Lucifer but also to all the demons under him.

It is helpful to understand that Satan has an army with powerful generals who have specific characteristics and those characteristics are mirrored in those demons that serve the general. For example, we have the Jezebel general and many Jezebel demons under this general and these Jezebel demons have varying power and authority.

It is helpful to know that many demons that we encounter are lower order demons e.g. the "privates" and "corporals" of Satan's army that have a hold on people. In some cases, you may encounter a demon(s) that are higher up the command chain.

Thus, the following use of Satan is a generic term to help us understand the nature of Satan and his army and make it easier to talk about. The good news is that what biblical truths apply to Satan, applies to every demon, at whatever level, under him.

The following has been helpful to me in the many years of deliverance ministry that I have undertaken.

Satan's Characteristics

Let us look at some of the major characteristics of Satan, which helps us to understand the enemy we face and so know how to stand against him.

1. **Satan is bound**:

Satan is a defeated foe who has no rightful authority over people. He is simply a usurper. The judgment was implemented at Calvary. He is bound; his power is curbed. He cannot prevent, although he can hinder, the spread of the gospel. He is not omniscient (all knowing) or omnipotent (all powerful) or omnipresent (everywhere present). He is a defeated foe and he cannot ultimately prevail. While he is a defeated foe because of Jesus, we should not underestimate him or take him for granted.

2. Satan is mighty:

Satan attacks the minds of people with doubts, fears and propaganda. He assails the spirits of people with lust, pride and hatred. He assaults the bodies of people with disease, torture, and death. He assails the institutions of society with structural evil bringing hurt and pain and destruction to people's lives. It is unwise to underestimate his power. He can be resisted and overcome through the name of Jesus, but any other name he can and does brush aside.

3. Satan is violent:

He loves bitterness, hatred, war and revenge. Violence is the result of his work whether it is through demonization of a person, sometimes throwing the person down to the ground or giving superhuman strength, or a state where it has given itself to evil and violence is the normal feature of its life.

4. Satan is highly intelligent:

He has massive mental powers. He does not create a situation but he corrupts it. He is uncannily crafty, subtle and cunning. He knows the scriptures and can twist them to his advantage. He knows the ways of God so that he can counter them.

5. Satan is a liar:

He is the master of misrepresentation where his lies subtly cover over or twist the real issue.
Two of the most effective lies are that
(1) he does not exist and that
(2) man is most free when in pursuit of
- "Free thought",
- "Free expression" and
- "Free love".

6. Satan can enter a person:

He entered into Judas Iscariot (Luke 22:3, John 13:27). He cannot do this without a person's free will but deliberate sin will allow entry.

7. Satan can dominate:

Paul tells of how his missionary plans were frustrated in 1 Thessalonians 2:17–18: "We endeavored the more eagerly, and with great desire, to see you face to face; because we wanted to come to you . . . but Satan hindered us."Satan hates evangelism and discipleship, and he will throw every obstacle he can in the way of missionaries and people with a zeal for evangelism.

8. Satan is persistent:

He does not give up easily in the pursuit of people. After the temptation of Jesus in the wilderness, when Jesus defeated the devil, the Scripture records that Satan withdrew, until an opportune time to attack Jesus (Luke 4:13).

His persistence can be in the form of a siege where there may be a prolonged assault on a person. This could be a severe illness, a car accident, or an ongoing depressed state. Or it could come as a surprise, leaving the person alone and lulling her/him into a false sense of security and then coming in the most unexpected way.

When we least expect him, he comes and seeks to bring us down. Usually this occurs just before or just after a time of blessing.

9. Satan counterattacks:

The ability of Satan to counterattack permeates nearly all the words of Jesus. One parable, (Luke 11: 24-26), where a demon having been cast out will return with seven others, more evil than the first, emphasizes this ability of Satan to counterattack (see also the parables of Jesus in Matthew 13:18-30 where God sows the good seed but the enemy strikes back by seeking to plunder it).

10. Satan is cowardly:

He fears the Name of his conqueror, Jesus Christ and those who stand in His Name.

Resist the devil and he will flee from you (James 4:7)

These are some of the characteristics of the Enemy of humankind. None of us can match him for his cunning, intelligence, power and hatred. Left to our own resources we would not have a hope.

But we have the victory of the Cross of Christ and when we stand on that victory and stand in the Name of Christ, the enemy runs away, a defeated foe.

Let us take a closer look at Satan and his army.

As Satan is a fallen angel, he is not omnipresent like God. He is limited in time and space. The book of Revelation in 12:3,4 points out that Satan was hurled down along with a third of the angels who followed him. As they are likened to stars, the implication is that there are too many to count.

Paul in Ephesians 6 describes them as rulers, powers, principalities, spiritual forces of evil, indicating an army with different leaders that have different authority, location and powers.

The gospels talk about demons. But they seem to be the lesser members of Satan's army though still powerful as they take a hold of people and control them.

Satan's Generals

Satan is a fallen archangel who took many other angels with him when he was caste out from heaven (Revelation 12). Since Satan is not omnipresent, he has many demons strategically placed around the world. Satan has an angel army that is like a country's army.

There are Generals and various commanders under them who are very powerful. They have responsibility over nations, regions and institutions. Then there are the foot soldiers, the demons that are sent out to attack humans that we encounter and send to the feet of Jesus for judgment.

Note that the demons that we encounter have a similar identity as the generals but they are not as powerful. Thus, for example, we have the general called Antichrist and foot soldiers called antichrist that we encounter.

Some of the major generals that we will come into contact in our battle are:

Antichrist - *(son of perdition, man of lawlessness, false Christ) Ref. Mark 13; 2 Thessalonians 2:10; Revelation 13; 16:12, 17; 19:19-21.*

Antichrist is a worldwide power as well as a ruling spirit. It is found both inside the church and outside it. It is the power that opposes God's kingdom. It is of the world and speaks about things of the world. People yielding to that spirit respond to the world, know the world, approve of the world, delve into the world, and appreciate the things of the world and the world responds to them.

In every area of our society, the Antichrist manifests its influence, infiltrates people's ideas of what is good and infects everything. Nothing is safe; entertainment, sport, industry, medicine, law, business.

Many Christians dip their feet into the world, compromising their values and going after prosperity and success.

In the church, the spirit manifests through constant deception and distortion of doctrine. Seducing spirits entice groups to follow charismatic leaders who twist the truth of God. Splits occur; people leave and start their own church, believing that they are right only to find, later on, that they get burnt.

The gateway for the Antichrist is self. Self in the church represents rebellion against authority, pride, stubbornness and lack of submission.

Antichrist works in conjunction with Jezebel (control), Beelzebub (mind control) and Leviathan (pride).

Apollyon - *(Abaddon) Ref. Revelation 9:11.*

It is the destroyer of human life through anger, hatred, violence, murder, destruction and death and war.

Its influence is seen in every country where murder and death are experienced. It works with Molech in the area of suicide and abortion.

Ashtaroth - *(Ashtoreth (Israel), Ishtar (Babylon), Ashtart (Aram), Astarte or Aphrodite (Greece), Venus (Rome)) Ref. Judges 2:12, I Samuel 7:3, 12:10, 1 Kings 11:5,33.*

It seeks to lure people away from God through perverted sex via pornography, homosexuality, lesbianism, and sodomy. It was worshipped in Canaan as a fertility goddess, and its name means "giver of life".

Asmodeus- *Ref. Tobit 3:17.*

It works against unity in marriages, families and churches through division, discord and dissent. It seeks to break down unity through the use of hurt, unforgiveness, unreconciled relationships and discontent within relationships.

Beelzebub- *Ref. Mark 3:20-27 (Matthew 10:25, Luke 11:15)* as the "prince of demons".

A high-ranking spirit in authority over other demons, it is "seen" with many flies crawling over it. It is behind the occult, witchcraft, new age practices, martial arts, mind control and drug addiction especially mind-altering drugs.

It has the spirit of *Mind Control* under it. This demon is often "seen' as a giant squid with ten tentacles that stick into the brain or over the head. Fear, ungodly meditation, hypnotism and other mind control practices are entry points.

Dagon-*Ref. Judges 16:23; 1 Samuel 5:2, 1 Chronicles. 10:10.*

Dagon was the Philistine god. It was in Dagon's temple that Samson pulled down the supporting pillars causing the whole building to topple on himself and the three thousand Philistines who were offering a great sacrifice to their god. (Judges 16:1-31)

When the Philistines had captured the ark of God, they took it to Ashdod and placed it in Dagon's temple setting it before the statue of Dagon. God afflicted the people of Ashdod with tumors until they removed the ark to Gath. (1 Samuel 5:12). They knew Baal, the god worshipped by the Canaanites and Phoenicians, as the son of Dagon.

Its influence is through sickness and infirmity, especially terminal illness.

Diana (Artemis *(Greece)) - Ref. Acts 19:24-35.*

It is said to have taken on the characteristics of Cybele, the mother goddess of fertility worshipped in Asia Minor and served by many prostitute priestesses. Diana is the adulteress of the book of Revelation, the woman who got drunk with the blood of the saints (Revelation 17:6). She is the one who kills them.

It is behind sexual immorality and sexual abuse through fornication, incest, prostitution, seduction and adultery.

Freemasonry

Released through the craft of Freemasonry and its associated lodges, it places a hood of deception over its followers. Primarily a secret society for men, but can be a separate society for women, based on the attainment of degrees, it has found its way in the life of mainline churches (Anglican (Episcopal), Methodist, Presbyterian and Uniting Churches in Australia (Methodist, Presbyterian and Congregational churches combines in 1977)) and the community.

It is a religion of good works. Many founding fathers were freemasons like George Washington (first American President), William Light (founder of Adelaide, South Australia) and many cities are based on Masonic principles and foundations. Many powerful and influential men in finance, business, police and law are freemasons.

It is based on ancient rites that go back to Egyptian, Babylonian and Canaanite gods. It opens up men (women), as they go up the "ladder", to satanic worship. It is a powerful spirit that continues to keep, in captivity, many men, women (and their families), churches, communities and cities, through sickness, poverty, untimely deaths, religiosity, retardation of spiritual growth and maturity, usurping of spiritual leadership.

Jezebel – *Ref. 1 Kings 16:22, 2 Kings 9, Revelation 2:18-29*

The Jezebel spirit manifests itself in the form of control, manipulation, intimidation and domination over people as typified by Queen Jezebel. Mainly found in women but it is also very present in ministers/pastors/elders/leaders of churches.

This control can be exercised by the leadership of a church as it tells the people what to wear, what to give, what to believe. There is no allowance for any discussion and healthy debate and it seeks to cut out any warning voices.

The seductive face of Jezebel is false flattery, laying a trap, pitting one against another. It includes strategic affiliation, dismantling a wall of prayer and false dreams and visions. It also involves carrying false burdens creating spiritual dependence in others, appearing more spiritual than others with a false humility. It also involves control, manipulation and emotional blackmail.

The deadly ploys used are defensive posturing, being unreasonable and unyielding, appealing to others. It organizes private prayer sessions, seeking others to teach, twisting scripture and reworking doctrines. It uses reckless words, false prophecy, seeks to impart and influence and appears religious. The experiences are dramatized. It looks to other men and seeks to undermine the husband.

Entry points are roots of rebellion, bitterness, bondage, fear, and pride.

It is linked to the *Queen of Heaven (ref. Revelation 18:7; a higher principality)* that delights in worship of it, primarily through Mary worship.

Leviathan - *Ref. Job 41, Psalm 74:14, 104:26, Isaiah 27:1.*

It is described in Job 41 as a serpent like sea monster. It is the king over all who are proud. (Job 41:34). It uses pride, spiritual pride to attack Christians and the Church. It is said that it sits in the

Holy place, counterfeits the furnishings, and blocks the entrance to the Holy of Holies (Job 41:18-20). It gives a false peace and sense of wellbeing by counterfeiting the gifts of the Spirit – false revelations, prophecies, words, visions and dreams.

It counterfeits the lamp stand and gives false understanding where Christians cling to favorite doctrines and beliefs and cause them to be unteachable. It counterfeits the table of showbread and gives a false word to support false doctrines and block them from seeing the light of God's word. It counterfeits with fire and smoke, the altar of incense, leading to unholy prayers and praises that are false (Parable of Pharisee and Tax collector (Luke 18:9-14)). Pride can stick up its ugly head and look around the church in the middle of praise and worship.

It has scales of pride (Job 41:15-17) that close up the person so that the wind of the Holy Spirit struggles to get in. It makes a deep boil, like a pot of ointment (Job 41:31), making a person act calm and peaceful in worship but vents the emotions after church, boiling over to family with intense emotions. It makes people stiff-necked (Job 41: 22-24) where they have a one-track mind and they cannot be changed.

It acts like a wet blanket over a church, smothering the Holy Spirit, the fruit in people's lives, and their gifts of ministry esp. the supernatural gifts, and keeps the church in spiritual kindergarten.

It is "seen" like a slug or snail: a corkscrew wrapped around and difficult to remove (Isaiah 27:1); multiple heads (Psalm 74:13, 14) (but we are not told how many heads and may be different heads in people and the church).

Molech *(Moloch, Malcham, Chemoch, Chemosh) Ref. Leviticus 18:21,20:2-5; Judges 11:24; 2 Kings 23:10. Chemoch (Chemosh) (Moab) Numbers 21:29; 1 Kings 11:7*

These were behind the gods that were worshiped through human sacrifice especially children, in ancient times. Now they are behind suicide, abortion, satanic ritual killing. It works with *Apollyon* to achieve its destructive forces. It gives the thoughts and plans to the person to produce the death of themselves or others.

Watcher and Listener Demons

In the book of Daniel there is the term watchers (Daniel 4:13,17,23 called holy ones) that refer to angels. In our ministry we have discovered that there exists watcher and listener demons whose job is to watch, listen and record what is being done and report it back to the demons above them.

They are there because these demons are limited in time and space i.e. not omnipresent but can travel fast. We pray and regularly remove them to the feet of Jesus for judgment and ask Jesus to destroy by fire all their looking, listening and recording devices that are present, spiritually, in the ceiling of the room.

Those with spiritual eyes can see them and specific prayer can remove them. (See prayers in the glossary of prayers at the end of the book)

Satan's Targets

Satan seeks to attack in a number of areas:

He attacks God:

He attacks God by opposing God, desiring and working towards having the power of God.

His game plan is to take over the world and be "God". He does this by seeking to break down love through hatred, life through death, light through darkness. He also attacks God by counterfeiting God's system of truth.

He seeks to deny the existence of God and His control or explain the world by substituting human progress for divine salvation, humankind's utopia for God's Kingdom, atheism, agnosticism, pragmatism, existentialism, relativism and wokery for God's Truth.

He also promotes counterfeit religions with their own false ministers, false doctrine and false Christ's seeking to deceive the innocent seekers of meaning in life. Cults, sects and eastern mystic religions have grown quite considerably in the western world under his encouragement.

We have seen this attack come through the New Age movement offering a false spirituality and false healing to a spiritually dry people.

We have seen this attack through novels like Da Vinci Code that attack the resurrection and divinity of Jesus. Jesus is portrayed only as a human being and not the Son of God. We have seen this attack through Post Modernism where there is a denial of absolute authority and truth. The Bible is now just one of many religious books that can teach truth.

He has false followers, professing to believe in Christ, but they are Satan's Sowers of evil. (Matthew 13:38-39). He seeks to counteract God's sovereignty through rebellion. Although he cannot step outside God's ultimate authority, he will work very hard within the limits given to him by God.

He attacks the nations:

He leads nations astray from the truth as it is in God and Christ through deception. He influences governments and their affairs to bring down the work of Christ. One way is the use of governments to hinder the spread of the gospel at home and abroad by persecution and murder of local Christians and the deportation of Christian missionaries.

He attacks those who are not saved:

He does this by preventing them from hearing the truth. He snatches away the gospel from their grasp (Luke 8:12) and blinds their minds to the gospel through a veil (2 Corinthians 4:3-4).

He indoctrinates the unsaved in false religions e.g. a salvation by human works, persuasion to a belief that there is no salvation, promotion of systems that deny sin and evil or lead people into various religions like the occult, the New Age, eastern mysticism.

He leads people into a false lifestyle, centered in themselves and based on pleasure, possessions and position.

Do not love the world or anything in the world. If anyone loves the world, love for the Father is not in them. For everything in the world—the lust of the flesh, the lust of the eyes, and the pride of life—comes not from the Father but from the world. (1 John 2:15,16)

He attacks Churches

In the letters of Paul to the churches and in John's letter of Revelation 2 and 3 we see the attack and downfall of many of the churches that were planted by the Apostles.

A closer look reveals the type of attack that came which the leadership of the church did not recognize or did nothing about. These issues, not dealt with lovingly and strongly, can affect the life of the church for generations.

These attacks come in the following way:
- Religion rather than relationship (Galatians; Ephesus; Sardis)
- Division and taking of sides (Corinthians)
- Sin especially sexual sin (Corinthians; Pergamum; Thyatira)
- Control and manipulation of people (Corinthians; Thyatira)
- Spiritual elitism (Corinthians)
- Infiltration of false teachers and teaching (Galatians; Pergamum; Thyatira)

Defense:
- *The pastor and the leaders of the church continue to encourage their people to love one another*
- *An intercession team is formed to pray for the church, the pastor and leaders, and the people*
- *The Bible is preached and holy lives led by everyone, learning the lessons of the churches in the NT.*
- *The pastor and the church members understand the ways of the enemy and how to counter him.*

He attacks Christians

(a) Satan attacks the Christian's *mind*

But I am afraid that just as Eve was deceived by the serpent's cunning, your minds may somehow be led astray from your sincere and pure devotion to Christ. (2 Corinthians 11:3)

The mind is part of the image of God where God communicates with you and reveals His will for you.

Satan's purpose is to make you ignorant of God's will for your life so that you will be robbed of all the blessings that God has for you; so that you will make wrong decisions or get involved with sinful activities and ultimately build the wrong life for you. He plants thoughts and ideas into our mind. Unless we put into place God's protection, we can be deceived.

Defense:
- *Capture every thought that comes to you and assess/discern its "truth" and source. (2 Corinthians 10:5)*
- *Put the wrong thoughts into container and take it to the cross.*
- *Command in the name of Jesus, every demon, attacking your mind, including deception and mind control, to go to the feet of Jesus for judgment*
- *Wear the helmet of salvation; part of the armor of God. (Ephesians 6:10-20)*
- *Set your minds on the things that are above (Colossians 3:1)*
- *Finally, brothers, whatever is true, whatever is honorable, whatever is fair, whatever is pure, whatever is acceptable, whatever is commendable, if there is anything of excellence and if there is anything praiseworthy-keep thinking about these things. (Philippians 4:8)*

(b)   Satan attacks the Christian's *body*.

Therefore, in order to keep me from becoming conceited, I was given a thorn in my flesh, a messenger of Satan, to torment me. Three times I pleaded with the Lord to take it away from me. But he said to me, "My grace is sufficient for you, for my power is made perfect in weakness." (2 Corinthians 12:7-9)

In the New Testament, Satan, through his demonic helpers, sought to destroy the bodies of various people.

He caused
- one man to be dumb (Matthew 9:32, 33) and
- a woman to be bent over and disabled for years. (Luke 13:11-17).

His purpose is to make you impatient with God's will. Patience and faith go hand in hand. Impatience can lead to costly errors or make you impulsive or lead you to do something stupid that can lead you and/or others into trouble.

Defense:
- *Check out whether there has been any sin in your life that has given Satan an opportunity to attack.*
- *Deal with any curses that may have come against you. Curses give Satan an opportunity to attack with sickness*
- *Forgive people who have hurt you and let go of all unforgiveness, bitterness and resentment.*
- *Command all spirits of sickness and infirmity to go to the feet of Jesus for judgment.*
- *Command in the name of Jesus, your body to be healed.*
- *Are you able to live by the grace of God, like Paul, if your body is not healed? (2 Corinthians 12:7—9)*

(c) Satan attacks the Christian's *will*

He must not be a recent convert, or he may become conceited and fall under the same judgment as the devil. He must also have a good reputation with outsiders so that he will not fall into disgrace and into the devil's trap. (1 Timothy 3:6,7)

Satan seeks to control us. His purpose is to make you independent of God's will for you. He wants you to act and think independently of God. He wants you to be self-sufficient rather than God-sufficient and he uses pride to achieve his own ends.

Warren Wiersbe (1) warns:

Beware when you feel you have arrived! Beware when you feel you are very important and that God could not get along without you! Beware when you start to rob God of some of the glory that belongs to Him.

Defense:
- *Confession of all pride, rebellion and control to Jesus*
- *Place this in a container and take it to the cross.*
- *Command Leviathan, Beelzebub and Jezebel with all their demons of pride, rebellion and control to go to the feet of Jesus for judgment.*
- *Submit and surrender to the will of God- "not my will but your will, Lord"*
- *Always give God the glory*

(d) Satan attacks the Christian's *heart and conscience.*

Now the serpent was more crafty than any of the wild animals the Lord God had made. He said to the woman, "Did God really say, 'You must not eat from any tree in the garden'? "The woman said to the serpent, "We may eat fruit from the trees in the garden, but God did say, 'You must not eat fruit from the tree that is in the middle of the garden, and you must not touch it, or you will die.'"

"You will not certainly die," the serpent said to the woman. "For God knows that when you eat from it your eyes will be opened, and you will be like God, knowing good and evil."

When the woman saw that the fruit of the tree was good for food and pleasing to the eye, and also desirable for gaining wisdom, she took some and ate it. She also gave some to her husband, who was with her, and he ate it. Then the eyes of both of them were opened, and they realized they were naked; so they sewed fig leaves together and made coverings for themselves.

Then the man and his wife heard the sound of the Lord God as he was walking in the garden in the cool of the day, and they hid from the Lord God among the trees of the garden. But the Lord God called to the man, "Where are you?" He answered, "I heard you in the garden, and I was afraid because I was naked; so I hid."

And he said, "Who told you that you were naked? Have you eaten from the tree that I commanded you not to eat from?" The man said, "The woman you put here with me—she gave me some fruit from the tree, and I ate it." Then the Lord God said to the woman, "What is this you have done? "The woman said, "The serpent deceived me, and I ate." (Genesis 3:1-13)

When a person has disobeyed God, Satan attacks her/him in the heart and conscience, accuses her/him and seeks to defeat the Christian by forcing the Christian to impute blame on another or by reinforcing the feelings of shame and remorse that one feels before God.

His purpose is to make one feel guilty, to feel regret and remorse but not repentance.

He keeps accusing the Christian so that the focus is on oneself and her/his sins rather than on God's love and forgiveness and God's desire to restore the Christian into fellowship with Him once again. Excessive guilt and sorrow can only lead to depression, despair and defeat and even destruction.

Satan also attacks the Christian when someone has sinned against her/him producing hurt in some form. This hurt can fester and can lead to bitterness and unforgiveness if the Christian has not forgiven the person(s) that have wronged her/him.

The end product of Satan's attack upon a Christian can sometimes be "demonization" where the Christian gives access to demonic influence in their life to such an extent that some of their words and actions are under the influence of demons and hence her or his actions can be held back through the use of fear and doubt.

Defense:
- *Confession of sin. Ask for forgiveness from God.*
- *Ask God to cleanse your sin by the precious blood of Jesus and the living water of God. Use the Container Prayer to remove all the poison of sin, guilt, false guilt, shame, regret and remorse.*
- *Command all demons attacking you to go to the feet of Jesus for judgment.*
- *Ask Jesus to remove all roots of bitterness and destroy them by fire* (see last chapter for details)
- *If we claim to be without sin, we deceive ourselves and the truth is not in us. If we confess our sins, he is faithful and just and will forgive us our sins and purify us from all unrighteousness. If we claim we have not sinned, we make him out to be a liar and his word is not in us. (1 John 1:8-10)*

Satan's Weapons

Satan's weapons are those, which are part of our fallen world, which he uses for his own ends. He uses our propensity to sin and the objects of our culture to enhance his work. He uses every sinful aspect of this world for his own desires.

He seems to be behind the massive, illicit use of drugs, the pornographic industry, the dehumanizing bondage to materialism, and the obscene violence that increasingly threatens our society. He seems to be behind the philosophy of post modernism where there is no absolute truth. He seems to be behind the philosophy of wokeism (politically liberal or progressive (as in matters of racial and social justice) especially in a way that is considered unreasonable or extreme but only chooses the causes that suit its purpose).

While the root of sin is in our own fallen natures where our sinful hearts have turned away from God, the extent of the corruption and evil indicates that there is "someone" using what is there and taking it further, in a very destructive way.

Through the various names and characteristics of Satan, we already have some insight into the weapons of Satan.

In the classic passage in Ephesians 6, Paul warns his readers about the "flaming darts of the evil one".

Let us look at some of the main "darts" which we face as Christians though these are not exclusively limited to Christians. We use the Container prayer found in Chapter 4 to help us.

(1) *Pride*:

Pride is the exaltation of self and one's own importance. It seeks to glorify the person and robs God of the glory that only He deserves. It was pride that led the Pharisee to go home saying *"God, I thank you that I am not like other people—robbers, evildoers, adulterers—or even like this tax collector." (Luke 18:11)* As someone has said" Pride is a strange illness - it makes everyone sick but the one who has it".

Defense:
- *Acknowledgment and confession of pride and complete surrender to the Lordship of Christ.*
- *Put all your prideful thoughts into a container and give it to Jesus at the cross to be destroyed. Wash away any remnants of destruction by the blood of Jesus.*
- *Command in the name of Jesus, Leviathan and all his demons of pride and false pride, attacking you to go to the feet of Jesus for judgment.*
- *Ask the Holy Spirit to manifest and increase humility (part of the fruit of the Holy Spirit) into your life.*
- *If it has become a stronghold in you, then you will need to have the cords to Pride to be dealt with. (See the section on cords in chapter 12)*

(2) *Lust:*

Lust is the strong, excessive desire for something or someone. It is usually linked with sexual indulgence but may not be only that.

The story of David and Bathsheba is a salutary reminder that position and experience in life is no safeguard against temptation. A casual sight of a naked woman that is inflamed into passionate desire that leads to treachery, complicity, disloyalty, murder, lying and disgrace is a powerful warning to us all of the power of lust.

Jesus said that looking lustfully at a woman is as good as committing adultery with her (Matthew 5:28).

John warns his readers against loving the world for all that is in the world is *the lust of the flesh and the lust of the eyes and the pride of life* (1 John. 2:16).

Satan seeks to lure the Christian away from God through lust. His strategies include extra-marital affairs, sexual promiscuity through the ready availability of contraception and abortion, pornography, homosexuality and advertisements of products by attractive females with few clothes on. Satan's strategies of lust also include material possessions, power and position.

Defense:
- *Acknowledgment and confession of lust and complete surrender to the Lordship of Christ.*
- *Put all your lustful thoughts into a container and give it to Jesus at the cross to be destroyed. Wash away any remnants of Lust by the blood of Jesus.*
- *Command in the name of Jesus, Diana and all demons of lust to go to the feet of Jesus for judgment.*
- *Ask Jesus to purify your eyes so that you see girls and women through the eyes of Jesus alone.*
- *If it has become a stronghold in you, then you will need to have the cords of Lust to be dealt with. (See the section on cords in chapter 12)*

(3) *Doubt*:
Satan loves to raise questions that cause people to doubt God and to doubt themselves.
"Did God say?" and "If you are...?"

With only rare exceptions, however, doubt in Scripture is seen as a negative attitude or action because it is directed toward God by man (or evil spiritual agents). The word connotes the idea of weakness in faith or unbelief.

If one accepts a typological understanding of Isaiah 14, doubt actually began in heaven in the heart of Lucifer. Here the object of doubt (and rejection) was the sovereignty and majesty of God (vv. 13-14). On earth doubt was conceived and given birth in the garden when the serpent cast doubt on God's character and goodness (Gen 3:1-5).

Tragically Eve and Adam bought into his deceptive plan and plunged humankind into the fall (vv. 6-19). In both instances doubt is clearly an aspect of sin; it is directed toward God and is characterized by rebellion and disobedience.

In the Gospels the word "doubt" consistently carries with it a negative aspect, and the object of doubt again is always the Lord in some sense. Peter doubted Christ's ability to keep him from drowning (Matt 14:31). Here doubt is small or weak faith. Peter became doubtful as to the Lord's reliability and power to sustain him. The Pharisees doubted Christ's Messiah ship and asked for another sign (Matt 12:38-42).

If we have faith in God and do not doubt, we can move mountains and receive our request through prayer (Matt 21:21 ; Mark 11:23). Here doubt is the antithesis of faith. In John 14:1 Jesus encourages the disciples to not have a troubled (doubting?) heart with regards to the future, but to believe in him, to trust him for their future needs. Some of the disciples, including Thomas, doubted the reality of the resurrected Lord (Luke 24:38 ; John 20:27).

Here doubt is not outright denial or unbelief, but an attitude or feeling of uncertainty. Thomas is not severely rebuked, but neither is his skepticism commended. "Stop doubting and believe" is the word of the Lord to his disciple.

Doubt in Scripture can be seen to be characteristic of both believers and unbelievers. In believers it is usually a weakness of faith, a wavering in the face of God's promises. In the unbeliever doubt is virtually synonymous with unbelief. Scripture, as would be expected, does not look at doubt philosophically or epistemologically. Doubt is viewed practically and spiritually as it relates to our trust in the Lord. For this reason, doubt is not deemed as valuable or commendable.

But when you ask, you must believe and not doubt, because the one who doubts is like a wave of the sea, blown and tossed by the wind. That person should not expect to receive anything from the Lord. Such a person is double-minded and unstable in all they do. (James 1:6-8)

> *Defense:*
> - *Confess all doubt to Jesus. Put them all into a container and give your doubts to Jesus at the cross to be destroyed. Wash away any remnants of doubts by the blood of Jesus.*
> - *Command in the name of Jesus, all demons of doubt to the feet of Jesus for judgment.*
> - *Know the Scriptures and know what you believe.*
> - *Develop a deeper trust in your relationship with Jesus so that you know for certain what He is telling you.*
> - *If it has become a stronghold in you, then you will need to have the cords to Doubt to be dealt with. (See the section on cords in chapter 12)*

(4) *Lies*:

"Does Job fear God for nothing?" Satan replied. "Have you not put a hedge around him and his household and everything he has? You have blessed the work of his hands, so that his flocks and herds are spread throughout the land. But now stretch out your hand and strike everything he has, and he will surely curse you to your face." The Lord said to Satan, "Very well, then, everything he has is in your power, but on the man himself do not lay a finger." Then Satan went out from the presence of the Lord. (Job 1:9-12)

Satan is the father of lies (John 8:44).

But Satan is no fool and he does not try to deceive us with outright lies. Much of what he says is true and he will mix truth and error in order to make it believable.

In Job 1:9-12, we get an insight to the way he works. He quotes God accurately. But he twists one thing and adds that Job will curse God. Job does become depressed and he did curse the day that he was born but Job did not curse God.

Note also that Satan brings into question the motives and intent of Job's heart. This is a common strategy where he seeks to give you lying accusations about your motives and intentions or another's motives and intentions.

Christians must be careful that they do not become passive recipients of these lies nor be deceived by the subtlety of Satan.

Mark Virkler (1) suggests a working formula to understand Satan's lies: 85% truth + 15% error + destructive intent =satanic accusation.

Defense
- *Test everything by the Holy Spirit, looking for confirmation by the same Spirit. (look at the way to test what you receive in chapter one)*
- *Place the lies into a container and give it to Jesus at the cross to be destroyed. Wash away any remnants of lies by the blood of Jesus.*
- *Command in the name of Jesus, Antichrist and all demons of lies and deception, to go to the feet of Jesus for judgment.*
- *Wear the belt of truth (Ephesians 6:10-20)*
- *Know God and Know His Word.*

(5) *Discouragement:*

Meanwhile, the people in Judah said, "The strength of the laborers is giving out, and there is so much rubble that we cannot rebuild the wall." Also, our enemies said, "Before they know it or see us, we will be right there among them and will kill them and put an end to the work." (Nehemiah 4:10-11)

The people were set the task of rebuilding the walls of Jerusalem. Everything was going well until Sanballat and Tobiah started to ridicule and oppose the Jews. They plotted with the Ammonites and Ashdodites to come together to fight and bring confusion to the rebuilding of the walls.

They became discouraged about the work that was needed to rebuild the walls as well as the threats of Sanballat and Tobiah. But Nehemiah rallied the people, set a guard to protect them day and night and stationed every family on the lowest parts of the wall with their weapons.

After I looked things over, I stood up and said to the nobles, the officials and the rest of the people, "Don't be afraid of them. Remember the Lord, who is great and awesome, and fight for your families, your sons and your daughters, your wives and your homes." (Nehemiah 4:14)

The word *discouragement* comes from the root word *courage*. The prefix *dis-*means "the opposite of." So, *dis*couragement is the opposite of courage. When we are discouraged, we have lost the motivation to press forward. The mountain seems too steep, the valley too dark, or the battle too fierce, and we lose the courage to continue.

Discouragement about how life and your situation are not working the way that it should, is an opportunity for Satan to attack.

Discouragement can be caused by fatigue that sets in when the goal seems far away. It can be caused by frustration when life with all its rubbish weighs us down. It can be caused by a sense of failure when everything does not go right.

Discouragement sets in when it seems our prayers are not being answered and God seems to have forgotten us.

Discouragement is dissatisfaction with the past, distaste for the present, and distrust of the future. It is ingratitude for the blessings of yesterday, indifference to the opportunities of today, and insecurity regarding strength for tomorrow. It is unawareness of the presence of beauty, unconcern for the needs of our fellowman, and unbelief in the promises of old. It is impatience with time, immaturity of thought, and impoliteness to God. - William Ward (1769– 1823)

Defense:
- *Confess your discouragement and dissatisfaction to Jesus. Put it all into a container and give to Jesus at the cross to be destroyed. Wash away any remnants of discouragement by the blood of Jesus.*
- *Command in the name of Jesus, all demons of discouragement to go to the feet of Jesus for judgment.*
- *Being thankful in all circumstances (Philippians 4:4-7)*
- *Know that in all things God works together for your good (Romans 8:28)*
- *If it has become a stronghold in you, then you will need to have the cords to Discouragement to be dealt with. (See the section on cords in chapter 12)*

(6) *Fear*:

Do not be afraid of what you are about to suffer. I tell you the devil will put some of you in prison to test you, and you will suffer persecution for ten days. Be faithful, even to the point of death, and I will give you life as your victor's crown. (Revelation 2:10)

Fear is a very effective weapon of Satan. It is one of the most paralyzing emotions that can overwhelm us. No other emotion can so effectively negate our faith, stifle our joy, disrupt our peace and manacle our walk with God. Related to fear are the emotions of anxiety and worry which are stirred up.

Elijah, after an exhausting day, against the prophets of Baal, received a death threat from Jezebel and he was afraid (I Kings 19:1-3).

The fundamental and original idea of fear covers a semantic range from mild easiness to stark terror, depending on the object of the fear and the circumstances surrounding the experience.

There is no separate Hebrew of Greek lexeme describing fear of God so presumably such fear was from earliest times, the same kind of reaction as could be elicited from any encounter with a surprising, unusual, or threatening entity.

However, sometimes we are afraid, sometimes this "spirit of fear" overcomes us, and to overcome it we need to trust in and love God completely. *There is no fear in love. But perfect love drives out fear, because fear has to do with punishment. The one who fears is not made perfect in love (1 John 4:18)*.

No one is perfect, and God knows this. That is why He has liberally sprinkled encouragement against fear throughout the Bible. Beginning in the book of Genesis and continuing throughout the book of Revelation, God reminds us to "Fear not."

For example, Isaiah 41:10 encourages us, *So do not fear, for I am with you; do not be dismayed, for I am your God. I will strengthen you and help you; I will uphold you with my righteous right hand*. Often, we fear the future and what will become of us.

But Jesus reminds us that God cares for the birds of the air, so how much more will He provide for His children? *So don't be afraid; you are worth more than many sparrows. (Matthew 10:31)*.

Just these few verses cover many different types of fear. God tells us not to be afraid of being alone, of being too weak, of not being heard, and of lacking physical necessities. These admonishments continue throughout the Bible, covering the many different aspects of the "spirit of fear."

In Psalm 56:11 the psalmist writes, *In God I trust; I will not be afraid. What can man do to me?* This is an awesome testimony to the power of trusting in God. Regardless of what happens, the psalmist will trust in God because he knows and understands the power of God.

The key to overcoming fear, then, is total and complete trust in God. Trusting God is a refusal to give in to fear. It is a turning to God even in the darkest times and trusting Him to make things right. This trust comes from knowing God and knowing that He is good. As Job said when he was experiencing some of the most difficult trials recorded in the Bible, *though he slay me, yet will I hope in him (Job 13:15)*

Once we have learned to put our trust in God, we will no longer be afraid of the things that come against us. We will be like the psalmist who said with confidence *let all who take refuge in you be glad; let them ever sing for joy. Spread your protection over them, that those who love your name may rejoice in you (Psalm 5:11)*.

Defense:
- *Confess all your fears to Jesus. Put them into a container and give to Jesus at the cross to be destroyed. Wash away any remnants of fear by the blood of Jesus.*
- *Command in the name of Jesus, all demons of fear to go to the feet of Jesus for judgment.*
- *Don't be afraid for God is by your side*
- *Recite out loud and believe Psalm 23 and 91*
- *Trust God*

- *If it has become a stronghold in you, then you will need to have the cords to Fear to be dealt with. (See the section on cords in chapter 12)*

(7) *Low Self-Esteem:*

For by the grace given to me I ask every one of you not to think of yourself more highly than you should think, rather to think of yourself with sober judgment on the measure of faith that God has assigned each of you. (Romans 12:3)

One of Satan's greatest psychological weapons is a gut-level feeling of inferiority, inadequacy and low self-worth. This feeling shackles many people including many Christians, in spite of their spiritual experience and their faith and knowledge of God. They are tied up in knots, bound by a terrible feeling of inferiority and chained to a deep sense of worthlessness.

Defense:
- *Confess and renounce all vows of worthlessness and inferiority. Put them all into a container and give it to Jesus to be destroyed at the cross. Wash away any remnants of worthlessness and inferiority by the blood of Jesus.*
- *Command in the name of Jesus, all demons of worthlessness and inferiority to go to the feet of Jesus for judgment.*
- *Know that you are a child of God and who you are in Christ*
- *If it has become a stronghold in you, then you will need to have the cords to Pride, Worthlessness and Inferiority to be dealt with. (See the section on cords in chapter 12)*

(8) *Our Old Nature:*

Put to death, therefore, whatever belongs to your earthly nature: sexual immorality, impurity, lust, evil desires and greed, which is idolatry. Because of these, the wrath of God is coming. You used to walk in these ways, in the life you once lived. But now you must also rid yourselves of all such things as these: anger, rage, malice, slander, and filthy language from your lips. Do not lie to each other, since you have taken off your old self with its practices and have put on the new self, which is being renewed in knowledge in the image of its Creator. (Colossians 3:5-10)

Satan uses much of our old nature to ensnare us and stop our effectiveness for Christ.

Paul encourages the Christians of Ephesus, Colossae, and Rome to "put off" the old nature and "put on" the new nature.

In all cases Paul lists a number of areas that need to be remedied and a number of characteristics that need to be adopted.

Christians cannot afford to compromise nor underestimate the power and activity of Satan and the enticement and heart-hardening power of sin. There must be a willingness to change the clothing of sin for the clothing of Christ's righteousness.

Defense:
- *Moral inventory of your attitude and behavior. Write them down.*
- *Confess your sin and put it into a container and give it to Jesus at the cross to be destroyed. Wash away any remnants of sin by the blood of Jesus.*
- *Command in the name of Jesus, all demons of ………. (name of the sin(s)) to go to the feet of Jesus for judgment.*
- *Repent of your sin i.e. choose to do the opposite.*
- *Invite the Holy Spirit to transform your old nature to the nature of Christ.*

Be alert and of sober mind. Your enemy the devil prowls around like a roaring lion looking for someone to devour. Resist him, standing firm in the faith (1 Peter 5:8,9).

(9) *Suicide*

The thief comes only to steal and kill and destroy. I have come that they have life, and have it to the full. (John 10:10)

There are seven unambiguous examples of suicide in the Bible:
- Abimelech, mortally wounded by a millstone, ordered his armor-bearer to dispatch him to avoid the suggestion he had been slain by the woman who had thrown the stone (Judges 9:52-54)
- the prophet Ahithophel hanged himself after betraying David (2 Samuel 17:23)
- Zimri burned down his house around himself after military defeat (1 Kings 16:18)
- The familiar stories of Saul and his armor-bearer (1 Samuel 1:1-6; 1 Chronicles 10:1-6)
- Samson, (Judges 16:28)
- Jesus' disciple Judas—although it is only in Matthew's Gospel where he kills himself (Matthew 27:3-5; compare with Acts 1:18).

However, there is an ongoing debate about whether suicide is a sin or not. Can God forgive a person who commits suicide? Can God forgive a Christian who commits suicide?

This is not the place to debate this. It has been my experience as a counsellor and a minister who has conducted funerals for people who have committed suicide that one needs to understand the depths that the person has found themselves in to cause them to take their life.

The family that has been left behind want answers and question how they missed the signs.

Suicide has become a major killer in the western world. I have had to counsel many a person who have contemplated suicide because they feel depressed and hopeless about their life and want to take it.

I have come to understand, over many years, that when a person feels low, they are open to a demonic attack by Molech, Apollyon and their demons of suicide and death. Sometimes they have thought about taking their own life but have not done so. They return to life but fail to understand that they may be vulnerable to attack later in life.

This has been the case for a number of our clients who came to Walkingfree for help.

Suddenly they are having suicidal thoughts and wonder why they are having these thoughts.

These thoughts are a spiritual attack to prevent them from seeking help. Though they have not had these thoughts for years, they now come to haunt them. It is not just the thoughts but includes the plans and methods to take one's life!

We have had to pray for them to release them from this attack. Then we had to deal with their damaged lives and allow Jesus to heal them so that they enemy can't use their damaged emotions against them

Defense:
- *Confess every word, deed, thought and plan that is related to suicide. Put them all into a container and give them to Jesus to be destroyed at the cross.*
- *Cleanse the ground given to suicide by Jesus' blood*
- *Command in the name of Jesus, Molech, Apollyon and their demons of suicide and death to go to the feet of Jesus for judgment.*
- *Reclaim the ground by asking Jesus to fill you with His Presence, Peace and Power.*
- *Close all doors that have let suicide in.*
- *Change your perspective about your life and future because Jesus is at the center of it.*

Bondage by Satan – what Jesus discovered

A look at Jesus' encounters with demons gives us insight to how demons gain bondage over an individual. It gives us some understanding of the nature of this bondage and how Jesus dealt with them

Jesus encounter with Satan in the wilderness - Mark 1:12,13; Matthew 4:1-11, Luke 4:1-12

The first test for Jesus was His encounter with Satan in the wilderness. Mark summarizes this encounter in a verse but Matthew and Luke expand this encounter of Jesus with Satan, giving us insight to the nature of the temptation.

Firstly, Satan appears after Jesus' was full of the Holy Spirit through His baptism by John. God spoke to Him and He was on a "spiritual high". Then Satan came to challenge Him. The lesson to be learned is that Satan (or his demons) often attacks us after we have experienced a spiritual encounter with God to test us.

Secondly, Satan appears to Jesus after a period of fasting for forty days when he was quite vulnerable. Matthew makes this clear for Jesus was at the end of the time of fasting. Luke suggests that the encounter lasted forty days. Whatever was correct, Jesus was in a frail, vulnerable place when Satan came to try and take advantage of his condition. The lesson to be learned is that we have to be careful when we are vulnerable and weak because that is when Satan (or his demons) may attack us.

Thirdly, Satan challenges and questions Jesus' identity. *"If You are the Son of God…"* and wants Him to prove it in some miraculous way. Jesus knew that He was the Son of God. He did not have to prove it. He was secure in the revelation of who He was given to Him at His baptism. The lesson to be learned is that we need to be secure in who we are, viz, a child of God, and we don't have to prove ourselves in any miraculous way. We know who we are thorough our confession of faith and our baptism.

Fourthly, Satan shows that he has a knowledge of Scripture that is quite extensive but he has the ability to "cherry pick" it and twist it for his own ends. Jesus countered Satan with Scripture that went to the heart of the issue, viz, God's power for His own ends and worshipping someone or something other than God. The lesson to be learned is to know the Scriptures and to know that we are the creature and not the Creator and everything is under God's sovereignty.

The man with an unclean spirit – Mark 1:21-28, Luke 4:31-37

This is the first encounter and the earliest account with a person afflicted by a demon. We note that
- Expulsion took place in public (synagogue/church)
- There was no particular symptom and he was like any other person present
- Demon manifested when Jesus' presence, power and authority was present
- Demon talked to Jesus through the person
- Demon silenced and commanded to come out by Jesus
- Demon went but there were convulsions and loud shrieks but no harm to man

Gerasene Demoniac - Mark 5:1-20, Matthew 8:28-34, Luke 8:26-39
- Extreme case where every area of his life was affected: social relationships were nonexistent; physically he cut himself and tore chains apart; emotionally and mentally he was in torment often crying out loud; spiritually he was far from God, but he had a desire to be set free.
- Evil spirit controlled him only at certain times. He still had the will and freedom to see Jesus and run to him.
- Many demons but one acted as spokesmen
- Manifest presence of God through Jesus brings them out into the open.
- Demons shriek loudly, hide and have names. Can be identified.

- Demons seem to have a geographic allocated area of operation. They did not want to leave the area for some reason.
- The demons wanted to go into a herd of pigs which Jesus granted.
- Demons need to live in bodies, preferably human because they must express their personality and lusts through the body of the person.
- Man was released from demons. His sanity, sense of dignity, his emotional life was all restored. Other people were also affected by the healing

The child with an evil spirit – *Mark 9:14-29; Matthew 17:14-21; Luke 9:37-45*
- Symptoms of demons were epilepsy, speech robbed and violent convulsions that nearly killed him
- Disciples failed because they did not understand that prayer and fasting was needed for this type of demon.
- Presence of Jesus caused demon to manifest.
- Faith is an important factor not piety
- Done in relative privacy to avoid excess emotion, spectator mentality, dissipation of faith, unhealthy interest in the demonic and gloating over boy's demise
- Demon was a deaf and dumb spirit not just a dumb spirit.
- Demons put up battle

A Crippled woman – *Luke 13:10-17*
- She was bent over, could not straighten her back, crippled for 18 years, a physical condition
- She was a daughter of Abraham, a woman of faith
- She had an evil spirit, bound by Satan for 18 years
- Jesus spoke a word of freedom
- Laid hands on her and her back straightened

Bondage by Satan – what we have discovered

- Many illnesses can be caused by demonic influence or have demonic influence. To be healed of the illness, in many cases, involves the deliverance of demons.
- Demonic influence affects most aspects of a person (spiritual, mental, emotional, physical and social).
- The expulsion of demonic presence or influence leads to the healing of all infected areas.
- The presence of demons can be discerned through:
    - Natural discernment by the demon manifesting its presence or by the person being aware that he/she has a demon or through a definite pattern of compulsive behavior (bondage) (e.g. drug addiction, alcoholism, sexual perversion of all kinds, self-destructive thoughts and behavior to name a few) or stronghold that cannot be overcome through natural means.

- The spiritual gift of discernment between spirits (1 Corinthians 12:10)
- The spiritual gift of the word of knowledge (1 Corinthians 12:8)
- Knowledge of Satan, his army and his ways of operating in the world.
- General spiritual sensitivity and experience and awareness of symptoms when you see them.
- The Greek word used in the NT (diamonizomai-demonized) does not define the extent of the influence. It becomes clearer from the nature of the person's problem.
  - Possession or "control" is not common unless a person has given themselves totally to Satan. Most of the time "control" is temporary when the demon seizes the person. A Christian cannot be demon "possessed" because it implies ownership. Christians are born of God and have His Spirit living within us.
  - "Affliction", "Oppression", "Bondage", "Stronghold", "Foothold" are words to describe demonization. This implies varying degrees of demonic influence in certain areas of a person's life. This can be likened to a military invasion of a city where friendly forces may occupy and control the city, isolated areas can remain under enemy domination. Christians can be demonized at these levels if they allow themselves to be. (e.g., 1 Corinthians 10:20-22; 2 Corinthians 10:3-6; Ephesians 4:26,27; 1 Timothy 4:1-3)
- The works of the flesh mentioned by Paul (Galatians 5:19-21; Colossians 3:5-9) must be dealt with by repentance and self-discipline; but if they are not dealt with, they can eventually become demonic strongholds.
- Sin is the way that Satan and his demons enter a person's life and affects them. This sin is either by the person sinning or the person is a victim of another person's sin or there is family history of certain sin that gives permission for the demon to have a hold.
- Unconditional forgiveness of the person who has sinned against you and caused the entry points of the demons is also needed. Confession and repentance of all known sin is needed to release the demons' oppression. This includes (thoughts, deeds, words, knowing (and unknowing), participation in unholy (anti-Christian) practices) or occult involvement
- Deliverance prayers are to begin with a prayer of protection where we pray to cover ourselves with the blood of Jesus, bind, in the name of Jesus, all demons over the person, including pride, rebellion and control, place them in chains unbreakable and command in the name of Jesus all retribution from Satan to be turned back on him so that the person, team and all creation will not be affected by the ministry.
- Demonic manifestation may occur in people who are highly demonized. This can happen if they are coming out a life of witchcraft or satanic involvement or heavily involved with some sexual sin like pornography, homosexuality. We have seen people writhe on the ground, have faces distorted, growling coming from their mouths, speak with a voice from the client that is not their natural voice, their eyes rolled back, a coldness coming over the client, an increase

in the presence of fear. We have also seen people cough, sneeze as the demons are released from them. In some cases, people have felt sick or even dry vomit.
- Demonic manifestation is controlled by binding all demons of pride, control and rebellion and all strongmen (demons) that have a hold over the person. If there are manifestations, then don't fear but ask Jesus to manifest His power and stop the manifestations. We have found that there is little or no manifestations when we bind the demons of pride, rebellion and control.
- Deliverance of demons is to be ministered to Christians only or those who have Jesus' ownership or those who are willing to believe in Jesus and commit their life to Jesus (Matthew 12:43-45). In some cases, Jesus will allow deliverance of demons from a person who may be a non-believer so that they may know and experience that Jesus is real and has power over the enemy.
- Demons normally influence people in teams. They rarely act alone and even when there is only one type, e.g. infirmity, there are multiple demons e.g. spirits of infirmity. So, command all demons of ……..to go to the feet of Jesus for judgment.
- Demons are expelled by a command in the name of Jesus. Sometimes they will challenge our authority but we do not stand on our authority but the authority of Jesus Christ.
- It is helpful to name the demon(s) that you are casting out. If you are unsure of their name, then name the demons according to the sin or sickness that has been exposed and prayed into.
- It is better to work in teams as there is greater spiritual authority, insight, power and protection (spiritual and legal). However, there may be occasions when you have no team and you just have to pray for the person to deliver them from the control of a demon(s).
- The demons need to be sent somewhere or else they will return, making things worse, as Jesus pointed out (Matthew 12:43-45). While Jesus sent Legion into a herd of pigs (Mark 5:12,13), he did not send them anywhere on other occasions that has been recorded. However, the threat of return making things worse by the demons causes us to send them away. Some ministries send the demons to the pit, their final destination. We have chosen to send them to the feet of Jesus for judgment and then Jesus can decide their fate.
- The person who has been healed from demonization is not properly whole until all areas of healing are covered and support systems (small group, care, counseling, church worship and assimilation) fill the void in the person's life.
- We should not adopt the attitude of "seeking after demons" ("ghost busters") or being focused on them. Our eyes must be on Jesus and walking close to Him in holiness but if demons are present, then we should deal with them.
- When praying for the demonized, we should be compassionate and non-judgmental for "there by the grace of God go I".
- The principles of delivering people from the hold of Satan can be applied to property, churches, communities, businesses and countries. You need God's permission, repentance of

Chapter 6: Unlocking the Power to Defeat Demons

sin (by people in authority or owner(s) of the property) and enough prayer power to expel the powerful demons over them. (see Chapter 9)

Remove the right, then Satan has no might!

In the beginning days of deliverance ministry, a great deal of time, energy and trauma for the client was experienced as demons were commanded to go. It became apparent that unless you deal with the right (the reason) that the demon has claimed to be there, there is a tug of war trying to remove the demon(s) with the person exhausted at the end.

So now we focus on "pulling the rug from under the feet" of the demon through understanding the sin(s) entry point and dealing with that sin through confession and repentance of those sins. Using the Container Prayer helps remove the ground.

Once the person has confessed that sin and asked for forgiveness from Jesus, you can then wash that person with the blood of Jesus and remove the right that the demons have had. Then you can command the demons of ……………… (the area of sin) to go to the feet of Jesus for judgment.

If it has become a stronghold and the above prayer is not effective, then there is a demonic cord that needs to be dealt with. This way of praying is described in chapter 12.

Prayer to remove Sin and Satan

The following prayer needs to be prayed by the person to remove the sin that has given the demons a hold.

Lord Jesus, I confess to you my sin(s) of ……………… I ask for your forgiveness through your precious blood and I ask you to wash away my sin(s) and its affect upon every part of my being and relationships. I thank you that you died on the cross for my sin(s), that I am forgiven and been given a clean slate and I surrender again my life to you, Lord Jesus. Help me not to repeat these sin(s) any more. In Jesus name Amen.

The following prayers can be used to protect you, the person and dispel the demons. Once the person has confessed the sin then the right for the demons to have a hold is removed.

Lord Jesus, I thank you for Your healing and delivering power. I cover us here by the blood of Jesus. I cover all our family and friends, pets, possessions and property, wherever they are and whatever they are doing by the blood of Jesus. I ask you to station your guardian angels about them and us during this prayer/ministry time.

We put on the whole armor of God. On our heads, we place the helmet of salvation to protect our minds, upon our hearts the breastplate of Christ's righteousness, around our waists the belt of truth, on each of our feet the gospel shoes of peace, on one arm, the shield of faith and in the other hand the sword of the Spirit.

In the name of Jesus, I bind and gag all demonic spirits including pride, rebellion and control. I confound all their prayers; stop up their ears, blindfold their eyes, shine the light of the Lord on them and shrink them down to their proper size.

In the name of Jesus, I command all demons of ……….. (name the sin) who have a hold on …… (name of person) to go to the feet of Jesus for judgment

Prayer to counter and cleanse the person of suicidal thoughts

The person prays:

I confess to you every thought and word, deed and plan related to suicide. I ask you Jesus to forgive me, wash me clean by your precious blood, take back the ground that Molech and Suicide have taken and fill those places with your Presence, Peace and Power. I repent of all words and deeds, thoughts and plans related to suicide. I choose life and not death. I choose Jesus who is the Way, Truth and Life.

It is very helpful for another person to hear the confession and then pray the following prayers. Theses prayers can be used to protect you and dispel demons once the person has confessed their sin which has given the right for the demons to have a hold.

Lord Jesus, I thank you for Your healing and delivering power. I cover us here by the blood of Jesus. I cover all our family and friends, pets, possessions and property, wherever they are and whatever they are doing by the blood of Jesus. I ask you to station your guardian angels about them and us during this prayer/ministry time.

I (We) put on the whole armor of God. On our heads we place the helmet of salvation to protect our minds, upon our hearts the breastplate of Christ's righteousness, around our waists the belt of truth, on each of our feet the gospel shoes of peace, on our arm the shield of faith and in the other hand the sword of the Spirit.

In the name of Jesus, I bind and gag all demonic spirits including pride, rebellion and control. I confound all their prayers; stop up their ears, blindfold their eyes, shine the light of the Lord on them and shrink them down to their proper size.

Jesus, please wash away very thought, word, deed and plan related to suicide by your precious blood. In the name of Jesus, I command in the name of Jesus Molech, Apollyon and all their demons of suicide and death to go to the feet of Jesus for judgment. I fill every place with the Presence, Peace and Power of Jesus and close every door that has been used by demons to get in.

We now turn to know how to pray for the sick.

7

UNLOCKING THE POWER TO HEAL THE SICK

As soon as they left the synagogue, they went with James and John to the home of Simon and Andrew. Simon's mother-in-law was in bed with a fever, and they immediately told Jesus about her. So, he went to her, took her hand and helped her up. The fever left her and she began to wait on them. That evening after sunset the people brought to Jesus all the sick and demon possessed. The whole town gathered at the door, and Jesus healed many who had various diseases. He also drove out many demons, but he would not let the demons speak because they knew who he was. (Mark 1:29-34)

In September, 1998, my wife, Liz, was diagnosed with Uterine cancer. She had a hysterectomy in the hope that the uterus that contained the cancerous growth would be removed and she would be fine. Unfortunately, the cancer had entered into the blood stream. This we found out in February, 1999, when she started coughing at work. The cancer had now become lung cancer.

We attended a number of healing services. On one occasion, a friend in the congregation, received a word from Jesus: forgive. Liz had to forgive her Christian female doctor for not pursuing what Liz had felt inside her. This was in May, 1998, and there was the likelihood that the cancer would have been confined to the uterus and the operation would have removed the cancer. The delay gave the opportunity for the cancer cells to move further into her body through the blood stream.

This cancer was a malignant mixed Mullerian tumor (MMMT), also called a carcinosarcoma It is a type of cancer that contains two types of cancer cells - carcinoma and sarcoma. This was not good and the likelihood of survival was very small.

So, she and the oncologist decided to hit it hard with chemotherapy. We decided to hit it hard with prayer in the hope that Jesus would heal her. A group prayed for her every Sunday after church. We set up special anointing sessions and prayer for her.

Healing was supposed to be my gifting and expertise and I had seen many people healed through my praying. But this was another level. I believed and had faith that my wife would be healed but whether I was the agent, I did not know.

A few months had passed when one Sunday, after church, a lady from a Catholic church visited. She asked to join the prayer time for Liz. She placed her hand on Liz's chest and Liz felt the healing power of God come inside of her and the cancerous cells in her lung began to disappear.

She finished the chemotherapy treatment and everything was on the improve. But then, it was discovered that she had a brain tumor. It was the same cancer. For a few days, this was the last straw for Liz and she gave up on God. But after a few days, she realized she could not give up on God. She bargained with God that she needed to be alive to look after the children and see her grandchildren. She believed that I would struggle to be a parent and a minister of a church.

The good news about the tumor, (if there is any good news), was that it was operable. But prior to her operation, the tumor caused an epileptic fit. She was admitted to hospital where the tumor was removed. The downside was that she could not drive because of the epileptic fit. Her driving was restored later with a lot of convincing of the doctor.

Today, 25 years later, she is still alive, though the consequences of a brain tumor are now starting to take effect. They include balance and memory issues. However, she is determined not to let this defeat her and is doing many exercises to help her balance and memory.

I tell this story to help people understand that healing from life threatening illness is a mixture of miracle, medical knowhow, faith and determination.

God has a healing program for all disease. The challenge is in understanding the nature of the disease, its causes and asking God how He wants to heal the disease. It is never a one size fits all!

Too many people want to go down the 'miracle way' and get disappointed when God does not seem to want to heal them.

Healing is a journey and it involves miracles, medical science, faith, identifying and dealing with possible causal issues of the disease. It also requires determination and a willingness to accept what God wants to give as healing. For some the healing will be eternity where there is no more pain and suffering. (Revelation 21:3-4)

WHAT YOU NEED TO KNOW ABOUT SICKNESS

Medical science teaches us that there are three basic classes of human illness:
1. Organic,
2. Functional
3. Mental or psychic illness.

Organic illness: Is where the structure or tissue of the body is damaged in some way such as leprosy, blindness or lameness of the body.

Functional illness: Is where there is a malfunction of one organ or part of the body such as heart disease, peptic ulcers and high blood pressure.

Mental illness can be understood in terms of:
- Psychosis - a retreat from reality.
- Psychoneurosis - Can't break with reality but experience an extremely troubled mind characterized by anxiety, compulsiveness or depression.
- Hysteria
- Psychogenic physical states where there is no organic damage but an unconscious idea that the organic part cannot be used.

Emotional illness can be caused by trauma of life through
- Abuse (physical, emotional, verbal, sexual and spiritual)
- Drug, alcohol, gambling, pornography
- Events like car accidents, natural disasters
- Participation in war zones
- Abandonment or Rejection or Betrayal by significant other e.g. parent
- Symptoms include anger, bitterness, resentment, jealousy, low self-esteem, rebellion, control issues.
- Broken Heart (splintering of heart/soul called dissociation to take away the pain but can be triggered later and come to the surface)

Although it is clear that the healings of Jesus occurred in all areas, there is no specific record of Jesus healing someone in the area of functional illness. This may be due to how body function and illness was perceived / understood in those times.

It seems that the gospel writers were selective in their recording of Jesus' healing ministry partly because there were so many of them (John 20:30, 31) and partly because they wished to focus on the more dramatic and those which had a teaching function for their readers.

Sickness and Sin

From an Old Testament perspective, there was a direct correlation between sickness and sin.
Sickness was seen as a consequence of sin and a punishment for sin from God.

In Numbers 12:1-15, Miriam and Aaron oppose Moses and experience God's anger for talking against Moses. Miriam is covered with leprosy and Moses ends up appealing to God on her behalf for forgiveness. She is forgiven and healed but she must stay out of the camp until the period of cleansing according to the Law is completed.

Sin was also seen in the Old Testament as not simply breaking a commandment but also destroying a relationship through the breaking of trust with another person and/or with God.

A.H. Becker (1) in his book *Guilt- Curse or Blessing* comments:

It is not simply the breaking of a commandment. It is to render oneself untrustworthy in human relationships, and ultimately it is an act of rebellion against God. Sin is not simply passive. It is best understood not merely as weakness or ignorance, unwillingness or inability to obey a commandment. Sin is also an intentional, purposeful stance of active rebellion against another person (or persons) and against God. It is a declaration of self-sufficient strength, as well as an expression of weakness. It is decision, not vacillation. It is resistance, not just oversight. It is rejection of love, trust, or human interdependence. When we sin, we do not simply break rules or laws; we fracture our bonds with people and with God.

When Jesus comes onto the scene, a man blind from birth comes to Jesus (John 9). The disciples pose the question; *Rabbi, who sinned, this man or his parents that he was born blind?*

Jesus replied, that neither was the case but this was an opportunity for God's work and power to be displayed.

Jesus negated the traditional view that sickness was the direct consequence of sin. If someone was sick, it did not necessarily mean that sin was the cause of the sickness. Yet on some occasions, Jesus' final response *"Go, sin no more"* (John 5:1-15) or His declaration that the person's sins are forgiven (Mark 2:1-12) indicated that the sickness was attributed to some form of sin.

This could be:
- Unforgiveness,
- bitterness and resentments,
- willful sin,
- unconfessed sin,
- neglect of our relationship with God and His people
- other sinful acts can cause a sickness within that may have some outward physical and/or emotional symptoms as well as a sickness of the person's spirit.

We should never underestimate the power of sin within us and over us and its consequences to us. Sin destroys our relationship with God and with others and this brokenness can manifest itself in some form of sickness.

Sickness and the Heart:

Sickness of the heart deals with our emotional reactions to situations in which we have been hurt either by what someone has said, or done to us, or as a result of some experience from the past that was traumatic to that person.

These hurts affect people in the present, in the form of:
- bad memories
- weak and wounded emotions.

This in turn leads them into various negative forms of living:
- sins of the flesh (Galatians 5:19-21),
- depression
- a sense of worthlessness and inferiority
- unreasoning fears and anxieties
- Anger and hostility
- Psychosomatic and other illnesses.

The origin of past hurts ranges from those inflicted by persons we love (parents, spouses and siblings) to hurts caused by living in a sinful world and include hurts that are self-inflicted because of the wrong choices that one makes or because of the sin that one commits and hurts that are passed down from one generation to another.

Hurts that are inflicted by the ones we love can either be intentional or unintentional, actual or perceived. They often arise through failed expectations by the other at a special time of vulnerability. These hurts can be experienced in the womb and reinforced by further experiences as the child grows up.

The most common feelings that are manifested are:
- a sense of rejection
- anger
- resentment
- bitterness
- low self esteem
- envy
- jealousy
- rebellion
- fear
- unworthiness

Hurts that are experienced from living in a sinful world include the experiences of:
- hurt as a result of incidents of history,
- accidents of nature,
- disease and poverty.

Some of the feelings that are associated with such hurts are:
- fear, terror, anxiety
- rejection
- abandonment
- worthlessness
- shame
- insecurity
- defilement
- hopelessness
- hatred

Self-inflicted hurts are those which occur through sin and/or wrong choices or decisions. The feelings that surface are:
- guilt and failure
- shame and self-condemnation.
- hatred and self-hatred
- fear
- anger

These bottled-up feelings have, in many cases, produced chronic health disorders like chronic fatigue, fibromyalgia, auto-immune disease, allergies, stress disorders, heart conditions.

Jesus came to heal the "broken-hearted" (Isaiah 61:1; Luke 4: 18) Jesus came to heal those that have been shattered in heart and mind. This has resulted in the fragmentation or splintering of the soul. We discuss this in Chapter 12 and how Jesus can heal this.

Jesus came to forgive our sin so that we might forgive others who have wronged us and that we fight forgive ourselves (Matthew 6:14,15).

Unresolved sin can grow into bitter roots in the heart that can affect people's relationships with others and themselves. We discuss this in Chapter 12 and how Jesus can heal this.

Jesus came to redeem us (Galatians 3:13) from the curse of the law.

The words spoken by others to us or spoken by us to ourselves have the ability to bless or curse.

With the tongue we praise our Lord and Father, and with it we curse human beings, who have been made in God's likeness (James 3:9).

These curses or inner vows can lock a person into a life of sickness. We discuss the issue of curses and inner vows in Chapter 8.

Sickness and Satan

We have seen in the previous chapter; how demonic affliction is connected with many forms of sickness.

One of the most common ailments dealt with by the New Testament was what is described and translated as "*demon possession*". However, the use of the term *demonization* is perhaps better to be described as affliction, oppression or bondage by demons. Christians cannot be possessed by Satan because they are possessed by Jesus! However, Christians can give demons a hold because of unrepentant sin in some form.

There are a number of biblical examples that indicate some of the ways that an evil spirit can cause sickness.

(1) The most extreme case is the Gerasene Demoniac (Mark 5:1-20) where every area of his life is affected.
- Socially he had no relationships.
- Physically he had superhuman strength that enabled him to break his chains.
- Emotionally and mentally, he was in torment and would cry out in a loud voice.
- Spiritually he was away from God but saw in Jesus the hope of freedom.

(2) There is the case of the boy in Mark 9:14-29 where eight disciples tried to heal him. The father recognized that there was an evil spirit present. The symptoms were:
- His speech was robbed;
- He was thrown to the ground in a fit,

- He foamed at the mouth indicating a form of madness.
- Jesus discerned the presence of not only a dumb spirit but also a deaf one as well

(3) Yet on another occasion Mark 7:31-35, Jesus encountered a deaf and dumb man and healed him but there was no presence of demons. This indicates that we must be careful to discern which sickness is physical and which sickness is caused by demons.

We are seeing the presence of demons in the area of mental illness like
- Depression
- Anxiety disorders such as generalized anxiety disorders, social anxiety disorders, panic disorders, and phobias
- Obsessive-compulsive disorder (OCD)
- Bipolar disorder
- Post-traumatic stress disorder (PTSD)
- Schizophrenia
- Personality disorders such as borderline personality disorder, narcissistic personality disorder, and antisocial personality disorder

We are also seeing the presence of demons in many chronic health disorders like chronic fatigue, fibromyalgia, auto-immune disease, allergies, stress disorders, heart conditions.

In many cases of the above, the demons are not the cause of the illness but have "piggy-backed" onto the cause of the illness. The cause needs to be addressed and dealt with and then the demons can be dispelled. Remember it is the right that gives the demons the might.

Remove the right and they do not have a leg to stand on! But like many causes, the issues are complex and all need to be addressed.

Sickness and Forgiveness

The major issue for people is to forgive those who have wounded or hurt them.

For many people it is very hard to forgive because of what has happened to them, especially abuse in all its forms (sexual, verbal, bullying, physical and spiritual etc.)

For Christians, it is unforgivable not to forgive! Yet for many people including Christians, it is hard to forgive because the hurt runs deep!

For if you forgive other people when they sin against you, your heavenly Father will also forgive you. But if you do not forgive others their sins, your Father will not forgive your sins. (Matthew 6:14,15)

Christians are commanded to get rid of all bitterness, anger, and resentment in our lives and forgive those who hurt us.

Reverend John Lucas, DMin

Get rid of all bitterness, rage and anger, brawling and slander, along with every form of malice. Be kind and compassionate to one another, forgiving each other, just as in Christ God forgave you (Ephesians 4:31,32)

We need to forgive others so that Satan cannot take advantage of us. As Paul said:

Anyone you forgive, I also forgive. And what I have forgiven—if there was anything to forgive—I have forgiven in the sight of Christ for your sake, in order that Satan might not outwit us. For we are not unaware of his schemes. (2 Corinthians 2:10,11)

What is Forgiveness? Neil T Anderson (2) offers this insight about forgiveness in his book *Steps to Freedom in Christ*

Forgiveness

- It is not merely forgetting. Don't wait to forget to forgive. It will not happen.
- It is a choice, a decision of the will. Hurt places chains on you. Unforgiveness puts on a padlock.
- By forgiving you unlock the padlock and release the chains around you and the person from your hook to God's hook.
- It is agreeing to live with the consequences. Noone truly forgives without accepting and suffering the pain of another's sin.
- It comes from the heart. We can intellectualize our forgiveness but it must also travel from the head to the heart (Matthew 18:35)
- It is choosing not to hold someone's sin against him or her. Do not gunnysack! - bring up sins from the past
- It is not waiting to feel like forgiving. You will never get there!

CASE STUDY: The elderly widow

An elderly lady came forward for prayer on the Saturday of our seminar. She was a widow in her seventies. She explained that she had had a bad back for years. Now, she had one leg longer than the other and needed a raised shoe to enable her to walk. Prayer was offered for her back and leg but nothing happened! We sought the Lord.

The Lord spoke and said to a team member, *Ask her about her husband.* She burst into tears. She started to tell her story. Though her husband was now dead, she had found out his secret before they were married.

The man, who she had married, had a fling with another girl while they were engaged. She found out about it but did not call off the marriage. She carried that hurt for many years and now it affected her physically in her back. Not only that, but now she walked with a severe limp with one leg shorter than the other.

We led her in a prayer for forgiveness of her husband. We used the container prayer to download all the hurt and pain that she had carried for all the years. The container was taken to the cross and was destroyed by fire.

We continued to pray and the pain in her back disappeared.

The next day, she came to church where I preached. The pain was not there but she walked still with a severe limp.

After the service, I invited her to come forward for further prayer. I asked her to sit down and give me her two legs. As I raised them up, it was obvious that one was shorter than the other.

I then commanded in the name of Jesus for the shorter leg to come out. After a pause, the leg began to shake and move out until the leg was level with the other.

Now she had another problem but a good one! She needed a new pair of shoes because the one that had been raised with an increased sole and heel was not needed anymore.

In many cases, when a person asks for prayer for a certain issue, there are underlying issues that need to be addressed before the physical healing can happen.

UNDERLYING ISSUES

Many people present with various pain in their bodies. As you pray for the pain but it does not seem to go then look for possible underlying issues.

Back and Neck Pain- Stress could be the underlying issue. This stress could be generated from work or difficult relationships with spouse or other family members.

Cancer- In many cases, you might need to cut off the family history of cancer. We have found also that the roots of cancer can be bitterness, resentment and unforgiveness due to hurt that has built up and not been released. We have found that breast cancer may be related to issues with the mother or mother-in-law. The use of the Container Prayer (see Chapter 4) will be needed to download the emotional feelings.

Auto-immune diseases- The possible underlying issues can be linked to an unloving spirit that produces feelings of not being loved or accepted. This leads to self-rejection, self-hatred, self-bitterness and guilt that breaks down the nervous system. The use of the Container Prayer (see Chapter 4) will be needed to download the emotional feelings.

Heart Disease- The possible underlying issues are anger, hostility, rage, fear, anxiety, stress and hardness of heart. The use of the Container Prayer will be needed to download the emotional feelings.

Stress Disorders - The possible underlying issues are fear, anxiety, stress, guilt and shame. The use of the Container Prayer will be needed to download the emotional feelings.

Depression and Mental Illness - The possible underlying issues are the issues of the self: self-pity; self-accusation; self-centeredness; generations of unlovingness and demons.

This is not a comprehensive list but points to the fact that physical and mental illnesses are not simple and, in many cases, are connected to relationship and emotional issues that are played out in our physical bodies.

Exposing the Spiritual Roots of Disease by Dr. Henry W. Wright (3) is a wonderful resource to discover the spiritual roots that may be behind the physical diseases that you may be praying for. For many physical healings, the physical is the symptom but not the cause of the body breaking down. Pray for the spiritual cause then pray for the physical healing of the body.

HEALING THE WHOLE PERSON

I have come that they may have life, and have it to the full. (John 10:10)

This is good, and pleases God our Savior, who wants all people to be saved and to come to a knowledge of the truth. (2 Timothy 2:3,4)

A close look at the Greek word used, sodzo, means both to save and to heal
Here are some principles of Christian healing that provide the framework for our praying for the sick.

1. It is God's will and desire to heal and save people.
2. God's first priority is salvation in Jesus Christ. Any opportunity to pray for the sick is an opportunity to ask about a person's salvation in Christ or relationship with Jesus Christ.
3. God's healing covers all areas of life including the physical, the emotional, the mental, the spiritual, the relational, the social, the world.
4. A person is a complex personality consisting of physical, mental, emotional, spiritual, relational and social attributes which are inter-related and where one area can affect other areas. Ken Blue (4) in his book *Authority to Heal* sums it up in this way: *The human being is a kind of ecosystem, a complex interdependent whole. Pollution in one part contaminates all, and dealing with the pollution at its source heals all.*
5. God's healing can be instantaneous or a process. Even when it is instantaneous, it will take a period of time to counsel, understand the person's needs and pray for them.
6. There is a **mystery** in the way that God heals and we need some handles to help us understand why people may not be healed when you pray for them. The following may be some explanations:
    i. Lack of Faith
    ii. Not praying specifically
    iii. Faulty diagnosis
    iv. Redemptive suffering
    v. Sin
    vi. Lack of Forgiveness
    vii. Fear
    viii. Unbelief
    ix. Refusal to see medicine or doctors as a way God heals
    x. Not using the natural means of preserving health

xi. Now is not the time
   xii. A different person is to be the instrument of healing
   xiii. The social environment prevents healing from taking place
   xiv. Demons
   xv. Don't know
7. There are reasons why some people are not healed. Caution, compassion and the Spirit's insights are needed before we decide upon the reason. The first place to look is your ministry, viz. your discernment of the problem, your method of praying and your openness to God's leading. But in the end God knows best and we need to have a mystery box to put all our unanswered prayers and questions in.
8. Any healing will be only temporary, as we all in the end must die.
9. The final healing is through death and eternal life with Jesus.
10. The way that a Christian counsels and prays for healing reflects God's love, compassion and gentleness.
11. The healing ministry can take place anywhere and is not limited to a specific church healing service.
12. The healing ministry includes the work of doctors and other medical professions and each can make a unique contribution to the health of a person. Both a Christian in the healing ministry and a doctor have limitations and only know "in part" for " we all see in a mirror dimly" (1 Corinthians 13:12).

HOW TO PRAY FOR THE SICK

Praying for the sick has its challenges for the one who prays.

Firstly, it is important to have faith and belief that God can heal and that He can use you and your faith. The one who is needing prayer, usually, has a loss of faith as they may have prayed and asked for healing but it has not happened or the sickness has taken hold and they have struggled to have faith and belief.

The challenge for the one who is praying is not to be overwhelmed by the issue that is being presented. Praying for a person who has cancer can have a different impact upon the person who is praying than praying for a headache. Cancer is seen as almost impossible to heal. But the healing of a person is not dependent upon the one who is praying but on God. God just asks for one who believes and is open to God's Spirit and His leading.

Your faith and belief in God who can heal will be enough. Then it is up to God. If there is no healing, then it is up to you to seek God for a reason. Some of these reasons are found in the previous section- Healing the Whole Person.

Secondly, it is important to have the ability to listen to the Holy Spirit and understand what He is saying to show you where He may be working and healing. It is important to discern the "words", scriptures, senses, pictures, that the Holy Spirit uses to communicate where and how to pray. The information becomes the content of the praying.

On one occasion, while praying to heal chronic fatigue, I was given the word "root". This became the content of my prayers when I asked Jesus to remove and destroy the root of chronic fatigue in the person.

As you develop the skills of listening to the Holy Spirit (outlined in Chapter One), as you learn more about the ways of praying (outlined in the chapter on Prayer Tools) and the possible underlying issues of some physical diseases (outlined in this chapter), you develop a bank of knowledge that can be used by the Holy Spirit to enable you to pray more effectively for a sick person.

Thirdly, it is important to be comfortable laying your hands upon the sick area of the person. **Be careful where you place your hands.** While we are cognizant that some areas are personal and private, you can ask the person to place their hands on that personal part of the body (e.g. the breast if they have breast cancer) and then ask permission to lay your hand upon their hand that is on that personal part.

This gives a sense of assurance to the person being prayed for, raises the faith of the pray-er (it takes a lot of faith to put out one's hand expecting God to heal), allows the Spirit to "flow" through pray-er to the client and helps the pray-er to discern what the Spirit is doing through the tingling or heat sensations which may be felt through the hands. One can feel the intensity of the Spirit's presence increase and subside.

Fourthly, the first prayer that is made is *Come Holy Spirit!* We invite the Holy Spirit to lead, guide the praying and become the vehicle of healing for the person. It is a recognition that healing can only happen with the presence of God through the Holy Spirit.

Fifthly, the command prayer, commanding the body part to be healed, in Jesus' name, becomes your weapon to bring healing to the person. It sometimes needs to be repeated. The command prayer is used in conjunction with the authority that Jesus has given you and so you command not just in the name of Jesus but with the authority Jesus has given you. It is like commanding a dog to sit with a voice that means what it is saying.

In some cases, the command prayer will be needed to command any demons of sickness and infirmity to release the sick part of the person and then you send them to the feet of Jesus for judgment.

Sixthly, the more you pray for the sick, the more you get better at praying, the more that your faith increases and the more confident you become to work with the Holy Spirit to bring God's healing to a person.

It is important to develop a method of praying. John Wimber (4) in his book, *Power Healing* offers a process that I have used and modified over the years. This is my modification.

*(1) **THE INTERVIEW:*** The interview seeks to answer the question "Where does it hurt? What do you want me to pray for?"

While you do not want a medical history, some detail like where it hurts, how long have you had this condition, what happened to cause this?

*(2) **DIAGNOSTIC DECISION:*** The diagnostic decision seeks to answer the question "Why does this person have this condition?" This is a crucial step as it determines the type of prayer that is needed to bring healing.

Remember a person is a complex being and there is an inter-connectedness of aspects of life. Although there may be a physical symptom, the root issue may be a relationship hassle. Once the relationship has been prayed for, then the physical issue can be prayed for.

If you are working in a team, it is helpful for one person to lead. Those with any of the spiritual gifts of discernment, prophecy, Word of Knowledge should listen to the Spirit for any understanding of the issue. The leader, after listening to the client's story, invites those with any insights from the Spirit to share their insights in the team.

The value of a team approach comes into play when deciding the right prayer to use. Members can combine their insights and a joint decision can be made. Do not spend a lot of time deciding which prayer to pray. If you are unsure, go with what you know, especially what the person has shared and the Holy Spirit will take it from there and give you further insight.

*(3) **PRAYER SELECTION:*** This step answers the question "What kind of prayer is needed to help this person?" Once you have diagnosed the issue, you are now ready to pray for the person. There are different approaches of prayer for each condition.

(a) If it is a prayer for physical healing, you are getting ready to lay hands upon the injured part and preparing to command that part to be healed in Jesus' name.

(b) If the physical problem is the symptom of a deeper issue like sin, then the person needs to be led in a prayer of confession for the sin and then the container prayer used to download the sin and its poison inside the person.

If the cause is a relationship issue, then a prayer of forgiveness for that person followed by the container prayer to download the poison of that relationship needs to be prayed before prayer for physical healing.

(c) If it is a prayer for deliverance, you are encouraging the person that God is in control; God will free the person and so they do not need to be anxious. Begin by binding in the name of Jesus, the spirits of pride, rebellion and control to stop all demonic manifestations (see the previous chapter with the exact prayers to pray) Bind in the name of Jesus also all spirits of sickness and infirmity. Then name the demons of the sickness affecting the person and command them by name to go to the feet of Jesus for judgment.

*(4) **PRAYER ENGAGEMENT:*** This step answers the question, "How effective are the prayers?" Here the pray-ers are to recognize what God is doing through the Holy Spirit and cooperate with the Holy Spirit.

Once the appropriate posture is taken, a prayer is prayed to the Holy Spirit inviting Him to come upon the person and release His healing power. This prayer should be prayed with the eyes OPEN by at least one person so that you can see how the Holy Spirit is manifesting Himself upon the person, if at all.

There are a number of ways that the Holy Spirit manifests himself: fluttering of the eyelashes, appearance of engagement with God like the nodding of the head as if the person was understanding what the Spirit was saying to them, "sheen" on the face, flushes around the neck, feeling of heat, shaking, trembling, deep breathing, weeping, laughing, peace, falling down and resting in the Spirit, tingling sensation like pins and needles.

These manifestations are not ends in themselves nor are they indicators of healing. The manifestations are some of the ways that the Spirit reveals Himself to the client and pray-er. Thus, the pray-er and the client should not be surprised when the Spirit does come and uses one of these manifestations to show that He is present.

The aim is to understand where God is working and to bless His work. Jesus said: *"Very truly I tell you, the Son can do nothing by himself; he can do only what he sees his Father doing, because whatever the Father does the Son also does. (John 5:19)*

Dialogue with the person to see if they are feeling anything. The purpose of this is

    (a) To understand what the Spirit may be doing

    (b) To explain to the person what may be happening to them

    (c) To ask questions to see if the root cause is different

    (d) To help and guide the person through the healing process with the Holy Spirit. For example, I have had to lead the person through a prayer of forgiveness for a person before the Spirit can continue.

Keep listening and working with the Spirit, keep dialoguing with the person until it appears the ministry time is over either because the person is healed or feels better or has received as much as he or she can handle for the night or the person does not wish to go further because the pain is too much or there is hidden sin.

During prayer engagement it is helpful to pray both in English and tongues. If pray-ers have the gift of tongues it is beneficial for them to use the gift. Ask the person's permission for tongues to be used. It may be that you pray your tongue under your breath.

Explain the use of tongues, viz.

    (a) It helps the pray-ers to be open to the Spirit;

    (b) It unlocks the needs of the person who is being prayed for;

    (c) It speaks to any demons that may be trying to stop the healing

    (d) It can command any demon that may be oppressing the person to leave.

In all the cases except when dealing with the demonic, the tongues tend to be soft and gentle. In the case of demons, the tongues, when used by the pray-er, may be either soft and gentle or, in some cases, come out quite harsh, loud, speaking strongly to the demons to go.

Ask the person whether they have any objection to tongues being used. If he/she has, then tongues may hinder the healing process and it is better to keep to English.

If a deliverance prayer is to be used, pray the following:

In the name of Jesus, I command the spirit(s) of .... to come out and go to the feet of Jesus for judgment.

Make sure that you have reclaimed any ground that Satan has by leading the person in a prayer for repentance of any sin. You may need to ask the Holy Spirit to reveal any sin that is there before you can deal with it.

There are some indicators when the ministry is finished. The anointing declines as the Holy Spirit lifts His power, the sensations like the warmth or tingling diminish or the person indicates that it is over.

The client will know if there has been any healing. They will sense a difference to their life. They will feel better. There is no need to claim any healing that has not happened.

(5) POST-PRAYER DIRECTIONS: This step seeks to answer the questions "What should they do to keep their healing or What should they do if they were not healed?"

In the case of being healed, one counsels them

    (a) To praise God and continue to praise and thank God for His healing
    (b) To allow God to continue His process of healing
    (c) To consult a doctor to confirm any physical healing or before stopping any medication
    (d) Not to fall into sin by breaking with old habits
    (e) Start or continue the spiritual disciplines such as prayer, bible reading, worship and service to the Lord
    (f) Join a small group for fellowship and support
    (g) Prepare for the enemy's counter-attack

In the case of not being healed, one:

    (a) Encourages the person that God still loves them and has not forgotten them
    (b) Assures them that they should not feel guilty or blame themselves
    (c) Admits that there may be areas that the pray-ers have not discerned
    (d) Agrees to continue to pray for the person so that there may be further insight
    (e) Encourages the person to continue to seek God and not give up so that they may get further insight to their issue
    (f) Encourage the person to seek further prayer at a later date

Finally close in prayer giving praise to God and asking God to bless, care for and protect the person in the days and weeks ahead.

Whenever you pray for the sick remember to treat the person as a whole person. John Wimber (4) wisely comments:

Keeping in mind that we pray for persons and not simply conditions, ensures the protection of people's dignity. When I pray for a person's healing my goal is to, leave her or him feeling more loved by God than before I prayed.

PRAYERS TO PRAY FOR PHYSICAL HEALING

Come Holy Spirit upon ...... (name of person)

In the name of Jesus, I command the .... (body part) *of* .... (person) *to be healed* (may need to be repeated)

In the name of Jesus, I command every demon of sickness and infirmity including Dagon to go to the feet of Jesus for judgment.

8

UNLOCKING THE POWER TO CANCEL CURSES

If you fully obey the Lord your God and carefully follow all his commands I give you today, the Lord your God will set you high above all the nations on earth. All these blessings will come on you and accompany you if you obey the Lord your God. (Deuteronomy 28:1,2)

However, if you do not obey the Lord your God and do not carefully follow all his commands and decrees I am giving you today, all these curses will come on you and overtake you. (Deuteronomy 18:15)

With the tongue we praise our Lord and Father, and with it we curse human beings, who have been made in God's likeness. Out of the same mouth come praise and cursing. My brothers and sisters, this should not be. (James 3:9,10)

We live in the world of the internet and social media where words have become a weapon to attack people. The attack can be vicious and demeaning and can cause people to have mental health issues and even consider taking their own lives.

Emily A. Vogels (1) reports for the Pew Research Center of December 15, 2022 that 46% of US teens have experienced at least one type of cyber bullying: offensive name-calling; spreading of false rumors; receiving explicit images that they did not ask for; constantly being asked where they are, what they are doing and physical threats.

While bullying existed long before the internet, the rise of smartphones and social media has brought a new and more public arena into play for this aggressive behavior.

In our ministry, we are constantly undoing the toxic messages that people of all ages have received during their life that have had a huge impact upon them.

The Bible has a lot to say about curses and the harmful impact upon people's lives. It has also a lot to say about blessings and the positive impact that they can have on people's lives

There are many words in the Old Testament that are translated curse. They include *"qabab"* (to malign, stab with words), *"arar"* (to execrate or bitterly curse). In the NT there are also a number of words that include *"kataraomai"* (to doom) *kakologeō* (to *revile*: - speak evil of)

The main vehicles of curses and blessings are words: spoken, written, prayed and uttered inwardly. With the advent of social media, there is another platform for people to be cursed. We see this platform contain racial slurs, images that are used against another, comments that bully another person and so the list goes on.

Deuteronomy 27 and 28 describe the many blessings and curses that can come upon a person. James, in speaking about the tongue and its evil power, describes the tongue this way;

With the tongue we praise our Lord and Father, and with it we curse human beings, who have been made in God's likeness. Out of the same mouth come praise and cursing. My brothers and sisters, this should not be. (James 3:9,10)

CURSES OF GOD

Deuteronomy distinguishes between the curses that God places upon a person and their succeeding generations through sin and disobedience to God and the curses that others (and ourselves) place upon us.

In Deuteronomy 27:11-26 and 28:15-68, Moses lists God's curses and their consequences. The list in Deuteronomy 27:11-26 covers many specific issues that violate the Ten Commandments. The consequences are found in Deuteronomy 28:15-68 and include diseases and pestilences on people, towns and land, victory for the enemies of Israel, loss of crops and animals, exile to a foreign country, fear and terror, overwhelming anxiety, hopelessness and despair.

Many Christians struggle with this concept. But God is a Holy God and when people break God's laws, i.e., they sin and there are consequences of that sin. These consequences not only affect the individual who has committed the sin but also others. Some may feel that they are innocent but they can experience the consequences of that sin.

Imagine you are driving through an intersection and another car goes through the red light and collects you. Your car will be damaged but also you and/or the driver and maybe passengers get injured or maybe killed. One person has broken the law but they have impacted others who were going about their own business.

In the same way, when God's laws are broken, it is not just the breaker of the law but possibly innocent victims who get hurt.

Sadly, we have seen this in families where the sin is repeated through the generations. Consequently, the health, finances and relationships of many family members are caught up, and some are innocent victims.

Legitimate curses from God come upon a family when a family member in a previous generation has disobeyed or broken God's Laws. Idolatry, sexual sin, murder and occult activity seem to have the most impact on the next generations.

The good news is that Jesus became a curse for us and all these curses from God have been dealt with and defeated by the cross of Jesus.

These curses need to be brought to the cross by the family member(s) who have been affected by this. They are to stand in the gap on behalf of their family, repent of the sin and disobedience of the family member(s) and ask God to lift His curses off the family because of Jesus. As families can be complicated, one must include the family members through not only birth but adoption, step or fostered situations.

The following can be prayed to deal with God's curses.

Lord Jesus, I stand in the gap for the sin of my (birth/adoptive/step or foster) family members, past and present who have broken the Law of God, through their disobedience that has become a curse upon my family line.

I repent of this sin, on behalf of my family members, past and present, and I ask you to forgive them.

I bring the power of the blood of Jesus and the oil of the Holy Spirit against every curse of God that has come upon my (birth/adoptive/step or foster) family members and me through their sin and I ask you, God, to remove these curses from me and my present and future generations because of Jesus' death on the cross.

In the name of Jesus, I bind every demon attached to the curses and command them to go to the feet of Jesus for judgment.

CURSES BY OTHERS

The other types of curses come from person to person through direct words spoken or through some prayer activity when the person who receives the curse is not present.

These are word curses that can have a huge impact upon the person: e.g., the pointing of the bone by an aboriginal to another aboriginal or non-aboriginal; the cursing through words from many European/Catholic cultures; name calling; bullying and labels (e.g.: stupid, bossy, dresses to attract males) spoken over people.

These words can be spoken by parents and significant adults like teachers or church leaders or school students. We are seeing an increase of this type of cursing through social media like Facebook, TikTok and SMS messages.

These words can be prayers that are being prayed against Christians by occult groups, religious cults and people in alternative religions.

These words have enormous power in a person's life and can affect every aspect of their life: emotional; physical; relational and financial.

We have sponsored the building of churches in Hindu villages. We have found that individual Hindus did not want these churches to be built. They prayed and cursed the building project and told lies to the authorities to block and stop the building.

We have also seen the emotional damage to people's lives through verbal abuse that has occurred in their childhood, or work life or marriage.

The old saying, *"Sticks and stones may break my bones but words will never harm me"* is completely wrong. Words have been and still are a powerful weapon that can destroy a person's life. The power of a curse is not just in the words that are used but also the context of how the prayers were made.

Those who make curses add power to the curses through shedding some form of blood because there is power in blood. Blood is so important to God that it is mentioned in the Bible around 700 times. David referred to the "incorruptible" blood. Peter spoke of the "precious" blood, and John wrote of the "overcoming" power of the blood.

We're told in Leviticus 17:11 that *the life of the flesh is in the blood.* This is true in both spiritual and physical realms.

The blood of Jesus has great power. Let me remind you of what I have said earlier. The blood of Jesus

- **Provides forgiveness of your sins.** *In fact, the law requires that nearly everything be cleansed with blood, and without the shedding of blood there is no forgiveness. (Hebrews 9:22)*
- **Gives you life.** *Jesus said to them, "Very truly I tell you, unless you eat the flesh of the Son of Man and drink his blood, you have no life in you." (John 6:53)*
- **Brings you close to God.** *But now in Christ Jesus you who once were far away have been brought near by the blood of Christ. (Ephesians 2:13)*
- **Cleanses your conscience.** *How much more, then, will the blood of Christ, who through the eternal Spirit offered himself unblemished to God, cleanse our consciences from acts that lead to death, so that we may serve the living God! (Hebrews 9:14)*
- **Gives you boldness to approach God.** *Therefore, brothers and sisters, since we have confidence to enter the Most Holy Place by the blood of Jesus (Hebrews 10:19)*
- **Sanctifies you.** *And so Jesus also suffered outside the city gate to make the people holy through his own blood. (Hebrews 13:12)*
- **Cleanses you.** *But if we walk in the light as He is in the light, we have fellowship with one another, and the blood of Jesus Christ, His Son, cleanses us from all sin.* (*1 John 1:7*)
- **Heals you.** *"He himself bore our sins" in his body on the cross, so that we might die to sins and live for righteousness; "by his wounds you have been healed." (1 Peter 2:24)*
- **Enables you to overcome the devil and his works.** *They triumphed over him by the blood of the Lamb and by the word of their testimony; they did not love their lives so much as to shrink from death. (Revelation 12:11)*

There is power in the blood of Jesus and those in the know seek to copy and replicate that power by shedding blood in the making of their curses through cutting of animals or themselves and sometimes taking the next step through a sacrifice to their god. This sacrifice in some cases can be human!

To cancel the power of the curses made with and through blood, that shed blood used in the making of these curses needs to be covered and cancelled by covering that shed blood with the blood of Jesus.

Power is also gained to a lesser extent through the use of particular objects. People who are involved with alternative religions can offer up food or objects deemed sacred by the religious group. They can be burnt offerings.

People who are involved in the occult or satanic practices add power to their curses through the use of a person's photograph or a doll in the person's image (voodoo idol). They can use a piece of the person's clothing or hair or fingernail to curse them. Feathers, bones and other inanimate objects are also used in the making of curses.

We have found that behind every curse is a cause: *Like a fluttering sparrow or a darting swallow, an undeserved curse does not come to rest. (Proverbs 26:2)*

The primary causes that we have come across are:
- False gods like new age and eastern religions
- Moral and ethical sins including rebellion, disrespect for parents, oppression and injustice against the weak and helpless, illicit and unnatural sex, stealing, cheating and shifting property boundaries
- Anti-Semitism (speaking against the Jews)
- Legalism and carnality i.e. trusting man, rules and self and not God
- Theft, perjury and robbing God where people have property and debt upon their lives
- Cursing authority figures like leaders of government and churches
- Secret society oaths esp. Freemasonry
- False Christian sects like Jehovah Witnesses, Mormons, Scientology etc.
- Ruler of country places a curse upon you and/or family line
- Aboriginal injustice
- Aboriginal (Australian first people) Gadjiva men or tribal Indigenous person or witchdoctor placing a curse on someone.
- Blasphemy especially cursing or blaming God for a death, illness or misfortune
- Objects from overseas trips which have had curses placed upon them
- Entering places of non-Christian worship e.g. temples or shrines and walking inside them.
- Land and buildings where curses (Aboriginal (or Nation's first people) and non-Aboriginal (Indigenous) and Satanist) have been placed upon them or there have been sinful actions like murder or genocide that has defiles them
- Spoken words over a person through witchcraft, voodoo sympathetic magic, Satanist ceremonies
- Spoken words by significant others (parents, grandparents, employers, employees, ministers, teachers, Sunday school teachers etc.) like *"you're hopeless, an idiot, dumb, no good, won't amount to much or achieve anything"*

The evidence of a curse in a person's life may be found in:
- Mental and emotional illness and breakdowns
- Chronic or repeated sickness
- Barrenness or a tendency to miscarry or period problems
- Breakdown of marriage or family alienation

- Poverty or financial difficulties or insufficiency
- Accident prone
- History of suicide or untimely or unnatural deaths

A lady came for ministry. She had unexplained sickness that the doctors could not diagnose. Some days she was sick and some days she was OK. Further questioning revealed that she had been overseas recently where she had bought some clothes. Further questioning revealed that she only became sick when she was wearing a certain dress.

The team sought the Lord and it was revealed that the dress had been cursed by the one who made it. Thus, when the dress was worn, the curse of sickness came upon the wearer.

The team sought further the Lord about what to do. Sometimes the cursed object can be prayed for it so that all the curses are destroyed. Sometimes the cursed object needs to be disposed of in such a way that it cannot be worn or used by another.

In this case the Lord guided the team and the lady to dispose of the dress. Special prayers need to be made to counter these curses.

Normally curses can be broken by any individual as they cover them with the blood of Jesus, asking Jesus to retrieve any blood that has been shed then break the power of the curse by calling on the fire of God to destroy them (or ask Jesus to destroy the curses by fire) and send their ashes to the pit. Then we ask the Lord to return the object to its God given purpose.

To pray to break the curses that have come against you, your family, then pray:

In the name of Jesus, I cover with the blood of Jesus, all curses, hexes, spells and ungodly prayers against me or my family.

In the name of Jesus, I negate them all, ask Jesus to retrieve any blood that was shed in the making of them and return it to Himself. I pull out all instruments used in the making of these curses, put them in a pile and call down the fire to God to destroy all instruments.

In the name of Jesus, I negate all curses/oaths/vows/inner vows and with the sword of the Spirit, sever them all from me or my family, call down the fire of God to destroy them all and collect their ashes and send them to the place that Jesus has appointed.

In the name of Jesus, I bind every demon attached to the curses and command them to go to the feet of Jesus for judgment.

PRAYERS TO BREAK THE CURSE ON THE WOMB

In our ministry we have come across a number of women who are struggling to get pregnant or have a history of miscarriages. We have found that the cause of the problem is a curse that has been placed upon the womb by family members from previous generations on either or both sides of the woman or husband through their participation in the Occult. We have also found that the cause comes from people known to the person who have been jealous or dislike the person and wish them the worse.

The following is a prayer to cancel out the curse and restore the womb to its godly use and fruitfulness.

Lord Jesus, has there been a curse placed upon the womb of............ (name of person) to cause barrenness or miscarriages.

If yes or unsure, pray:

In the name of Jesus, I cover with the blood of Jesus, all curses, hexes, spells and ungodly prayers that have been placed upon the womb of............(name of person)

In the name of Jesus, I negate them all, ask Jesus to retrieve any blood that was shed in the making of them and return it to Himself.

I pull out all instruments used in the making of these curses, put them in a pile and call down the fire to God to destroy all instruments.

In the name of Jesus, I negate all curses/oaths/vows/inner vows and with the sword of the Spirit, sever them all from the womb of ...., call down the fire of God to destroy them all and collect their ashes and send them to the place that Jesus has appointed.

In the name of Jesus, I bind every demon of barrenness, miscarriage and infertility attached to the curses and command them to go to the feet of Jesus for judgment.

In the name of Jesus, I restore the womb of ....(name of person) back to its godly use.

In the name of Jesus, I speak healing, life and fruitfulness into the womb of ....(name of person). Amen.

Reverend John Lucas, DMin

FREEMASONRY

Freemasonry is a collection of pagan rites and initiations base on the religions and worship of Egypt. It is syncretistic, an amalgamation of various religions and practices. It involves the worship of the three pagan gods from Egypt, Babylon and Canaan though many do not realize this.

It has enough biblical terminology to deceive the unsuspecting. It considers itself to be universal and does not acknowledge the uniqueness of Jesus Christ as the Son of God. It is a religion of good works and good fellowship where they look after their own kind. It gives away much money and seeks to earn a reputation of looking after the elderly and other community projects.

There are many different lodges that are based on Freemasonry. These include the Buffalo Lodge, the Blue Lodge, Orange Lodge and the Shriners (USA). While it is primary male based, there are female versions of Freemasonry.

We have prayed for many people who have a history of Freemasonry in the family or may have been Freemasons themselves. We have found that the following may be in the family or family line as a result of Freemasonry:

- The spiritual separation of husbands and wives through oaths of secrecy.
- The release of lust in both sexes: for sex (including perversions), for power, for money, and for control of others.
- The release of sickness and infirmity in families often linked to the words of the oaths that are made.
- The release of bitterness and anger in women who tend to learn to control and manipulate the family. This is often linked to a controlling spirit or else they become docile and passive and experience all kinds of sicknesses.
- The release of a curse of religion in which a form of religion is maintained without faith in Jesus as Lord. They tend to disagree with godly leadership.
- The release of curses into family and family line: e.g. lust, uncleanness, illegitimacy, infirmity, death, destruction (esp. first-born son)
- Difficulty for the gospel to mature in every part of the person and church.
- Mirror-image effect where leaders see a problem but before anything can be done, they are blamed for it. Often results in removal of pastoral authority and desertion or betrayal of close friends and colleagues.
- Release of a poverty spirit where a person struggles to get ahead financially.
- Barrenness of the womb because of a curse being placed upon it.

These consequences fall not only on the individual involved with Freemasonry but their family and future family members. They are connected to the oaths and ceremonies in the initiation and future progress in the Order.

The ceremonies that are a part of Freemasonry initially begin with the oaths of induction. These oaths are made to bind the person to the Lodge with the additional consequences of life-threatening outcomes if these oaths are broken. They are made with a hood over their head, rope around their neck and one arm of the shirt cut.

While it is claimed that these life-threatening consequences may not happen if the person leaves the Lodge, the person is spiritually bound and leaving the Lodge does release spiritual negative outcomes.

As the individual progresses through the 33 Degrees of Freemasonry, further oaths and promises are made that hook them and their families and future generations. Like all counterfeit religions, Freemasonry copies and corrupts the way of God.

We have found three things that need to be dealt with to free the person and their family, present and future from the impact of Freemasonry and the curses associated with it.

Firstly, as all Christians have their name written in the Book of Life in Heaven, Freemasons and their families, past, present and future, have their names written in the Book of Freemasonry to claim ownership of the family. To free the family members, their names are to be removed by Jesus through His blood, His fire and His power.

Secondly, as Christians are the bride of Christ with Christ the bridegroom, so family members are "married" with rings and certificates. To free the family, the rings and certificates used in the ceremonies need to be removed and burnt by God's fire.

Thirdly, the instruments of Freemasonry, used in the ceremonies like ropes and daggers, the books and Masonic aprons need to be destroyed by God's fire.

This gives the family members total freedom from the bondage of Freemasonry over the family, past, present and future and goes deeper than just declaring out loud the renouncements of every level of Freemasonry.

Sadly, many Christians, including ministers, have been deceived and have joined their ranks. They do not understand the spiritual implications and consequences of their joining for themselves, their families and future generations!

Prayers to cancel Freemasonry in the family line

Lord Jesus, is there Freemasonry in the family line?

If you have the sense of Yes, then proceed. (Sometimes you may not have a sense of Yes or No, so assume that there is present)

Lord Jesus, has the name been written in the Freemasonry Book?

If yes, (Sometimes you may not have a sense of Yes or No, so assume that there is present)

Then pray:

Lord Jesus, please remove the family name and all names of the family from the Book and destroy the page(s) on which they have been written.

Then wait. Then pray: *Jesus has it been done?* Wait for His Yes

Lord Jesus, are there any marriage rings and certificates?

If yes, (Sometimes you may not have a sense of Yes or No, so assume that there is present)

Lord Jesus, please remove all rings and certificates, destroy them by fire and put the ashes into the pit.

Then wait. Then pray: *Lord Jesus, has it been done?* Wait for His Yes.

Lord Jesus, are there any books and Masonic instruments and paraphernalia like ropes, daggers etc.?

If yes, (Sometimes you may not have a sense of Yes or No, so assume that there is present)

Lord Jesus, please remove all books and Masonic instruments and paraphernalia, destroy them by fire and put the ashes into the pit.

Then wait. Then pray: *Lord Jesus, has it been done?*

Wait for His Yes.

Cults, Occult and Satanic groups.
We live in a world where secret groups attract many people, especially young people who are struggling in their lives and so offers a way of living and having power in their lives that makes them feel better about themselves.

They find an identity, acceptance and belonging that they did not have in their family or school or life. But they get caught up with people who lord it over them, control them, and use them for no good ends.

Through the use of indoctrination, teaching and psychological techniques, they come under the control of the leader in various ways.

To set these people free, there needs to be an understanding of their involvement, the ceremonies used and the degree of trauma that they have experienced so that the prayers used, target the issues and through Jesus sets the person free, slowly and methodically.

It takes numerous sessions being aware of all that has been planted inside the person. It needs people with supernatural gifting by God to spiritually see and unlock the person from the grasp of Satan and his followers.

This type of praying is not for most Christians but those called by God to set people free from these groups.

INNER VOWS

For as he thinks in his heart, so is he. (Proverbs 27:3 NKJV)

Our thinking influences the way we feel and behave. Events/situations that occur in the outside world do not usually cause feelings or behavior; rather it is an individual's interpretation (or thoughts) about those events that will directly lead to their feelings and subsequent actions. In some cases, the thoughts that they have about a particular situation can be quite unhelpful.

Often, the unhelpful thoughts happen so quickly in response to trigger events that people do not even realize what is happening. That is why these thoughts are often referred to as 'automatic'. Usually, people suddenly realize that they are experiencing something wrong. These feelings are often a signal that they have slipped into automatic pilot and allowed a trigger situation to lead to an unhelpful thought about that situation.

This leads to a range of thinking that leads people to make vows that lock them to wrong thinking. They become a curse that they have said over them.

This leads them to wrong thinking in the following way:

- **Black and white thinking**: Examples of black and white thinking include: *"If I fail partly, it is as bad as being a complete failure"*, or *"I never get what I want so it's foolish to want anything"*. In particular, *"even if I sin again, I'm a failure, so why bother"* or *"I can't change, so it's pointless trying at all"*.
- **Jumping to negative conclusions**: For example, they might think: *"Things just won't work out the way I want them to"*, or *"I never get what I want so it's stupid to want anything"*, or *"There's no use in really trying to get something I want because I probably won't get it"*. In relation to drug use, people with this pattern of thinking may believe *"I'll never be able to change my drug using, it'll never be any different"*.
- **Catastrophizing**: For example, *"If I fail this test, I will never pass school, and I will be a total failure in life." "If I don't recover quickly from this procedure, I will never get better, and I will be disabled my entire life."*
- **Personalizing**: For example, *"My brother has come home in a bad mood, it must be something that I have done"* or *"I feel stupid, so I am stupid"*. People with this pattern of thinking often put themselves down, and think too little of themselves, particularly in response to making a mistake. They may think things like *"I'm weak and stupid, there's no way I'll be able to resist."*. In response to a slip, personalizers will often say to themselves: *"see, I knew I'd never be strong enough to resist, I'm such a terrible person."*
- **Shoulds/oughts**: For example, *"I must not get angry"*, *"He should always be on time"*, and especially, *"I should be strong enough to never even experience a craving – I should just be able*

to stop. " 'Should' statements can cause a person to experience anger and frustration when that person directs these statements at others.

People then make vows that control their life.

A vow is a solemn promise or assertion by which a person is bound to act, service or condition. The vow needs to be unbound. An inner vow is a determination set by the mind and the heart into all the being in early life (and usually forgotten). The distinctive mark of an inner vow is that it resists the normal maturation process. Vows lay a trap for us in creating a burden that we, in our weakness and finiteness cannot keep.

There are a number of reasons for this:
- Vows are about actions in the future, and the future is something over which we have little or no control.
- Vows are solemn and sacred and involve powerful heavenly realities that we should not mess with.
- Some people e.g. the Pharisees, used vows to make people trust them so they could trick and cheat others.
- Breaking a vow can result in judgment (James 5:12) and the destruction of the work of our hands (Ecclesiastes 5:4-6).
- We may make a vow that depends on the actions of another person, and that person may act in such a way to make fulfilling the vow impossible - such as a vow to be responsible for another person's debts.
- Our circumstances may change so that we cannot keep the vow or pledge e.g. we may lose our job and be unable to pay the pledge to the church.
- We may construct the vow in absolute terms using words such as 'always" or "never" and in reality, life is too complex to say we will "always" do X or "never" do Y.
- We may make an open-ended vow that traps us with its consequences using terms such as "whatever".

Inner vows can result from traumas / embarrassments / rejections and be such as:
- I will never speak in public, never develop breasts, never grow up, never have any friends
- Never to give of self / clothes / personal space / time
- Never fail / be the best ever / never try again / be perfect How could I be so dumb? I am a failure.
- I should I couldn't I can't I will never forgive myself.
- I am not good enough I hate myself I am ugly I am dumb
- Jesus gives a solemn warning about the danger of words used carelessly.

But I tell you that everyone will have to give account on the day of judgment for every empty word they have spoken. (Matthew 12:36)

RENOUNCING INNER VOWS

The following process helps us to unlock any inner vows that we have made in our life.

Lord Jesus, reveal to me an inner vow that I have made.

I renounce the inner vow ……………………… And I announce the truth that …………….. (Announcing the truth involves the opposite of the vow plus a bible verse or truth. Repeat the above process until all the inner vows have been revealed for that ministry.

For Example:

- Inner Vow – I am dumb, no intelligence etc. ……
Announced truth …I am created in the image of God and He has given me the mind of Christ

- Inner Vow -- I can't …..... etc………..
Announced Truth…I can do all things through Christ who strengthens me

- Inner Vow I am ugly etc. ………
Announced Truth …I am a child of God and God says that I am beautiful

- Inner Vow I am not worthy -------
Announced Truth…. I am a precious child of God and extremely valuable to Him

Reverend John Lucas, DMin

9

UNLOCKING THE POWER TO SET YOUR PROPERTY FREE

Do not pollute the land where you are. Bloodshed pollutes the land, and atonement cannot be made for the land on which blood has been shed, except by the blood of the one who shed it. Do not defile the land where you live and where I dwell, for I, the Lord, dwell among the Israelites. (Numbers 35:33,34)

However, if you do not obey the Lord your God and do not carefully follow all his commands and decrees, I am giving you today, all these curses will come on you and overtake you: You will be cursed in the city and cursed in the country. Your basket and your kneading trough will be cursed. The fruit of your womb will be cursed, and the crops of your land, and the calves of your herds and the lambs of your flocks. You will be cursed when you come in and cursed when you go out. The Lord will send on you curses, confusion and rebuke in everything you put your hand to, until you are destroyed and come to sudden ruin because of the evil you have done in forsaking him. (Deuteronomy 28:15-20)

Say to rebellious Israel, 'This is what the Sovereign Lord says: Enough of your detestable practices, people of Israel! In addition to all your other detestable practices, you brought foreigners uncircumcised in heart and flesh into my sanctuary, desecrating my temple while you offered me food, fat and blood, and you broke my covenant. Instead of carrying out your duty in regard to my holy things, you put others in charge of my sanctuary. (Ezekiel 44:6-8)

We moved to Coolangatta, Queensland, (north-eastern state of Australia) in 2010, where I was invited to come to a property to pray for it. Two brothers owned a cattle property in eastern NSW near the border with Qld. They contacted us because their property was not thriving and the cattle were having all sorts of problems producing calves. Liz and myself came with a friend Diane to pray for the property.

As we walked around the property, and talked to the owners, and sought the Lord, we discovered a number of issues that had prevented the property from flourishing.

In the history of the property, a man committed suicide in one of the sheds. The other major issue happened at the creek bed. There were a number of deaths from aboriginal tribes fighting each other and then later rapes and deaths committed by white people against the local aboriginal tribes.

We asked the two owners to pray with us, confessing the sin that had happened on their land and the subsequent lack of productivity. We had to stand in the gap and ask forgiveness for the deaths of aboriginals by each other, by white people and the rapes so that the curse of death could be removed and the land restored to productivity again.

One year later, the two brothers gave us a report of what had happened. Firstly, the pastures regrew and became bountiful again. Secondly, the cattle began to produce calves to not only replenish the stock but also be available to send to market for their meat. Thirdly, their finances were restored and much of their debt had been paid back.

In our ministry over the years, we have been called to pray through farms, people's homes where things go "bump in the night" and churches to remove the blockages that were there.

We need to recover what local indigenous people know that the land is significant to our life. But we need a biblical understanding of the land and how it can be defiled.

BIBLICAL PERSPECTIVE OF LAND

The bible gives us the foundations for understanding the land.

1. God created the Land

In the beginning God created the heavens and the earth (Genesis 1:1)

2. God's creation was good

God saw all that he had made, and it was very good. And there was evening, and there was morning—the sixth day. (Genesis 1:31)

3. God gave man the role to be a steward (keep, protect, guard, watch over like a watchman) of the creation

God blessed them and said to them, "Be fruitful and increase in number; fill the earth and subdue it. Rule over the fish in the sea and the birds in the sky and over every living creature that moves on the ground." (Genesis 1:28)

4. God remained the owner. Man was only a tenant.

"'The land must not be sold permanently, because the land is mine and you reside in my land as foreigners and strangers. (Leviticus 25:23)

5. The land can be polluted by people

The earth is defiled by its people; they have disobeyed the laws, violated the statutes and broken the everlasting covenant. Therefore, a curse consumes the earth; its people must bear their guilt. Therefore, earth's inhabitants are burned up, and very few are left. (Isaiah 24:5,6)

6. People are affected by the condition of the land

Hear the word of the Lord, you Israelites, because the Lord has a charge to bring against you who live in the land: "There is no faithfulness, no love, no acknowledgment of God in the land. There is only cursing, lying and murder, stealing and adultery; they break all bounds, and bloodshed follows bloodshed. Because of this the land dries up, and all who live in it waste away; the beasts of the field, the birds in the sky and the fish in the sea are swept away. (Hosea 4:1-3)

DEFILEMENT OF OUR STEWARDSHIP

The Bible also gives us an understanding of how we may defile the land. We bring defilement into our life and work in at least three ways:

1. By what we do (e.g. Cain in Genesis 4:1-16)
2. By what others do and say to us and our subsequent reactions (Samson and Delilah in Judges 16)
3. By what our ancestors in earlier generations have passed on. *You will perish among the nations; the land of your enemies will devour you. Those of you who are left will waste away in the lands of their enemies because of their sins; also because of their ancestors' sins they will waste away. (Leviticus 26:38,39)*

DEFILEMENT OF LAND THROUGH SIN

God gave Israel the Promised Land. But they were to honor the land that was given to them. However, over time, they defiled the land through their sinful practices, breaking the commandments that were given through Moses.

The following are ways that the prophets and others outlined how defilement of the land occurs.

- Not obeying God's words (Jeremiah 25:8,11)
- Breaking Covenant (Isaiah 24:5,6)
- Shedding of Blood (Psalm 106:37-39)
- Sexual Sins. These things include: uncovering nakedness, adultery, child abuse/abortion, homosexuality and bestiality. (Leviticus 18:24)
- Idolatry (Ezekiel 36:18)
- Lack of intercession for the land (Jeremiah 12:10,11)
- Divorce (Jeremiah 3:1)
- Indifference (Jeremiah 12:4)
- Injustice (Zechariah 7:8-14)
- Unfaithfulness and treachery (Ezekiel 14:12-14)
- Not giving honor to God (Malachi 2:1-3)
- Stealing and lying (Zechariah 5:3)
- Dishonoring parents (Exodus 20:12)

Reverend John Lucas, DMin

DEFILEMENT OF LAND THROUGH CURSES

Another way that the land was defiled was through curses.

A curse (Hebrew arar) means "to bind with a spell, to encircle with obstacles, to render powerless or make infertile". Dictionary meaning adds "expressing or feeling abhorrence toward something". Another interpretation is "calling forth mischief or injury on someone or something else" In its simplest form it means "removal of God's favor and presence from His people.

The main understanding of curses comes from Deuteronomy 28-30. It is a list of blessings and curses from God.

The blessings include Exaltation, Health, Reproductivity - family, livestock, crops, business and exercise of creative talents.

The curses include: Humiliation, Barrenness, Unfruitfulness, Mental and Physical Sickness, Family Breakdown, Poverty, Defeat, Oppression, God's Disfavor.

We struggle with the notion of God cursing people and the land because we have this notion, primarily from the New Testament that God is love. However, we fail to appreciate the consequences when we break God's law.

This was what Moses was warning the people about. Breaking God's commandments through disobedience and sin have enormous consequences not just for the present generation but also for future generations. Unless that sin and disobedience is addressed through repentance and cleansing by blood, the consequences and the fall out remain.

Finally, man has the ability to curse the land and people through his words and prayers. We find Jesus cursing the towns of Chorazin and Bethsaida for their rejection of Jesus and his works of power.

"Woe to you, Chorazin! Woe to you, Bethsaida! For if the miracles that were performed in you had been performed in Tyre and Sidon, they would have repented long ago, sitting in sackcloth and ashes. (Luke 10:13)

Then Jesus curses the fig tree (Matthew 21:18-22) and it withered and died. It was an acted parable to prove two things.

It was fruitfulness that counts rather than the outward potential. Also, it is faith with no doubts that can perform miracles.

Later in the New Testament, James in chapter 3 outlines the power of the tongue that has the ability to destroy.

With the tongue we praise our Lord and Father, and with it we curse human beings, who have been made in God's likeness. (James 3:9)

We have seen that cursing has an enormous impact upon the land as many indigenous tribes seek to combat the takeover of their land down through the centuries.

JUDGMENT OF GOD ON LAND

The history of Israel in the Old Testament shows the experience of God's judgment upon the land and people because of sin and disobedience.

The prophet in Ezekiel 14:12-23 outlines God's judgment that comes to the land because of the people's sin and disobedience.

The word of the Lord came to me: "Son of man, if a country sins against me by being unfaithful and I stretch out my hand against it to cut off its food supply and send famine upon it and kill its people and their animals, even if these three men—Noah, Daniel and Job—were in it, they could save only themselves by their righteousness, declares the Sovereign Lord.

Or if I send wild beasts through that country and they leave it childless and it becomes desolate so that no one can pass through it because of the beasts, as surely as I live, declares the Sovereign Lord, even if these three men were in it, they could not save their own sons or daughters. They alone would be saved, but the land would be desolate.

Or if I bring a sword against that country and say, 'Let the sword pass throughout the land,' and I kill its people and their animals, as surely as I live, declares the Sovereign Lord, even if these three men were in it, they could not save their own sons or daughters. They alone would be saved.

Or if I send a plague into that land and pour out my wrath on it through bloodshed, killing its people and their animals, as surely as I live, declares the Sovereign Lord, even if Noah, Daniel and Job were in it, they could save neither son nor daughter. They would save only themselves by their righteousness.

For this is what the Sovereign Lord says: How much worse will it be when I send against Jerusalem my four dreadful judgments—sword and famine and wild beasts and plague—to kill its men and their animals! Yet there will be some survivors—sons and daughters who will be brought out of it. They will come to you, and when you see their conduct and their actions, you will be consoled regarding the disaster I have brought on Jerusalem—every disaster I have brought on it. You will be consoled when you see their conduct and their actions, for you will know that I have done nothing in it without cause, declares the Sovereign Lord. (Ezekiel 14:12-23)

God's judgment for sin and unfaithfulness was famine (not just of food but also the Word of God), ecological devastation, war and disease.

The book of Revelation adds the present and future judgment of God.

I looked, and there before me was a pale horse! Its rider was named Death, and Hades was following close behind him. They were given power over a fourth of the earth to kill by sword, famine and plague, and by the wild beasts of the earth. (Revelation 6:8)

Reverend John Lucas, DMin

DEFILEMENT OF BUILDINGS

In the book of Leviticus, chapter 14:33-57, God gives detailed instructions regarding the defiling of a house by mold, mildew or fungus that God had spread in the land. The priest was to check what the contamination was like and give orders to close the house for seven days. If it was still there then contaminated bricks had to be removed and walls scraped and, in some cases, pulled down and all the building materials taken to an unclean place.

In Leviticus, chapter 15, people would defile the home if they were unclean. This uncleanness was from bodily discharge by a man or a woman. Where ever they sat on, whatever they touched or leaned upon became unclean. There were specific instructions for both men and women to address their uncleanness.

In Leviticus, chapter 11, the clean and unclean food was itemized so that the people of God would not eat unclean food and refrain from touching it.

This notion of being clean or unclean determined whether they could bring their sacrifices to the priest at the Tabernacle and then later to the Temple when that was built. This notion also applied to who they should and should not marry.

The people were not to take the local idols into their home for that was idolatry and frowned upon by God.

Rachel in Genesis 31 escaped with the family idols, put them in the saddle bag and sat upon them when Laban came to retrieve them. Michal, in 1 Samuel 19, placed an idol in the bed to pretend that it was David to buy time for his escape. In both cases the wife of a godly man continued to be influenced by pagan spiritual practices that carried over from her father's family.

It became a real problem for Solomon who married many foreign women and who brought their gods with them. The writer of Kings comments

King Solomon, however, loved many foreign women besides Pharaoh's daughter— Moabites, Ammonites, Edomites, Sidonians and Hittites. They were from nations about which the Lord had told the Israelites, "You must not intermarry with them, because they will surely turn your hearts after their gods." Nevertheless, Solomon held fast to them in love. He had seven hundred wives of royal birth and three hundred concubines, and his wives led him astray. As Solomon grew old, his wives turned his heart after other gods, and his heart was not fully devoted to the Lord his God, as the heart of David his father had been. He followed Ashtoreth the goddess of the Sidonians, and Molech the detestable god of the Ammonites. So, Solomon did evil in the eyes of the Lord; he did not follow the Lord completely, as David his father had done. (1 Kings 11:1-6)

Later when the Temple was built, desecration happened in two ways. Firstly, when the people of God failed to repent of their idolatry and sinful practices and dared to enter the Temple to present their sacrifices to the Lord. The prophets Ezekiel and Jeremiah were quite scathing.

"The people of Israel and Judah have done nothing but evil in my sight from their youth; indeed, the people of Israel have done nothing but arouse my anger with what their hands have made, declares the Lord. From the day it was built until now, this city has so aroused my anger and wrath that I must remove it from my sight. The people of Israel and Judah have provoked me by all the evil they have done—they, their kings and officials, their priests and prophets, the people of Judah and those living in Jerusalem. They turned their backs to me and not their faces; though I taught them again and again, they would not listen or respond to discipline. They set up their vile images in the house that bears my Name and defiled it. They built high places for Baal in the Valley of Ben Hinnom to sacrifice their sons and daughters to Molek, though I never commanded—nor did it enter my mind—that they should do such a detestable thing and so make Judah sin. (Jeremiah 32:30-35)

Secondly, the temple was desecrated when conquerors of Israel destroyed the Temple and took away the Temple treasures. Later in the days of Jesus, the money lenders desecrated the Temple by their practices. Then the Romans placed their idols in the Temple itself, causing the Jewish rebellion of 70AD when the Temple, built by King Herod, was destroyed.

Throughout history, the land and the buildings upon it, continued to be desecrated by what was done by local tribes against each other. Conquering armies from other nations continued the process of rape and pillage and the worship of false idols devastating the local people and all that they built.

MODERN DAY DESECRATION

The Bible describes how the land that God gave and the structures placed upon it, especially the Temple, were desecrated by sin, the shedding of blood, idolatry and word curses.

But what about today! My journey of understanding of this idea began in 1990 when I was doing my Doctorate of Ministry from Fuller Seminary. I was introduced to this concept by Dr Peter Wagner and the associated reading I had to do on Church Growth. My thesis topic was on the healing and deliverance ministry of Christ and how it could be applied to my denomination. I was living in a small country town in the north of South Australia called Peterborough.

In the years that followed, the Lord brought people to my doorstep who needed healing and deliverance. In my rural and railway community, some young people committed suicide and through my research I discovered that suicide was a repeat problem. I attended a seminar interstate that focused on Suicide and discovered that there was a forest nearby that was the site of a number of suicides and that people would drive there, some from a distance, to take their lives.

The elders and myself walked around the boundaries of the community, prayed and had communion to seek to address the strongholds of suicide and death. We were very raw in this way of praying and we hoped that we had made a difference to these strongholds. At the same time, I was writing my dissertation and people were coming for healing. We had a team learning as we prayed and saw God healing.

Reverend John Lucas, DMin

We also prayed through the church that I was a pastor of, dealing with the past sin that we found through local knowledge and revelation from God and began to see some small signs of growth.

I moved to a church in suburban Adelaide, Tusmore Park Uniting Church. I taught the series Communion with God by Mark Virkler and discovered a small group of people who were given the spiritual insight and giftedness, though immature, to help me pray through the church.

Reading the history of the church and its council meetings and through spiritual insight I discovered a number of issues that continued to appear again and again; conflict and anger at church meetings; a religious spirit and a lack of prayer to change things.

We brought all the sinful ways of the past before God, confessed them and ask the church to be cleansed and its angel to be restored in its rightful place. We set up a prayer meeting for the church and its ministry and facilitated people with prayer points to pray at home.

The fruit of such praying was that people on the fringe of the church rediscovered a vital faith in Jesus. A second modern service was started with the young people becoming the music team and new people coming to church. Prayer became a central part of church life.

People started to come to church for healing prayer and a healing ministry called Pools of Healing was established with teams comprised of people from other churches wanting to pray for the sick. I developed a way of praying so that ordinary people could form a team and pray for the sick.

In 2004, my wife and I moved to Toowoomba, Queensland, to lead Freedom Life Centre that prayed for people face to face and over the phone. I expanded the teams to pray for healing and ran three annual conferences, upheld by intercessory prayer where the Holy Spirit manifested His presence in a powerful life changing way.

I was invited to go to a house on the Gold Coast to pray for a house that had disturbances and problems. The man who lived there was not a Christian but asked the local church to help. The local church invited my wife and I to help out.

We prayed and the Lord showed us that the home was used as a brothel and a person had been murdered there. We prayed and dealt with the blood that was spilt, the sin that went on in the house and removed all demons to the feet of Jesus for judgment.

The man was so pleased and noted the difference immediately. We invited him to receive Jesus as Lord and Savior and he did! Praise God!! We then had lunch together to celebrate the healing of the house and his decision to follow Christ.

In our time at Toowoomba, we were invited to churches to teach, heal and pray for people. In some cases, we prayed for the church to free it from the past sins and restore its Angel in its rightful place. On one occasion we prayed for the angel and found it tied up in the back room! We asked Jesus to free it and restore it and invited the local people to look after the church and its angel by not tolerating sin and filling the place with worship and praise.

In 2010, we moved to Coolangatta, Queensland. We were contacted by the local radio station whose breakfast announcers were talking about what was happening in the home of one of the announcers: lights were going off and on, noises were heard and the wife felt uncomfortable in their home.

We went with a team and found that demons had followed them from Bali, attached to the merchandise that they brought back. We asked the owners to confess the sin and we removed all the demons from the home. They reported that nothing now was happening!

EARTHBOUND SPIRITS?

A man heard the account on the radio and invited us to his home. His elderly Mum was hearing voices and talking to a young woman. His house was filled with antique furniture. We prayed for the house. We found that the "young woman" was an earthbound spirit that was locked to one of antique wardrobes. She was not a demon but the spirit of a person who had died before her time and was connected to the antique furniture.

We were not able to get the full story but we asked Jesus to come and talk to her and give her the gospel. After a short period of time, she was willing to go with Jesus and she left the home. The man reported that his elderly mother complains that everything is now quiet!

We were also invited to a business where each morning they would come into the office and all the papers that were neatly piled on the desks, the previous night, were now scattered on the floor. We prayed and found another earthbound spirit, an elderly lady, who was unhappy that her church had moved and become this business. We again invited Jesus to meet her and talk to her. She responded and went with Jesus. The office workers reported to us that the problem was not a problem anymore.

Earthbound spirits are spirits of humans who roam this earth. Some have died before their time and others have unfinished business. We have found these spirits near a railway crossing where a collision between a car and a train occurred.

Earthbound Spirits are seen by some as very contentious, even not true!

But look at 1 Peter 4:6

For this is the reason the gospel was preached even to those who are now dead, so that they might be judged according to human standards in regard to the body, but live according to God in regard to the spirit.

And the story of Saul and the witch of Endor who brings up the spirit of Samuel in 1 Samuel 28:3-25 gives us the affirmation that what the Lord has shown us is true and not something made up.

For the people concerned who were not believers, they were not interested in the contentious theology but a solution that our praying gave them. From my point of view, the fact that we have encountered these phenomena on a number of occasions, the way that we prayed as Jesus had shown us, seeing these spirits being taken away by Jesus and His angels and then being told that the problem is not a problem anymore confirms that we saw was real and what we did was right.

All these experiences led us to a way of understanding about the desecration of land, churches and buildings and a prayer process to pass on to others.

Reverend John Lucas, DMin

WHAT MAY YOU FIND ON YOUR LAND/BUILDINGS/BUSINESS?

Is your land, home, church or business flourishing? If not, there may be some defilement holding it back.

Your historical knowledge and seeking the Lord to show you will help you discern what has happened. While this schema is for Australia, you can easily apply the same schema to the land in other countries.

You can substitute Aboriginal with Indigenous tribes that first inhabited the land. Knowledge of the way the land was colonized and the early conflicts is helpful. It will add to the revelation that God will give by His Spirit.

The following is a checklist to help you discover what may have defiled your land or home or church or business.

DEFILED BY SIN!

The following ways whereby the land can be defiled by sin.
1. Shed blood
    a. Aboriginal v Aboriginal through tribal wars (Indigenous tribal wars)
    b. Aboriginal (Indigenous) v White through early settlement and colonization
    c. White v Aboriginal (Indigenous) through early settlement including rape of women
    d. White v other culture through violence and murder.
    e. White v White through violence and murder
    f. Suicide
    g. Abortion
2. Idolatry
    a. Aboriginal
    b. Occult
    c. Secret Societies
    d. Man
3. Sin
    a. Sexual sin though rape, incest, fornication, adultery and prostitution
    b. Stealing of titles or goods
    c. Boundary shifting or removal of boundary
    d. Tampering with the natural water courses
    e. Marriage problems
    f. Child abuse
    g. Pornography

DEFILED BY CURSES

The following are ways that curses can defile the land:
1. Aboriginal (Indigenous) curses by Gadjiva men or witchdoctors
2. Occultic curses by covens
3. Curses spoken by neighbors or other humans against the new owner.
4. Talismans (objects or stones or engraved rings that have power) that are placed on the land either physically or spiritually.

UNWANTED RESIDENTS

The following can be found defiling the land.
1. Demons
2. Earthbound spirits
3. Indigenous witchdoctors or Gadjiva men whose spirits have stayed on earth for some nefarious reason.

HEALING THE LAND

When praying for the land and your buildings, the following is needed to be effective in setting your land and property free.

1. Dealing with sin on land and in buildings
- Take your authority. (As legal owner, you have authority to deal with defilement that you have inherited on your land and buildings)
- Pray for the Lord's protection and put on your gospel armor. (see the prayers below in this section)
- Bind all demonic spirits and place them in chains unbreakable especially the spirit of control. Bind all earthbound spirits and place them in a group with the angels guarding them
- Stand in the gap and repent of all sin that has been committed on the land. Take your time. You may have to deal with the sin separately.
- Ask Jesus to cover the sin with His blood and wash it clean.
- Where blood has been shed, ask Jesus to cover the shed blood with His blood and ask Jesus to remove the blood and return it to Him.
- Where instruments have been used i.e. any weapons or talismans, ask Jesus to remove them and cast them into the fiery pit.
- Send all demonic spirits to the feet of Jesus for judgment
- Ask Jesus to send His angels and take them to the place that he has appointed (heaven or hell)
- Ask Jesus to send down His Holy Fire to purify the land
- Wash the land with the blood of Christ and the living water of God

- Reclaim the land for Jesus by placing his cross on it
- Pray to ask Jesus to place His angels around the boundary (Regular pray and thank God for them and make sure that they are OK and not beaten up by the enemy's forces)

2. Dealing with curses
- Cover all curses with the blood of Jesus
- Ask Jesus to cover all blood that was shed in the making of curses with His blood and return to Himself
- Cover all instruments used in the making of curses with the blood of Jesus and ask Jesus to throw them into the fire of the pit.
- Negate all curses and ask Jesus to send His fire to destroy them
- Bind all demons with chains unbreakable and cast them into the flames of the pit
- Seek Jesus about the presence of any Earthbound Spirit or Indigenous witchdoctor (Gadjiva man). If present ask Jesus to speak to them and share the gospel with them. Once they have heard and made their decision to go with Him or not, ask Jesus to send His angels to take them to the place that He has appointed.

3. Anoint the Land and Buildings

After prayer has been given and the land has been cleansed, walk and pray around the boundary of the property anointing with olive oil, consecrated to the Lord, on the corners of the property.

After you have prayed through the building, anoint the doors and windows with holy anointing oil to secure the property.

Ask the Lord for His allocated angels to stand at the corners of the property and over the building(s)

PRAYER FOR LAND AND BUILDINGS

It is best to pray with a team who have spiritual giftings and faith.
Pray prayers of protection

Lord Jesus, I thank you for Your healing and delivering power. I cover us here by the blood of Jesus. I cover all our family and friends, pets, possessions and property, wherever they are whatever they are doing by the blood of Jesus. I ask you to station your guardian angels about them and us during this prayer time.

I put on the whole armor of God on all of us. On our heads I place the helmet of salvation to protect our minds, upon our hearts the breastplate of Christ's righteousness, around our waists the belt of truth, on each of our feet the gospel shoes of peace, on our arm the shield of faith and in the other hand the sword of the Spirit.

Prayer for the land
Invite the owner to pray the following prayer by repeating after you, the leader

Lord Jesus, I stand in the gap for the sin that has been committed on this land by aboriginal to aboriginal (aboriginal to white) (white to aboriginal) (white to white). I cover this sin by the blood of Jesus and the oil of the Holy Spirit and I ask you to forgive all the sin that was committed on this land.

The leader prays:

Lord Jesus, has there been any sin committed by aboriginal to aboriginal (aboriginal to white) (white to aboriginal) (white to white) on this land?

If yes, pray:

In the name of Jesus, I the cover all sin with the blood of Jesus and I ask Jesus to forgive the sin. I wash away all sin by Your blood and the living water of God committed on the land.

Lord Jesus, has there been any blood shed on this land through that sin?

If yes or unsure, pray the next prayer:

In the name of Jesus, I cover all blood shed on this land with the blood of Jesus. I ask you, Lord Jesus, to retrieve all the blood that was shed and return it to yourself.

Lord Jesus, has there been any objects (earthly or spiritual) placed in the ground to contaminate the ground?

If yes or unsure, pray the next prayer:

In your name, Lord Jesus, I cover with your blood all earthly and spiritual objects that have been planted in this land, cancel their power and ask Jesus to remove them from the land and dispose of them.

Lord Jesus, are there any earthbound spirits on the land?

If yes or unsure, pray the next prayer:

Lord Jesus, send your angels and bring all earthbound spirits to you. Then speak to them, explain who you are and share the gospel with them.

If there are then wait until Jesus says that they are ready to go. When they are ready, pray:

Reverend John Lucas, DMin

Lord Jesus, ask your angels to take the earthbound spirits to the place that you have designated.

Houses/buildings

Invite the owner to pray the following prayer by repeating after you, the leader.

Lord Jesus, I stand in the gap for the sin that has been committed on/in this house/building by previous owners and occupants. I cover this sin by the blood of Jesus and the oil of the Holy Spirit and I ask you to forgive all sin that was committed on/in this house/building.

The leader prays:

Lord, has there been any sin committed by aboriginal to aboriginal (aboriginal to white) (white to aboriginal) (white to white) on/in this house/building?

If yes:

In the name of Jesus, I name the cover all sin with the blood of Jesus and I ask Jesus to wash away all sin with the blood of Jesus and the living water of God committed on/in the house/building.

Has there been any blood shed on/in this house/building through that sin?

If yes or unsure, pray the next prayer:

In the name of Jesus, I cover all blood shed on/in this house/building with the blood of Jesus. I ask you, Lord Jesus, to retrieve all the blood that was shed and return it to yourself.

Have there been any objects (earthly or spiritual) placed on/in the house/building to contaminate the house/building?

If yes or unsure, pray the next prayer:

In your name, Lord Jesus, I cover with your blood all earthly and spiritual objects that have been placed on/in this house/building, cancel their power and I ask Jesus to remove them and dispose them.

I bind all head spirits and principalities that are associated with all sin on/in the house/building, and in the name of Jesus, I command them to go to the place that Jesus has appointed without hurting anyone or harming anyone.

I take back the ground that Satan had and I ask you Jesus to restore the house/building to its original Godly use.

I ask you, Lord Jesus, for angels to take up their position over the house/building.

Cursed Buildings and Cursed Land

Invite the owner to pray the following prayer by repeating after you, the leader.

Lord Jesus, I stand in the gap for the one who has sinned and placed a curse upon this land/building. I ask you for your forgiveness. I cover the land/building with the blood of Christ and the anointing oil of the Holy Spirit.

The leader prays:

Lord Jesus, has there been any blood shed because of sin or in the making of curses?

If yes or unsure:

In the name of Jesus, I cover all curses made with blood, with the blood of Jesus. I ask you, Lord Jesus, to retrieve all the blood and return it to yourself.

Lord Jesus, have there been any instruments used to make curses?

If Yes or unsure:

In the name of Jesus, I remove all instruments used to make curses, and call down the fire of God to destroy them.

In the name of Jesus, I cancel every curse, break their power and call upon the fire of God to destroy them.

I bind all head spirits, in the name of Jesus, principalities and all demons that are associated with this curse upon land/building, and I command them, in the name of Jesus, to go to the feet of Jesus for judgment. I ask you, Lord Jesus, to take back the ground that Satan had.

I ask you, Lord Jesus, to cleanse the land/building with Your blood and the living water of God and restore it to its original and Godly use. I ask you, Lord Jesus, for angels to take up their position over the land/building.

I ask you, Lord Jesus, for angels to take up their position over the land/building.

Prayers to cleanse Cursed Businesses

Invite the owner to pray the following prayer by repeating after you, the leader.

Lord Jesus, I stand in the gap for the one who has sinned and placed a curse upon this business. I confess all sin that has been committed by this business, past and present including former owners. I ask you for your forgiveness. I cover the business with the blood of Christ and the anointing oil of the Holy Spirit.

The leader prays:

Lord Jesus, has there been any blood shed because of sin or in the making of curses?

If yes or unsure:

In the name of Jesus, I cover all sin and curses made with blood with the blood of Jesus. I ask you, Lord Jesus, to retrieve all the blood and return it to yourself.

Lord Jesus, have there been any instruments used to sin or make curses?

If yes or unsure:

In the name of Jesus, I remove all instruments used to sin or make curses, and call down the fire of God to destroy them. In the name of Jesus,

I cancel every curse, break their power and call upon the fire of God to destroy them.

I bind, in the name of Jesus, all head spirits and principalities that are associated with this curse upon this business, and I command them to go to the feet of Jesus for judgment. I ask you, Lord Jesus, to take back the ground that Satan had.

I ask you, Lord Jesus, to cleanse the business with the blood of Jesus, the living water of God and restore it to its original and Godly use.

I ask you, Lord Jesus, for your designated angels (s) to cover and protect the business.

TEACHER'S PRAYERS FOR THE CLASSROOM

The classroom is more about conflict and managing conflict than teaching. With the advent of children coming to school with anxiety, depression and autism challenges, the class room becomes more a battlefield than a learning environment.

The children come with all their struggles and the enemy takes advantage of this to stir up trouble in the classroom.

The following are prayers that I have given to teachers to minimize the conflict and enable teaching to occur. This prayer will need to be prayed each day before the children come into the class or at home before you leave to work.

TEACHER'S PRAYERS FOR THE CLASSROOM

Prayer of protection and binding to begin the day.

Lord Jesus, I thank you for your healing and delivering power. I cover my students and myself with the blood of Jesus. I ask you to station your guardian angels about them and me for this day.

I put on the whole armor of God. On my head, I place the helmet of salvation to protect my mind, upon my heart the breastplate of Christ's righteousness, around my waist the belt of truth, on each of my feet the gospel shoes of peace, on my arm the shield of faith and in the other hand the sword of the Spirit.

I bind, in the name of Jesus, all head spirits, powers and principalities over my students. I bind their power and their control in the name of Jesus. I place them in chains unbreakable and cover them with the blood of Christ and the anointing oil of the Spirit.

In the name of Jesus, I bind the spirits of control, the spirits of deception, the spirits of culture, the spirits of pride, the spirits of rebellion and lawlessness, the spirits of mental illness and autism, the spirits of gossip and criticism and all blocking, distracting spirits.

I bind them in chains unbreakable covered with the oil of the Spirit and the blood of Christ. In the name of Jesus, I blindfold their eyes, stop up their ears, gag their mouths, confound their prayers and command them to stay as one group in a sound proof room, outside my classroom and I command them, in the name of Jesus, to stay there for the whole day and not to interfere with my students or any other students.

I ask you, Lord Jesus, to station your angels about them and guard them until the end of the day.

In the name of Jesus, I take my sword of the Spirit and cut off all power cords from Satan and his army that are feeding my students and I ask Jesus to destroy them by fire.

I invite Jesus to come into the center of this classroom, and take control of it, for you are the teacher. I ask the Holy Spirit to come to lead me and guide me this day and bring conviction to the hearts of my students in everything that I say and do.

I thank you, Lord Jesus for your power and authority that you have given to me. I ask you to help me to use that power and authority in a wise way.

Prayer to cleanse the classroom

In the name of Jesus, I stand in the gap for all sin that has been committed in this classroom by all teachers and students and I ask for your forgiveness, Lord Jesus. I ask that you wash clean this classroom clean of all sin through your blood shed on the cross and your living water.

I renounce any allegiance given to false gods or spirits by other occupants. I renounce any claim on this room by Satan based on the activities of past or present occupants, including me.

In the name of Jesus and the authority that He has given me, I command all evil spirits to leave this place and go to the feet of Jesus for judgment.

I ask you, Lord Jesus, to station your holy warring angels to protect my class and me.

I ask you, Lord Jesus, to station all the angels that you have allocated for my classroom so that I might teach and disciple my students.

Prayers to bring cleansing and freedom from curses

In the name of Jesus, I cover all words, thoughts and actions, prayers, hexes and spells that have become a curse/oath/vow upon me (my class) with the blood of Jesus and the oil of the Spirit.

Lord Jesus, have there been any curses made with blood?

If yes or unsure, pray the next prayer:

In the name of Jesus, I cover all curses made with blood with the blood of Jesus. I ask you, Lord Jesus, to retrieve all the blood and return it to yourself.

Lord Jesus, have there been any instruments used to make curses?

If yes or unsure, pray the next prayer

In the name of Jesus, I remove all instruments used to make curses and I ask Jesus to destroy them by fire.

In the name of Jesus, I negate all curses/oaths/vows and I take the sword of the Spirit and sever them all from me (my class). I call down the fire of God to destroy them all and I collect their ashes and send them to the place that Jesus has appointed.

I ask you, Lord Jesus, to cleanse all the areas where curses have been through the blood of Christ and the living water of God.

I take back the ground that Satan has gained and I fill every place with the love, joy and peace of the Holy Spirit where all curses/oaths/vows have been.

I cover every door, window and opening with the blood of Jesus where all curses/oaths/vows/inner vows have been, and I close them all, never to be opened again.

I bind all head spirits and principalities that are associated with these curses against my class and me. In the name of Jesus, I command them to go to the feet of Jesus for judgment.

I take back the ground that Satan had and restore it to Jesus.

The next chapter is about praying for protection from all that may be used against us by the enemy.

Reverend John Lucas, DMin

10

UNLOCKING THE POWER TO PROTECT ONESELF AND OTHERS

Then the Lord said to Satan, "Have you considered my servant Job? There is no one on earth like him; he is blameless and upright, a man who fears God and shuns evil." "Does Job fear God for nothing?" Satan replied. "Have you not put a hedge around him and his household and everything he has? You have blessed the work of his hands, so that his flocks and herds are spread throughout the land. But now stretch out your hand and strike everything he has, and he will surely curse you to your face. (Job 1:8,9)

If you say, "The Lord is my refuge," and you make the Most High your dwelling, no harm will overtake you and no disaster will come near your tent. For he will command his angels concerning you to guard you in all your ways (Psalm 91:9-11)

When I first started out in the deliverance ministry of Jesus, I knew in my heart that the Evil One would not like it and would do his best to attack me and my family

God has honored my request but it has not been easy. I have had to face many challenges. My wife nearly died of cancer but through mountains of prayer by many, God's presence and medical help she remains alive today. In September 25, 2023, we celebrate 25 years of being cancer free. Praise God!

I had a growth on my voice box that could have been cancer. I contracted shingles during the time my wife was recovering from cancer. But God healed and protected me as He prepared me for a further stage of my ministry.

In 2006, I lost my dream job through a number of circumstances. I felt that my termination was not warranted but others had a different opinion. I was not prepared to give the church my material and so my payout was less than it should have been. But God had another purpose. Walking Free was born and the church later paid up in full what I was owed and then some.

When we ask for God's protection, what do we mean and hope for? Do we look to have a trouble-free life where nothing goes wrong and we sail into life and eternity with no problems?

Certainly, a close look at Jesus and his apostles, Stephen and Paul and the record of church history shows that life as a Christian is not trouble free.

Yet Psalm 91 promises the Lord's protection to all who dwell in the shelter of the Almighty, who take refuge in the Lord, then no harm will befall you. (Psalm 91:9,10)

So how can we appropriate this shelter so that no harm will befall us?

In my ministry, I have sought to understand how this shelter can be put in place not just for me but for everyone. Over the years I have developed a Prayer of Protection that seeks to cover and protect an individual from all that may come against them.

For those who are struggling with many issues, I invite them to pray the prayer when they first get up and before they go to sleep at night. The enemy works 24/7 and does not rest but seeks an opportune time to attack, especially when our defenses are down because we have been lulled into a false sense of security.

Thus, this prayer contains elements of warfare praying because we are not just coming against flesh and blood but powers and principalities. (Ephesians 6:12)

The following is the prayer of protection and I will explain each section of the prayer.

Prayer of protection and binding. (To be prayed out loud)

Lord Jesus, I thank you for Your healing and delivering power. I cover us here by the blood of Jesus. I cover all our family and friends, pets, possessions and property, wherever they are and whatever they are doing by the blood of Jesus.

I ask you to station your guardian angels about them and us during this prayer time. In the name of Jesus, I ask you Jesus to send any angels that You have allocated to surround my home, my family and me.

I put on the whole armor of God. On my head I place the helmet of salvation to protect my mind, upon my heart the breastplate of Christ's righteousness, around my waist the belt of truth, on each of my feet the gospel shoes of peace, on my arm the shield of faith and in the other hand the sword of the Spirit. Lord Jesus, please repair or replace any part of my armor that has been damaged or is now non-existent due to the warfare that I have been knowingly or unknowingly involved in.

I confess all sin committed by me, including fear, anxiety, doubt, unbelief, frustration, anger and lack of trust in Jesus, knowingly or unknowingly. I ask you Jesus to forgive me and wash me clean by Your precious blood and take back the ground that I have given to Satan.

I bind, in the name of Jesus all head spirits, powers and principalities. I bind their power and their control in the name of Jesus. I place them in chains unbreakable and cover them with the blood of Christ and the anointing oil of the Spirit.

In the name of Jesus, I bind and gag all demonic spirits and confound all their prayers; I stop up their ears, blindfold their eyes, shine the light of the Lord on them and shrink them to their proper size.

In particular I bind, in the name of Jesus, in chains unbreakable, the strongmen over me, my family and my house and all their minions including all spirits of control, subversion and deception, lying, negativity, interfering and blocking, culture, infirmity and sickness, confusion, fear, anxiety, lack of trust, doubt and unbelief. (add any that the Lord tells you)

In the name of Jesus, I bind all watcher and listener spirits sent by Satan. I bring the power of the blood of Jesus Christ and the oil of the Holy Spirit against all watcher and listener spirits, bind them in chains unbreakable, erase their memories and I command them to go to the feet of Jesus for judgment.

I call down the fire of God to destroy all looking, listening and scrambling devices that they have left behind and send their ashes to the flames of the pit.

In the name of Jesus, I command all demons to go to the feet of Jesus for judgment. (Repeat this command if you have a sense that they have not all gone)

In the name of Jesus, I cover with the blood of Jesus, all curses, hexes, spells and ungodly prayers against me, my family, my property and possessions. In the name of Jesus, I negate them all, ask Jesus to retrieve any blood that was shed in the making of them and return it to Himself. I pull out all instruments used in the making of these curses, put them in a pile and call down the fire to God to destroy all instruments and curses and send their ashes to the flames of the pit.

In the name of Jesus, I pray against all retribution from Satan because of this prayer and turn it back on him.

Come Kingdom of God into my heart and life. Come Kingdom of Peace into my heart and life. Come Kingdom of Love into my heart and life. Come Kingdom of Joy into my heart and life. Come King Jesus into my heart and life and take over.

Lord Jesus, I surrender all of me including all my fears and doubts, all my unbelief and lack of trust in you and ask you to take control of all my fragment parts and me.

I declare "in that coming day no weapon forged against me will prevail, and I will refute every tongue that accuses me. This is my heritage as a servant of the Lord, and this is the servant's vindication from Me, declares the Lord." (Isaiah 54:17)

Prayer of protection and binding. (To be prayed out loud)

Lord Jesus, I thank you for Your healing and delivering power. I cover us here by the blood of Jesus. I cover all our family and friends, pets, possessions and property, wherever they are and whatever they are doing by the blood of Jesus. In the name of Jesus, I ask you Jesus to send any angels that You have allocated to surround my home, my family and me.

There is spiritual power in praying out loud. It engages the pray-er in the whole prayer and invites the person to pray in faith, believing in what they are praying. The danger with all written prayers is that people tend to read them or skim read them whether to themselves or out loud. But the written prayers give us words to pray especially when we don't know what to pray.

We are to pray in such a way that we are fighting for our wellbeing and we are taking up arms against the enemy. We are embracing the authority we have in Christ and standing in that authority.

We are not to be passive but we are doing our part so that God can do His part!

As this is a warfare prayer, we must use the protection that God has given us to go into battle for our situation. If you or a team are praying for a person, to go into battle against the enemy who has the person in their grips without any spiritual protection is foolish. Many a person has suffered at the hands of demons because they have gone into battle unprotected.

As I have written in chapter Four, pleading the blood of Jesus is a means of being protected. As Satan is a legalist, this prayer is to cover everyone and everything that is connected with you. Thus, we cover everyone and everything that is near and dear to you, including your pets! Nothing is excluded from the attacks of the enemy. As Jesus says *the thief comes only to steal and kill and destroy. (John 10:10)*

As Jesus is the commander of the hosts of angels, we ask for angelic protection for all that is near and dear to us claiming the words of Psalm 91: *For he will command his angels concerning you to guard you in all your ways (Psalm 91:11)*

I put on the whole armor of God. On my head I place the helmet of salvation to protect my mind, upon my heart the breastplate of Christ's righteousness, around my waist the belt of truth, on each of my feet the gospel shoes of peace, on my arm the shield of faith and in the other hand the sword of the Spirit. Lord Jesus, please repair or replace any part of my armor that has been damaged or now non-existent due to the warfare that I have been knowingly or unknowingly been involved in.

Paul, writing to the Ephesian Church, explains that we are not fighting against flesh and blood but powers and principalities. We are entering a spiritual battle. He uses the Roman soldier's armor as a type of spiritual armor to wear.

The helmet is to protect our minds. The Roman helmet had flaps that went over the ears of the soldier. Our helmet needs flaps to cover our ears and block the whispering of demons entering our mind.

The breastplate is to protect our hearts from the hurts of others. The belt of truth is to give us spiritual discernment. The shoes of the Roman soldier had sprigs to enable the soldier to grip the ground, make a stand and not be pushed over. So, in the same way we need sprigs to grip our spiritual ground and make our stand. Paul repeats a number of times that we should stand our ground.

The shield that is as tall as us, is to block the prayers, words and curses from the demons and from people being used by Satan, knowingly or unknowingly to counter or undermine what we are doing.

The sword is the Word of God that can penetrate the darkness and bring down the lies of the enemy. Sometimes you will be given scriptures to pray out loud to counter and penetrate the enemy's stronghold over your situation or the person you are praying for.

As we are involved in warfare over our lives, our armor can be beaten and battle bruised making us vulnerable to attacks from the enemy. Thus, it is helpful and needed to ask God to repair or replace your armor, especially after a period of warfare whether it has been in the natural realm like a struggle in your life or warring in prayer for someone or something.

I confess all sin committed by me, including fear, anxiety, doubt, unbelief, frustration, anger, lack of trust in Jesus, knowingly or unknowingly. I ask you Jesus to forgive me and wash me clean by Your precious blood and take back the ground that I have given to Satan.

Sin is an open door that the enemy walks through. To counter his attack and close the door is to confess the sin(s) that opened the door and gain the cleansing power of Jesus' blood.

Confession of sin, committed knowingly or unknowingly, then washed away by the blood of Jesus keeps the pray-er safe from the attack of the enemy. We need to be honest with God and ourselves about the sin that lies deep within. Naming the sin that you struggle with, bringing it to Jesus, asking for forgiveness and cleansing, keeps our lives clean before the Lord and gives no opportunity to the enemy to attack us.

As the enemy uses fear and anxiety as a way of attack, we must confess our fear and anxiety and ask for cleansing by the blood of Jesus to close the door to the enemy. As the enemy uses doubt and unbelief, we need to give our doubts and unbelief to Jesus, so that the blood of Jesus can cleanse them.

Confessing our sin and cleansing by the blood of Jesus is an essential way to protect us from the attack of the enemy and closes the door to attack.

I bind, in the name of Jesus all head spirits, powers and principalities. I bind their power and their control in the name of Jesus. I place them in chains unbreakable and cover them with the blood of Christ and the anointing oil of the Spirit.

In the name of Jesus, I bind and gag all demonic spirits and confound all their prayers; I stop up their ears, blindfold their eyes, shine the light of the Lord on them and shrink them to their proper size.

We enter now into prayers of binding the powers of darkness that want to come against us.

Firstly, we bind the enemy in the name of Jesus. We use the name of Jesus because there is power and authority in the name of Jesus who defeated the enemy on the Cross. As we have discussed in Chapter Four, there is power in the name of Jesus for every knee has to bow to Jesus (Philippians 2:9-11)

Jesus reminds us that we need to bind the enemy to limit his power (Matthew 12:29). We begin by naming all the head spirits, powers and principalities that are over our lives. As stated in chapter five, there is a hierarchy of demons that come against us from the most powerful to the least powerful.

We place them in chains unbreakable to limit their activity. We have found that this prayer does not last forever as the demons have the ability to unlock the chains but they can't do it straight away. We add the covering of the blood of Jesus and the anointing oil of the Holy Spirit to increase the power to contain them.

As demons have the capacity to speak, including praying against God and His people, we seek to limit all this by specifically gagging their mouths, covering their ears so that they can't hear what is being shared, and stop them seeing by covering their eyes. We also ask for the light of Jesus to expose them for they hide in the darkness and they can't stand being in the Light. Finally, we shrink them down to their proper size as they seek to pretend to be bigger and more powerful than they truly are.

We do all this in the name of Jesus because we have no authority or power other than what Jesus has given us. Using His name indicates that we are acting in and with His power that has been won on the cross.

In particular I bind, in the name of Jesus, in chains unbreakable, the strongmen over me, my family and my house and all their minions including all spirits of control, subversion and deception, lying, negativity, interfering and blocking, culture, infirmity and sickness, confusion, fear, anxiety, lack of trust, doubt and unbelief. (add any that the Lord tells you)

We now become more specific about the identity of the strongmen, the powerful demons that are attacking us.. We again name them not just ourselves but for our home and family. We are marking our territory before the demons and saying that there is a no-go zone. As the demons act in groups and there is a designated power structure in the demonic group, we address the whole army: the leaders and all those that are under their orders.

We now name the areas of attack that the demons use to attack us. Control because life is all about power and control and who has it. Subversion and deception highlight what the demons try and do. Lying because Satan is a liar. Negativity because the demons seek to pull us down by emphasizing that we can't rather than we can. Interfering and blocking highlight another aspect of their methodology.

Culture because in every culture, Satan has penetrated to corrupt what God has made and seek to destroy that culture. In my Australian culture, there is a predilection to betting, gambling and alcohol. (What are the sinful characteristics of your culture?) Infirmity and sickness are another way that Satan attacks God's people to pull them down.

Confusion, doubt, unbelief and lack of trust go back to the Garden of Eden (Genesis 3) where the serpent questions what God has said, twisting the truth to sow confusion, doubt, unbelief and lack of trust in God. The demons continue to use the same strategy and we continue to fall for this attack.

Finally fear with its associated feelings of anxiety is another tactic used to undermine our lives. However, we can add more areas that we are struggling with like low self-esteem, rebellion or specific attacks through drugs or pornography or suicidal thoughts or any other area that is sinful in the sight of God.

In the name of Jesus, I bind all watcher and listener spirits sent by Satan. I bring the power of the blood of Jesus Christ and the oil of the Holy Spirit against all watcher and listener spirits, bind them in chains unbreakable, erase their memories and I command them to go to the feet of Jesus for judgment.

I call down the fire of God to destroy all looking, listening and scrambling devices that they have left behind and send their ashes to the flames of the pit.

As Satan is not omnipresent like God, he relies on a network of demons to listen, record and relay all the information about what we are doing, what we are struggling with and how we may be or not be relying upon Jesus. He seeks the information to know when to attack.

In the name of Jesus, I command all demons to go to the feet of Jesus for judgment. (Repeat this command if you have a sense that they have not all gone)

Finally, we command in the name of Jesus all the demons that are attacking us to go to the feet of Jesus for judgment. We speak in such a way to show the demons that we mean what we are say and pray. Ask Jesus, if they have all gone. If not, repeat the prayer.

There needs to be an authority and a belief in our voice. I liken this voice and its tone as one that gives orders like ordering a dog to sit or stay.

As we pray this prayer, we harness the protection that God can give us.

In the name of Jesus, I cover with the blood of Jesus, all curses, hexes, spells and ungodly prayers against me, my family, my property and possessions. In the name of Jesus, I negate them all, ask Jesus to retrieve any blood that was shed in the making of them and return it to Himself. I pull out all instruments used in the making of these curses, put them in a pile and call down the fire to God to destroy all instruments and curses and send their ashes to the flames of the pit.

Western Christians underestimate the power of words and prayers that can come against them. The sources can be fellow Christians who have issues with you, non-Christians who don't like you, religions whose practice is to curse Christians, and even people involved with the Occult or Witchcraft.

Western Christians underestimate the power of curses coming against them. If you travel overseas, visiting temples of foreign religions and their gods, you are vulnerable for curses being attached to you.

Chapter 8 deals in length with curses.

Reverend John Lucas, DMin

In the name of Jesus, I pray against all retribution from Satan because of this prayer and turn it back on him.

Jesus said that the *enemy comes to steal, kill and destroy* (John 10:10). He seeks to counter what Jesus is doing in a Christian's life, especially if they are effective for the Kingdom. He seeks to bring harm to an individual or family or church or business when they are being effective for Jesus.

All Christians should be effective for Jesus and become a target for the enemy to apply his harm. But praying against that harm will prevent very bad things happening to effective Christians.

Come Kingdom of God into my heart and life. Come Kingdom of Peace into my heart and life. Come Kingdom of Love into my heart and life. Come Kingdom of Joy into my heart and life. Come King Jesus into my heart and life and take over.

The role of this prayer is to re-orientate our life under the Lordship of Jesus and His Kingdom purposes. We invite the King of Kings to re-establish His peace, love and joy into our heart. It is sometimes helpful to repeat this to allow Jesus to come deeper into our heart and life.

For the kingdom of God is not a matter of eating and drinking, but of righteousness, peace and joy in the Holy Spirit, because anyone who serves Christ in this way is pleasing to God and receives human approval. (Romans 14:17,18)

Lord Jesus, I surrender all of me including all my fears and doubts, all my unbelief and lack of trust to you and ask you to take control of all my fragment parts and me.

As Christians, there are vulnerable parts of our lives that the enemy can attack. His weapons are fear and doubt and questioning God's care and provision. Then the enemy challenges our trust and belief in God to care and provide. Thus, we need to recognize these vulnerabilities and surrender these to Jesus so that the enemy does not infiltrate our mind and heart.

For many people, their soul has fragmented because of the trauma and abuse that they have experienced. This has caused fragmentation that can come to the surface and take over at unexpected times. They do this by intensifying the feelings caused by the trauma and abuse that are buried. If this is a problem, Jesus will need to take control or else the fragment parts will be triggered off and take control. (I have explained this in the final chapter 12 re dissociation/fragmentation)

I declare "in that coming day no weapon forged against me will prevail, and I will refute every tongue that accuses me. This is my heritage as a servant of the Lord, and this is the servant's vindication from Me, declares the Lord." (Isaiah 54:17)

This scripture is a declaration of what God will do. This needs to be embraced by the one who prays and believes that God will protect the person. This verse needs to be declared out loud to affirm that the protection and victory belongs to the Lord.

In the next chapter, we now turn to one of the heart-breaking situations that we can face when a loved one turns their back on you and the Lord and walks away.

How can they return to you and the Lord? Only by prayer that is targeted to bring them back to you and the Lord.

Reverend John Lucas, DMin

11

UNLOCKING THE POWER TO BRING BACK REBELS

Jesus continued: There was a man who had two sons. The younger one said to his father, 'Father, give me my share of the estate.' So, he divided his property between them. "Not long after that, the younger son got together all he had, set off for a distant country and there squandered his wealth in wild living. After he had spent everything, there was a severe famine in that whole country, and he began to be in need. So, he went and hired himself out to a citizen of that country, who sent him to his fields to feed pigs. He longed to fill his stomach with the pods that the pigs were eating, but no one gave him anything.

"When he came to his senses, he said, 'How many of my father's hired servants have food to spare, and here I am starving to death! I will set out and go back to my father and say to him: Father, I have sinned against heaven and against you. I am no longer worthy to be called your son; make me like one of your hired servants.' So, he got up and went to his father. "But while he was still a long way off, his father saw him and was filled with compassion for him; he ran to his son, threw his arms around him and kissed him "The son said to him, 'Father, I have sinned against heaven and against you. I am no longer worthy to be called your son.' (Luke 15:11-21)

In my third year at Tusmore Park Uniting Church, a lady came to my office very distraught. Her young daughter had eloped with an older man and they were in a motel somewhere. She did not know what to do.

Just recently I had come cross some information about praying for the lost. I read the material and formulated a pro forma prayer for the lady to pray for her daughter on a daily basis.

A month passed and I received a phone call from the mother. Her daughter had returned home and sat on the bed with her mother and apologized for what she had done. The mother and daughter were reconciled and everything was now happy.

I formulated this prayer in 1999 and in the subsequent 24 years, we have seen many prodigals return home. While it is not foolproof with a 100% success rate, this prayer has proved to be very successful as people prayed for spouses and family members to return home and in many cases find Jesus.

The Prayer is the following:

Reverend John Lucas, DMin

PRAYERS TO COVER REBEL LIVES

Prayer of Agreement (Matthew 18:19)

I cover with the blood of Jesus myself, my family, my possessions, property and pets where ever they are and whatever they are doing. (Exodus 12:7,13)

I put on the whole armor of God. On my head I place the helmet of salvation to protect my mind, upon my heart the breastplate of Christ's righteousness, around my waist the belt of truth, on each of my feet the gospel shoes of peace, on my arm the shield of faith and in the other hand the sword of the Spirit. Lord Jesus, please repair or replace any part of my armor that has been damaged or now non-existent due to the warfare that I have been knowingly or unknowingly been involved in. (Ephesians 6:10-20)

I confess all sin committed by me, including fear, anxiety, doubt, unbelief, frustration, anger, lack of trust in Jesus, knowingly or unknowingly. I ask you Jesus to forgive me and wash my clean by Your precious blood and take back the ground that I have given to Satan. (1 John 1:9)

I ask you, Lord Jesus, to lift the veil over (2 Corinthians 4:4)

I ask that the Holy Spirit will hover over ....

I pray for godly people to be put in their pathway to speak to them.

In the name of Jesus, I cast down anything that would exalt itself against the knowledge of God, specifically pride, rebellion and control.

In the name of Jesus, I pull down all known strongholds including thought patterns, belief systems, opinions on religion, materialism, fear (add anything that God reveals to you)

In the name of Jesus, I bind all head spirits including pride, rebellion, deception and control (add any others that the Lord has shown you) *over ....*

And I command them to be still and silent and not to interfere in any way with (Mark 3:27; Matthew 18:18)

I bind all wicked thoughts and lies that Satan and his army would try to place in the mind of ....

I place the hedge of thorns around .... (Hosea 2:6,7)

I ask the Holy Spirit to bring conviction of guilt with regard to sin, judgement and righteousness to .... (John 16:8-11)

I ask the Holy Spirit to bring conviction that God loves them and that Jesus died on the cross for their sin and sickness. (Isaiah 53:4,5)

I ask the Holy Spirit to speak to _____ and release God's healing and blessings upon _____ (Matthew 16:19)

    Then BLESS the person: *their Body*
                                              their Labor
                                              their Emotional life
                                              their Social life
                                              their Spiritual Life   *(Luke 6:27-31)*

This prayer is a type of warfare prayer to claim back the person from Satan's grasp.

Prayer of Agreement (Matthew 18:19)

"Again, truly I tell you that if two of you on earth agree about anything they ask for, it will be done for them by my Father in heaven.

    The promise of Jesus in this verse is that if two agree about anything, the Heavenly Father will do it. Thus, when praying this prayer, the power of this verse is to pray with another person who joins with you to bring the rebel home.

    It could be another family member or friend or prayer partner but the power of agreement releases the power of God. This other person needs to be a follower of Jesus who has faith and belief.

    Also, this prayer should be prayed together out loud. There is power in the spoken word. But this prayer should not just be read together but prayed together.

    There is a difference in reading something out loud and praying out loud. Praying out loud raises the faith and belief level, uses the authority we have in Christ and brings an earnestness and pleading that is released.

    It is the difference between reading something and meaning what you are reading. You don't have to shout but you actually believe in the words and in the prayer.

    The danger with anything written down is that it can be just parrot read without taking hold of the power of the words that are written.

    It is the same with a worship liturgy. You can just read the words or believe in the words and be drawn into the encounter with God through the Holy Spirit.

I cover with the blood of Jesus myself, my family, my possessions, property and pets where-ever they are and whatever they are doing. (Exodus 12:7,13)

As this is a warfare prayer, we must use the protection that God has given us to go into battle for the person. To go into battle against the enemy who has the person in their grips without any spiritual protection is foolish. Many a person has suffered at the hands of demons because they have gone into battle unprotected.

As I have written in chapter Four, pleading the blood of Jesus is a means of being protected. As Satan is a legalist, this prayer is to cover everyone and everything that is connected with you. Thus, we cover everyone and everything that is near and dear to you, including your pets! Nothing is excluded from the attacks of the enemy. As Jesus says *the thief comes only to steal and kill and destroy. (John 10:10)*

I put on the whole armor of God. On my head I place the helmet of salvation to protect my mind, upon my heart the breastplate of Christ's righteousness, around my waist the belt of truth, on each of my feet the gospel shoes of peace, on my arm the shield of faith and in the other hand the sword of the Spirit. Lord Jesus, please repair or replace any part of my armor that has been damaged or now non-existent due to the warfare that I have been knowingly or unknowingly been involved in. (Ephesians 6:10-20)

Paul, writing to the Ephesian Church, explains that we are not fighting against flesh and blood but powers and principalities. We are entering a spiritual battle. He uses the Roman soldier's armor as a type of spiritual armor to wear.

The helmet is to protect our minds. The Roman helmet had flaps that went over the ears of the soldier. Our helmet needs flaps to cover our ears and block the whispering of demons entering our mind.

The breastplate is to protect our hearts from the hurts of others. The belt of truth is to give us spiritual discernment. The shoes of the Roman soldier had sprigs to enable the soldier to grip the ground, make a stand and not be pushed over. So, in the same way we need sprigs to grip our spiritual ground and make our stand. Paul repeats a number of times that we should stand our ground.

The shield that is as tall as us, is to block the prayers, words and curses from the demons and from people being used by Satan, knowingly or unknowingly to counter or undermine what we are doing.

The sword is the Word of God that can penetrate the darkness and bring down the lies of the enemy.

As we live in a state of warfare, our armor can be damaged or destroyed. On many occasions, in seminars, I have asked the Lord Jesus to show people their armor. Many are surprised to find damage like an axe sticking out of their helmet or part of their armor not there!

I confess all sin committed by me, including fear, anxiety, doubt, unbelief, frustration, anger, lack of trust in Jesus, knowingly or unknowingly. I ask you Jesus to forgive me and wash my clean by Your precious blood and take back the ground that I have given to Satan. (1 John 1:9)

Sin is an open door that the enemy walks through. To counter his attack and close the door is to confess the sin(s) that opened the door and gain the cleansing power of Jesus' blood.

Confession of sin committed knowingly and unknowingly that is then washed away by the blood of Jesus keeps the pray-er safe from the attack of the enemy. We need to be honest with God and ourselves about the sin that lies deep within. Naming the sin that you struggle with, bringing it to Jesus, asking for forgiveness and cleansing, keeps our lives clean before the Lord and gives no opportunity to the enemy.

As the enemy uses fear and anxiety as a way of attack, we confess and receive cleansing by the blood of Jesus to close the door. As the enemy uses doubt and unbelief, we need to give our doubts and unbelief to Jesus so that the blood of Jesus can cleanse them.

Confession of sin and cleansing by the blood of Jesus is an important way to protect us from the attack of the enemy and closes the door to those attacks.

As I have previously indicated, I recommend using the container prayer, as described in Chapter 4, to give to Jesus all that you are struggling with. I also recommend commanding in the name of Jesus all associated demons to go to the feet of Jesus for judgment.

I ask you, Lord Jesus, to lift the veil over .... and burn it by holy fire (2 Corinthians 4:4)

The god of this age has blinded the minds of unbelievers, so that they cannot see the light of the gospel that displays the glory of Christ, who is the image of God. (2 Corinthians 4:4)

Paul warns the Corinthians that the enemy has blinded the minds of unbelievers. He has covered their minds with a spiritual veil that has blinded them so that they cannot see the glory of Christ.

If the enemy has done that, we ask the Lord Jesus, to lift this veil off the person and destroy it so that the person can begin to see and understand the truth of the gospel for themselves.

I ask that the Holy Spirit will hover over ....

We now invite God, the Holy Spirit to connect with the prodigal and hover over their life and begin to work in their life. It is the work of the Holy Spirit to bring conviction of the truth to set the prodigal free in the way that the Holy Spirit chooses.

I pray for godly people to be put in their pathway to speak to them.

So often the prodigals have shut off their family members along with their help and advice. They refuse to listen. So, we ask God to send people in their pathway that the prodigal will listen to. It may be a friend or a stranger, a believer or even an unbeliever!

It does not matter who as long as that person gets through to them. We do not know who God will use but we need the help of another person to speak to the prodigal. We need at least one person whom they will listen to.

In the name of Jesus, I cast down anything that would exalt itself against the knowledge of God, specifically pride, rebellion and control. In the name of Jesus, I pull down all known strongholds including thought patterns, belief systems, opinions on religion, materialism, fear (add anything that God reveals to you)

In the name of Jesus, I bind all head spirits including pride, rebellion, deception and control (add any others that the Lord has shown you) *over* ....

And I command them to be still and silent and not to interfere in any way with (Mark 3:27; Matthew 18:18)

We now enter into the war over the prodigal's life. Taking the authority and power of Jesus, we pray to bring down the strongholds over the person's life as Paul indicated to the Corinthian Church in the verse above.

In the heart, we have the strongholds of pride, rebellion and control that are the core of sin and our flesh. These are the driving force that pushes people away from God and encourages them to do what they want to do.

Pride is just not arrogance but for many it is a focus on themselves and how the world is against them and they don't feel acceptable or good enough. It is a problem of the heart for this is where the hurt enters in.

Rebellion is a rejection of the authority of another and a decision to be their own authority. Rebellion causes them to be stubborn and refuse to believe the truth.

Control, for many, is the desire to be in control and seek to control all the circumstances that have caused them pain. The lie is that the only way to control the pain and our circumstances is to be in control.

For some people, control is all about power and wanting the power. They want to be their own god. This was the reason that Satan was kicked out of heaven.

In the mind of the prodigal, we ask Jesus to bring down the wrong thinking and beliefs about God and themselves. We ask Jesus to bring down all the world's influences upon the person's thinking.

We leave a space for those who are praying to name all the thinking that they are specifically aware of in the prodigal that they are praying for.

In both cases, we pray in the name of Jesus for there is power in the name of Jesus.

In the name of Jesus, I bind all head spirits including pride, rebellion, deception and control (add any others that the Lord has shown you) over ………….And I command them to be still and silent and not to interfere in any way with ………… (Mark 3:27; Matthew 18:18)

I bind all wicked thoughts and lies that Satan and his army would try to place in the mind of ……………. (Matthew 12:29)

We now enter the war over the person by binding specifically the demons that are controlling/influencing the heart, the mind and the behavior of the person.

We name before the Lord the specific areas that the person is now involved with. If it is drugs, we bind the demons of all drugs. If the sin is pornography, then we bind the demons of pornography. Remember that the demons work in teams and so we use the plural. If we just use the single form, then only one demon will be addressed.

In binding them we also command them to be still and silent and not interfere with the person. This needs to be done so that the voice of Jesus can be heard.

We also bind the voice of the demons seeking to spread their lies and thoughts into the mind and life of the prodigal. We cannot underestimate the ways of the enemy as he sows lies and twisted truth in to the mind of the prodigal as he did in the garden of Eden when he raised doubts and lies in the mind of Eve, questioning the goodness of God and that He could not be trusted. (Genesis 3:1-5)

I place the hedge of thorns around ………. (Hosea 2:6,7)

Therefore behold, I will hedge your way with thorns, and wall up her wall, that she shall not find her paths. And she shall follow after her lovers, but she shall not overtake them. She shall seek them, but shall not find them. Then she shall say, I will go and return to my first husband, for then it was better with me than now. (Hosea 2:6, 7)

The Lord commanded Hosea to marry Gomer who would be an adulteress. It was to be a prophetic marriage signifying Israel and her adulteress ways with foreign gods. It was a difficult time for Hosea as Gomer would go back to her old ways.

The Lord then told Hosea that he would place a hedge of thorns around Gomer. This would have the effect of

- Not finding her paths of unrighteousness
- Not find her lovers
- Returning to her husband because she realized there is no place like home.

We pray the hedge of thorns around the prodigal so that they can realize that they are going the wrong way, getting involved with the wrong people and things and realizing that life is better at home.

I ask the Holy Spirit to bring conviction of guilt with regard to sin, judgement and righteousness to ………. (John 16:8-11)

I ask the Holy Spirit to bring conviction that God loves them and that Jesus died on the cross for their sin and sickness. (Isaiah 53:4,5)

I ask the Holy Spirit to speak to …………. And release God's healing and blessings upon ………. (Matthew 16:19)

We have spent time praying against the enemy's hold on the prodigal and blanket the blockages that are there.

We now call upon the Holy Spirit to work to bring conviction.

Firstly, in the area of guilt: not in the form of accusation and condemnation but a realization of being wrong and doing wrong. It is to make the prodigal stand up and think about what they have done and the people they have hurt. It is a healthy guilt that allows the person to seek forgiveness and healing. It is what the prodigal felt in Jesus' parable when he was feeding the pigs.

He longed to fill his stomach with the pods that the pigs were eating, but no one gave him anything. "When he came to his senses, he said, 'How many of my father's hired servants have food to spare, and here I am starving to death! I will set out and go back to my father and say to him: Father, I have sinned against heaven and against you. I am no longer worthy to be called your son; make me like one of your hired servants (Luke 15:16-19)

It is the guilt and conviction that enables a person to come to their senses.

So often we want to rescue the prodigal from doing damage to themself but in our desire to rescue we fail to allow the Holy Spirit to bring the person to their senses. This can be hard for a parent but unless we allow the person to get to the bottom of the pit so that they can come to the top, they will quickly go back to their old ways because they have not come to their senses.

Secondly, we invite the Holy Spirit to give them an encounter with Jesus as Savior and friend. We have two equal goals: bring the prodigal back from the pit and bringing the prodigal into a living relationship with Jesus where they know and experience His salvation and healing.

For God wants all people to be saved not just from their pit but for eternity.

Thirdly, we ask the Holy Spirit to speak to the prodigal and begin the journey back to restoration, healing and God's life and destiny for them.

The Holy Spirit will use any means that He can to speak. Sometimes but not often, it will be an audible voice. But in many cases, He will use people of all persuasions, social media, electronic media, songs, whatever to get His message across to the prodigal.

In the message that is received by the prodigal, the healing and restoration will begin.

Then BLESS the person:	*their Body*
	their Labor
	their Emotional life
	their Social life
	their Spiritual Life (Luke 6:27-31)

We bless the prodigal not only for his/her sake but more importantly for our sake. In the Bible, blessings signify an intimate relationship with the blesser and the blessed.

The purpose of blessing is really for the one who wants the prodigal to return home. But there has been a lot of water gone under the bridge, words said that can't be taken back, hurt felt, pain and sorrow, many a sleepless night.

Over time, if we are not careful, bitterness, resentment and anger can build up and if not dealt with before the prodigal returns, it can push the prodigal away again.

Blessing the prodigal pushes our heart towards them rather than pushing them away. It keeps our heart and mind, attitude and perspective in the proper place ready to receive the prodigal in the same way, as in Luke 15, where the father ran towards the estranged son and received him with open arms and gave him a ring and a party!

So, we bless every aspect of the prodigal's life, not just while he is away but making her/him ready to start the new journey when they return.

Praying the Rebel (Prodigal) Prayer each day until they return gives God the ammunition to speak and to help the prodigal to return.

The challenge is that we live in an instant world wanting instant results. But the return of the prodigal will take time, faith and trust that the Lord is working even if there seems to be no apparent results. In many cases, it gets worse before it gets better.

What I have found is that the person needs to get to rock bottom before they come to their senses. It is not a great place to be and it is the greatest fear of the family. But if the person does not come to their senses, they will not implement the changes needed to never return to that place.

So, continue to pray for the prodigal, using the prodigal prayer. Be faithful and do not give up praying. Then give God the glory and throw a party that the one who was once dead, is now alive; they were lost but now are found.

The final chapter is the prayer model/process that I have developed to bring freedom and healing in every area of a person's life.

Some of the areas have been covered in previous chapters but I now expand the prayers to cover all that has caused captivity and prevented people from total freedom.

Reverend John Lucas, DMin

12

UNLOCKING THE POWER TO SET THE CAPTIVE FREE

The Spirit of the Sovereign Lord is on me, because the Lord has anointed me to proclaim good news to the poor. He has sent me to bind up the broken-hearted, to proclaim freedom for the captives and release from darkness for the prisoners (Isaiah 61:1)

Jesus replied, "Very truly I tell you, everyone who sins is a slave to sin. Now a slave has no permanent place in the family, but a son belongs to it forever. So, if the Son sets you free, you will be free indeed. (John 8:34-36)

In 1996 I moved into a new understanding of healing. Previously I had a deliverance ministry at Peterborough, South Australia, setting people from the captivity of demons. Then I moved to Adelaide, capital of South Australia, and God brought more people to my doorstep with more complex problems caused by trauma, especially by some form of abuse.

These people were severely damaged yet managed to survive in society. These people had intense emotional and mental health issues that took over their lives and in some cases were difficult to handle. They needed Jesus to help them.

I needed to understand how these people became broken and then how to pray so that Jesus could put them back together again. Thus, again, I was on a journey to develop a way of praying to help these people be healed. Not only that, I needed to develop a prayer method that could be used by people other than me.

This I did, by God's grace, and I set up Pools of Healing at my church with a number of teams equipped to bring Jesus' healing to those who were broken.

This continued when the Lord moved me to Toowoomba, Queensland, to Freedom Life Centre. While it only lasted three years, I was brought into contact with people coming out of PTSD, ritual abuse and satanic ritual abuse who needed Jesus' healing.

Jesus, in his first sermon, in Nazareth, took the scroll and opened it up at Isaiah 61, read the first verses and then declared that this scripture was fulfilled in their hearing. (Luke 4:14-21)

In the OT passage, the Hebrew word translated broken hearted means shattered in heart and mind. This shattering of heart and mind is the shattering of the soul that splinters to cope with the trauma that has been experienced.

Reverend John Lucas, DMin

The following explains how people become imprisoned by their sickness and brokenness and how they can be set free. The following is a prayer process (model or method) to set the captives free but like any prayer process and method, they are tools to work with the Holy Spirit who guides the process.

This means that you will need to be flexible and open to the Spirit to lead you into using the prayers that He wants you to use in the order that He determines.

Thus, being familiar with all the tools of prayer and confident in using them will enable the Holy Spirit use your praying so that Jesus can set the person free.

The prayer model begins with the prayer of protection that has been outlined in the prayer tools chapter. **It is essential that the prayer of protection is prayed to cover both the team and the person being prayed for.**

Then we tackle the Generational sin and any captivity through Freemasonry or the Occult practice by former family members. We name out loud the patterns of sickness including mental health and sin especially what has happened to the person e.g. abuse, control, fear etc.

We then go through all the Curses that has come upon the individual, including God's Curses, Curses from others, Self-Curses, Unforgiveness of others and self. We do a general cleanup before we go to the specific issues.

We check out the inner vows that still control the person, unlocking them specifically (as the chapter on Curses indicates and the section below details also). These inner vows are also planted in the "garden" where the bitter roots are and they need to be removed. For example, the inner vow of feeling worthless has a tree(s) of worthlessness in the "garden" that need to be removed.

We then deal with individuals that have hurt the person through forgiveness and the container prayer. We then check to see if there are any negative spiritual cords to that person and if so, we deal with them (as the section below details).

We then ask Jesus to remove the Switch in the brain and remove the negative files that are stored in the person's memory that remind them of all the bad!

We then check the garden where the bitter roots have grown and ask Jesus to remove the vines and trees that are growing there that control the person.

We then check the house where the fragment parts live, asking Jesus to go into each room to find them and heal them. (The process is explained in the section below on Dissociation)

Please note that in the first 90-minute session we will have time to go through the Generational Sin, the Curses, some inner vows and forgiveness of a person that has hurt them that includes the container prayer and maybe the cord to the person and the brain healing.

As this is a deep ministry of Jesus, it is good to take it slow with the person.

As these are prayer tools to tackle specific issues, they can be used on an individual basis as the Lord leads you to specifically help the person and especially if you only have a short time.

For example, a person comes to the front of the church for ministry. The altar call is to forgive a person that has hurt you. You can pray with them by leading them in a prayer of forgiveness, then use the container prayer to download the hurt, and command in the name of Jesus every demon that is connected to the hurt to go to the feet of Jesus for judgment. This should take about ten minutes or less.

Or a person comes to you for prayer with a family issue. In your talking to them, it becomes obvious that there is a family pattern that needs to be dealt with. Thus, you lead them through the Family sin confession prayer, name the issues, cleanse the family line by the blood of Jesus and command all demons to go in the name of Jesus to the feet of Jesus for judgment.

We say to the client that the session would take about 90 minutes and will need 3-5 ministries in deal with everything. Some more complex situations will take longer. The length of time will depend upon the person willing to work with Jesus to deal with their issues. We normally have a two-week gap between ministries so that the person can process what they have experienced and then give Jesus time to prepare the person for the next ministry by raising the next issue. However, we still ask Jesus when the next ministry is to take place.

The following is the total prayer model to bring deep healing to broken lives that a short prayer at the altar cannot do because of the complex issues that the person has. The success of this model is that one person, with authority, faith and knowledge of what to pray, leads the "client" through the prayers and another has the Holy Spirit gifts of word of knowledge, discernment of spirits, and the ability through vision or word to "see" what Jesus is saying and doing.

This is especially true for healing the fragment parts of the soul. It is more than just saying the words but working with Jesus through spiritual sight to heal the parts of the soul. It is deep spiritual surgery of the person's soul.

My hope is that individuals and church ministry teams will use this model of praying to upskill their prayer healing ability and learn how to set people free through the power of Jesus.

CAPTIVE TO FAMILY SIN

You shall not bow down to them or worship them; for I, the Lord your God, am a jealous God, punishing the children for the sin of the parents to the third and fourth generation of those who hate me. (Exodus 20:5)

We are all born into a family and that family has a history of health, good and bad. Many now have an idea of their family history as they are familiar with their parents and grandparents. Some are not so familiar with their family history because they have been adopted or fostered. Some people are step children because one of both parents have separated and/or divorced.

But whatever your situation, patterns of ill health and behavior are passed down the family line through your birth family line and also through your adopted/step/foster family line.

Moses warned the people in Exodus 20:5 of the consequences of idolatry in one generation visiting succeeding generations. Later in Deuteronomy 28, we again are warned of the consequences of disobedience to God and His laws to people.

In the life of David, we see the consequences of his adultery with Bathsheba and the ways he tried to cover it up that affected his children and grandchildren where sexual sin, rape and murder, insurrection and idolatry ending up splitting up the nation into two, Israel and Judah, and the patterns of his sin continuing through successive kingships of Israel and Judah and the people.

When you go to a doctor or psychologist or psychiatrist for the first time, they usually ask for your family history. For they know that your family history may impact your life in exactly the same way as previous generations.

So, what is in your family history that may be affecting you?

- There are patterns of disease that can destroy the body like various cancers, heart disease and diabetes.
- There are patterns of mental illness like depression, anxiety, phobias, suicidal ideations.
- There are patterns of abuse like verbal, mental, physical, sexual and spiritual.
- There are patterns of addictions like gambling, drugs (illegal and prescriptive) alcohol, pornography and various eating disorders.
- There are patterns of broken relationships like divorce, adultery, affairs producing unforgiveness, bitterness and resent, anger and hatred, envy and jealousy.
- There are patterns of abuse, fear, control, manipulation and perfectionism.
- There are patterns of pride, rebellion and control that are the essential components of our sinful nature.
- There are patterns of sickness caused by previous family members participating in ungodly practices like various forms of Witchcraft or Occult practices and Freemasonry. In this last area, Occult and Freemasonry, there are complications that need to be dealt with spiritually by Jesus.

All the patterns need to be recognized and named before Jesus so that which was hidden is now brought out into the light so that Jesus may deal with it.

In the Occult and Freemasonry, they seek to gain power over the individual and succeeding families. Thus, we need to ask Jesus to deal with the power that they seek to gain.

In the Occult, it is their practices of witchcraft that include the use of specific ceremonies, instruments like photographs, hair, feathers and shells etc. from the person, and in some cases sacrifices of animals or humans where blood is shed to gain power. For they know that there is power in the blood of Jesus and they seek to replicate that in some way.

While we may not know exactly what has been done, as we pray simply and specifically, this allows Jesus to deal with and cancel out what they have done.

In the area of Freemasonry, it seeks to gain power by replicating Christian truths to gain power and control over the family line. As our name is written in the Lambs Book of Life, they seek to "write" the family names in their book. As we are married to the Lamb, their ceremonies seek "marriage" through the presentation of rings and certificates.

Chapter 12: Unlocking the Power to Set the Captive Free

Finally, they use ropes, daggers and various Masonic paraphernalia like books and aprons that symbolize ownership and recitation of various vows that have a bad consequence if broken.

Again, while we may not know all the detail of what is there, Jesus does and asking Him what may be present and then asking Him to deal with it, cuts off the negative impact on the family and future family lines.

The way to deal with this pattern of captivity is the individual to stand in the gap to confess all the sin in the family line. Then another person to pray to cut off everything that has a hold on them, dealing with all the possibilities.

It is important to name out loud, every pattern of sickness from the mental health to the emotional health to the physical health.

It is helpful if two people pray to remove the captivity; one to pray the words and one to listen to Jesus to hear his answers and see that he has done what you have prayed and asked Him to do.

Thus, one person is designated the leader to primarily lead the person through the process and the other is the "seer" who sees and hears what Jesus is doing and communicates that to the leader.

Please note that the prayers assume everything. Even though the person may not have children at the moment or may not be able to have children, we pray *any children that they may have* to cover the situation of marrying later a person who has children. Hence those children may be affected by the family sin of the step parent.

Don't be quick to pray, but wait to make sure that Jesus has done what you have asked Him to do.

The following prayer was highlighted in Chapter 4. Prayer is made by two people. One confesses the sin of their family line. The other person prays to allow Jesus to cancel and remove the destructive patterns in the family line.

The person prays:

I stand in the gap, on behalf of my family, and repent of all sin committed by previous generations on my (birth/adoptive/step or foster) mother's side and my (birth/adoptive/step or foster) father's side.

I ask, Lord God, for Your forgiveness through the blood of the Lord Jesus Christ.

In particular I name the patterns of ....
(physical illness like cancer or heart disease),
(mental illness like depression and anxiety, dementia etc.),
(relationship issues like abuse (all forms), abandonment, control etc.)
(financial issues)
(suicide)
(addiction to alcohol, gambling, pornography etc.)
(participation in Freemasonry, alternative religions, New Age and witchcraft/occult groups)

I ask you, Jesus, to cleanse my family line through Your blood, through my (birth/adoptive/step or foster) mother's side and my (birth/adoptive/step or foster) father's side to my children _____ (names of any children) (or any children that I may have) and every succeeding generation.

I ask you, Lord Jesus to take back the ground that Satan has gained through my family line on my (birth/adoptive/step or foster) mother's side and my (birth/adoptive/step or foster) father's side and fill every place with the presence, power, love, joy and peace of the Holy Spirit.

In Jesus' name, Amen.

The leader person prays:

I cover by the blood of Jesus the family line of .... (name) through the (birth/adoptive/step or foster) mother's side and the (birth/adoptive/step or foster) father's side back to the beginning of the generations.

Lord, has there been any blood shed in any of the generational lines?

If yes, pray:

In the name of Jesus, I cover all blood shed, with the blood of Jesus and I ask Jesus to recover all the blood and return it to Himself?

Lord, have there been any instruments used in the generational lines?

If yes, pray:

In the name of Jesus, I cover all instruments used, with the blood of Christ and I ask Jesus to remove them and throw them into His holy fire to be destroyed.

Then pray:

In the name of Jesus, I break the power of all generational sin in every area that Satan has had a hold on the family line of _____ (name) on the (birth/adoptive/step or foster) mother's side and the (birth/adoptive/step or foster) father's side, through the (birth/adoptive/step or foster) children (names of any children) ...., ...or any children that they may have and to every succeeding generation.

In the name of Jesus, I take the sword of the Spirit and I sever all negative generational connections from the (birth /adoptive/step or foster) mother's side and the (birth/adoptive/step or foster) father's side through the (birth/adoptive/step or foster) children (names of any children) ...., ... or any children that they may have and to every succeeding generation.

In the name of Jesus, I command every demon attached to the family line to go to the feet of Jesus for judgment.

I ask you Jesus to take back the ground that Satan has gained in the family line and fill those places with Your presence, power, love and peace.

CAPTIVITY BY WORDS OR CURSES

What are curses?

However, if you do not obey the Lord your God and do not carefully follow all his commands and decrees I am giving you today, all these curses will come on you and overtake you. (Deuteronomy 28:15)

"Again, you have heard that it was said to the people long ago, 'Do not break your oath, but fulfill to the Lord the vows you have made.' But I tell you, do not swear an oath at all: either by heaven, for it is God's throne; or by the earth, for it is his footstool; or by Jerusalem, for it is the city of the Great King. And do not swear by your head, for you cannot make even one hair white or black. All you need to say is simply 'Yes' or 'No'; anything beyond this comes from the evil one. (Matthew 5:33-37)

Curses are words spoken, written or uttered inwardly by yourself and others. We have explored in detail the nature of curses in chapter 8. This is a condensed version to focus on the prayers that need to be made.

Curses can come as a consequence of family members breaking the law of God. We have covered in depth this issue in chapter on curses.

They are called God's curses and are outlined in Deuteronomy 28.

The consequences of breaking God's laws can be reaped by future generations if they are not dealt with by asking for God's forgiveness of what has happened.

Curses can come from other people who speak negatively over our lives in some way. Curses come from Satan's followers who seek to break down Christians, their marriages and their churches.

We bring those curses to Jesus where family members, past and present, have broken the laws of God and now individuals are wearing the consequences of those curses.

The good news is that Jesus has died on the cross for all the curses and consequences of those curses through the breaking of God's law.

We also have to contend against the cursing by others from the past and present. We bring all those curses before God to be destroyed through standing in the gap and confessing those curses, known and unknown.

The following prayers need to be prayed by the individual who wants to cancel out all the curses on their life.

Please note that in some cases, blood has been shed in the making of the curse to gain power over the person. Note, also, that instruments are normally words that are like spears and arrows to the heart but they can be the occultic use of shells, crystals and other objects.

Then another person needs to pray to cancel them and destroy them. This person can use the prayer titled **LEADERS PRAYERS TO BREAK CURSES, VOWS OF SECRECY AND INNER VOWS.**

This prayer can be prayed once the person has prayed the prayers from **To Break Legitimate Curses from God; to Break Illegitimate Curses from Others and Inner Vows.**

BREAKING LEGITIMATE CURSES FROM GOD

The person prays:

Lord Jesus, I stand in the gap for the sin of my (birth/adoptive/step or foster) family members, past and present who have broken the Law of God, through their disobedience, which has become a curse upon my family line.

I repent of this sin, on behalf of my family members, past and present, and I ask you to forgive them.

I bring the power of the blood of Jesus and the oil of the Holy Spirit against every curse of God that has come upon my (birth/adoptive/step or foster) family members and me through their sin and I ask you to remove these curses from me and my present and future generations.

BREAKING ILLEGITIMATE CURSES FROM OTHERS.

The person prays:

I bring the power of the blood of Jesus and the oil of the Holy Spirit against every word, thought, prayer, hex and spell curse that has become a curse against me, including those coming through previous generations and those placed upon me in my life since I was conceived, to this point in time. I ask you Jesus to destroy them by fire.

WHAT ARE VOWS OF SECRECY AND SILENCE?

Again, you have heard that it was said to the people long ago, 'Do not break your oath, but fulfill to the Lord the vows you have made.' But I tell you, do not swear an oath at all: either by heaven, for it is God's throne; or by the earth, for it is his footstool; or by Jerusalem, for it is the city of the Great King. And do not swear by your head, for you cannot make even one hair white or black. All you need to say is simply 'Yes' or 'No'; anything beyond this comes from the evil one. (Matthew 5:33-37)

Vows of secrecy and silence are promises that an individual makes so that they or people that they love are not harmed.

These promises are normally made by people who have been abused in some way. Part of the abuse is the threat to life if they tell anyone.

These vows can put the person in denial that nothing had really happened. These vows trap the person into lies, deceit and secrecy. These vows keep that which is bad, secret and hence Satan has a hold on anything that is hidden.

The process is similar. Two people are needed. One to confess and one to break the power of the vows.

BREAKING VOWS OF SECRECY AND SILENCE

The person prays:

Heavenly Father, in the name of Jesus, I renounce all vows of secrecy and silence, including all threats against me or my family to hurt me or them if I ever reveal what has been done to me in secret. I ask you to release me through the power of your name.

WHAT ARE INNER VOWS?

For as he thinks in his heart, so is he. (Proverbs 23:7) (NKJV)

The heart of inner vows is either adopting what another has said about us that is negative or that we judge the behavior in another person and we make a promise to ourselves not to be like that.

The inner vows' strength is such that it affects the mind, will, emotions, soul and body.

Inner vows mainly fall into five categories:

I am .... stupid, hopeless, not beautiful, worth anything

I shall never.................. marry a man like my father, trust a ...., be a missionary, have children, depend on others, give in, be taken advantage of...

I shall always.... be strong, be in charge, be on my guard, be wealthy, be nice, be submissive, be safe, be an expert on everything....

I must .... **or else** .... get 100% or I am a total failure.

If I ever .... **then I'll** .... make a mistake in public - I will die..., If I get married – I will go crazy,

The problem with such vows is that they remain a permanent part of our psyche and affect our future actions.

Reverend John Lucas, DMin

RENOUNCING INNER VOWS

Lord Jesus, reveal to me an inner vow that I have made.

I renounce the inner vow .... And I announce the truth that ....

(Announcing the truth involves the opposite of the vow plus a bible verse or truth. Repeat the above process until all the inner vows have been revealed for that ministry.)

For example;
Inner Vow – I am dumb, no intelligence etc. ......
Announced truth ...I am created in the image of God and He has given me the mind of Christ
Inner Vow -- I can't .... etc...........
Announced Truth...I can do all things through Christ who strengthens me

Inner Vow I am ugly etc. ....
Announced Truth ...I am a child of God and God says that I am beautiful

Inner Vow I am not worthy ....
Announced Truth I am precious child of God and extremely valuable to Him.

LEADERS PRAYERS TO BREAK CURSES, VOWS OF SECRECY AND INNER VOWS

In the name of Jesus, I bring the power of the blood of Jesus and the oil of the Holy Spirit against all words, thoughts and actions, prayers, hexes and spells that have become a curse/oath/vow/inner vow or bitter root upon .... (name) life both from previous generations and from the time of conception to now.

Lord Jesus, have there been any curses made with blood?

If yes or unsure,

In the name of Jesus, I bring the power of the blood of Jesus against all curses made with blood. I ask you, Lord Jesus, to retrieve all the blood that was shed and return it to yourself.

Lord Jesus, have there been any instruments used to make curses?
If yes or unsure,

In the name of Jesus, I remove all instruments used to make curses and throw them into the pit and call down the fire of God to destroy them

In the name of Jesus, I negate all curses/oaths/vows/inner vows and with the sword of the Spirit, sever them all from ...., and I call down the fire of God to destroy them all and collect their ashes and send them to the place that Jesus has appointed.

In the name of Jesus, I bind all demons attached to the curses with chains unbreakable. I shrink them down to their proper size and I cover them all with the blood of Christ. I command them to go to the feet of Jesus for judgment.

CAPTIVITY BY UNGODLY CONNECTIONS

Is not this the fast that I have chosen: to loose the bonds of wickedness, to undo the bands of the yoke, and to let the oppressed go free, and that you break every yoke? (Isaiah 58:6)

We were praying for a person who was having difficulties. They had been overseas as a tourist and ventured into local religious temples. They had taken off their shoes and walked with the guide through the temple. They were asked to acknowledge the idol that was seated at the front.

Unbeknown to them, an ungodly connection and attachment was created and they were connected to the demon/idol that they acknowledged.

We prayed for them and we had to disconnect them from the demonic presence causing all the problems that they were experiencing back home in Australia.

Ungodly connections produce a stronghold on a person that can affect their physical and emotional health. They are created through sin, either by the person or other people, present or past. Satan uses the connections to gain power over the person to injure their life.

They can come in through the generations. They can come in through the damage to people by organizations and institutions including churches and their pastors. They can come in when a person has visited foreign countries or from places where they have participated in religious activities with groups, sects or cults.

They can be generated by chronic behavior patterns like anger, jealousy, fear, control, bitterness and resentment. They can be connected to strongholds of addictions and mental illness.

They are also connected to people who have abused or wounded another in some way.

We see them, spiritually, as a cord that has its origins in the source of the stronghold that goes into the person controlling the person's heart, mind and will. We see them as wires, hooks and programs inside the person.

In some cases, if the cord has been there for a long time, that is there is a long history of the stronghold, there is a root system attached to the cord that Jesus has to excavate and remove to free the cord to cut and put into the fire.

As the enemy has created this cord, he cunningly puts a security system on the cord, the root system, the wires, hooks and programs. This security system is full of trips, traps and triggers. He places inside the person, hooks, wires and programs to control and influence the person. This security system is active and can cause trouble for the individual. It must be made powerless by Jesus and disconnected before the cord can be cut.

Before we are able to tackle the cord, we need to address the reason it was created. This is to be done by a prayer of confession for participating knowingly or unknowingly in a sinful practice that has caused the cord to be formed. In the case of a cord from a person who has wounded the individual in some way, a prayer of forgiveness will need to be made.

After the prayer of confession, the container prayer needs to be employed to download all the poison of the sin or wounding and then placed at the Cross for Jesus to destroy it. We have described the Container Prayer in chapter 4.

Finally, as this cord is a demonic cord, we need to command all the demons attached to the cord to go to the feet of Jesus for judgment.

You will find that wherever there is a stronghold in a person's life, there will be a demonic cord that needs to be cut!

Thus, the prayer process is simply

Confess the sin or forgive the person

Container for the poison

Cross to destroy the container, full of poison, by taking the Container to the Cross for Jesus to destroy the container and contents.

Cut the Cord

Command the demons to go to the feet of Jesus for judgment.

It is helpful to again pray in a team of two or more where one is the person needing healing and freedom. One needs to be the leader to take their authority and faith to pray for freedom from the enemy. It is very helpful to have a third person who can spiritually "see" what is there and what Jesus is doing. It could be via a picture or being able to hear Jesus explaining what he is doing or at least checking with Jesus to see if every step has been completed.

The following prayers are helpful to deal with any cord created by sin and used by Satan.

CONFESSION PRAYER

Lord Jesus, I confess to you my sin(s) of .... or

Lord Jesus, I confess to you that I have participated in ...._

I ask for your forgiveness through your precious blood and I ask you to wash away my sin(s) and its affect upon every part of my being and relationships. I thank you that you died on the cross for my sin(s), that I am forgiven and have been given a clean slate and I surrender again my life to you, Lord Jesus. Help me not to repeat these sin(s) anymore. In Jesus name Amen.

FORGIVENESS PRAYER

I choose to forgive .... (name of the person, themselves, church, institution) *for all that they said and did* (Invite person to name any specific sins that have ruined their life) *and for all that has not been said and done* (Invite person to name any specific sins that should have been said and done that have ruined their life).

I release my judgment of them to you, Jesus, and I place them and the situation into your hands. Jesus, wash me clean by your blood of all hurt and pain, bitterness and resentment, envy and jealousy, criticism and judgment, frustration, anger and rage. In Jesus name. Amen.

CONTAINER PRAYER

Lord Jesus, I ask for a container for ....

Ask the person to describe what the container looks like.
Has it got a lid? (Lids need to be open)

Lord Jesus, could you please tell .... *who or what this container is for* ....

In the name of Jesus, I bring the power of the blood of Jesus and the oil of the Holy Spirit against all ungodly soul ties that .... *has had with* .... (other people) *I cut them off with the sword of the spirit and put them into the container.*

Once this is indicated,

Lord Jesus, Please download everything that has happened between .... *and* .... (e.g. Thoughts, words, hurts, feelings, traumas issues with other people or groups)

Ask the person if they need another container or a bigger one, especially if they see it overflow.
Ask the person to tell you when the container is full.
Ask Jesus to close and seal the container.

Lord Jesus, please help .... *to take the container to the cross.*
(If too heavy you can ask Angels or Jesus to help the person take it to the cross.)

Is the container at the cross yet? Ask the person. Do they sense or see it there?

Lord Jesus, please destroy it with all its contents.

Once it is destroyed, ask the person how it has been destroyed (e.g. fire, disappeared crushed or exploded)

Lord, please put anything that is left over (like ashes) in the place that you have appointed. I wash the area clean with the blood of Jesus and the living water of God. I close and seal that place with the blood of Jesus. Amen.

LEADERS PRAYER TO BREAK THE POWER CORDS THAT ARE CONNECTED TO THE PERSON

As the leader is praying this prayer, the other team member who "sees in the Spirit" checks that all the cutting and dismantling is actually happening and confirms that to the leader as indicated in the prayer.

I cover by the blood of Jesus and the oil of the Holy Spirit the power of cord from .... (person or a stronghold like fear or anger or depression etc. or organization) to .... (person)

I ask you, Lord Jesus to deal with any blood that was shed and the instruments used.

Lord Jesus, has that been done? (team member confirms this)

Lord Jesus, I ask that you deactivate, dismantle and dispose of all trips, traps, triggers.

Lord Jesus, has that been done? (team member confirms this)

In the name of Jesus, I cut the power cord(s) from .... (i.e. the source) and I cap it. I cut the cord from the .... (the person) and I ask you Jesus to destroy the cord by fire. I ask You, Jesus, to excavate and remove any root system attached to the cord(s) and burn it by fire.

Lord Jesus, have they all been cut, any roots removed and all cords and roots burnt? (If no, seek the Lord about what is the problem. There may be confession or forgiveness issues that are connected. There may be cords hidden underground that need to be exposed and dealt with. They need to be pulled up. Occult cords are usually silver and need a laser cut by Jesus)

I cover the connector, wiring, hooks and programs inside the person with the blood of Jesus.

Lord Jesus, has that been done? (team member confirms this)

Lord Jesus, I ask that you deactivate, dismantle and dispose of all trips, traps, triggers.

Lord Jesus, has that been done? (team member confirms this)

In the name of Jesus, I cover all the blood shed on the wiring, hooks and programs with the blood of Jesus and I ask Jesus to recover all the blood that was shed and return it to Himself?

Lord Jesus, has that been done? (team member confirms this)

In the name of Jesus, I cover all instruments used with the blood of Christ and I ask Jesus to remove them and throw them into His holy fire to be destroyed.

Lord Jesus, has that been done? (team member confirms this)

I ask you, Lord Jesus, to gently remove any pieces of cord, connector plugs, wiring, hooks and any programs that are attached to the person and destroy them by fire.

Lord Jesus, has that been done? (team member confirms this)

I ask you, Lord Jesus, to cleanse the areas where the wiring, hooks and programs have been with your blood, the oil of the Holy Spirit and the living water of God.

I ask you, Lord Jesus, to take back the ground that Satan had gained through all power cords and fill every place with the presence, power, love, joy and peace of the Holy Spirit.

I apply the balm of God to heal and seal any damage that has been caused inside ....

I cover every door, window and opening with the blood of Jesus where the cords have been, I close them shut, never to be opened again.

In the name of Jesus, I bind all powers and principalities with chains unbreakable and cover them with the blood of Christ that gained access through the power cords and I command them to go to the feet of Jesus for judgment. In Jesus name, Amen.

I ask the Holy Spirit to fill every place where Satan has had a hold with Your love, joy and peace.

*Lord Jesus, has all that been done? (*team member confirms this*)*

CAPTIVE BY SIN

For all have sinned and fall short of the glory of God (Romans 3:23)

If we claim to be without sin, we deceive ourselves and the truth is not in us. But if we confess our sins, God is faithful and just to forgive us all our sins and cleanse us from all unrighteousness. (1 John 1:8,9)

Reverend John Lucas, DMin

In 1988 I went to a John Wimber Conference in Melbourne, Australia. On the night before the last session, God gave me a dream that was quite disturbing. This dream then played out the next day. My problem of sin was lust and during that final day, my eyes locked onto a number of young women in the conference. No matter how hard I try to shift my gaze, a power took over and I was looking again.

I went forward for prayer and was delivered.

On the way home, we stopped in the gardens of Ballarat and my companions prayed for me. It was a very long session and during that session God brought to me all the idols that I had in my heart. It was a sobering experience because I thought I was OK!

If I was going to serve the Lord in His healing ministry, I had to be cleansed of all my sins. Not only that, the Lord wanted me to take sin very seriously so that I knew the devastating results that sin could have in my life and in other people's lives.

Paul, in his letters, had to address the sins of the people and churches that he had founded. He called them the sins of the flesh and he was happy to call them out in his letters. Peter, James and John, in their letters, would continue to identify specific sins that had not only enmeshed people but also the life of the church.

It is worth reading the letters to take an inventory of your life and see what sins may lie deep within your heart; what sins you have ignored or been complacent with.

The bible solution to sin is the cross of Jesus where all sin has been placed on the shoulders of Jesus and been paid for by the blood of Jesus that was shed on the cross.

When we focus on the cross and the price that was paid for sin, we can realize how serious God is about sin and its consequences. We can also realize that we need to take seriously sin in our life and deal with it immediately or else it will have catastrophic effects in our life.

The Jesus way of dealing with sin is through confession of sin and asking for cleansing by the blood of Jesus.

We have found the best way to deal with sin is a prayer of confession, followed by the container prayer to empty out all the sin and its consequences in the container and then take it to the cross to be destroyed.

In many cases, the sin has become a stronghold of Satan, especially if the sin has become an addiction. Thus, it has become a stronghold with the cord to that sin that needs to be cut, the wires, hooks and programs need to be removed and everything destroyed by fire. (I have spoken, previously, about the captivity of cords and how to deal with them)

CONFESSION PRAYER

Lord Jesus, I confess to you my sin(s) of .... or
Lord Jesus, I confess to you that I have participated in ....

I ask for your forgiveness through your precious blood and I ask you to wash away my sin(s) and its affect upon every part of my being and relationships. I thank you that you died on the cross for my sin(s), that I am forgiven and been given a clean slate and I surrender again my life to you, Lord Jesus. Help me not to repeat these sin (s) any more. In Jesus name Amen.

CONTAINER PRAYER

Lord Jesus, I ask for a container for...............

Ask the person to describe what the container looks like.
Has it got a lid? (Lids need to be open)

Lord Jesus, could you please tell .... who or what this container is for ....

In the name of Jesus, I bring the power of the blood of Jesus and the oil of the Holy Spirit against all ungodly soul ties that .... has had with .... (other people) I cut them off with the sword of the spirit and put them into the container.

Once this is indicated,

Lord Jesus, please download everything that has happened between ....and .... (e.g. Thoughts, words, hurts, feelings, traumas issues with other people or groups)

Ask the person if they need another container or a bigger one.
Ask the person to tell you when the container is full.
Ask Jesus to close and seal the container.
Lord Jesus, please help............. to take the container to the cross.

(If too heavy you can ask Angels or Jesus to help the person take it to the cross.)
Is the container at the cross yet? (Ask the person if it is there. Do they sense or see it there?)

When it is there, pray:

Lord Jesus, please destroy it and all its contents.

Once it is destroyed
Ask the person how it has been destroyed (e.g. fire, disappeared crushed or exploded)

Lord, please put anything that is left over (like ashes) in the place that you have appointed. I wash the area clean with the blood of Jesus and the living water of God. I close and seal that place with the blood of Jesus. Amen.

LEADERS PRAYER TO BREAK THE POWER CORDS THAT ARE CONNECTED TO THE PERSON

As the leader is praying this prayer, the other team member who "sees in the Spirit" checks that all the cutting and dismantling is actually happening and confirms that to the leader as indicated in the prayer.

I cover by the blood of Jesus and the oil of the Holy Spirit the power of cord from .... (person or a stronghold like fear or anger or depression etc. or organization) *to .... (person)*

I ask you, Lord Jesus to deal with any blood that was shed and the instruments used.

Lord Jesus, has that been done? (team member confirms this)

Lord Jesus, I ask that you deactivate, dismantle and dispose of all trips, traps, triggers.

Lord Jesus, has that been done? (team member confirms this)

In the name of Jesus, I cut the power cord(s) from .... (i.e. the source) and I cap it. I cut the cord from the .... (the person) and I ask you Jesus to destroy the cord by fire. I ask You, Jesus, to excavate and remove any root system attached to the cord(s) and burn it by fire.

Lord Jesus, have they all been cut, any roots removed and all cords and roots burnt? (If no, seek the Lord about what is the problem. There may be confession or forgiveness issues that are connected. There may be cords hidden underground that need to be exposed and dealt with. They need to be pulled up. Occult cords are usually silver and need a laser cut by Jesus)

I cover the connector, wiring, hooks and programs inside the person with the blood of Jesus.

Lord Jesus, has that been done? (team member confirms this)

Lord Jesus, I ask that you deactivate, dismantle and dispose of all trips, traps, triggers.

Lord Jesus, has that been done? (team member confirms this)

In the name of Jesus, I cover all the blood shed on the wiring, hooks and programs with the blood of Jesus and I ask Jesus to recover all the blood that was shed and return it to Himself?

Lord Jesus, has that been done? (team member confirms this)

In the name of Jesus, I cover all instruments used with the blood of Christ and I ask Jesus to remove them and throw them into His holy fire to be destroyed.

Lord Jesus, has that been done? (team member confirms this)

I ask you, Lord Jesus, to gently remove any pieces of cord, connector plugs, wiring, hooks and any programs that are attached to the person and destroy them by fire.

Lord Jesus, has that been done? (team member confirms this)

I ask you, Lord Jesus, to cleanse the areas where the wiring, hooks and programs have been with your blood, the oil of the Holy Spirit and the living water of God.

I ask you, Lord Jesus, to take back the ground that Satan had gained through all power cords and fill every place with the presence, power, love, joy and peace of the Holy Spirit.

I apply the balm of God to heal and seal any damage that has been caused inside ....

I cover every door, window and opening with the blood of Jesus where the cords have been, I close them shut, never to be opened again.

In the name of Jesus, I bind all powers and principalities with chains unbreakable and cover them with the blood of Christ that gained access through the power cords and I command them to go to the feet of Jesus for judgment. In Jesus name, Amen.

I ask the Holy Spirit to fill every place where Satan has had a hold with Your love, joy and peace.

Lord Jesus, has all that been done? (team member confirms this)

CAPTIVE BY PEOPLE, CHURCHES, GROUPS AND ORGANIZATIONS

For if you forgive other people when they sin against you, your heavenly Father will also forgive you. But if you do not forgive others their sins, your Father will not forgive your sins. (Matthew 6:14-15)

We live in a world where abuse has become more prominent. Initially it was verbal abuse. But sexual abuse has now become more common. We now have abuse of power in families, churches, groups and organizations/businesses. Added to that is the toll of abuse through social media where people's persona is attacked.

This abuse wounds the individually deeply. They struggle to forget, let alone forgive the one who has hurt and abused them.

The wounding and hurt puts the individual in a prison that they struggle to get out of. The only way out is through unconditional forgiveness.

Jodi Picoult (2) in her book *The Storyteller* writes:

Forgiving isn't something you do for someone else. It's something you do for yourself. It's saying 'You're not important enough to have a stranglehold on me.' It's saying, 'You don't get to trap me in the past. I am worthy of a future'

When Jesus was asked by Peter (Matthew 18:21-35) how many times do I need to forgive a person, Jesus replied not seven times but seventy times seven that is unlimited.

When Jesus was crucified, he said Father, forgive them, for they do not know what they are doing. (Luke 23:33,34)

In chapter 4, Prayer Tools, I talked about what forgiveness looks like. But we need to add the container to remove all the experience and the pain of abuse

FORGIVENESS

I choose to forgive .... (name of the person, themselves, church, institution) *for all that they said and did* (Invite person to name any specific sins that have ruined their life) *and for all that has not been said and done* (Invite person to name any specific sins that have ruined their life).

I release my judgment of them to you, Jesus, and I place them and the situation into your hands. Jesus, wash me clean by your blood of all hurt and pain, bitterness and resentment, envy and jealousy, criticism and judgment, frustration, anger and rage. In Jesus name. Amen.

CONTAINER PRAYER

See above

LEADERS PRAYER TO BREAK THE POWER CORDS THAT ARE CONNECTED TO THE PERSON

See above

CAPTIVE BY YOUR BRAIN.

Do not conform to the pattern of this world, but be transformed by the renewing of your mind. Then you will be able to test and approve what God's will is—his good, pleasing and perfect will. (Romans 12:2)

The mind or brain is a complex organ that has been created by God to help us think and move. The brain also stores information that we can use at a later date for all sorts of purposes. The brain remembers all that has happened to you and stores it for later use. You may not be aware of some of these events. The brain warns you of potential danger and processes that potential danger.

You take a walk and you encounter a black dog ahead of you. Your brain warns you through its amygdala, the alarm switch. It then goes to your memory files (the hippocampus) to the file that says "black dog". In that file are the memories of your experiences with a black dog or any dog. Those experiences are processed and recalled in your brain so that you can make a quick decision to continue walking towards the black dog or go across the road to avoid the black dog. It happens almost instantaneously!

Your decision will be based on what your brain has revealed to you from past experiences and what feels comfortable for you.

In many cases it is good to remember the past experiences and it is helpful that certain things like photos or food, sounds, smells, similar experiences can trigger good memories and also bad memories.

But in the area of abuse and brokenness the brain remembers all that has been done to you. Most of us would like not to remember the bad that has been done. The problem with this is that the brain can be reactivated or triggered by further or similar events, sounds, smells etc. to remember and further traumatize the individual.

The trigger mechanism is the **amygdala** and the **hippocampus** is the filing system that remembers and recalls the trauma.

We can pray and ask Jesus to remove the switch that is activated by an event or a person and then remove the files in our memory that are connected with the trauma associated with the individual and/or the experience (s).

For example, a man, wearing a certain aftershave, sexually abuses a girl. This abuse can be buried inside the person. But it can later emerge when this girl - now a woman - goes out with a different man who wears the same aftershave as her abuser. This can be very traumatic for the woman as the memory of the abuse "screams" inside her. Her male friend wonders why she is now reacting to him in a very negative way.

For the woman to be set free from this experience, she has to be healed by the prayer process described above; namely, forgiving her abuser, putting all the hurt and pain into a container and giving it to Jesus at the cross, removing the power cord between her abuser and her.

The final release from captivity by this person is to remove the switch that is set off by her abuser and the removal of all the files that include the memory of the abuse and all the sights and sounds connected to the abuse and the abuser.

This is what Jesus needs to do. So, after praying the prayer process described above, we add the following to heal the brain and the memories.

Jesus, will you please go into the brain and remove the switch (amygdala) that is connected to ....then reset or replace it please. Thank you, Lord (Watch and wait and ask Jesus when he has done this. Some pray-ers are able to see this spiritually)

Jesus, will you go into the filing system (hippocampus) and remove all the files connected to..........and burn them by fire. Then fill with new files containing your Word. (Watch and wait and ask Jesus when he has done this. Some pray-ers are able to see this spiritually)

The other aspect of the brain is the **hypothalamus.** It is the watchdog of your endocrine system. It soaks up the real and imagined fear, anxiety and stress in the person. It controls sleep patterns. When it senses stress, it will not rest until the stress issue is resolved.

Resolution of your fear, anxiety and stress through confession, the container prayer, removing the cords and commanding, in the name of Jesus, the demons of stress, fear and anxiety to go to the feet of Jesus for judgment will need to be dealt with. Then asking Jesus to give rest to the hypothalamus so that it is not on constant alert.

In peace I will lie down and sleep, for you alone, Lord, make me dwell in safety. (Psalm 4:8)

CAPTIVE BY YOUR "WEEDS", "VINES" AND "TREES"

See to it that no one falls short of the grace of God and that no bitter root grows up to cause trouble and defile many. (Hebrews 12:15)

A client came to us and told us their experience of growing up. Dad was very critical and judgmental of the client and their performance at school, sport, girlfriends etc. These words of criticism and judgment were planted in the person's heart and had a devastating impact upon the person's life.

So much so, that they became critical and judgmental to their family and friends.

The seed was planted by the father and was nurtured to become a tree in the person's life that "kicked in" when they did not want it to.

The seed became a tree and then a forest. The garden of the person's life became a forest of unwanted trees that controlled the person. They became bitter roots as the writer of Hebrews warns.

What comprises these "*bitter roots?*" They consist of traumatic experiences of pain, distress, disappointment, guilt, etc. That starts *the seed of bitterness growing.* And without a good resolution to that trauma, once afflicted, the bitter memories and how we represent those memories in our minds and bodies can keep a person continually torn up with pain as much as if the person continued to go through that experience. And so, it grows like a poisonous root. And as it does, it makes more and more facets of the person's life toxic and bitter.

Grief, guilt, bitterness, low self-esteem, co-dependency, sexual compulsions, eating disorders, etc., indicate bitter roots at work in people's lives. These pains almost always hark back to some specific event, interaction, or hurt *and* then continue to grow and take on a life of their own by the way we internally represent them ("as a man thinks in his heart...." so he increasingly becomes!).

Yes, a person can love Jesus and live as a devout Christian and still have bitter roots of hurt and ugliness continue to control one's emotions, states, and behaviors. For that very reason, the Hebrew writer wrote that we should "see to it" that we don't miss out on the grace of God due to some poisoning, toxifying bitter root.

These bitter roots, for the most part, work unconsciously within us and so often require therapeutic assistance in uncovering and resolving them.

Bitterness is an unresolved anger response to the unfair use of power.

Fathers do not embitter your children, or they will become discouraged. (Colossians 3:21)

Honor your father and your mother, so that you may live long in the land the Lord your God is giving you. (Exodus 20:12)

The power of bitter roots comes from the unchangeable laws of God, which cause us to reap in kind what we have sown. Bitter root judgements are far more powerful than bitter root expectancies. Judgements operate by God's laws; whereas repeated incidents form patterns of expectancy that operate only on the psychological level. Both judgements and expectancies rob us of the abundant life Jesus came to give us.

First, it's **a response to the unfair use of power**. As such it is often aimed at people in positions of authority (like dads and moms), or others in positions of power (perceived or real). This is very clearly true in this command coming from Colossians 3.

Fathers, in the time that Colossians was written, had absolute power over their families. The very life of their children was in their hands. If a father, for whatever reason choose to use that power in unfair ways the child had no recourse. There was no way a child could get back at a father. There was no higher law that a child could appeal to, and disobedience could cost a child his life. If a child chose to respond in anger, it would have to be repressed or swallowed, because there was no way at getting back at dad.

What was true in Paul's day is still true today. Granted parents don't have such absolute power. But like in Paul's day, parents still use or apply the power they have in unfair ways. They use power unfairly because they are merely human, they are imperfect, they don't see issues as we see them as children, they are not given all the information. Whatever the reason, in the minds of children, a parent's application of power will at times be unfair. I suspect that every parent here has heard at least some of his children give the response: *"That's not fair."*

Just as in Paul's day, children in this day and age respond to what they perceive to be the unfair use of power over them and sometimes they respond in anger, judging their parents for being the imperfect sinful people they are. And if they do not find a way or choose not to resolve their anger, they bury it and go on with life only to find out they have sown a seed that will affect them for years to come. That is called a root of bitterness - something we find referred to in Hebrews 12.

Bitterness shapes our character.

What happens when in response to the unfair use of power we bury our anger? It becomes what the scriptures would call a root of bitterness. The anger buries itself deep in our character. We think that by pushing it far down, we have gotten rid of it, "out of sight and out of mind," but in truth, it is like a seed that we bury. That seed in time springs forth roots and over time it comes to the surface maybe with a whole variety of shoots showing itself in many ways, often shaping our character, shaping who we are for years to come.

Bitterness binds us to reactionary decisions and repeating behavior patterns

Do not judge, or you too will be judged. For in the same way you judge others, you will be judged, and with the measure you use, it will be measured to you. (Matthew 7:1,2)

The simple truth is, when we judge someone and we do not resolve our anger but let it become a bitter root within our lives, what goes around comes around because we have let the very thing that we have judged shape our characters so that we also become worthy of judgment.

There can be bitter roots of rejection, shame, self-hatred, anger and fear to name a few.

Bitterness keeps us from others (and God)

These roots of bitterness cause us to react and interpret wrongly people's comments. It causes us to go down the sin path, hardening our hearts to God and His power.

Bitterness "defiles" others

The fruit of bitter roots is the impact upon others. As you speak out in your anger and frustration, judge them unfairly, misinterpret what they have said, you can curse the other person or estrange yourself from them.

Guard your heart

How do we guard our heart? The word "keep" in the Strong's Lexicon is the Hebrew word *natsar* and is defined as "to protect, maintain, and obey". The instructions from the father to his son in this proverb were:

My son, pay attention to what I say; turn your ear to my words. Do not let them out of your sight, keep them within your heart; for they are life to those who find them and health to one's whole body. Above all else, guard your heart, for everything you do flows from it. (Proverbs 4:20- 23)

We can protect our hearts from the negative things that try to enter through offense by attending to the Word of God, consenting and submitting to its instructions. God told Joshua to meditate on the Word, day and night. We may not be able to keep a Bible in our laps all day long, but we can meditate on the Word all day.

The word "meditate" is the Hebrew word *hagah* and it means to murmur, to ponder, imagine, mutter, speak, study, talk, utter. If we keep the Word of God in the center of our hearts and humbly consent and submit to its instructions, we can keep our hearts free from the things that would try to enter and defile it, making it polluted and unclean. (See Matthew 15:18-20)

What has been planted in your heart? What lies have grown up inside you? What has taken a deep root in your life that is affecting you? These have become a default position in your heart and now you have become that person.

Look at the following and see whether one or some have been planted in your heart and is still affecting you today:

Fear; Anxiety; Anger; Bitterness; Resentment; Criticism; Judgment; Guilt; Shame; Envy; Jealousy; Worthlessness; Rejection; Hopelessness; Inferiority; Pride; Perfectionism; Lust; Hatred; Revenge; Drivenness; Low Self Esteem; Control; Rebellion; Unrealistic Expectations

How is your garden growing? The Lord has given us a spiritual metaphor to use to pray for bitter roots. It is the metaphor of a garden. The garden has the tree of Life (tree of the Holy Spirit) in the center.

In the garden there are flowers that represent the spiritual gifts and ministries that God has planted. They are either growing well or have some problems: not enough water (i.e. Holy Spirit or the Word); weeds or vines that are strangling it (represent cares of the world or problems that are starting to grow); unwanted plants and trees (represent the bitter roots that have been planted and now are growing and destroying the garden).

The ground may be barren (needs to be the cultivated and fertilized by God's Word).

Some gardens need Jesus and the angels to do a backyard blitz!

The object of the prayer is for Jesus to remove all the bitter roots seen as weeds, vines and trees that should not be there.

Reverend John Lucas, DMin

Prayer to cleanse the Bitter Roots.

Lord Jesus, is there any bitter root system over ....'s heart?

If yes, then pray (to be confirmed by another person who sees and hears Jesus well):

Lord Jesus, reveal the nature of the trees and vines that are present.

In the name of Jesus, I ask Jesus to remove all trees and vines of ...., excavate all the roots attached and burn it all with your holy fire.

In the name of Jesus, I command all demons of .... (related to the roots) to go to the feet of Jesus for judgment.

I ask you, Lord Jesus, to cultivate and fertilize where the trees and vines have been. Water it with your Word. Strengthen the Tree of the Holy Spirit (the Tree of Life) in this person's garden/heart. (to be confirmed by another person who sees and hears Jesus well)

CAPTIVE BY YOUR SHATTERED SOUL.

The Spirit of the Sovereign Lord is on me, because the Lord has anointed me to proclaim good news to the poor. He has sent me to bind up the broken-hearted, to proclaim freedom for the captives and release from darkness for the prisoners (Isaiah 61:1)

In the synagogue of Nazareth, Jesus opened the scroll of Isaiah to chapter 61 and read the passage out. He said that this scripture was fulfilled in their hearing.

Jesus came to bind up the broken-hearted. This word comes from two Hebrew words: *shavar* and *lev*.

First, *"shavar"* in Hebrew means: to break, destroy, crush, to be smashed, shatter, to bring to breakthrough, break in pieces, quench. *"Lev"* in Hebrew means: heart, by extension the inner person, the self, the seat of thought and emotion, conscience, courage, mind, understanding, wisdom. In English we think of our heart as just being our emotions. In Hebrew, it is our thoughts, mind, courage, understanding and emotions all rolled into one.

Thus, broken-hearted is being shattered in heart and mind. The heart and mind are seen to be part of our soul from the Greek perspective. This shattering comes when we experience some form of trauma in our life.

Understanding Trauma and Dissociation

James (not his real name) came to me seeking help. He was 40 years of age. It turned out that he was sexually abused as a child. Now as an adult the pain of that abuse and the anger that was buried came to the surface. The anger would be expressed by smashing objects. The experience was so severe that sometimes he would dissociate into another identity that would "run away". It was not unusual for James to "wake up" and find himself miles away from his home, not knowing how he got there.

Susan (not her real name) came to us for help. She was 61 years of age. She grew up with alcoholic parents and was the carer of her siblings. This led to a life of being used and abused. She had two failed marriages where the husbands continued the pattern of abuse. She had four children but now there were issues, personally and with her relationships. A few years back she had a meltdown in church. Now she was suffering with depression, compulsive behaviors, anger and poor eating habits.

Whenever a person is subjected to severe trauma, a fragmenting of the person's soul may occur. It is an automatic coping mechanism for the protection and survival of that person. Depending upon the severity of the trauma, this fragmentation can be either partial or total. The medical term is "dissociation". The extreme outcome of this trauma may be a person with multiple personalities.

Fragmentation/Dissociation is God's defense mechanism where the soul of the person shatters into pieces or parts as the soul can't process the fear and trauma that the body has or is experiencing. The soul separates into parts and some of the parts carry the pain and trauma with their associated feelings of fear, anxiety, anger, shame, guilt, depression, bitterness and resentment and they hide themselves inside the person.

However, they do come to the surface sometime later, triggered off by words, events, pictures, similar experiences, but they come to surface with all their hurt and pain and the associated emotions. It becomes quite difficult for the person to manage and carry on with their lives. The person may, in some situations, act in a regressed (to an earlier age) way rather than as expected in an adult.

We need to see that dissociation or fragmentation of the soul is on a spectrum. We all have the capacity to dissociate to a greater or lesser extent.

We can be listening to a lecture or sermon where the person drones on! We switch off to what is being said and think of something better: the meal that you are looking forward to or the holiday that starts in a few days' time etc. While we are physically there, our mind is elsewhere. We have dissociated to a small extent. When the person has finished, we come back together again with mind and body in sync.

Now in the case of trauma, the person goes through a severe experience that shatters the soul.

The Australian Psychological Society (1) defines trauma as *very frightening or distressing events that may result in psychological harm. This harm is called trauma, and can affect a person's ability to cope or function normally.*

This trauma can be what a person has experienced, witnessed, or was confronted with in an event or events that involved actual or threatened death or serious injury, or a threat to the physical and emotional integrity of self or others. The person's response involved intense fear, helplessness, or horror.

It can be:

Impersonal - accidents, natural disasters

Interpersonal - assault, rape, sexual harassment, stalking, sexual tourism, war, terrorism, slavery, and political violence

Combined impersonal and interpersonal -transportation accidents, human-made disasters

Attachment/developmental

- Occurs in attachment relationships with caregivers
- Insecurity of response and availability
- Non-response of caregiver
- Caregiver as the source of both fear and comfort
- Domestic and child abuse of all types
- Neglect, abandonment, non-protection, sexual and physical assault and violence, verbal assault

Symptoms of Dissociation

- Awareness of strong physical, emotional and mental response when prayer is given in a certain area.
- An awareness of child/teenage/adult feelings which are foreign to the adult
- Adult/surface person reacting to ministry with feelings: This isn't real, is this really me, I feel like a fool, this is embarrassing, where does this come from, laughing, getting up, walking away etc.
- An awareness of other's emotions most of the time.
- Sleep disturbances including nightmares.
- Relationship problems and marriage problems.
- Immaturity of behavior. Inappropriate behavior e.g. silliness.
- Prolonged lack of concentration.
- Depression, misery, sadness, suicidal feelings (endogenous (growing from within) depression as distinct from reactive depression which is tied to circumstances).
- Thoughts of suicide
- Anxiety and panic attacks
- Flashbacks or abreaction (expression and consequent release of a previously repressed emotion) – a sense of reliving previous traumatic events
- Unresolved physical, emotional and spiritual problems that never seem able to be resolved
- Anger problems where anger rises to the surface in a disproportionate way relative to the incident
- Driving to a destination and being able to recall leaving and arriving, but unable to recall some or all details of the journey
- Variation in handwriting styles

- Feeling the need when dressing to go out, to change clothes several times because "this isn't me!"
- Little or no memory of childhood years
- Eating disorders (Anorexia or Bulimia etc.)
- Awareness of inner voices or dialogue (strong controlling thoughts within head)

Dissociative Identity Disorder

Total fragmentation occurs when a separate personality is born with entirely separate will, emotions, and reasoning power. In these alternate personalities, there are stored hurts and traumas of the occasion together with demonic spirits that caused the problem.

There appears to be a continuum commencing with dissociation, moving on to fragmentation, multiple personality and deliberate splitting of the personality through mind control techniques and ritual abuse e.g. Ritual Satanic Abuse.

When counselling people with DID (Dissociative Identity Disorder), it is important to realize that they may mentally leave the real-life counselling session and have to be brought back by specifically speaking to them by name or shaking them gently on the shoulder as you speak When this happens, they are using an automatic coping mechanism to cut them off from the trauma and the memories that are associated.

The original or host personality may have no knowledge of the event or events that caused the splitting. This knowledge is locked away in another personality (known, psychiatrically, as "alters"). Trigger mechanisms can vary from smells, facial appearances, places or things or sounds. This partial memory can surface ten, twenty or thirty years later.

Treatment of such a person is complex and requires love, patience and perseverance from the person undertaking the task. It can be very draining. It involves a degree of experience of praying in this area.

This is at the extreme end of dissociation. These people may be diagnosed as Borderline Personality Disorder or Schizophrenia or some other mental illness.

Sadly, these people are a growing cohort in our society. Some come to our churches seeking the help and healing of Jesus. We must have a strategy in place to help them and maybe pray for them.

We must be careful to encourage these people to continue the medical advice and medication that they are on. Like all prayer ministry, the people must only go off any medication in consultation with their doctor.

IT MUST BE RECOGNISED THAT THIS IS AN AREA FOR THOSE WHOM GOD HAS CALLED AND HAVE EXPERIENCE IN PRAYING FOR PEOPLE.

I include this area to help people know that in some cases, the total healing of a person requires the healing of their shattered soul. In many cases a person can only move forward when their shattered soul is healed.

The following information about how to heal dissociation/ fragmentation of the soul is for those called by Jesus to pray for people in this way. It is a delicate prayer operation that needs a person in the team to "see" the Parts and "see" what Jesus is doing and be able to inform the prayer leader as what is happening.

There needs to be some experience by the team to work with Jesus to bring healing to people in the ways that I have outlined in the previous chapters like physical healing and deliverance of demons from a person.

Healing of Dissociation/ Fragmentation

The dissociative Parts (alters) form a defense system within the person. It is helpful to understand this defense system as a complex layered system that seeks to look after the person when things go haywire or are triggered to the surface when something is said, seen or done that has some similarity to what has happened in the past.

It is helpful to see these as "little ones" or Parts that are being looked after by "Big Protectors" whose job is to guard them. The Lord has shown us that these Parts and Big Protectors reside inside the person in a house with many rooms, including an attic and a basement. Sometimes the rooms have a secret room attached. Sometimes there is an outhouse that is used to house the parts.

These Parts stay the age at which the trauma (splintering of the soul) has taken place. Sometimes there are multiple ages because of successive trauma e.g. sexual abuse over a number of years.

These Parts carry a range of emotions and illnesses like fear, rejection, shame, guilt, grief, sickness, depression to name a few. They can be many ages.

These Parts affect the whole person when they come to the surface. They "take over" the person and magnify the emotion that has been triggered off. They have the capacity to hear you and speak to you through the person. We have the capacity, through the Holy Spirit, to "hear" them talking and speaking.

These Parts are very sensitive and can be hostile. Great care needs to be taken. Sometimes, if they are reluctant to come out, you can ask the person to take authority in the name of Jesus and call them out to meet Jesus.

We have worked in a team of two or three to pray for the healing of these people. One will take the role of ministry leader to lead the process and to pray out loud the various prayers to release the people. One who has the gift of seeing (called a seer) will take the role of listening to Jesus through the Holy Spirit and even seeing what is happening spiritually.

The role of the ministry seer is to look at what Jesus is doing and informing the ministry leader. Using that information, the ministry leader prays out loud for Jesus to heal the Parts, to speak the word of salvation so that the Parts may become Christian like the host person, command the demons to leave the Parts and ask Jesus to remove all imposters and saboteurs (demons that want to upset the healing process).

Chapter 12: Unlocking the Power to Set the Captive Free

We then ask Jesus to wash them clean by giving the female Parts a bubble bath or the male Parts a shower. Then we ask Jesus to give them new armor, new clothes and give everything else that they need to help the person find their destiny. We ask Jesus to send any angels to collect any left behind and once all out and healed, we ask Jesus to dismantle and dispose of the room.

People who are dissociated/ fragmented can be put back together again by the Healing Power of God. But it may take 3-5 ministries to bring total healing of the brokenness. In some cases, it has taken over a year, maybe more, of praying to bring total healing of the broken-ness that has happened.

The process is a step-by-step one, guided by the Holy Spirit. It is **very important** that you do **exactly** what the Spirit directs you to do. It is highly recommended that you **double-check** with each other and with God on every step!

The steps should not be rushed. You may need to agree as a team that God through Jesus has completed each step before you go to the next step.

The steps are as follows.

The Leader prays:

Lord Jesus, is there any fragmentation?

Yes/No or you get a picture that symbolizes brokenness like a shattered mirror or a picture that symbolizes many parts?

Lord Jesus, do we have your permission to pray into this area?

Yes/No. If No, there might be another area that needs to be addressed first and the Holy Spirit will reveal that to you when you ask Him.

I invite all the Parts carrying ………. (An emotion like anger or that have been affected by) ………. (a person or organization), *to come out and listen to what Jesus has to say and receive His healing love.*

Ask the seer to tell you what is happening. Has the door opened? Has Jesus gone in? If the door has not opened, is there a demonic security system on the door that needs to be removed by Jesus.
If there is security system present,

Lord Jesus, please deactivate the security system on the door and then open the door.

Once the door has opened and Jesus has entered,

Lord Jesus, please remove all the imposters and saboteurs to your feet for judgment. Lord Jesus, remove all the strongmen of .... (the primary emotion that the Parts are carrying)

(The enemy has placed demons called saboteurs or imposters to infect and affect the Parts and seek to boycott what Jesus wants to do)

Lord Jesus, please remove all the lies and deception from the Parts.

Lord Jesus, please speak to the Parts, convince them that .... (the person) *wants them back and minister healing to them. Speak the word of salvation to any who may not be Christian and invite them to follow You as Lord and Savior* (some of the Parts may have been splintered off before the person became a Christian).

Parts, hand over everything that you are carrying to Jesus including any weapons.

(These Parts are holding on to all the hurt, pain and associated emotions. Sometimes Jesus shows us that they are carrying backpacks and suitcases of all that has been experience. If these are seen, then name what you see and encourage the Parts to hand it all to Jesus)

Lord Jesus, please remove the second skin of .... (the emotion like fear or anger etc.) *off the Parts.*

(On some occasions the emotion like anger has been around a long time and embedded into the parts like a second skin that has to be removed)
We wait now for a minute while Jesus talks with the Parts and gets them ready for the next stage of healing

Lord Jesus, please send your angels to collect any ones left behind.

(Sometimes, not all the Parts come out and need to be collected. Sometimes, you can lead the person to pray.)

In the name of Jesus, I command all my Parts to come out and meet my friend and Savior Jesus.

(Once all the Parts have all come out, met with Jesus, given their lives to Him, handed all that they are carrying to Jesus and been healed by Him, they are now ready for the next step)

Lord Jesus, are they ready for a bubble bath/shower?

(Wait for permission. If permission is not given, then ask Jesus the reason. It may be there are more wanting to come out. Sometimes the parts are not ready and need more time to be with Jesus for healing.)

If no, then wait. If yes, then pray:

I join all the Parts back to .... (name of person) and grow them to the same age as .... (name of person) is today.

As there may be a number of rooms with Parts, the process is repeated until all the rooms are emptied. This may not happen in the one ministry if the fragmentation is severe. It may take a number of sessions for total healing of all the Parts.

Once all the rooms have been cleared, including the attic and the basement (normally filled with demons to be removed but occasionally there are Parts), we then invite all the Big Protectors to come out. These Big Protectors are Parts of the person designated to look after the house containing all the parts inside the rooms. They normally come out last when all the rooms are cleared.

The leader prays:

I invite the Big Protectors to come out to Jesus. Lord Jesus, please speak to them and thank them for the great job that they have done to protect the Parts. Lord Jesus, please speak your word of salvation and heal them.

When ready, Lord Jesus, please give them a bath/shower.

Lord Jesus, do I have your permission to join the Protectors back to ....?

(Wait for permission. If permission is not given, then ask Jesus the reason. It may be there are more wanting to come out. Sometimes the Parts are not ready and need more time to be with Jesus for healing.)

If no, then wait. If yes, then pray:

I join all the Protectors back to .... (name of person) and grow them to the same age as .... (name of person) is today.

Lord Jesus, is the house emptied and ready to be demolished.

(The house represents the old life that has been damaged and needs to be replaced with a new house representing the new life that Jesus wants to give.)

If yes, then pray:

Lord Jesus, please demolish this house and replace it with a new one.

Some additional notes

- As there may be a number of layers, repeat the above process until all Parts and Protectors are integrated back.
- In some layers both Protectors and their Parts come out together and you will pray one lot of prayers that include the Parts as well.
- In some layers there will be a lot and in some there will be a few
- Sometimes the Protectors will hide some of their Parts to see if this is the real Jesus. We ask Jesus to reveal himself to the Protectors. (There may be a false Jesus in the system. Or it may be fragmentation caused by an occult member pretending to be a Christian) Say to them that Jesus has shown you that there are some hidden away. Thank them for their caution and invite them to go and collect them. Then continue the process.
- Sometimes we ask the angels to look and see if we have missed any!
- In some layers there will be a lot of brokenness or damage, or pain or anger or hurt and you may need to wait until they are ready. Sometimes they come out with weapons (anger/rage) or dressed in different clothes or acting differently. Be creative in your praying by undoing what is described.
- Sometimes the Parts have many questions about what has happened or why it happened or where was Jesus? Do not enter into a discussion but ask Jesus to talk to them!
- In some cases, there are inner vows, bitter roots and forgiveness issues that will need to be addressed before the Parts can come out and be healed.
- In many cases you will need a number of ministries to deal with all the Dissociative Parts.
- For those who have been involved with Ritual Abuse or Satanic Ritual abuse, the house with all the Parts is more complex. It is like a video game where you follow Jesus through the passage ways, mazes and rooms, being aware of what has been placed to hinder the healing process.
- For those who have had occult/Satanic involvement, there will most likely be some form of program or booby trap or bomb on, at or near the door to where these Parts are housed. These must be dealt with FIRST by Jesus. Cover them with the blood of Jesus and ask Jesus to disarm, dismantle and dispose of them to the fire of God to be destroyed.
- The last layer is normally the Big Protectors with their Parts who have held it all together
- There will be differences in the way that a person"sees"them in the Spirit and how it works with the person. There is no ONE-WAY of seeing.
- There will be occasions when Jesus will lead you to pray for these Parts in one area. We prayed for a lady who came forward for prayer at a church at the altar. She admitted to being sexually

abused by her father. As we had only a short time, we led the lady in a prayer for forgiveness, then the container prayer, disconnecting the cord from the father and then praying for the abused Parts to come out and be healed.

Remember to be led by the Holy Spirit and be familiar with the process of healing and the prayers. The above healing method for fragment Parts has worked over many years. As you become proficient with the process, then more flexibility with the Holy Spirit can be employed.

Captive by Satan

When Jesus got out of the boat, a man with an impure spirit came from the tombs to meet him. This man lived in the tombs, and no one could bind him anymore, not even with a chain. For he had often been chained hand and foot, but he tore the chains apart and broke the irons on his feet. No one was strong enough to subdue him. Night and day among the tombs and in the hills, he would cry out and cut himself with stones. When he saw Jesus from a distance, he ran and fell on his knees in front of him. He shouted at the top of his voice, "What do you want with me, Jesus, Son of the Most High God? In God's name don't torture me!" For Jesus had said to him, "Come out of this man, you impure spirit!"

Then Jesus asked him, "What is your name?" "My name is Legion," he replied, "for we are many." And he begged Jesus again and again not to send them out of the area. (Mark 5:2-10)

Over the many years of ministry, we have had to deal with the lives of people and places that have been captive by Satan and his army of demons as Jesus discovered in His ministry.

I remember praying for a female Salvation Army officer where demons of lust and seduction manifested. They took over her features and sought to seduce me as I was praying. We had to deal with the root cause so that these demons could be released from her. She continues to be an active Officer with a fruitful ministry without the problems of lust and seduction that came from her pre-Christian experience.

We have found that where there is a stronghold of thinking, behavior or sin that can't be released through confession and human effort, there are always some demons present. Unless these demons are dealt with, then there is no freedom from the stronghold. Chapter Six gives in detail what you need to know about the Enemy and His ways.

He attacks us in some way to stop us from walking with Jesus in victory. He attacks our bodies and our minds through what has happened to us through our own sinful ways. He attacks our bodies and minds using the sinful ways of others that have affected us. Our inability to deal with this attack through unforgiveness, bitterness and resentment (to name a few) may complicate the damage. As Jesus has warned us in John 10:10; *The enemy comes to steal, kill and destroy.*

While the enemy is not behind every bush, he is behind most bushes. We need to pray deliverance prayers to command the enemy to leave and go to the feet of Jesus for judgment every time that we pray for another or ourselves.

Even if you do not have the gift of discernment of spirits, you can be assured that if a person is struggling with an issue, a demon or two is involved that needs to be dealt with.

Remove the right then Satan has no might. What is the reason for the demonic affliction. Once discovered and dealt with, then the demons have no right to be there. So, command all the demons to go to the feet of Jesus for judgment.

Peter reminds his readers and us,

Be alert and of sober mind. Your enemy the devil prowls around like a roaring lion looking for someone to devour. Resist him, standing firm in the faith, because you know that the family of believers throughout the world is undergoing the same kind of sufferings. And the God of all grace, who called you to his eternal glory in Christ, after you have suffered a little while, will himself restore you and make you strong, firm and steadfast. To him be the power for ever and ever. Amen. (1 Peter 5:8-11)

Setting the Captives Free

For many people, it is not just one thing that has held them in captivity. It is a range of areas that need to be checked out and prayed through as we have indicated above. In most cases where there are strongholds, demons need to be released.

Jesus came to set the captive free. He has given us the authority to heal the sick, cast out demons and resurrect the dead. He has given us the Holy Spirit to enable us to do so.

This book or prayer manual has given you tried and true teaching, and prayers for you to pray effectively, specifically and supernaturally to set all that you love free.

If the Son has set you free, you will be free indeed. (John 8:36)

All you have to do is to UNLOCK THE POWER!

GLOSSARY OF PRAYERS

PRAYING THE BLOOD OF JESUS

We can pray for its protection.
I(We) cover us here by the blood of Jesus. I(We) cover all our family and friends, pets, possessions and property, wherever they are and whatever they are doing by the blood of Jesus for our and their protection

We can pray for its saving power.
I(We) confess all sin committed by me(us), including fear, anxiety, doubt, unbelief, frustration, anger, lack of trust in Jesus, knowingly or unknowingly. I ask you Jesus to forgive me and my parts and wash me (us) clean by Your precious blood and take back the ground that I (We) have given to Satan

We can pray for its healing power.
Lord Jesus, I ask you to place your blood on every cancer cell to destroy the power of cancer that is controlling this person. Lord Jesus, pour your blood through the diseased parts of the body of .... (name of person) so that the body may be healed.

We can pray for its delivering power.
I(We) bind, in the name of Jesus all head spirits, powers and principalities. I(We) bind their power and their control in the name of Jesus. I(We) place them in chains unbreakable and cover them with the blood of Christ and the anointing oil of the Spirit. In the name of Jesus, I(We) bind and gag all demonic spirits and confound all their prayers; I(We) stop up their ears, blindfold their eyes, shine the light of the Lord on them and shrink them to their proper size.

We can pray for the cancelling of curses.
In the name of Jesus, I(We) cover with the blood of Jesus, all curses, hexes, spell and ungodly prayers against us. In the name of Jesus, I(We) negate them all and ask Jesus to retrieve any blood that was shed in the making of them and return it to Himself. I(We) pull out all instruments used in the making of these curses, put them in a pile and call down the fire to God to destroy all instruments and curses and send their ashes to the flames of the pit.

PRAYER OF CONFESSION

Lord Jesus, I confess to you my sin(s) of .... I ask for your forgiveness through your precious blood and I ask you to wash away my sin(s) and its affect upon every part of my being and relationships. I thank you that you died on the cross for my sin(s) and invite you to come into my life and be my Savior and Lord. Help me not to repeat these sin(s) any more. In Jesus name.

If they are a Christian but need help to confess, the following prayer that you memorize is helpful:

Lord Jesus, I confess to you my sin(s) of .... *I ask for your forgiveness through your precious blood and I ask you to wash away my sin(s) and its affect upon every part of my being and relationships. I thank you that you died on the cross for my sin(s), that I am forgiven and been given a clean slate and I surrender again my life to you, Lord Jesus. Help me not to repeat these sin(s) any more. In Jesus name Amen.*

PRAYER OF FORGIVENESS

I choose to forgive .... (name of the person, themselves, church, institution) *for all that they said and did (*Invite person to name any specific sins that have ruined their life*) and for all that has not been said and done (*Invite person to name any specific sins that have ruined their life*).*

I release my judgment of them to you, Jesus, and I place them and the situation into your hands. Jesus, wash me clean by your blood of all my hurt and pain, bitterness and resentment, envy and jealousy, criticism and judgment, frustration, anger and rage. In Jesus name. Amen.

PRAYER OF IDENTIFICATION CONFESSION/REPENTANCE TO CLEANSE THE FAMILY LINE

I stand in the gap, on behalf of my family, and repent of all sin committed by previous generations on my (birth/adoptive/step or foster) mother's side and my (birth/adoptive/step or foster) father's side. I ask, Lord God, for Your forgiveness through the blood of the Lord Jesus Christ.

In particular I name the patterns of _____
(physical illness like cancer or heart disease),
(mental illness like depression and anxiety, dementia etc.),
(relationship issues like abuse (all forms), abandonment, control etc.)
(financial issues)
(suicide)
(addiction to alcohol, gambling, pornography etc.)
(participation in Freemasonry, alternative religions, New Age and witchcraft/occult groups)

I ask you, Lord Jesus, to cleanse my family line through Your blood, through my (birth/adoptive/step or foster) mother's side and my (birth/adoptive/step or foster) father's side to my children _____ (names of any children) *(or any children that I may have) and every succeeding generation.*

I ask you, Lord Jesus, to take back the ground that Satan has gained through my family line on my (birth/adoptive/step or foster) mother's side and my (birth/adoptive/step or foster) father's side and fill every place with the presence, power, love, joy and peace of the Holy Spirit. In Jesus' name, Amen.

PRAYERS TO CANCEL FREEMASONRY IN THE FAMILY LINE

Lord Jesus, is there Freemasonry in the family line?

If you have the sense of Yes, then proceed. (Sometimes you may not have a sense of Yes or No, so assume that there is present)

Lord Jesus, has their name been written in the Freemasonry Book?

If yes, (Sometimes you may not have a sense of Yes or No, so assume that there is present)

Then pray:

Lord Jesus, please remove the family name and all names of the family from the Book and destroy the page(s) on which they have been written

Then wait. Then pray:

Lord Jesus, has it been done?

Wait for His Yes.

Lord Jesus, are there any marriage rings and certificates?

If yes, (Sometimes you may not have a sense of Yes or No, so assume that there is present)

Lord Jesus, please remove all rings and certificates, destroy them by fire and put the ashes into the pit.

Then wait. Then pray:

Lord Jesus, has it been done?

Wait for His Yes.

Lord Jesus, are there any books and Masonic instruments and paraphernalia like ropes, daggers etc.?

If yes, (Sometimes you may not have a sense of Yes or No, so assume that there is present)

Lord Jesus, please remove all books and Masonic instruments and paraphernalia, destroy them by fire and put the ashes into the pit.

Then wait. Then pray:

Lord Jesus, has it been done?

Wait for His Yes.

PRAYER TO CANCEL THE OCCULT/ WITCHCRAFT INFLUENCE IN THE FAMILY LINE

Lord Jesus, is there Occult/Witchcraft in the family line?

If you have the sense of Yes, then proceed. (Sometimes you may not have a sense of Yes or No, so assume that there is present)

Lord Jesus, are there ceremonies still present in the family line?

If yes, (Sometimes you may not have a sense of Yes or No, so assume that there is present)

Then pray:

Lord Jesus, please destroy all ceremonies by fire and put the ashes into the pit!

Then wait. Then pray:

Lord Jesus, has it been done?

Wait for His Yes.

Lord Jesus, are there any instruments still active in the family line?

If yes, (Sometimes you may not have a sense of Yes or No, so assume that there is present)

Lord Jesus, please remove all instruments, destroy them by fire and put the ashes into the pit.

Then wait. Then pray:

Lord Jesus, has it been done? Wait for His Yes.

Lord Jesus, are there any sacrifices still active in the family line?

If yes, (Sometimes you may not have a sense of Yes or No, so assume that there is present)

Lord Jesus, please destroy all sacrifices by fire and put the ashes into the pit.

Then wait. Then pray:

Lord Jesus, has it been done? Wait for His Yes.

CONTAINER PRAYER

Lord Jesus, I ask for a container for..............

Ask the person to describe what the container looks like.
Has it got a lid? (Lids need to be open)

Lord Jesus, could you please tell .... what this container is for.

In the name of Jesus, I bring the power of the blood of Jesus and the oil of the Holy Spirit against all ungodly soul ties that .... has had with................ (other people). I cut them off with the sword of the spirit and put them into the container.

Once this is indicated:

Lord Jesus, please download into the container everything that has happened between .... and .... (e.g. Thoughts, words, hurts, feelings, traumas issues with other people or groups)

Ask the person if they need another container or a bigger one.
Ask the person to tell you when the container is full.
Ask Jesus to close and seal the container.

Lord Jesus, please help............. to take the container to the cross.

(If too heavy you can ask Angels or Jesus to help the person take it to the cross.)

Is the container at the cross yet? Ask the person. Do they sense or see it there?

If it is there, pray:

Lord Jesus, please destroy the container with all its contents.

Once it is destroyed, ask the person how it has been destroyed (e.g. fire, disappeared crushed or exploded)

Lord Jesus, please put anything that is left over (like ashes) in the place that you have appointed. I wash the area clean with the blood of Jesus and the living water of God. I close and seal that place with the blood of Jesus. Amen.

COMMAND PRAYER

In the name of Jesus, I command ....
- *the body to be healed*
- *The headache to leave.........(name of person)*
- *The demons of ....to go to the feet of Jesus*
- *The mountain of .... (e.g. confusion, boss's attitude or hindrances in your life) to be moved into the sea.*

PRAYER OF THE LORD'S NET

In the name of Jesus, I place the net of Christ over all demons attacking and afflicting ...... (person's name) and I send them to the feet of Jesus for judgment.

PRAYER OF BINDING

In the name of Jesus, I bind all head spirits, powers and principalities. I bind their power and their control in the name of Jesus. I place them in chains unbreakable and bring the power of the blood of Jesus and the oil of the Holy Spirit against them and shrink them to their proper size.

In the name of Jesus, I bind all the strongmen of pride, rebellion and control, sickness and infirmity, doubt and unbelief, deception and Antichrist, lying and blocking Spirits.

In the name of Jesus, I bind and gag all demonic spirits and confound all their prayers; I stop up their ears, blindfold their eyes and command them not to interfere with anyone on earth.

In the name of Jesus, I bind all watcher and listener spirits sent by Satan to spy and report back what we are doing. I bring the power of the blood of Jesus and the oil of the Holy Spirit against them, and I bind them in chains unbreakable, erase their memories and I command them to go to the feet of Jesus for judgment.

I call down the fire of God to destroy all listening, scrambling, recording and looking devices and all infrastructure that they have left behind and send their ashes to the flames of the pit.

PRAYERS OF PROTECTION

Lord Jesus, I thank you for Your healing and delivering power. I cover me (us) here by the blood of Jesus. I cover all my (our) family and friends, pets, possessions and property, wherever they are and whatever they are doing by the blood of Jesus. I ask you to station your guardian angels about me (us) and them during this prayer time.

I (We) put on the whole armor of God. On my (our) head I place the helmet of salvation to protect my (our) minds, upon my (our) heart(s) the breastplate of Christ's righteousness, around my (our) waist the belt of truth, on each of my (our) feet the gospel shoes of peace, on my (our) arm the shield of faith and in the other hand the sword of the Spirit. Lord Jesus, please repair or replace any part of my (our) armor that has been damaged or now non-existent due to the warfare that I (We) have been knowingly or unknowingly been involved in.

PRAYER FOR GOD'S ANGELS

Lord Jesus, I ask you to appoint angels on the boundary markers and over my house for protection. I ask you to strengthen them and renew them during times of personal struggle and attacks from the enemy.

PRAYER FOR THE HEDGE OF PROTECTION

Lord Jesus, I ask that you place your hedge of protection around my family, property, friends and business

PRAYER TO COUNTER SUICIDE OR SUIDCIDAL THOUGHTS

The person prays:

I confess to you every thought and word, deed and plan related to suicide. I ask you Jesus to forgive me, wash me clean by your precious blood, take back the ground that Molech and Suicide have taken and fill those places with your Presence, Peace and Power. I repent of all words and deeds, thoughts and plans related to suicide. I choose life and not death. I choose Jesus who is the Way, Truth and Life.

It is very helpful for another person to hear the confession and then pray the following:

Lord Jesus, please wash away every thought, word, deed and plan related to suicide by your precious blood. In the name of Jesus, I command Molech, Apollyon and all their demons of suicide and death to go to the feet of Jesus for judgment. I fill every place with the Presence, Peace and Power of Jesus and close every door that has been used by demons to get in.

PRAYERS TO HEAL THE BODY

Come Holy Spirit upon ....

In the name of Jesus, I command the .... of (person) *to be healed*

In the name of Jesus, I command every demon of sickness and infirmity to go to the feet of Jesus for judgment.

PRAYERS TO CANCEL CURSES

In the name of Jesus, I cover with the blood of Jesus, all curses, hexes, spells, ungodly prayers against me (us).

In the name of Jesus, I negate them all, ask Jesus to retrieve any blood that was shed in the making of them and return it to Himself. I pull out all instruments used in the making of these curses, put them in a pile and call down the fire to God to destroy all instruments.

In the name of Jesus, I negate all curses/oaths/vows/inner vows and with the sword of the Spirit, sever them all from me (us), call down the fire of God to destroy them all and collect their ashes and send them to the place that Jesus has appointed.

In the name of Jesus, I bind every demon attached to the curses and command them to go to the feet of Jesus for judgment.

PRAYERS TO BREAK THE CURSE ON THE WOMB

Lord Jesus, has there been a curse placed upon the womb of............. (name of person) to cause barrenness or miscarriages.

If yes or unsure, pray:

In the name of Jesus, I cover with the blood of Jesus, all curses, hexes, spells and ungodly prayers that have been placed upon the womb of............(name of person)

In the name of Jesus, I negate them all, ask Jesus to retrieve any blood that was shed in the making of them and return it to Himself.

I pull out all instruments used in the making of these curses, put them in a pile and call down the fire to God to destroy all instruments.

In the name of Jesus, I negate all curses/oaths/vows/inner vows and with the sword of the Spirit, sever them all from the womb of ...., call down the fire of God to destroy them all and collect their ashes and send them to the place that Jesus has appointed.

In the name of Jesus, I bind every demon of barrenness, miscarriage and infertility attached to the curses and command them to go to the feet of Jesus for judgment.

In the name of Jesus, I restore the womb of ………(name of person) back to its godly use.

In the name of Jesus, I speak healing, life and fruitfulness into the womb of ……………(name of person). Amen.

PRAYERS TO RENOUNCE INNER VOWS

Lord Jesus, reveal to me an inner vow that I have made.
I renounce the inner vow …………………………And I announce the truth that ………………
(Announcing the truth involves the opposite of the vow plus a bible verse or truth. Repeat the above process until all the inner vows have been revealed for that ministry.
Vow – I am dumb, no intelligence etc. ……I am created in the image of God and He has given me the mind of Christ

- I can't …..... etc……….. I can do all things through Christ who strengthens me
- I am ugly etc. ……….I am a child of God and he says that I am beautiful
- I am not worthy ------- I am a child of God and Jesus makes me worthy.

PRAYERS TO CLEANSE THE LAND

This prayer has been made in the Australian context. If you are from another country, you can substitute first people or name of the tribe for aboriginal to identify the original people on the land.

Prayers for Protection need to be prayed before you start praying for the land, house or buildings.

The owner of the land needs to pray the prayer. You will need to seek Jesus to know who has sinned. It may be all: aboriginal to aboriginal; aboriginal to white; white to aboriginal; white to white.

Lord Jesus, I stand in the gap for the sin that has been committed on this land by aboriginal to aboriginal (aboriginal to white) (white to aboriginal) (white to white). I cover this sin by the blood of Jesus and the oil of the Holy Spirit and I ask you to forgive all sin that was committed on this land.

Lord, has there been any sin committed by aboriginal to aboriginal (aboriginal to white) (white to aboriginal) (white to white) on this land?

If yes, pray:

I ask you, Lord Jesus, to forgive the sin and cleanse this land through your blood and the living water of God and I call down the fire of God to purify this land.

Lord Jesus, has there been any blood shed on this land through that sin?

If yes or unsure, pray the next prayer:

In the name of Jesus, I cover all blood shed on this land with the blood of Jesus. I ask you, Lord Jesus, to retrieve all the blood that was shed and return it to yourself.

Lord Jesus, have there been any objects (earthly or spiritual) placed in the ground to contaminate the ground?

If yes or unsure, pray the next prayer:

In your name, Lord Jesus, I cover with your blood all earthly and spiritual objects that have been planted in this land, cancel their power and ask Jesus to remove them from the land and dispose of them.

Lord Jesus, are there any earthbound spirits on the land?

If yes or unsure, pray the next prayer:

Lord Jesus, send your angels and bring all earthbound spirits to you. Then speak to them, explain who you are and share the gospel with them.

If there are then wait until Jesus says that they are ready to go. When they are ready, pray:

Lord Jesus, command your angels to take the earthbound spirits to the place that you have designated.

I bind all head spirits and principalities that are associated with all sin on the land, and in the name of Jesus, I command them to go to the place that Jesus has appointed without hurting anyone or harming anyone.

I take back the ground that Satan had and restore it to Jesus and I ask you Jesus to restore this land to its original Godly use.

I ask you, Lord Jesus, for angels to take up their position around the corners of the land.

Houses/buildings

Invite the owner to pray the following prayer by repeating after you, the leader.

Lord Jesus, I stand in the gap for the sin that has been committed on/in this house/building by previous owners and occupants. I cover this sin by the blood of Jesus and the oil of the Holy Spirit and I ask you to forgive all sin that was committed on/in this house/building.

The leader prays:

Lord Jesus, has there been any sin committed by aboriginal to aboriginal (aboriginal to white) (white to aboriginal) (white to white) on/in this house/building?

If yes or unsure, pray the next prayer:

I ask you, Lord Jesus, to forgive the sin and cleanse this house/building through Your blood and the living water of God.

Has there been any blood shed on/in this house/building through that sin?

If yes or unsure, pray the next prayer:

In the name of Jesus, I cover all blood shed on/in this house/building with the blood of Jesus. I ask you, Lord Jesus, to retrieve all the blood that was shed and return it to yourself.

Lord Jesus, have there been any objects (earthly or spiritual) placed on/in the house/building to contaminate the house/building?

If yes or unsure, pray the next prayer:

In your name, Lord Jesus, I cover with your blood all earthly and spiritual objects that have been planted on/in this house/building, cancel their power and I ask Jesus to remove them and dispose them.

Lord Jesus, are there any earthbound spirits in the house/ building?

If yes or unsure, pray the next prayer:

Lord Jesus, send your angels and bring all earthbound spirits to you. Then speak to them, explain who you are and share the gospel with them.

If there are then wait until Jesus says that they are ready to go. When they are ready, pray:

Lord Jesus, command your angels to take the earthbound spirits to the place that you have designated.

I ask you, Lord Jesus, to cleanse this house/building through your blood and the living water of God and I call down the fire of God to purify this house/building.

I bind, in the name of Jesus, all head spirits, principalities and demons that are associated with all sin on the house/building, and I command them to go to the place that Jesus has appointed without hurting anyone or harming anyone.

I take back the ground that Satan had and restore it to Jesus and I ask you Jesus to restore this house/building to its original Godly use.

I ask you, Lord Jesus, for angels to take up their position over the house/building.

Cursed Buildings and Cursed Land

Invite the owner to pray the following prayer by repeating after you, the leader.

Lord Jesus, I stand in the gap for the one who has sinned and placed a curse upon this land/building. I ask you for your forgiveness. I cover the building with the blood of Christ and the anointing oil of the Holy Spirit.

The leader prays:

Lord Jesus, has there been any blood used in the making of curses?

If yes or unsure:

In the name of Jesus, I cover all curses made with blood, with the blood of Jesus. I ask you, Lord Jesus, to retrieve all the blood and return it to yourself.

Lord Jesus, have there been any instruments used to make curses?

If yes or unsure:

In the name of Jesus, I remove all instruments used to make curses, and call down the fire of God to destroy them.

In the name of Jesus, I cancel every curse, break their power and call upon the fire of God to destroy them.

I bind, in the name of Jesus, all head spirits and principalities that are associated with this curse upon land/building, and I command them to go to the feet of Jesus for judgment. I ask you, Lord Jesus, to take back the ground that Satan had.

I ask you, Lord Jesus, to cleanse the land/building with the blood of Jesus, the living water of God and restore it to its original and Godly use.

I ask you, Lord Jesus, for angels to take up their position over the land/building.

Prayers to cleanse Cursed Businesses

Pray the Prayer of protection and binding to begin the prayer for the business

Invite the owner to pray the following prayer by repeating after you, the leader.

Lord Jesus, I stand in the gap for the one who has sinned and placed a curse upon this business. I confess all sin that has been committed by this business, past and present including former owners. I ask you for your forgiveness. I cover the business with the blood of Christ and the anointing oil of the Holy Spirit.

The leader prays:

Lord Jesus, has there been any blood shed because of sin or in the making of curses?

If yes or unsure:

In the name of Jesus, I cover all sin and curses made with blood with the blood of Jesus. I ask you, Lord Jesus, to retrieve all the blood and return it to yourself.

Lord Jesus, have there been any instruments used to sin or make curses?

If yes or unsure:

In the name of Jesus, I remove all instruments used to sin or make curses, and call down the fire of God to destroy them.

In the name of Jesus, I cancel every curse, break their power and call upon the fire of God to destroy them.

I bind, in the name of Jesus, all head spirits and principalities that are associated with this curse upon this business, and I command them to go to the feet of Jesus for judgment. I ask you, Lord Jesus, to take back the ground that Satan had.

I ask you, Lord Jesus, to cleanse the business with the blood of Jesus, the living water of God and restore it to its original and Godly use.

I ask you, Lord Jesus, for your designated angels(s) to cover and protect the business.

TEACHER'S PRAYERS FOR THE CLASSROOM

Prayer of protection and binding to begin the day.

Lord Jesus, I thank you for your healing and delivering power. I cover my students and myself with the blood of Jesus. I ask you to station your guardian angels about them and me for this day.

I put on the whole armor of God. On my head, I place the helmet of salvation to protect my mind, upon my heart the breastplate of Christ's righteousness, around my waist the belt of truth, on each of my feet the gospel shoes of peace, on my arm the shield of faith and in the other hand the sword of the Spirit. Lord Jesus, please repair or replace any part of my armor that has been damaged or now non-existent due to the warfare that I have been knowingly or unknowingly been involved in.

I bind, in the name of Jesus, all head spirits, powers and principalities over my students. I bind their power and their control in the name of Jesus. I place them in chains unbreakable and cover them with the blood of Christ and the anointing oil of the Spirit.

In the name of Jesus, I bind the spirits of control, the spirits of deception, the spirits of culture, the spirits of pride, the spirits of rebellion and lawlessness, the spirits of mental illness and autism, the spirits of gossip and criticism and all blocking, distracting spirits.

I bind them in chains unbreakable covered with the oil of the Spirit and the blood of Christ. In the name of Jesus, I blindfold their eyes, stop up their ears, gag their mouths, confound their prayers and command them to stay as one group in a soundproof room, outside my classroom and I command them, in the name of Jesus, to stay there for the whole day and not to interfere with my students or any other students.

I ask you, Lord Jesus, to station your angels about them and guard them until the end of the day.

In the name of Jesus, I take my sword of the Spirit and cut off all power cords from Satan and his army that are feeding my students and I ask Jesus to destroy them by fire.

Glossary of Prayers

I invite Jesus to come into the center of this classroom, and take control of it, for you are the teacher.

I ask the Holy Spirit to come to lead me and guide me this day and bring conviction to the hearts of my students in everything that I say and do.

I thank you, Lord Jesus for your power and authority that you have given to me. I ask you to help me to use that power and authority in a wise way.

Prayer to cleanse the classroom

In the name of Jesus, I stand in the gap for all sin that has been committed in this classroom by all teachers and students and I ask for your forgiveness, Lord Jesus. I ask that you wash clean this classroom clean of all sin through your blood shed on the cross and your living water.

I renounce any allegiance given to false gods or spirits by other occupants. I renounce any claim on this room by Satan based on the activities of past or present occupants, including me.

In the name of Jesus and the authority that He has given me, I command all demons to leave this place and go to the feet of Jesus for judgment.

I ask you, Lord Jesus, to station your holy warring angels to protect my class and me.

I ask you, Lord Jesus, to station all the angels that you have allocated for my classroom so that I might teach and disciple my students.

Prayers to bring cleansing and freedom from curses

In the name of Jesus, I cover all words, thoughts and actions, prayers, hexes and spells that have become a curse/oath/vow upon me (my class) with the blood of Jesus and the oil of the Spirit.

Lord Jesus, have there been any curses made with blood? (If yes or unsure)

In the name of Jesus, I cover all curses made with blood with the blood of Jesus. I ask you, Lord Jesus, to retrieve all the blood and return it to yourself.

Lord Jesus, have there been any instruments used to make curses? (If yes or unsure)

In the name of Jesus, I remove all instruments used to make curses and I ask Jesus to destroy them by fire.

In the name of Jesus, I negate all curses/oaths/vows and I take the sword of the Spirit and sever them all from me (my class). I call down the fire of God to destroy them all and I collect their ashes and send them to the place that Jesus has appointed.

I ask you, Lord Jesus to cleanse all the areas where curses have been through the blood of Christ and the living water of God.

I take back the ground that Satan has gained and I fill every place with the love, joy and peace of the Holy Spirit where all curses/oaths/vows have been.
I cover every door, window and opening with the blood of Jesus where all curses/oaths/vows/inner vows have been, and I close them all, never to be opened again.

I bind all head spirits and principalities that are associated with these curses against my class and me. In the name of Jesus, I command them to go to the feet of Jesus for judgment.

I take back the ground that Satan had and restore it to the Lord Jesus.

PRAYER OF PROTECTION AND BINDING. *(To be prayed out loud)*

Lord Jesus, I thank you for Your healing and delivering power. I cover us here by the blood of Jesus. I cover all our family and friends, pets, possessions and property, wherever they are and whatever they are doing by the blood of Jesus.

I ask you to station your guardian angels about them and us during this prayer time. In the name of Jesus, I ask you, Lord Jesus, to send any angels that You have allocated to surround my home, my family and me.

I put on the whole armor of God. On my head, I place the helmet of salvation to protect my mind, upon my heart the breastplate of Christ's righteousness, around my waist the belt of truth, on each of my feet the gospel shoes of peace, on my arm the shield of faith and in the other hand the sword of the Spirit. Lord Jesus, please repair or replace any part of my armor that has been damaged or is now non-existent due to the warfare that I have been knowingly or unknowingly involved in.

I confess all sin committed by me, including fear, anxiety, doubt, unbelief, frustration, anger and lack of trust in Jesus, knowingly or unknowingly. I ask you, Lord Jesus, to forgive me and wash me clean by Your precious blood and take back the ground that I have given to Satan.

I bind, in the name of Jesus all head spirits, powers and principalities. I bind their power and their control in the name of Jesus. I place them in chains unbreakable and cover them with the blood of Christ and the anointing oil of the Spirit.

Glossary of Prayers

In the name of Jesus, I bind and gag all demonic spirits and confound all their prayers; I stop up their ears, blindfold their eyes, shine the light of the Lord on them and shrink them to their proper size.

In particular I bind, in the name of Jesus, in chains unbreakable, the strongmen over me, my family and my house and all their minions including all spirits of control, subversion and deception, lying, negativity, interfering and blocking, culture, infirmity and sickness, confusion, fear, anxiety, lack of trust, doubt and unbelief. (add any that the Lord Jesus tells you)

In the name of Jesus, I bind all watcher and listener spirits sent by Satan. I bring the power of the blood of Jesus Christ and the oil of the Holy Spirit against all watcher and listener spirits, bind them in chains unbreakable, erase their memories and I command them to go to the feet of Jesus for judgment.

I call down the fire of God to destroy all looking, listening and scrambling devices that they have left behind and send their ashes to the flames of the pit.

*In the name of Jesus, I command all demons to go to the feet of Jesus for judgment. (*Repeat this command if you have a sense that they have not all gone*)*

In the name of Jesus, I cover with the blood of Jesus, all curses, hexes, spells and ungodly prayers against me, my family, my property and possessions. In the name of Jesus, I negate them all, ask Jesus to retrieve any blood that was shed in the making of them and return it to Himself. I pull out all instruments used in the making of these curses, put them in a pile and call down the fire to God to destroy all instruments and curses and send their ashes to the flames of the pit.

In the name of Jesus, I pray against all retribution from Satan because of this prayer and turn it back on him.

In the name of Jesus, I ask you, Lord Jesus, to send any angels that You have allocated to surround my home, my family and me.

Come Kingdom of God into my heart and life. Come Kingdom of Peace into my heart and life. Come Kingdom of Love into my heart and life. Come Kingdom of Joy into my heart and life. Come King Jesus into my heart and life and take over.

Lord Jesus, I surrender all of me including all my fears and doubts, all my unbelief and lack of trust in you and ask you to take control of all my fragment parts and me.

I declare "in that coming day no weapon forged against me will prevail, and I will refute every tongue that accuses me. This is my heritage as a servant of the Lord, and this is the servant's vindication from Me, declares the Lord." (Isaiah 54:17)

Reverend John Lucas, DMin

PRAYERS TO BRING BACK REBELS/PRODIGALS

Prayer of Agreement (Matthew 18:19)

I cover with the blood of Jesus myself, my family, my possessions, property and pets wherever they are and whatever they are doing. (Exodus 12:7,13)

I put on the whole armor of God. On my head I place the helmet of salvation to protect my mind, upon my heart the breastplate of Christ's righteousness, around my waist the belt of truth, on each of my feet the gospel shoes of peace, on my arm the shield of faith and in the other hand the sword of the Spirit. Lord Jesus, please repair or replace any part of my armor that has been damaged or now non-existent due to the warfare that I have been knowingly or unknowingly been involved in. (Ephesians 6:10-20)

I confess all sin committed by me, including fear, anxiety, doubt, unbelief, frustration, anger, lack of trust in Jesus, knowingly or unknowingly. I ask you, Lord Jesus, to forgive me and wash me clean by Your precious blood and take back the ground that I have given to Satan. (1 John 1:9)

I ask you, Lord Jesus, to lift the veil over .... (2 Corinthians 4:4)

I ask that the Holy Spirit will hover over ....

I pray for godly people to be put in their pathway to speak to them.

In the name of Jesus, I cast down anything that would exalt itself against the knowledge of God, specifically pride and rebellion.

In the name of Jesus, I pull down all known strongholds including thought patterns, belief systems, opinion on religion, materialism, fear (add anything that God reveals to you)

In the name of Jesus, I bind all head spirits including pride, rebellion, deception and control (add any others that the Lord has shown you) over ....And I command them to be still and silent and not to interfere in any way with .... (Mark 3:27; Matthew 18:18)

I bind all wicked thoughts and lies that Satan and his army would try to place in the mind of ....

I place the hedge of thorns around .... (Hosea 2:6,7)

I ask the Holy Spirit to bring conviction of guilt with regard to sin, judgement and righteousness to .... (John 16:8-11)

I ask the Holy Spirit to bring conviction that God loves them and that Jesus died on the cross for their sin and sickness. (Isaiah 53:4,5)

*I ask the Holy Spirit to speak to ....And release God's healing and blessings upon ....
(Matthew 16:19)*

    Then BLESS the person: their Body
their Labor
their Emotional life
their Social life
their Spiritual Life (Luke 6:27-31)

PRAYERS TO SET THE CAPTIVES FREE

The following prayers are the Prayer Method to cover all the areas that need to be covered to free the person totally by the power of Jesus.

Prayer of protection and binding to begin each ministry session

The leader prays:

Lord Jesus, I thank you for Your healing and delivering power. I cover us all here by the blood of Jesus. I cover all our family and friends, pets, possessions and property, wherever they are and whatever they are doing by the blood of Jesus. I ask you to station your guardian angels about them and us during this ministry and prayer time.

We put on the whole armor of God. On our head, we place the helmet of salvation to protect our mind, upon our heart the breastplate of Christ's righteousness, around our waist the belt of truth, on each of our feet the gospel shoes of peace, on our arm the shield of faith and in the other hand the sword of the Spirit. Lord Jesus, please repair or replace any part of our armor that has been damaged or now non-existent due to the warfare that we have been knowingly or unknowingly been involved in.

In the name of Jesus, I bind all head spirits, powers and principalities. I bind their power and their control in the name of Jesus. I place them in chains unbreakable and bring the power of the blood of Jesus and the oil of the Holy Spirit against them.

In the name of Jesus, I bind in chains unbreakable, the strongmen over this ministry and prayer session with .... (name) and all their subordinates naming all spirits of
    • *Pride, rebellion, control and rejection*
    • *Antichrist and deception lying, interfering and blocking spirits,*
    • *Culture, infirmity and sickness,*
    • *Confusion, fear, doubt, and unbelief.*
    • *Witchcraft, occult and Freemasonry*

Add any that the Lord tells or shows you or what the person has shared about their family life and struggles.

In the name of Jesus, I bind and gag all demonic spirits and confound all their prayers; I stop up their ears, blindfold their eyes and command them not to interfere with anyone on earth.

In the name of Jesus, I bind all watcher and listener spirits sent by Satan. I bring the power of the blood of Jesus and the oil of the Holy Spirit against them, and I bind them in chains unbreakable, erase their memories and I command them to go to the feet of Jesus for judgment.

I call down the fire of God to destroy all listening, scrambling, recording and looking devices and all infrastructure used to put them in place that they have left behind and send their ashes to the flames of the pit.

In the name of Jesus, I bring the power of the blood of Jesus, against all curses, hexes, spells, ungodly prayers, negative words brought against this ministry team and prayer session.

In the name of Jesus, I negate them all, and ask you Jesus to retrieve any blood that was shed in the making of them and return it to yourself.

I pull out all instruments used in the making of these curses, and call down the fire of God to destroy them and send their ashes to the flames of the pit.

In the name of Jesus, I pray against all retribution from Satan because of this ministry and prayer session with............and turn it back on him.

In the name of Jesus, I ask for an open heaven over this ministry and prayer time. I ask that you open up the channel of communication between the throne room and us. I ask that you place the cross in the center of this channel and place angels around it to watch over it.

In the name of Jesus, I ask you Jesus to send any angels that You have allocated for this ministry and prayer time to come and take their position.

I invite the Lord Jesus to be the center of this ministry and prayer time and ask the Holy Spirit to guide us.

I pray that Your purposes will be achieved in every aspect for this ministry and prayer time for...............................Amen.

Phone or Zoom Ministry: *I cover with the blood of Jesus the phone (zoom) connection between ………and us and I command all demons attached to the phone, phone line or internet to go to the feet of Jesus for judgment.*

Person with strong occult connections: Ask Jesus to provide a soundproof room in a safe place. Command all demons over the client to go to that room and ask Jesus to station angels to guard them.

PRAYERS TO BREAK THE FAMILY LINE

The person prays:

I stand in the gap, on behalf of my family, and repent of all sin committed by previous generations on my (birth/adoptive/step or foster) mother's side and my (birth/adoptive/step or foster) father's side.

I ask, Lord God, for Your forgiveness through the blood of the Lord Jesus Christ.

In particular I name the patterns of _____
(physical illness like cancer or heart disease),
(mental illness like depression and anxiety, dementia etc.),
(relationship issues like abuse (all forms), abandonment, control etc.)
(financial issues)
(suicide)
(addiction to alcohol, gambling, pornography etc.)
(participation in Freemasonry, alternative religions, New Age and witchcraft/occult groups)

I ask you, Lord Jesus, to cleanse my family line through Your blood, through my (birth/adoptive/step or foster) mother's side and my (birth/adoptive/step or foster) father's side to my children - (names of any children) _____, (or any children that I may have) and every succeeding generation.

I ask you, Lord Jesus, to take back the ground that Satan has gained through my family line on my (birth/adoptive/step or foster) mother's side and my (birth/adoptive/step or foster) father's side and fill every place with the presence, power, love, joy and peace of the Holy Spirit. In Jesus' name, Amen.

The other person/team leader prays:

I cover by the blood of Jesus the family line through the (birth/adoptive/step or foster) mother's side and the (birth/adoptive/step or foster) father's side back to the beginning of the generations.

Lord, has there been any blood shed in any of the generational lines?

If yes or unsure, pray:

In the name of Jesus, I cover all blood shed, with the blood of Jesus and I ask Jesus to recover all the blood and return it to Himself?

Lord Jesus, have there been any instruments used in the generational lines?

If yes or unsure, pray:

In the name of Jesus, I cover all instruments used, with the blood of Christ and I ask Jesus to remove them and throw them into His holy fire to be destroyed.

Lord Jesus, is there Freemasonry in the family line?

If you have the sense of Yes, then proceed (sometimes you may not have a sense of Yes or No, so assume that there is present).

Lord Jesus, is the name been written in the Freemasonry Book?

If yes, (Sometimes you may not have a sense of Yes or No, so assume that there is present)

Then pray:

Lord Jesus, please remove the family name and all names of the family from the Book and destroy the page(s) on which they have been written

Then wait. Then pray:

Lord Jesus has it been done?

Wait for His Yes.

Lord Jesus, are there any marriage rings and certificates?

If yes, (Sometimes you may not have a sense of Yes or No, so assume that there is present)

Lord Jesus, please remove all rings and certificates, destroy them by fire and put the ashes into the pit.

Then wait. Then pray:

Jesus has it been done?

Wait for His Yes.

Lord Jesus, are there any books and Masonic instruments and paraphernalia like ropes, daggers etc.?

If yes (sometimes you may not have a sense of Yes or No, so assume that there is present):
Lord Jesus, please remove all books and Masonic instruments and paraphernalia, destroy them by fire and put the ashes into the pit.

Then wait. Then pray:

Lord Jesus has it been done? Wait for His Yes.

Lord Jesus, is there Occult/Witchcraft in the family line?

If you have the sense of Yes, then proceed (sometimes you may not have a sense of Yes or No, so assume that there is present).

Lord Jesus, are there ceremonies still present in the family line?

If yes (sometimes you may not have a sense of Yes or No, so assume that there is present), Then pray:

Lord Jesus, please destroy all ceremonies by fire and put the ashes into the pit!

Then wait. Then pray:

Lord Jesus has it been done?

Wait for His Yes.

Lord Jesus, are there any instruments still active in the family line?

If yes (sometimes you may not have a sense of Yes or No, so assume that there is present):

Lord Jesus, please remove all instruments, destroy them by fire and put the ashes into the pit.

Then wait. Then pray:

Lord Jesus has it been done?

Wait for His Yes.

Lord Jesus, are there any sacrifices still active in the family line?

If yes (sometimes you may not have a sense of Yes or No, so assume that there is present).

Lord Jesus, please destroy all sacrifices by fire and put the ashes into the pit.

Then wait. Then pray:

Lord Jesus has it been done?

Wait for His Yes. Then pray:

In the name of Jesus, I break the power of all generational sin in every area that Satan has had a hold of the family line of .... (name) on the (birth/adoptive/step or foster) mother's side and the (birth / adoptive/step or foster) father's side and through the (birth/adoptive/step or foster) children (names of any children) ...., ...*or any children that they may have and to every succeeding generation.*

In the name of Jesus, I take the sword of the Spirit and I sever all negative generational connections from the (birth/adoptive/step or foster) mother's side and the (birth/adoptive/step or foster) father's side through the (birth/adoptive/step or foster) children (names of any children) ...., ...*or any children that they may have and to every succeeding generation.*

In the name of Jesus, I command every demon attached to the family line to go to the feet of Jesus for judgment.

I ask you, Lord Jesus to take back the ground that Satan has gained in my family line and fill those places with Your presence, power, love and peace.

CAPTIVITY BY WORDS OR CURSES

BREAKING LEGITMATE CURSES FROM GOD

The person prays:

Lord Jesus, I stand in the gap for the sin of my (birth/adoptive/step or foster) family members, past and present who have broken the Law of God, through their disobedience, which has become a curse upon my family line.

I repent of this sin, on behalf of my family members, past and present, and I ask you to forgive them.

I bring the power of the blood of Jesus and the oil of the Holy Spirit against every curse of God that has come upon my (birth/adoptive/step or foster) family members and me through their sin and I ask you to remove these curses from me and my present and future generations.

BREAKING ILLEGITIMATE CURSES FROM OTHERS.

The person prays:

I bring the power of the blood of Jesus and the oil of the Holy Spirit against every word, thought, prayer, hex and spell curse that has become a curse against me, including those coming through previous generations and those placed upon me in my life since I was conceived, to this point in time. I ask you, Lord Jesus, to destroy them by fire.

BREAKING VOWS OF SECRECY AND SILENCE

The person prays:

Heavenly Father, in the name of Jesus, I renounce all vows of secrecy and silence, including all threats against me or my family to hurt me or them if I ever reveal what has been done to me in secret. I ask you to release me through the power of your name.

LEADERS PRAYERS TO BREAK CURSES, VOWS OF SECRECY AND INNER VOWS

In the name of Jesus, I bring the power of the blood of Jesus and the oil of the Holy Spirit against all words, thoughts and actions, prayers, hexes and spells that have become a curse/oath/vow/inner vow or bitter root upon .... life both from previous generations and from the time of conception to now.

Lord Jesus, have there been any curses made with blood? (If yes or unsure, then pray)

In the name of Jesus, I bring the power of the blood of Jesus against all curses made with blood. I ask you, Lord Jesus, to retrieve all the blood that was shed and return it to yourself.

Lord Jesus, have there been any instruments used to make curses? (If yes or unsure, then pray)

In the name of Jesus, I remove all instruments used to make curses and throw them into the pit and call down the fire of God to destroy them

In the name of Jesus, I negate all curses/oaths/vows/inner vows and with the sword of the Spirit, sever them all from ...., call down the fire of God to destroy them all and collect their ashes and send them to the place that Jesus has appointed.

In the name of Jesus, I bind all demons attached to the curses with chains unbreakable. I shrink them down to their proper size. I cover them all with the blood of Christ. I command them to go to the feet of Jesus for judgment.

RENOUNCING INNER VOWS

Lord Jesus, reveal to me an inner vow that I have made.

I renounce the inner vow .... And I announce the truth that ....

(Announcing the truth involves the opposite of the vow plus a bible verse or truth. Repeat the above process until all the inner vows have been revealed for that ministry.

CAPTIVITY BY UNGODLY CONNECTIONS

The prayer process is simply:
Confess the sin or forgive the person
Container for the poison
Cross to destroy the container, full of poison, by taking the Container to the Cross for Jesus to destroy the container and contents
Cut the Cord
Command the demons to go to the feet of Jesus for judgment.

CONFESSION PRAYER

Lord Jesus, I confess to you my sin(s) of .... or
Lord Jesus, I confess to you that I have participated in ....

I ask for your forgiveness through your precious blood and I ask you to wash away my sin(s) and its affect upon every part of my being and relationships. I thank you that you died on the cross for my sin(s), that I am forgiven and have been given a clean slate and I surrender again my life to you, Lord Jesus. Help me not to repeat these sin(s) anymore. In Jesus name Amen.

FORGIVENESS PRAYER

I choose to forgive .... (name of the person, themselves, church, institution) for all that they said and did (Invite person to name any specific sins that have ruined their life) *and for all that has not been said and done* (Invite person to name any specific sins that should have been said and done that have ruined their life).

I release my judgment of them to you, Jesus, and I place them and the situation into your hands. Jesus, wash me clean by your blood of all hurt and pain, bitterness and resentment, envy and jealousy, criticism and judgment, frustration, anger and rage. In Jesus name. Amen.

CONTAINER PRAYER

This should read:

Lord Jesus, I ask for a container for...............
Ask the person to describe what the container looks like.
Has it got a lid? (Lids need to be open)

Lord Jesus, could you please tell .... what this container is for.

In the name of Jesus, I bring the power of the blood of Jesus and the oil of the Holy Spirit against all ungodly soul ties that ....has had with................ (other people)

I cut them off with the sword of the spirit and put them into the container.

Once this is indicated,

Lord Jesus, Please download everything that has happened between ....and ....
(e.g. Thoughts, words, hurts, feelings, traumas issues with other people or groups)

Ask the person if they need another container or a bigger one.
Ask the person to tell you when the container is full.
Ask Jesus to close and seal the container.

Lord Jesus, please help............. to take the container to the cross.
(If too heavy you can ask Angels or Jesus to help the person take it to the cross.)

Is the container at the cross yet? Ask the person if it is there. Do they sense or see it there?

When it is there, pray:

Lord Jesus, please destroy it and all its contents.

Once it is destroyed, ask the person how it has been destroyed (e.g. fire, disappeared crushed or exploded):

Lord Jesus, please put anything that is left over (like ashes) in the place that you have appointed. I wash the area clean with the blood of Jesus and the living water of God. I close and seal that place with the blood of Jesus. Amen.

Reverend John Lucas, DMin

LEADERS PRAYER TO BREAK THE POWER CORDS THAT ARE CONNECTED TO THE PERSON

As the leader is praying this prayer, another team member who "sees in the Spirit" checks that all the cutting and dismantling is actually happening and confirms that to the leader as indicated in the prayer.

I cover by the blood of Jesus and the oil of the Holy Spirit the power cord from ....(person or a stronghold like fear or anger or depression etc. or organization) to ....(person)

I ask you Jesus to deal with any blood that was shed and the instruments used.

Lord Jesus, has that been done? (team member confirms this)

Lord Jesus, I ask that you deactivate, dismantle and dispose of all trips, traps or triggers.

Lord Jesus, has that been done? (team member confirms this)

In the name of Jesus, I cut the power cord(s) from .... (i.e. the source) and I cap it. I cut the cord from the .... (the person) and I ask you Jesus to destroy the cord by fire. I ask You, Jesus, to excavate and remove any root system attached to the cord(s) and burn it by fire.

Lord Jesus, have they all been cut, any roots removed and all cords and roots burnt? (If no, seek the Lord about what is the problem. There may be confession or forgiveness issues that are connected. There may be cords hidden underground that need to be exposed and dealt with. They need to be pulled up. Occult cords are usually silver and need a laser cut by Jesus)

I cover the connector, wiring, hooks and programs inside the person with the blood of Jesus.

Lord Jesus, has that been done? (team member confirms this)

Lord Jesus, I ask that you deactivate, dismantle and dispose of all trips, traps and triggers.

Lord Jesus, has that been done? (team member confirms this)

In the name of Jesus, I cover all the blood shed on the wiring, hooks and programs with the blood of Jesus and I ask Jesus to recover all the blood that was shed and return it to Himself?

Lord Jesus, has that been done? (team member confirms this)

In the name of Jesus, I cover all instruments used with the blood of Christ and I ask Jesus to remove them and throw them into His holy fire to be destroyed.

Lord Jesus, has that been done? (team member confirms this)

I ask you, Lord Jesus, to gently remove any pieces of cord, connector plugs, wiring, hooks and any programs that are attached to the person and destroy them by fire.
Lord Jesus, has that been done? (team member confirms this)

I ask you, Lord Jesus, to cleanse the areas where the wiring and hooks have been with your blood, the oil of the Holy Spirit and the living water of God

I apply the balm of God to heal and seal any damage that has been caused inside ....

I ask you, Lord Jesus, to take back the ground that Satan had gained through all power cords and fill every place with the presence, power, love, joy, peace of the Holy Spirit.

I cover every door, window and opening with the blood of Jesus where the cords have been, I close them, never to be opened again.

In the name of Jesus, I bind all powers, principalities and demons that have gained access through the power cords with chains unbreakable, cover them with the blood of Christ and I command them to go to the feet of Jesus for judgment. In Jesus name, Amen.

I ask the Holy Spirit to fill every place where Satan has had a hold with Your presence, power, love, joy and peace.

Lord Jesus, has all that been done? (team member confirms this)

CAPTIVE BY YOUR BRAIN.

Lord Jesus, can you please go into the brain and remove the switch (amygdala) that is connected to .... (either the emotion or the person who has harmed them in some way)

Then reset it or replace it please. Thank you, Lord Jesus (Watch and wait and ask Jesus when he has done this. Some pray-ers are able to see this spiritually)

Lord Jesus, can you go into the filing system (hippocampus) and remove all the files connected to .... (either the emotion or the person who has harmed them in some way) *and burn them by fire.*

Then fill with new files containing your Word. (Watch and wait and ask Jesus when he has done this. Some pray-ers are able to see this spiritually)

CAPTIVE BY YOUR "WEEDS", "VINES" AND "TREES"

Lord Jesus, is there any bitter root system over ....'s heart? If yes, then pray

Lord Jesus, reveal the nature of the trees and vines that are present.

In the name of Jesus, I ask Jesus to remove all tress (and vines) of .... (name the emotions like fear, doubt, criticism, judgment, etc.) *excavate all the roots attached and burn it all with your holy fire.*

In the name of Jesus, I command all demons of .... (related to the nature of the trees and vines eg, fear, doubt, etc.) *to go to the feet of Jesus for judgment.*

I ask you, Lord Jesus, to cultivate and fertilize where the trees and vines have been. Please water it with your Word and strengthen the Tree of the Holy Spirit (the Tree of Life) in this person's garden/heart.

CAPTIVE BY THE SHATTERED SOUL

Lord Jesus, is there any fragmentation?

Yes/No or you get a picture that symbolizes brokenness like a shattered mirror or a picture that symbolizes many Parts?

Lord Jesus, do we have your permission to pray into this area?

Yes/No. If No, there might be another area that needs to be addressed first and the Holy Spirit will reveal that to you when you ask Him.

I invite all the Parts carrying .... (An emotion like anger or that have been affected by .... a person or organization), *to come out and listen to what Jesus has to say and receive His healing love.*

Ask the seer to tell you what is happening. Has the door opened? Has Jesus gone in? If the door has not opened, is there a demonic security system on the door that needs to be removed by Jesus.

If there is security system present,

Glossary of Prayers

Lord Jesus, please deactivate the security system on the door and then open the door.

Once the door has opened and Jesus has entered,

Lord Jesus, please remove all the imposters and saboteurs to your feet for judgment. Lord Jesus, please remove all the strongmen of .... (the primary emotion that the Parts are carrying)

The enemy has placed these demons called saboteurs or imposters to affect the Parts and to boycott what Jesus wants to do

Lord Jesus, please remove all the lies and deception from the Parts.

Lord Jesus, please speak to the Parts, convince them that .... (the person) wants them back and minister healing to them. Speak the word of salvation to any who may not be Christian and invite them to follow you as Lord and Savior.

Some of the Parts may have been splintered off before the person became a Christian.

Parts, hand over everything that you are carrying to Jesus including any weapons.

These Parts are holding on to all the hurt, pain and associated emotions. Sometimes Jesus shows us that they are carrying backpacks and suitcases of all that has been experience. If these are seen, then name what you see and encourage the Parts to hand it all to Jesus.

Lord Jesus, please remove any second skin of .... (the emotion like fear or anger etc.) off the Parts.

On some occasions the emotion like anger has been around a long time and embedded into the Parts like a second skin that has to be removed
We wait now for a minute while Jesus talks with the Parts and gets them ready for the next stage of healing.

Lord Jesus, please send your angels to collect any ones left behind.

Sometimes, not all the Parts come out and need to be collected. Sometimes, you can lead the person to pray:

In the name of Jesus, I command all my Parts to come out and meet my friend and Savior Jesus.

Lord Jesus, are they ready for a bubble bath/shower? If no, then wait. If yes, then pray:

(The Parts from a female person normally like to be cleansed in a bubble bath while Parts from a male person normally prefer a shower. Sometimes we see the Parts go under a waterfall for cleansing.)

Lord Jesus, please wash them clean, baptize them into the new life that you have for them, then give them new armor of God and new clothes and give them all that they need to help .... fulfil their destiny.

Once out of the bath/shower and have new clothes, then pray:

Lord Jesus, do I have your permission to join the Parts back to ....?

Wait for permission. If permission is not given, then ask Jesus the reason. It may be there are more wanting to come out. Sometimes the Parts are not ready and need more time to be with Jesus for healing.

If no, then wait. If yes, then pray:

I join all the Parts back to .... (name of person) and grow them to the same age as .... (name of person) is today.

As there may be a number of rooms with Parts, the process is repeated until all the rooms are emptied. This may not happen in the one ministry if the fragmentation is severe. It may take a number of sessions for total healing of all the Parts.

Once all the rooms have been cleared, including the attic, basement (normally filled with demons to be removed but occasionally there are Parts), we then invite all the Big Protectors to come out. These Big Protectors are Parts of the person designated to look after the house containing all the Parts inside the rooms. They normally come out last when all the rooms are cleared.

The leader prays:

I invite the Big Protectors to come out to Jesus. Lord Jesus, please speak to them and thank them for the great job that they have done to protect the Parts. Lord Jesus, speak your word of salvation and heal them.

When ready,

Lord Jesus, please give them a bath/shower.

When ready,

In the name of Jesus, I join the Big Protectors back to .... (the person) and grow them to the same age that .... (the person) is today.

Lord Jesus, is the house emptied and ready to be demolished.

The house represents the old life that has been damaged and need to be replaced with a new house representing the new life that Jesus wants to give.
If yes, then pray:

Lord Jesus, please demolish this house and replace it with a new one.

Reverend John Lucas, DMin

REFERENCES

CHAPTER ONE

1. Dialogue with God by Mark Virkler, Peacemakers Ministries Ltd, Woy Woy, NSW, Australia, 1986
2. Brent D Earles, (https://www.dailychristianquote.com/brent-d-earles/)
3. Mark Virkler, *Communion with God*, Peacemakers Ministries Ltd, Woy Woy, NSW, 1986. (I have used his key points but with my descriptions. I have used his description of testing. The test of belief is my addition.)

CHAPTER TWO

1. *Character out of Chaos,* David Dykes, Kregel Publications, Grand Rapids, Michigan, 2004

CHAPTER THREE

1. *Today in the Word*, MBI, January, 1990, p. 36.
2. Source: Signs of the Times, Copyright (c) September 19, 1900, Pacific Press
3. Orr, J. Edwin. *The Flaming Tongue*. Chicago: Moody, 1973
4. January 18, God Calling, a Daily Devotional, Arthur James Limited, 1953

CHAPTER FOUR

1. Jack Hayford (https://www.jackhayford.org/teaching/articles/pleading-the-blood/)
2. source unknown; sermonillustrations.com
3. Vine's Complete Expository Dictionary of Old and New Testament Words, Thomas Nelson, Nashville, 1985
4. Neil T Anderson, *The Steps to Freedom in Christ*, Revised Edition. Bethany House, Minneapolis, 2000.
5. Neil T Anderson, *The Steps to Freedom in Christ,* page 20
6. Pentecost in Arnhem Land, by Djiniyini Gondarra: https://renewaljournal.com/2016/02/27/pentecost-in-arnhem-land-bydjiniyini-gondarra/

CHAPTER FIVE

1. Dr. Paul Bragg and his daughter Patricia, *The Miracle of Fasting*, Health Science and Live Products, Santa Barbara, California, 2005
2. Barbara Gordon contributed by Devon Huss @SermonCentral.com on August 11, 2009

CHAPTER SIX

1. Mark Virkler, Counselled by God, Peacemakers Ministries Ltd, Woy Woy, 1983
2. Warren Wiersbe, *The Strategy of Satan*, Tyndale House Publishers, Illinois, 2011

CHAPTER SEVEN

1. A.H. Becker in *Guilt- Curse or Blessing*, Augsburg Pub. House, Minneapolis, 1977
2. Neil T Anderson *Steps to Freedom in Christ*, Bethany House, Minneapolis, Minnesota, 2000
3. Dr Henry W. Wright *Exposing the Spiritual roots of Disease*, Whitaker House, PA, 2019
4. Ken Blue *Authority to heal*, Intervarsity Press, Illinois, 1987
5. John Wimber, *Power Healing*, Harper and Row, San Francisco, 1987

CHAPTER EIGHT

1. Emily A. Vogels, Pew Research Center (https://www.pewresearch.org/) in December 15, 2022

CHAPTER TWELVE

1. The Australian Psychological Society (https://psychology.org.au/for-the-public/psychology-topics/trauma)
2. Jodi Picoult, *The Storyteller*, Atria Books, New York, 2013

For more information contact Reverend John Lucas

Adelaide, South Australia, Australia
johnlucas0253@gmail.com
www.revjohnlucas.com

To purchase additional copies of these books, visit our bookstore at: www.advbookstore.com

"we bring dreams to life"™
www.advbookstore.com

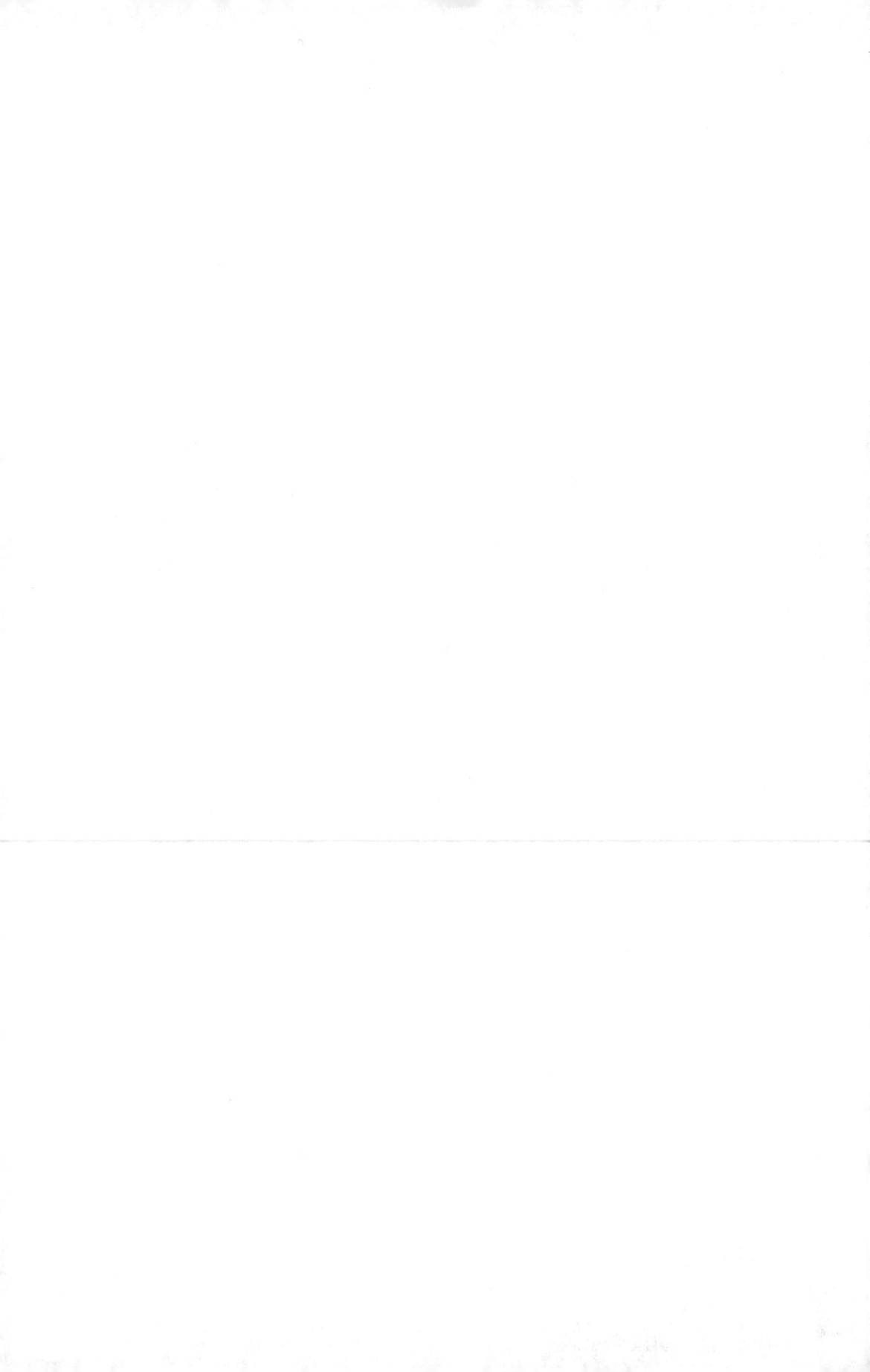

www.ingramcontent.com/pod-product-compliance
Lightning Source LLC
Chambersburg PA
CBHW081825230426
43668CB00017B/2374